RELIGION AND CULTURE IN ANCIENT ISRAEL

Religion & Culture in
ANCIENT ISRAEL

J. Andrew Dearman

HENDRICKSON
PUBLISHERS
PEABODY, MASSACHUSETTS 01961-3473

Copyright © 1992 by Hendrickson Publishers, Inc.
P. O. Box 3473
Peabody, Massachusetts, 01961–3473
All rights reserved
Printed in the United States of America

ISBN 0–943575–90–7

Library of Congress Cataloging-in-Publication Data

Dearman, John Andrew.
    Religion and culture in ancient Israel   /   John Andrew Dearman.
        p.   cm.
    Includes bibliographical references and indexes.
    ISBN 0–943575–90–7
    1. Judaism—History—To 70 A.D.   2. Jews—Civilization—To 70 A.D.
3. Bible. O.T.—Criticism, interpretation, etc.   4. Religion and culture—Palestine.   5. Palestine—Religion.   I. Title.
BM170.D32   1992
296.3'87'0933—dc20   92-33068
                                                                          CIP

The cover photo depicts Taanach, a terra cotta offering stand (late 10th
century B.C.E.) and is used courtesy of Zev Radovan, Jerusalem.

This volume is dedicated to John W. Dearman,
James R. Dearman, and Giles W. Dearman,
in thanksgiving for their presence with us.

TABLE OF CONTENTS

PREFACE

I WOULD LIKE TO EXPRESS MY THANKS to two institutions which assisted me in the preparation of these essays. They are Austin Presbyterian Theological Seminary and the Reformed Church of Bavaria in the Republic of Germany. Austin Seminary graciously granted me a sabbatical during the academic year 1989–90, as well as financial support and other forms of assistance. The Reformed Church of Bavaria offered me a stipend that allowed the Dearman family a priceless opportunity to live six months in Erlangen, Germany. I shall be forever grateful for their help.

While in Germany I had the privilege of using the resources of the Old Testament Seminar of the University of Erlangen-Nürnberg. Professor Ludwig Schmidt kindly allowed me full use of the library and its excellent resources. Dr. Alasdair I. C. Heron, professor of Reformed Theology at the University and a minister of the Reformed Church of Bavaria, was my host in Erlangen. He and his assistant, Dr. Robert R. Redman, were most gracious to us. I am grateful for all their help as well.

Readers will note that I have provided an English translation of several quotations from works written in German and a couple quotations written in French. This is for the benefit of my primary audience of English-speaking readers, since some of them have little facility in German or French. I have also made my own translations of ancient texts unless otherwise noted, and I have included a number of transliterated words for those who wish to explore the texts in more depth. On a few occasions I have included a semitic or Greek term in its native script. I sincerely hope that all of my translations and transliterations are both accurate and clear.

ABBREVIATIONS

AASOR	Annual of the American Schools of Oriental Research
AAT	*Ägypten und Altes Testament*
ABib	Analecta biblica
ADAJ	Annual of the Department of Antiquities of Jordan
AfO	*Archiv für Orientforschung*
AJSL	*American Journal of Semitic Languages and Literature*
AJBA	*Australian Journal of Biblical Archaeology*
ANET	*Ancient Near Eastern Texts Related to the Old Testament* (ed. J. B. Pritchard)
ANETS	*Ancient Near Eastern Texts and Studies*
AOAT	Alter Orient und Altes Testament
ASTI	*Annual of the Swedish Theological Institute*
AThANT	Abhandlungen zur Theologie des Alten und Neuen Testaments
AUSS	*Andrews University Seminary Studies*
BA	*Biblical Archaeologist*
BAR	*Biblical Archaeology Review*
BASOR	*Bulletin of the American Schools of Oriental Research*
BBB	Bonner biblische Beiträge
BET	*Beiträge zur evangelischen Theologie*
BETL	Bibliotheca Ephemeridum Theolgicarum Lovaniensium
BHT	Beiträge zur historischen Theologie
BN	*Biblische Notizen*
BS	*Biblische Studien*

BTB	*Biblical Theology Bulletin*
BWANT	Beiträge zur Wissenschaft vom Alten und Neuen Testament
BZ	*Biblische Zeitschrift*
BZAW	Beihefte zur Zeitschrift für die Alttestamentliche Wissenschaft
CB	*Coniectanea Biblica*
CBQ	*Catholic Biblical Quarterly*
CBQMS	Catholic Biblical Quarterly Monograph Series
CTM	*Calwer theologische Monographien*
EI	*Eretz Israel*
EQ	*Evangelical Quarterly*
FOTL	*Forms of Old Testament Literature*
FRLANT	*Forschungen zur Religion und Literatur des Alten und Neuen*
FTS	*Frieburger theologische Studien*
HDR	*Harvard Dissertations in Religion*
HR	*History of Religions*
HSM	*Harvard Semitic Monographs*
HSS	*Harvard Semitic Studies*
HTR	*Harvard Theological Review*
HUCA	*Hebrew Union College Annual*
IA	Iron Age
IEJ	*Israel Exploration Journal*
Int	*Interpretation*
IOS	*Israel Oriental Studies*
JAAR	*Journal of the American Academy of Religion*
JANESCU	*Journal of the Ancient Near Eastern Society of Columbia University*
JAOS	*Journal of the American Oriental Society*
JBL	*Journal of Biblical Literature*
JCS	*Journal of Cuneiform Studies*
JEA	*Journal of Egyptian Archaeology*
JETS	*Journal of the Evangelical Theological Society*
JJS	*Journal of Jewish Studies*
JNES	*Journal of Near Eastern Studies*
JNWSL	*Journal of Northwest Semitic Languages*
JPOS	*Journal of the Palestine Oriental Society*
JQR	*Jewish Quarterly Review*
JSJ	*Journal for the Study of Judaism*
JSOT	*Journal for the Study of the Old Testament*
JSOTSS	*Journal for the Study of the Old Testament Supplementary Series*
JSS	*Journal of Semitic Studies*
JTC	*Journal for Theology and the Church*
JTS	*Journal of Theological Studies*
KAI	*Kanaanäische und Aramaische Inschriften* (ed. Donner and Röllig)

LBA	Late Bronze Age
OBO	*Orbus Biblicus et Orientalis*
OTS	*Oudtestamentische Studien*
PEFA	*Palestine Exploration Fund Annual*
PEFQS	*Palestine Exploration Fund Quarterly Statement*
PEQ	*Palestine Exploration Quarterly*
QDAP	*Quarterly of the Department of Antiquities of Palestine*
RB	*Revue Biblique*
RevQ	*Revue de Qumrân*
RHPR	*Revue d'histoire et de philosophie religieuses*
RSR	*Religious Studies Review*
SANT	*Studien zum Alten und Neuen Testament*
SBM	*Stuttgarter biblische Monographien*
SBT	Studies in Biblical Theology
SEA	*Svensk Exegetisk Årsbok*
SEL	*Studi epigrafici e linguistici*
SFSHJ	South Florida Studies in the History of Judaism
SHANE	Studies in the History of the Ancient Near East
SJLA	Studies in Judaism of Late Antiquity
SO	*Studia Orientalia*
SOTSMS	Society of Old Testament Studies Monograph Series
SUNT	Studien zur Umwelt des Neuen Testaments
SWBA	Social World of Biblical Antiquity
TA	*Tel Aviv*
TDOT	*Theological Dictionary of the Old Testament*
Tl Gl	*Theologie und Glaube*
TLZ	*Theologische Literaturzeitung*
Transeu	*Transeuphrates*
TTS	*Trierer theologische Studien*
TTZ	*Trierer theologische Zeitschrift*
UF	*Ugaritforschungen*
VF	*Verkündigung und Forschung*
VT Sup	*Supplements to Vetus Testamentum*
VT	*Vetus Testamentum*
WMANT	Wissenschaftlichen Monographien zum Alten und Neuen Testament
WO	*Die Welt des Orients*
ZA	*Zeitschrift für Assyriologie*
ZAW	*Zeitschrift für die Alttestamentliche Wissenschaft*
ZDPV	*Zeitschrift des Deutsches Palästinas-Vereins*
ZTK	*Zeitschrift für Theologie und Kirche*

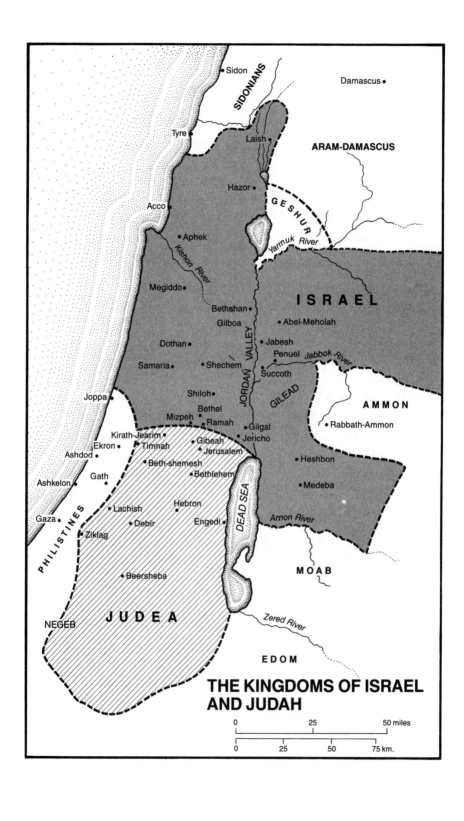

THE KINGDOMS OF ISRAEL
AND JUDAH

INTRODUCTION

THE ESSAYS IN THIS VOLUME deal with aspects of the relationship between religion and culture in the Old Testament. They are arranged in two parts. Part One devotes three chapters to the narrative traditions of Israel contained in Genesis through 2 Kings, 1–2 Chronicles, Ezra and Nehemiah, and 1–2 Maccabees. Part Two examines four phenomena in the OT: covenant instruction in Deuteronomy, pre-exilic prophecy, the wisdom movement, and apocalypticism.

DEFINING RELIGION AND CULTURE

Both religion and culture are deceptively simple terms and are not defined easily in deductive fashion. It is important, therefore, to begin with working definitions before proceeding more specifically to the task at hand. The following definitions come from Clifford Geertz, a noted anthropologist, whose proposals are widely known (and discussed) among scholars.[1] They are not designed to defend a particular theology. They apply to the analysis of literature as well as nonwritten historical remains. Geertz defines religion as

> a set of symbols which acts to establish powerful, pervasive, and long-lasting moods and motivations in men [sic] by formulating conceptions of a

---

[1] C. Geertz, *The Interpretation of Cultures. Selected Essays* (New York: Basic Books, 1973).

> general order of existence and clothing these conceptions with such an aura of factuality that the moods and motivations seem uniquely realistic.[2]

And for culture, he offers the following:

> it denotes an historically transmitted pattern of meanings embodied in symbols, a system of inherited conceptions expressed in symbolic forms by means of which men [sic] communicate, perpetuate, and develop their knowledge about and attitudes toward life.

These definitions themselves require some comment, especially as they pertain to the study of the OT. The term *symbol*, which is used in both definitions, is especially important in social science analysis.[3] Geertz defines a symbol as "any physical, social, or cultural act or object that serves as a vehicle for a conception."[4] Accordingly, the documents of the OT are themselves symbols[5] since they convey meaning to religious communities, just as material objects (altars, divine images) and ritual activity (prayer, animal sacrifice) were symbols which embodied or signified meaning in ancient Israel. Human communication clothes itself in symbolic action—whether the communication is written or unwritten—and culture is the social context in which human activity communicates meaning.

As part of a culture which communicates a particular understanding of life, religion has a double aspect. As Geertz defines religion, it typically provides adherents a conception of "the general order of existence," which then informs the particular choices and commitments they make in life.[6] On the one hand, religion can manifest an order (or

---

[2] This quote and the one that follows come from the essay, "Religion as a Cultural System," *The Interpretation of Cultures*, 89–90.

[3] See further, R. Firth, *Symbols: Public and Private* (Ithaca: Cornell University Press, 1973); V. Turner, *Dramas, Fields, and Metaphors: Symbolic Action in Human Society* (Ithaca: Cornell University Press, 1974); E. Leach, *Culture and Communication: The Logic by which Symbols are Communicated* (Cambridge: Cambridge University Press, 1976); J. Skorupski, *Symbol and Theory: A Philosophical Study of Theories of Religion in Social Anthropology* (Cambridge: Cambridge University Press, 1976).

[4] Taken from the essay, "Ideology as a Cultural System," *The Interpretation of Cultures*, 208.

[5] This has been stressed by W. G. Dever, perhaps the most prominent Syro-Palestinian archaeologist of the last two decades. See his *Recent Archaeological Discoveries and Biblical Research* (Seattle: University of Washington Press, 1990), 9: "It [the Bible] is a shaped material object that, like any other artifact, reflects the human thought and behavior that produced it. It is thus a symbol, the visible reality that points to an invisible reality beyond it."

[6] See also the widely discussed volume by P. Berger and T. Luckmann, *The Social Construction of Reality. A Treatise in the Sociology of Knowledge* (Garden City: Doubleday, 1966). The authors propose that what any person or group calls "reality" (something similar to Geertz's "general order of existence") is to some degree a social construction based on the particularities of their historical setting.

logic) that shapes itself to a particular culture, or similarly, that takes certain forms as a result of its cultural setting. On the other hand, religion can help shape a culture by the order it represents and by the world view it offers to its adherents who live in that culture. Both aspects are significant; religion is shaped by its larger cultural context, and it also helps interpret and shape its cultural context. There is, consequently, not just one form of relationship between religion and culture, but a wide variety of possible relationships between the two. In the case of the OT, the writers reflect a variety of approaches in their attempt to relate their faith to a particular cultural setting. In making such judgments about another time and place, modern investigators should always bear in mind, in the words of Geertz, "that what we call our data are really our own constructions of other people's constructions of what they and their compatriots are up to."[7] In proposing a model for the place of religion in a particular culture, one person offers an interpretation of another person's (or another community's) "conception of the general order of existence."

Religion, therefore, is not just a part of culture, but it is inseparable from it, providing symbols for the interpretation and legitimation of culture and also for its criticism. The two are symbiotically related, although a culture may be host to more than one religion with which it is intertwined. Geertz stresses that a religious critique figures prominently in a culture because it offers a perspective on the meaning of life both foundational and particular, even when the same culture offers other perspectives. This function has been observed by other sociologists who note religion's role in defining a person's or community's identity within a larger society.[8] And the symbiosis between religion and culture is manifested in other ways: both are the product of human interaction with a given socio-historical and geographical context, and both of them conserve and transmit values, giving shape and context to the continuing experience of their heirs.

INVESTIGATING RELIGION AND CULTURE IN ISRAEL

In ancient Israel the practice of religion took a variety of forms of social expression. In line with Geertz's definitions, the symbols for the

---

[7] Taken from the essay, "Thick Description: Toward an Interpretive Theory of Culture," *The Interpretation of Cultures*, 9.

[8] See the discussion of religion as the "sacralization of identity" in H. Mol, *Identity and the Sacred. A Sketch for a new Social-Scientific Theory of Religion* (New York: The Free Press, 1976); and the discussion of the importance of religion in defining the concepts of "meaning and moral order" in R. Wuthnow, *Meaning and Moral Order: Explorations in Cultural Analysis* (Berkeley: University of California Press, 1987).

religion of ancient Israel are known from two primary categories. The first is the Hebrew Bible (the Christian Old Testament), ancient Israel's literary testament. But as M. Coogan has observed: "it is essential to consider biblical religion as a subset of Israelite religion."[9] Hence the importance of the second category that also illustrates the practices of Israelite religion, namely, extrabiblical sources, including the material culture from within the approximate geographical and chronological boundaries of ancient Israel.[10] Extrabiblical sources from whatever provenance in the Middle East can provide illustrative material for reconstructing Israelite religion and culture. These sources include written and unwritten materials. The "stuff" of this material culture (its symbols) is derived primarily from the excavations of ancient sites.

It is obvious that no one approach or single volume can comprehensively analyze Israelite religion in its cultural context. The methodological questions and the sheer amount of data to interpret make comprehensive analysis impossible whether one deals primarily with the biblical text or with extrabiblical sources and material culture. Thus the goal of the present work is more modest and specific. The following essays treat aspects of the relationship between religion and culture in ancient Israel, using the working definitions of Geertz and adapting a typology of relationships first proposed by H. Richard Niebuhr for Christian faith in its cultural setting.[11] Part One is a summary in three chapters of aspects of Israelite religion in their cultural context. Its arrangement follows the "storyline" of the Old Testament, concentrating on the narrative portions and 1–2 Maccabees, and drawing comparisons and contrasts with the evidence from the relevant material culture and historical context. In chronological terms this covers a time span of more than a thousand years, from the transition of the Late Bronze Age (LBA, ca. 1500–1200/1150 B.C.E.) to the Hellenistic period (ca. 325–165 B.C.E.). The emphasis falls on the pre-monarchic and pre-exilic periods of the "storyline," following the lead of the biblical writers whose narrative traditions concentrate on the periods before the Babylonian Exile. Part Two devotes a chapter to each of the following: Deuteronomy, the pre-exilic writing prophets, the wisdom books (Proverbs, Ecclesiastes, Job), and the rise of apocalyptic literature (Daniel). Parts One and Two

---

[9] M. D. Coogan, "Canaanite Origins and Lineage: Reflections on the Religion of Ancient Israel," *Ancient Israelite Religion. Essays in Honor of Frank Moore Cross* (ed. P. D. Miller, Jr., P. Hanson, D. McBride; Philadelphia: Fortress, 1987), 115.

[10] Some scholars using social scientific approaches distinguish between the "domain of notions" in the biblical text and the "domain of actions" reflected in the material culture of ancient Israel. See J. F. Flanagan, *David's Social Drama: A Hologram of Israel's Early Iron Age* (SWBAS 7; Sheffield: Almond Press, 1988); P. McNutt, *The Forging of Israel. Iron Technology, Symbolism, and Tradition in Ancient Society* (SWBAS 8; Sheffield: Almond Press, 1990).

[11] *Christ and Culture* (New York: Harper & Row, 1951).

are designed to complement and reinforce each other. Cross references are employed to make these links explicit.

An assumption underlying each of the essays is that the relationship presupposed between Israelite religion and its larger cultural context varies among the documents of the OT. But the manner in which this assumption is worked out differs between Parts One and Two. The survey in Part One does not draw upon a comprehensive anthropological theory; instead, the basic definitions of Geertz are assumed, and the three chapters of Part One present an introduction to some significant symbols of the biblical text and, where appropriate, to the material culture in its variety. Part Two adapts the socio-historical typology of Niebuhr.[12] To summarize its chapters briefly: for Deuteronomy, covenantal religion must transform the cultural context of Israel in Canaan, or Israel suffers the consequences. Similarly the pre-exilic prophets depict a paradoxical relationship between faithful religion as they imagined it should be and the Israelite culture of their day in which the central social and religious institutions are perceived as failures. The wisdom movement in Israel tended to presuppose a more positive, synthetic relationship between religion and culture. Such a relationship best accounts for wisdom's universality, though the sapiential traditions of the OT sharply limit any comprehensive synthesis by which to judge all of human experience. The apocalyptic traditions from Israel, which reach maturity in the book of Daniel, are an outgrowth of the prophetic and sapiential movements in Israel as they encounter a dominating and often hostile culture. Thus the apocalyptic movement typically produced a religion-against-culture approach which assumed the continuing validity of older religious traditions in the face of their cultured despisers.

Niebuhr's work was devoted to the expression of Christian faith in specific types of cultural settings. Neither his general methodology nor his specific typology are taken over in this volume without adaptation. It seems true, however, that Niebuhr's typological approach has proved itself valuable over time in a way that more recent and more sophisticated social science analysis has yet to do. Part of the strength of his approach was its value as an angle of vision for modern investigation that was both broad in its grasp of a movement as a whole and specific in its search for those elements that made a movement distinctive and more readily understandable. Neither did he abdicate the tasks of the historian by way of his socio-historical typology. Furthermore, his approach did not exclude other methods of analysis or claim to be the definitive interpretation of either culture

---

[12] His models for relating Christian faith to its cultural context were: Christ against culture, The Christ of culture, Christ above culture, Christ and culture in paradox, Christ the transformer of culture.

or religion. And even where it is generally agreed that his analysis was wrong,[13] his overall approach still commends itself to many interpreters for its heuristic value. His typological approach remains a means to organize and interpret religious diversity in its cultural expression. There are two ways, however, in which these essays differ considerably from Niebuhr's approach.

1. One is the concern for the OT documents themselves, which Niebuhr largely ignored. Whatever the topic (wisdom movement, prophecy, political institutions, etc.), the goal of analysis is to understand the OT documents in their larger cultural context. The concern for the documents as primary symbols (to use Geertz's language) shares certain emphases with what is often called "canonical analysis."[14] It is Deuteronomy, the Deuteronomistic History, or Daniel, as documents, that receive most of the attention, not hypothesized sources which likely preceded them.

2. A second difference comes to expression in the attention paid to the material culture as it is known for ancient Israel (Part One). Anthropological analysis is a trend in biblical studies[15] and one that can assist a typological approach toward religion and culture. Geertz too underscores the relevance of material culture in his methodological approach; the study of religion is a study not about ideas alone but about the way the practice of religion works itself out in the larger cultural context. A tangible expression (symbol) of faithfulness requires scrutiny, whether it is a cult stand or a ritual, or whether it survives only through the medium of literature.

TRENDS IN THE INTERPRETATION OF THE OT

By way of introduction, it is instructive to compare the succession of volumes issued by the Society of Old Testament Studies in Great Britain for the different ways in which Israel's religion has been analyzed by scholars.[16] These volumes provide a useful survey of the variety of

---

[13] As an example, it is generally agreed that his assessment of gnosticism (*Christ and Culture*, 85–91) is inadequate.

[14] As two examples of this approach, see B. Childs, *Introduction to the Old Testament as Scripture* (Philadelphia: Fortress Press, 1979); R. Rendtorff, *The Old Testament. An Introduction* (Philadelphia: Fortress Press, 1986).

[15] The best introduction to this approach as regards Israel's material culture comes in the work of the archaeologist W. G. Dever. See his two works, *Recent Archaeological Discoveries and Biblical Research* (1990); "The Contribution of Archaeology to the Study of Canaanite and Early Israelite Religion," in Miller et al., eds., 209–47. There are further references in chapter 1, p. 30, note 91.

[16] *The People and the Book* (ed. A. S. Peake; Oxford: Clarendon Press, 1925); *Record and Revelation* (ed. H. Wheeler Robinson; Oxford: Clarendon Press, 1938);

approaches and the development of trends in interpretation. The subtitle of the most recent volume (edited by Clements) is a clear indication of current trends in scholarship. Two of its essays survey trends in the social scientific approach to the study of the OT.[17] They illustrate both the possibilities and the pitfalls of such methods in biblical studies. There is, for example, the danger of the biblical scholar's depending too heavily on one theory (which may be out of date or held in low regard by many in the social sciences). And there is also the problem that potentially useful theories imported from the social sciences are inadequately understood or imposed improperly on the data rather than being used to facilitate interpretation.

Other trends in the interpretation of the OT require comment. Along with the emphasis on social science analysis has come a certain skepticism in reconstructing Israelite history, especially regarding the pre-monarchical period. Caution has become the operative word in response to an overconfident use of archaeology to confirm aspects of biblical history. Renewed attention to literary detail in the analysis of biblical narratives has also contributed to the avoidance of historical reconstruction as well as a trend toward the late dating of primary biblical texts.[18] The present writer does not share the skepticism of those who reject the historical analysis of the biblical text in favor of a strictly anthropological approach to Israel's religion or the approach of those whose literary theory requires a strictly non-historical reading of the OT narratives. At the same time, he hopes he has learned some methodological cautions from both approaches.

Finally, the frequently used terms "official religion" and "popular religion" require brief comment. The meanings attached to the terms can vary considerably among scholars who enlist them in the investigation

---

The Old Testament and Modern Study (ed. H. H. Rowley; Oxford University Press, 1951); *Tradition and Interpretation* (ed. G. W. Anderson; Clarendon Press, 1979); *The World of Ancient Israel. Sociological, anthropological and political perspectives* (ed. R. E. Clements; Cambridge: Cambridge University Press, 1989). See also the essays in *The Hebrew Bible and Its Modern Interpreters* (ed. D. Knight, G. Tucker; Chico: Scholars Press, 1985), which come from members of the North American Society of Biblical Literature.

[17] J. W. Rogerson, "Anthropology and the Old Testament," 17–37; A. D. H. Mayes, "Sociology and the Old Testament," 39–63.

[18] See for examples, R. Alter, *The Art of Biblical Narrative* (New York: Basic Books, 1979), 23–46; M. Sternberg, *The Poetics of Biblical Narrative* (Bloomington: Indiana University Press, 1985); R. N. Whybray, *The Making of the Pentateuch. A Methodological Study* (JSOTSS 53; Sheffield: JSOT Press, 1987). And from different perspectives, see J. Van Seters, " 'Comparing Scripture with Scripture': Some Observations on the Sinai Pericope of Exodus 19–24," *Canon, Theology, and Old Testament Interpretation* (ed. G. Tucker et al.; Philadelphia: Fortress, 1988), 111–30; in the same volume, B. Long, "A Figure at the Gate: Readers, Reading, and Biblical Theologians," 166–86.

of Israelite religion.[19] Official Israelite religion is that religion supported by the state and practiced by its administrative leadership (e.g., ruler, monarch, high priest). It is possible, for example, that a state priesthood could represent religious practices which differed from that of the monarch (cf. the description of Athaliah and the Jerusalem priest Jehoiada in 2 Kings 11), and it is possible that a state might support more than one cult. Popular Israelite religion, in contrast, is essentially those practices and beliefs excluded by the state-sponsored and legitimated cult(s). Thus the term popular religion presupposes a variety of cultic pratices and beliefs. On occasion, aspects of popular religion may or may not differ appreciably from the practices of the official cult(s). Such a judgment requires a case by case examination.[20]

It is clear from comparisons between biblical texts and the material culture from Israel that the OT writers struggled to define who and what Israel should be over against a number of competing claims found both inside and outside the Israelite community. Something similar can be said for the ways in which non-biblical texts and the symbols from the material culture convey understandings of YHWH (Yahweh), the God of Israel. Both text and culture reflect substantial diversity in understanding. And neither biblical text nor material culture gives evidence of a golden age where Israel's faith was practiced in cultural isolation and Israel was free from the influence of competing world views or immune to the possibility of internal corruption. It is also clear that what the OT represents about God and Israel is the process of considerable reflection. The history of biblical interpretation demonstrates that it has had a marked effect on the identity of subsequent religious communities.[21]

---

[19] See the perceptive comments by P. D. Miller, Jr., "Israelite Religion," *The Hebrew Bible and its Modern Interpreters* (ed. D. Knight, G. Tucker; Chico: Scholars Press, 1985), 215–18.

[20] The terms "popular religion" and "popular piety" (*Volksfrömmigkeit* in German) are sometimes used pejoratively by commentators to describe naive and superstitious practices on the part of the common people.

[21] Although the approach taken in these essays differs considerably at points from that of J. A. Sanders, *From Sacred Story to Sacred Text* (Philadelphia: Fortress Press, 1987), the present writer has learned a great deal from two of his proposals: (1) that Israel had a fourfold process in the construction of the canon (what Sanders calls depolytheizing, monotheizing, Yahwizing and Israelitizing); (2) that in the canonical process, the influence of particular communities of faith is greater than that of particular individuals.

PART ONE

A SKETCH OF ISRAELITE RELIGION ACCORDING
TO THE BIBLICAL STORYLINE AND IN LIGHT OF
EXTRABIBLICAL SOURCES

PREMONARCHIC ISRAEL   1

ARLIEST ISRAEL WAS AN ASSOCIATION of tribes and clans that emerged in Canaan as a political entity after the breakup of the traditional powers of the Bronze Age. For Syria and Palestine the traditional powers had been the Egyptians and the Hittites from northern Syria and Anatolia. The demise of the traditional powers across the Fertile Crescent, Anatolia, and the Mediterranean took place in the thirteenth/twelfth centuries B.C.E.[1] and was followed by a period of readjustment for all population groups, some of which emerge in historical records for the first time in the Late Bronze Age (LBA) or even later. Israel falls into the latter category of emerging states, like Ammon, Moab, Edom, the Philistines, and some of the Aramean groups. These groups eventually form nation-states, that is, a political entity named primarily for a people and not a territory. The more commercially oriented cities along the Syrian coast fall more into the category of territorial states, each forming essentially a city-state of its own.[2] These people are the Phoenicians, whose two best known cities, Tyre and Sidon, were closely related to Israel through commerce, culture, and geographic proximity.

---

[1] H. Tadmor, "The Decline of Empires in Western Asia ca. 1200 B.C.E.," *Symposia Celebrating the Seventy-Fifth Anniversary of the Founding of the American Schools of Oriental Research [1900–1975]* (ed. F. M. Cross; Cambridge: ASOR, 1979), 1–14; W. H. Stiebing, "The End of the Mycenean Age," *BA* 43 (1980): 7–21.

[2] The distinction between nation-states and territorial states is that of G. Buccellati, *Cities and Nations of Ancient Syria* (Studi Semitici 26; Rome: University of Rome, 1967).

The tribal association of Israel was located primarily in the hill-country that now comprises the West Bank and Galilee regions. The earliest non-biblical reference to an "Israel" comes in the stela of the Egyptian Pharaoh Merneptah, which is late thirteenth century in date (ca. 1207 B.C.E.), and which assumes that Israel is the name of a people or group living in Canaan.[3] There is no extrabiblical evidence for an Israel anywhere outside of Canaan, though the OT preserves accounts linking Israel's ancestors with other areas in the Ancient Near East (ANE). Were it not for the brief reference to an Israel in the Merneptah stela, the earliest non-biblical references to Israel come in the ninth century B.C.E., in the annals of the Neo-Assyrian king Shalmaneser III and in the inscription of the Moabite king Mesha.[4] By this time Israel had progressed from a tribal association to a monarchical state and had even suffered internal division.

Israel's ancestral traditions in Genesis begin not with a tribal history but with accounts of the world's origin that move quickly into a family history. Interwoven in the world and family history are a number of genealogical and etiological traditions that establish Israel's identity in its larger cultural setting. Genealogies do far more than establish lines of kinship; especially in tribal societies without centralized institutions of power, they provide status and patterns of social accountability.[5] They are analogous to maps or diagrams which define social identity. The biblical accounts of a family-become-nation are a powerful symbol of Israelite identity and a pillar of the canonical "storyline."

The genealogies and birth stories in Genesis function etiologically to explain the names of the twelve tribes of Israel and their use as political and geographic designations. For example, the names Israel and Jacob can be used in the OT as a designation of the people as a whole or as a reference to a particular state (the northern kingdom of the divided monarchy) as distinct from the "brother" state of Judah. Ephraim, Manasseh, and (the house of) Joseph are also used to refer to this state, as is the name Isaac on two occasions.[6] In similar fashion, some of the ancestral genealogies claim kinship with various other states and peoples

---

[3] H. Engel, "Die Siegesstele des Merneptah," *Bib* 60 (1979): 373–99; G. Ahlström and D. Edelmann, "Merneptah's Israel," *JNES* 44 (1985): 59–61; L. Stager, "Merneptah, Israel and the Sea Peoples: New Light on an Old Relief," *EI* 18 (1985): 56–64; and D. Redford, "The Ashkelon Relief at Karnak and the Israel Stela," *IEJ* 36 (1986): 188–200. The hieroglyphic determinative used for the name Israel marks them as a people and not as a territorial state.

[4] *ANET*, 279, 320.

[5] R. R. Wilson, *Genealogy and History in the Biblical World* (New Haven: Yale University Press, 1977); T. J. Prewitt, "Kinship Structures and the Genesis Genealogies," *JNES* 40 (1981): 87–98.

[6] Amos 7:9, 16. Correspondingly, there are fewer ancestral stories about Isaac than about the other three primary ancestors.

known to Israel. Israel is related to Aramean elements in north Syria,[7] the three Transjordanian states of Moab, Ammon, and Edom,[8] and various Arab tribes.[9] Ancestral names such as Abraham and Jacob are not commonly used for personal names in later Israel and are among the oldest elements in the ancestral accounts.

THE RELIGION AND CULTURE OF THE ANCESTORS

The ancestral traditions in Gen 12–50 did not originate as a literary unity, and the various traditions now preserved cannot be dated to any single period. Recent literary and source analysis of the accounts has moved in two directions. One holds that the division of the ancestral accounts into discrete sources based on the use of divine names and other criteria has overlooked the importance of particular developments in the preservation of individual accounts.[10] Another dates the hypothetical source J—normally assumed to be the oldest Pentateuchal source— later and posits a date late in the Persian or early Hellenistic period for the final form of the Pentateuch.[11] The issue of dating is notoriously difficult because it requires many judgments of source and tradition analysis that are then used to support a reconstructed historical background. One suspects that a concern with precise dating of the ancestral stories in their literary setting is unlikely to result in a scholarly consensus. Ancestral stories *typically* contribute to preserving and interpreting a culture at any point in its development.[12] In the analysis which follows, the ancestral accounts are interpreted from a twofold cultural perspective; on the one hand, these accounts originate as stories of particular individuals who were the founders of families and clans, and whose descendants settled in Palestine. They define family and regional identities and preserve both archaic and archaizing elements in their

---

[7] Through Abraham and Jacob; Gen 22:20–24; 24:10; 25:20; 29:1–14.

[8] Moab and Ammon through Lot, the nephew of Abraham, Gen 19:30–38; Edom through Esau, the son of Isaac and the brother of Jacob, Gen 25:21–34; 32:3.

[9] Through Ishmael, the son of Abraham and his servant Hagar, Gen 16:1–16; 21:14–21; 25:12–18; and through Keturah, the wife of Abraham after the death of Sarah, Gen 25:1–6. Edom is linked to the Ishmaelites and other Arab elements in Gen 28:9; 36:1–43.

[10] E. Blum, *Die Komposition der Vätergeschichte* (WMANT 57; Neukirchen-Vluyn; Neukirchener Verlag, 1984).

[11] J. Van Seters, *Abraham in History and Tradition* (New Haven: Yale University Press, 1975); H. Vörlander, *Die Entstehungszeit des jehowistischen Geschichtswerkes* (Frankfurt: P. Lang, 1978). A useful survey of trends in Pentateuchal studies is provided by Whybray, *Making of the Pentateuch*.

[12] W. McKane, *Studies in the Patriarchal Narratives* (Edinburgh: Handsel Press, 1979).

literary expression. On the other hand, these same accounts take on the role of defining an incipient Israel as a family, a symbol that prefigures a national and even post-national identity.[13]

Etiological Accounts

Etiological accounts figure prominently in the stories of Israel's ancestors. Abraham builds altars for sacrificial worship at Shechem,[14] Bethel[15] and Hebron;[16] he plants a tree and worships at Beersheba;[17] and he prepares to sacrifice his son Isaac on an altar he builds on Mt. Moriah.[18] After defeating a coalition of raiders who kidnapped his nephew Lot, Abram gives a tenth of "all" to Melchizedek, priest of God Most High ('ēl 'elyôn) in Salem.[19] All of these sites named were centers of cultic and administrative activities in the monarchical period. Indeed, all but Beersheba have a long occupational history before there was an Israel. Such accounts show clearly the double role of the cultural process at work. The ancestors founded places of worship in the land which would, in turn, become key sanctuaries in the period of the monarchy. Moreover, some of the cultic practices described were no doubt used as warrants or explanations for later rites. Abraham's altars underline the importance of sacrificial worship, his gift of a "tenth" serves as a warrant for the practice of tithing, and the "non sacrifice" of Isaac (Gen 22) serves as a reason for substitution in the sacrificial system.[20]

Isaac and Jacob perform similar tasks, even at sites where Abraham had worshipped. Isaac builds an altar at Beersheba after an appearance of the "God of your father Abraham," and his servants dig a well there (Gen 26:23–25). Jacob twice encounters the "God of Abraham and Isaac" or "God Almighty" ('el šadday)[21] at Bethel. In Gen 28:10–19 he has a dream that convinces him that the place is the "house of God and the gate of heaven." In response he takes a stone pillar, raises it to a standing

---

[13] Z. Weisman, "National Consciousness in the Patriarchal Promises," *JSOT* 31 (1985): 55–73.

[14] At the "oak of Moreh," Gen 12:6–7.

[15] The place of worship is actually on the hill between Bethel and Ai, according to Gen 12:8. Cf. 13:4.

[16] At the "oak of Mamre," Gen 13:18. The MT has the plural "oaks" ('ēlōnê) but this likely the result of a textual error.

[17] Gen 21:33. There is no mention of an altar.

[18] Gen 22, especially vv. 2 and 9. In 2 Chron 3:1 Moriah is identified with the temple mount in Jerusalem.

[19] Like Moriah, Salem was later identified with Jerusalem, and the priesthood of Melchizedek was understood as an appropriate reference to the priestly duties of the king. Cf. Psa 110.

[20] The account in Gen 22 serves a prohibitive function, as a reason why Israel should not offer human sacrifice. Cf. the discussion on human sacrifice pp. 90–96.

[21] W. Wifall, "El Shaddai or El of the Fields," *ZAW* 92 (1980): 24–32.

position (*maṣṣēbāh*), anoints it with oil, and names the site Bethel (i.e., "the house of God").[22] In another account (35:6–15), he builds an altar there and erects a stone pillar (*maṣṣēbāh*), anointing it with oil and offering a drink libation. His name is then changed to Israel. The nurse of Rebekah dies at Bethel and is buried under the oak there subsequently named the "oak of weeping."[23] Jacob also erects a pillar at Shechem and calls on "*'El*, the god of Israel."[24] On the one hand, each of these accounts of Isaac and Jacob may have circulated independently in earlier forms, and even in their current context fit imperfectly in a connected narrative of the four ancestral generations. On the other hand, the various accounts all point to the importance of a particular sanctuary. This etiological function carries over to other accounts which do not have multiple versions of ancestral founding, such as Mahanaim (Gen 32:2), Peniel (Gen 32:24–32), and Mizpah (Gen 31:49). Each of these is linked to Jacob and is located in Transjordan.

Some of the cultic practices mentioned in these accounts fit well with what is known of Canaanite culture, though they diverge from later, Israelite orthodoxy. Prominent among the practices is the erecting of a standing stone or pillar (*maṣṣēbāh*) and its anointing with oil.[25] Other examples include the building of altars or the offering of sacrifice by non-priests. All of these cultic acts are best explained as illustrations of widely employed practices, particularly of personal and clan piety, which were pre-Israelite and continued to be practiced by Israelite and non-Israelite people alike long after the rise of Israel as a nation-state. Such rites had their roots in a combination of popular religion and individual clan traditions. These ancestral accounts are likely sources for much of the diversity in later Israelite religion. Family and clan worship centers would preserve distinctive customs more conservatively than larger temples or national theologies, since the latter represented the concerns of the dynasty and state, while the former were more oriented to the family life cycle and clan/village ethos.[26]

---

[22] According to Gen 28:19, Luz was the earlier name of Bethel.

[23] Cf. Gen 32:24–32.

[24] *'ēl 'elōhê yiśrā'ēl*, Gen 33:20 (cf. Gen 46:3). The MT records that he erected an altar (*mṣbḥ*), but the verb used (*nṣb*) better refers to the erection of a standing stone or pillar (*maṣṣēbāh*).

[25] C. Graesser, "Standing Stones in Ancient Palestine," *BA* 35 (1972): 34–63. Cf. Deut 7:5.

[26] B. Lang, "Persönlicher Gott und Ortsgott. Über Elementar-formen der Frömmigkeit im alten Israel," *Fontes Atque Pontes. Eine Festgabe für Hellmut Brunner* (AAT 5; ed. M. Görg; Wiesbaden: O. Harrassowitz, 1983), 271–301; R. Albertz, *Persönliche Frömmigkeit und offizielle Religion. Religionsinterner Pluralismus in Israel und Babylon* (CTM 9; Stuttgart: Calwer Verlag, 1978), 77–91.

Names and Epithets for God

One observes a similar phenomenon of cultural continuity/discontinuity with later Israel in the names and epithets for God. This was demonstrated in a seminal essay by A. Alt, who pointed out that a number of archaic, pre-Israelite elements are preserved in the existing accounts of the ancestors.[27] According to him, the ancestors were nomadic herdsmen who held to a form of tribal/clan religion honoring a patron deity. While these were not monotheistic clans in the modern sense, they depended upon a particular god of their father (e.g., 31:5), that is, the God who had appeared to the patriarch of their clan, and who moved about with them and protected them. This clan deity had no formal name. Alt accepted the scholarly judgment that references to the name YHWH (= יהוה in Hebrew, often "Yahweh" in English; see p. 21–24) in several of the ancestral accounts were secondarily added. But he also concluded that the references to 'El as a specific deity were also accretions to the stories that took place as the clans settled in Canaan and adopted the terminology of the local sanctuaries. In their earliest form the ancestral stories simply referred to the "God of your/my father" without reference to a particular sanctuary or the proper name of the ancestral deity.[28]

Thus Alt proposed that the accounts of the ancestors had passed through two major developments in the course of transmission. The anonymous "God of the father" was first identified with the manifestations of 'El known at the Canaanite sanctuaries. Subsequently 'El was identified with Yahweh the God of the Exodus and the tribal confederation of Israel. In the transmission of the stories some sources use the name Yahweh for the God who brought Abram and his descendants into the land;[29] for other sources the name Yahweh is first revealed to Moses as the God of the ancestors.[30] Subsequent research has essentially

---

[27] The essay by Alt appears in English as "The God of the Fathers," *Essays on Old Testament History and Religion* (Garden City: Doubleday, 1968), 3–86. The original essay is "Der Gott der Väter," *Kleine Schriften zur Geschichte des Volkes Israel* (vol. 1; Munich: Beck'sche, 1953), 1–78. An important update is that of F. M. Cross, *Canaanite Myth and Hebrew Epic* (Cambridge: Harvard University, 1973), 3–75.

[28] Alt and Cross provide many examples of the widespread use of the formula. It is even used in royal correspondence; cf. the phrase "Shamash, the God of my father," in a letter to the Pharaoh (EA 55:53) and in a letter to Hammurabi, "Adad, Lord of Al[eppo] and the God of your Father" (ARM X, 156:10–11).

[29] Gen 12:1. Part of the J or Yahwistic source of classical Pentateuchal analysis.

[30] Exod 3:15–16, part of the Elohistic source (E) which used the term *'elōhîm* for God until the revelation of the divine name to Moses; Exod 6:2–3, part of the P or Priestly source where the God of the ancestors is identified as *'ēl šadday* until the revelation to Moses.

confirmed that the name Yahweh has been introduced secondarily into the ancestral stories to make explicit the confession that Yahweh was the God of the ancestors.[31] But it is unlikely that the ancestral God(s) was anonymous until being identified with the god(s) of the Canaanite sanctuaries. This assumes too radical a distinction in religious terminology between supposedly nomadic groups such as the ancestral clans and the sedentary inhabitants of Canaan. The accounts depict an Abraham or Jacob extensively interacting with the sedentary population of Canaan without being fully intergrated in either the urban or the agrarian spheres. In fact, recent scholarship increasingly questions whether the concept of nomadism provides an appropriate model for the ancestral accounts. Clearly, too much emphasis was placed by earlier scholars on parallels with bedouin, and among some current scholars even the term nomad is rejected as inappropriate to describe Israel's ancestors.[32] More emphasis is being placed on the continuities between the religion of the ancestors and that practiced in Canaan.

It is possible to understand each Canaanite deity venerated at a sanctuary either as a local deity with a generic name ('ēl, "god") and an epithet, or as a local manifestation of the high god 'El. One doubts that the cults of the Canaanite sanctuaries represented a uniform opinion on this issue, but probably the majority of sanctuaries portrayed "their" deity as but one manifestation of 'El, the king of the gods.[33] Veneration of a high deity would not preclude the worship of other deities or the probability of a great deal of variety in the understanding of the worshippers. Multiple sanctuaries led inevitably to cultic diversity in Canaan throughout the second millennium B.C.E., where small city-states more often than not competed for local hegemony and influence with Egypt.

Among the names and epithets in Genesis for the ancestral deity are 'El 'Elyon, creator of heaven and earth (14:19); 'El Šaddai (17:1); and 'El 'Olam (21:2). Each of these names is comprised with a form of the word 'el, which in its singular and plural form ('elōhîm) can serve as a generic term for god. Epithets such as 'elyôn or šadday have parallels in

---

[31] G. Wenham, "The Religion of the Patriarchs," *Studies in the Patriarchal Narratives* (ed. A. Millard, D. J. Wiseman; Leicester: Inter-Varsity Press, 1980), 157–88.

[32] Bibliography and discussion in R. Neu, "Die Bedeutung der Ethnologie für die alttestamentliche Forschung," *Ethnologische Texte zum Alten Testament 1. Vor- und Frühgeschichte Israels* (ed. C. Sigrist, R. Neu; Neukirchen Vluyn: Neukirchener Verlag, 1989), 11–26. J. D. Martin, "Israel as a Tribal Society," in Clements, ed., *The World of Ancient Israel*, 95–117.

[33] So Cross, *Canaanite Myth and Hebrew Epic*, 46–60. On the importance of 'El as king among the other deities see E. T. Mullen, *The Assembly of the Gods. The Divine Council in Canaanite and Early Hebrew Literature* (HSM 24; Cambridge: Harvard, 1980).

a variety of extrabiblical sources. As noted above, it is unlikely that individuals or clans had personal deities known generically as the "God ('ēl) of my father" whom they did not also address directly and personally as 'El, usually with an epithet that marked some character of the deity.[34] We should be cautious, therefore, in making a clear-cut distinction between epithets which do not otherwise identify the deity—such as the "fear" (pahad) of Isaac (31:53) or the "strong one" ('abîr)[35] of Jacob (49:24)—and those references which identify a particular form of 'El. Because the ancestral accounts did not originate as a unity, and since they presuppose an extensive history of transmission, it is fruitless to look for one historical setting with which to compare these epithets for deity or to assume they are all uniform references to the high god 'El. They are probably not anachronistic for the second millennium, however, and with proper caution several aspects of the ancestral religion can be compared with what is known about the widespread phenomenon of personal gods in the ANE.[36] The "God of Abraham, Isaac, and Jacob" acts as the personal god of the respective families in times of crisis and at crucial times in the life cycle.

The Ancestors as a Wandering Family

The ancestral accounts depict generations of a family in their wandering and settling in the land of Canaan. Their god ('ēl) is identified with the god(s) of the Canaanite sanctuaries. As with all accounts of the past that are remembered and retold, those about the ancestors provided a sense of identity for the communities that transmitted them. A creative "give and take" existed between the ancestral accounts and the broader historical context of later Israel. It is not so much that the needs of later Israel invented the ancestral accounts as that the ancestral accounts helped Israel interpret who they were by passing along cultural reminders of who they had been.

Surprisingly, the ancestral accounts are strongly colored by the theme that Israel's origins are outside the land of Canaan. This identity has quite significant implications for the shape of Israel's religion, regardless of the historical truth or falsity of the theme; that Israel

---

[34] This is clear from the phrase 'El, the God of Israel, in Gen 33:20.

[35] The term can be translated as "bull" or "steer."

[36] H. Vorländer, Mein Gott. Die Vorstellung vom persönlichen Gott im Alten Orient und im Alten Testament (AOAT 23; Neukirchen-Vluyn: Kevelaer, 1975); Thorkild Jacobsen, The Treasures of Darkness, A History of Mesopotamian Religion (New Haven: Yale University Press, 1976), 147–64; F. M. Cross, "The Epic Traditions of Early Israel: Epic Narrative and the Reconstruction of Early Israelite Institutions," The Poet and the Historian. Essays in Literary and Historical Biblical Criticism (HSM 26; ed. R. E. Friedman; Chico: Scholars Press, 1983), 35.

originated outside Canaan is a primary symbol of the OT. The land of Canaan is remembered as a gift first promised to Israel's ancestors. The God who led the ancestors in their travels repeatedly revealed himself to them in the land. Israel originated from the "other side" of the Euphrates River. One account holds that Abram is from Ur of the Chaldees in southern Mesopotamia, though his strongest connections are with northern Syria (Gen 11:31). Isaac, the child of the promise, acquires a wife from these relatives in Syria, as does his son Jacob (Israel).[37] Joseph, the most prominent son of the fourth generation, spends virtually his whole life in Egypt and is brought back to Canaan only after his death.[38] Even the so-called table of nations in Gen 10, which arranges the peoples known to Israel according to descent from Noah's three sons, does not mention Israel directly! Israel is related to Eber, who is listed under the descendants of Shem. Perhaps "Hebrew," an early term used to describe Israelites, is related to the name Eber ('br = to cross over) and reflects an earlier non-sedentary status for some of the early tribal elements.[39] This "outsider" status of the ancestors remained a key symbol of later Israel's own sense of identity.

The Ancestral God of Promise and Blessing

Woven through the ancestral accounts as they now exist are powerful affirmations of the ancestral deity as the God of promise and blessing, the deity who personally intervened at crucial moments in the life cycles of the family. This God called Abram to leave his father's house and to come to Canaan, the land of promise. At the local sanctuaries in the land, this God appeared to bless and to protect and to judge. Particularly noteworthy is the self-binding oath made to Abram in promising him and his descendants the land of Canaan (Gen 15:1–21).[40] The details of the promise in Gen 15:13–18 presuppose knowledge of Israel's later history, and the whole chapter is a parade example of the national consciousness interpreting an earlier account.[41] There is no

---

[37] Gen 24; Gen 27–29.

[38] Gen 37, 39–50; Exod 13:19; Josh 24:32.

[39] Another possibility links the Hebrew term with a cognate term 'apiru, used to describe mobile classes of people who hired themselves out to clients. Cf. O. Loretz, *Habiru-Hebräer. Eine socio-linguistische Studie über die Herkunft des Gentiliziums 'ibrî vom Appellativum ḫabiru* (BZAW 160; Berlin: de Gruyter, 1984); and B. Oded, "The Table of Nations (Gen 10)—A Socio-cultural Approach," *ZAW* 98 (1986): 14–30. Loretz is skeptical about any links of the word "Hebrew" with early, non-biblical texts. Oded is more affirming with regard to the relationship of "Hebrew" with Eber (Gen 10:21). According to him, Eber represents the nomadic peoples in the table of nations.

[40] G. F. Hasel, "The Meaning of the Animal Rite in Gen. 15," *JSOT* 19 (1981): 61–78.

[41] R. E. Clements, *Abraham and David. Gen. 15 and its Meaning for Israelite*

compelling reason to assume, however, the whole account is the creation of the Deuteronomist or a later source.[42]

The unfolding generational history of the ancestors is designed to demonstrate the faithfulness of the ancestral God to the promised blessings of posterity and land (Gen 12:1–3, 7).[43] Both posterity and land are symbols of divine grace for the family of Israel. Ultimately the electing God, whose providence preserved the generations of one family or clan (mišpāḥāh), will use the descendants of that clan to bless all the families of the earth. In this most profound implication of the ancestral accounts, even a national history is only a prelude to the possibility of universal blessing dispensed by Yahweh.

In the canonical version the ancestral God is none other than Yahweh (יהוה), who would reveal his name to Moses and who would deliver the larger family of "outsiders" from Egypt and bring them into the land previously promised to their ancestors. Just as the ancestral name "Israel" was transmitted to an association of tribes and then later to the state, so the identity of the ancestral God of Abraham, Isaac, and Jacob was transmitted to Yahweh, the God of Israel. How this transmission took place is a fascinating question without a clear answer. One possibility is that Yahweh was originally an epithet of 'El which "hypostasized," i.e., developed into a personality of his own for early Israelite tribal elements.[44] This is perhaps the simplest way to account for the identification of 'El and Yahweh in the OT. Another possibility is that Yahweh is the name of a deity brought into Canaan from the outside who quickly absorbed not only the characteristics of the high god 'El but even his name.[45] And whatever the precise historical explanation for

---

Tradition (SBT 5; London: SCM Press, 1967); N. Lohfink, Die Landverheissung als Eid. Eine Studie zu Gen. 15 (SBS 28; Stuttgart: Katholisches Bibelwerk, 1967).

[42] For a late dating of the chapter see M. Anbar, "Genesis 15: A Conflation of Two Deuteronomic Narratives," JBL 101 (1982): 39–55; Van Seters, Abraham in History and Tradition, 249–69; J. Ha, Genesis 15. A Theological Compendium of Pentateuchal History (BZAW 181; Berlin: de Gruyter, 1989). Ha believes the passage is late and designed to serve as an introduction to the ancestral stories. The literary placement of the passage is not well suited for his hypothesis, and the contacts with other Pentateuchal traditions are best explained as redactional work on an older account of oath and covenant-making.

[43] Gen 12:1–3 is a literary "hinge" between the previous world history (Gen 1–11) and the ancestral accounts (Gen 12–50). It places the ancestral accounts under the theme of Yahweh's resolve to bless (brk).

[44] So Cross, Canaanite Myth and Hebrew Epic, 60–74. Part of the plausibility of this answer depends on the meaning attached to the epithet Yahweh. See pp. 23–24 below. Cross proposes the epithet was part of the phrase il ḏu yahwi ṣaba'ot, "El who creates the armies."

[45] So O. Eissfeldt, "El and Yahweh," JSS 1 (1956): 25–37. Although Eissfeldt too stressed the continuity between Yahweh and 'El in the biblical tradition, he believed Yahweh was originally a separate deity from 'El.

their identification, the first great cultural development for Israel comes with it.[46] 'El, widely recognized in Canaan as king of the gods, not only exercised special care for Israel's ancestors in Canaan, but in his identity as Yahweh, 'El redeemed them from Egypt and granted them an inheritance in the promised land. In theological terms, the identity between 'El and Yahweh helped Israel account for the fact that they were outsiders, yet that they were also culturally Canaanite.

THE ORIGINS OF YAHWISM

There are numerous studies on the meaning and signficance of the tetragrammaton YHWH (יהוה, Yahweh), used over six thousand times in the OT as the name of the God of Israel.[47] The earliest certain reference to the name in an extrabiblical text occurs in the ninth-century inscription of the Moabite king Mesha.[48] A number of earlier references have been proposed, though none of them are without problems. But even if references to the tetragrammaton are discovered that pre-date the OT, it should be remembered that the OT writers may attach significance to the name's meaning quite apart from its use elsewhere.

Extrabiblical Sources

Of the possible extrabiblical references, the most crucial for reconstructing the origins of Yahwism is a place name preserved in two Egyptian topographical lists of the LBA.[49] Apparently the place name

---

[46] The identification between Yahweh and 'El is an example of convergence in developing a religious tradition, according to M. S. Smith, *The Early History of God. Yahweh and the Other Deities in Ancient Israel* (San Francisco: Harper & Row, 1990), xxiii–xxiv, 7–40. See also J. C. De Moor, *The Rise of Yahwism. The Roots of Israelite Monotheism* (BETL 91; Leuven: University Press, 1990), 223–60; T. Mettinger, "The Elusive Essence. YHWH, El and Baal and the Distinctiveness of Israelite Religion," *Die Hebräische Bibel und ihre zweifach Nachgeschichte. Festschrift für Rolf Rendtorff* (ed. E. Blum, C. Macholz, E. Stegemann; Neukirchen-Vluyn: Neukirchener Verlag, 1990), 393–417.

[47] D. Freedman, D. O'Connor, H. Ringgren, "יהוה," *TDOT* 5.500–521; E. A. Knauf, "Yahwe," *VT* 34 (1984): 467–72; and his *Midian. Untersuchungen zur Geschichte Palästinas und Nordarabiens am Ende des Jahrtausends v. Chr.* (Wiesbaden: O. Harrassowitz, 1988), 43–48.

[48] ANET, 320.

[49] R. Giveon, *Les bédouins shosou des documents égyptiens* (Leiden: Brill, 1971), document 6a [Amenophis III, Soleb Temple] = t3 šsw yhw; and document 16a [Ramses II, Amarah West] = šsw yhw. Giveon proposes the site is located south or southeast of Palestine. Cf. L. E. Axelsson, *The Lord Rose Up From Seir. Studies in the History and Traditions of the Negev and Southern Judah* (CB/OT 25; Stockholm: Alqvist and Wiksell, 1987), 57–61.

should be translated "Yahweh in the Shasu land" and should be associated with the Shasu tribes south and east of Palestine. The name may even reflect a pre-Israelite form of Yahwism as well as indicate the location of Mt. Sinai.[50] These tribal nomads known as Shasu moved about in the areas east of the Egyptian Delta, south and southeast of Palestine, and even into Syria. If the translation and location are correct, they provide evidence for possible connections of the Shasu with the Midianites and Kenites of the OT, if not with early elements of Israel itself. They also provide an interesting tie-in with the biblical traditions that depict the revelation of the divine name to Moses at the mountain of God south of Palestine,[51] and with other texts that speak of Yahweh's appearance and "southern march" from the same region.[52]

Other biblical traditions presuppose a close relationship between Moses and the Midianites or Kenites who moved about in these areas.[53] Jethro, Moses' father-in-law, worships Yahweh and offers Moses advice on dealing with administrative problems. The so-called Kenite hypothesis links the origins of Yahwism to the relationship between Kenite or Midianite tribes and early Israelite elements.[54] H. Ringgren has rightly commented that of the various theories dealing with the origins of Yahwism it is the only one with much probability attached to it.[55] Nevertheless, the hypothesis is supported by a number of disparate elements comprised of fragmentary details. They cannot be mixed together arbitrarily in order to produce a more complete historical reconstruction; yet they can not be ignored either simply because gaps and questions remain. One can add to the evidence already mentioned the proposal that Midianite (i.e., northwest Arabian) elements[56] had sub-

---

[50] So Knauf, *Midian*, 48–63. He proposes a site in the region southeast of Akaba for the mountain.

[51] Exod 3:1, 19:2—mountain of God; Num 10:33—mountain of Yahweh.

[52] Judg 5:4–5; Psalm 68:6–8 (E, 7–8); Hab 3:3.

[53] Exod 2:16–22; 3:1; 18:1–27; Judg 4:11. Perhaps the earliest reference to Kenites in the Sinai region comes from a second millennium inscription; see M. Dijkstra, "The Statue Sinai Nr. 346 and the Tribe of the Kenites," *Wünschet Jerusalem Frieden* (ed. M. Augustin, K. D. Schunck; Frankfurt: P. Lang, 1988), 93–103.

[54] H. H. Rowley, *Joshua. Biblical Traditions in the Light of Archaeology* (London: British Academy, 1950), 149–56, has the best history of the discussion.

[55] H. Ringgren, *Israelite Religion* (Philadelphia: Fortress Press, 1966), 34. See also the approving comments of Mettinger, "The Elusive Essence," *Die Hebräische Bibel* (ed. E. Blum), 404–9. "We must then accept the core of the Midianite-Kenite hypothesis as basically correct" (p. 409).

[56] W. Dumbrell, "Midian—A Land or League?" *VT* 25 (1975): 323–37; M. Weinfeld, "The Tribal League at Sinai," in Miller, et al., eds., *Ancient Israelite Religion*, 303–13; F. M. Cross, "Reuben, First Born of Jacob," *ZAW* Sup 100 (1988): 46–63. Knauf, *Midian*, 48–114, gives the most detailed analysis of the possible connections between Midian, the biblical texts, and the origins of Yahwism. His own conclu-

stantial influence in the caravan routes of the Sinai and Transjordan in the thirteenth/twelfth centuries B.C.E. and the proposal that Kenite elements were closely related to the service of Yahweh in the Negev.[57]

The Significance of the Name Yahweh

The OT itself puts no great emphasis on a Kenite-Midianite connection with Israel, although it assumes that the mountain of God (Sinai/Horeb) lay south of the tribal boundaries and that life in Canaan was sedentary. Also, the OT reflects little interest in the geographic origin of the name Yahweh or its etymology, except as the latter has a bearing on the relationship between Yahweh and Israel. Exodus 3 is the primary account of the revelation of the divine name, and it preserves two claims. The first has already been mentioned; it is the identification of Yahweh with the ancestral God (3:6, 13, 15). The second is the connection between the Hebrew verb "to be" (היה or הוה) and the name Yahweh (יהוה) as it is employed in 3:12, 14. This derivation is assumed in the promise of God to Moses in v. 12: "I will be (אהיה) with you." When Moses then asks for the name of the God who is sending him back to Egypt, God replies: "I will be (אהיה) whom I will be (אהיה)," and instructs Moses to tell the Israelites "I will be (אהיה) has sent me to you."[58] The following verse (3:15) is an explanatory comment that Yahweh (יהוה), the God of the ancestors, is sending Moses to the Israelites and that Yahweh will be God's name throughout all generations.

Scholars have devoted considerable energy to the questions of tense and translation of the verb "to be" as it relates to the revelation of the divine name. Should the form be translated: (a) "I am," "I will be," (b) or in the causative sense, "I cause to be" or "I create," (c) or perhaps more philosophically, "I am the one who exists"? These are legitimate questions, especially in the context of a history of religions approach or a search for the origins of the name outside of the OT, but they should not obscure what the account in Exod 3 preserves about the name's significance. Yahweh is the God who intends *to be* for Israel. This significance is further illustrated in Hos 1:8–9 and Exod 6:2–8. The Hosea

---

sions about Moses (a Semitic official of Egypt who fails to capture the throne and escapes with one or two hundred men), and the victory at the sea (Miriam, a Midianite, saw one or two chariots sunk southeast of Aqaba) are hardly persuasive.

[57] B. Mazar, "The Sanctuary of Arad and the Family of Hobab the Kenite," *JNES* 24 (1965): 297–303; and his "YHWH Came out from Sinai," *Temples and High Places in Biblical Times* (ed. A. Biran; Jerusalem: HUCA, 1981), 5–9. One should note in this connection that the Negev and Sinai regions do not show any sedentary occupation in the LBA. The Negev has a few early Iron settlements, but Iron Age (IA) settlements in the Sinai region date to the tenth century B.C.E. and later.

[58] The phrase can also be translated "I AM who I AM."

reference is a double play on names. Gomer's third child is named "Not My People," since Yahweh declares to a disobedient Israel "you (plural) are not my people and I Am (אֶהְיֶה) Not for you."[59] The verse might be paraphrased to bring out the play on names: "You are named Not My People, and my name is I Am Not for you."

Exodus 6:2–8 is a parallel text (attributed to the P source) to the revelation of the divine name in Exod 3. Yahweh is identified as the ancestral God who established his covenant (bərît) with them, who has now heard Israel's cries in slavery and remembers his covenant[60] with the ancestors to give their descendants the land of Canaan. The name Yahweh is revealed to Moses in the context of the claim that the ancestral God will deliver (nṣl) Israel from slavery. In 6:7 there is a play on the verb "to be" expressed in the statement, "I will take you for myself as a people and I will be (וְהָיִיתִי) your God."[61] Thus both texts, Hos 1:9 and Exod 6:2–8, concern the importance of the divine name as it indicates the relationship between Yahweh and Israel.[62]

The chief value of the Kenite hypothesis in terms of cultural analysis is its implication that major elements of early Yahwism and of early Israel originated outside of Canaan. It provides nothing of significance to the translation of the name Yahweh. Historically, treatments of Israelite religion have placed much emphasis on the bedouin ethos or desert monotheism of early Israel in distinction to the more developed culture of Canaan. Much of early Israel's supposed distinctiveness was accounted for by this emphasis among earlier scholars. If the overdrawn elements in this contrast are ignored,[63] it is still historically plausible that some of Israel's ancestors and the origins of Yahwism come from outside Canaan. In any case, the location of Mt. Sinai outside the land of Canaan is a powerful symbol of Yahweh's identity in the OT and of the significance of the divine name. It is the place where Yahweh met Israel in the desert and instructed them in the ways of righteousness.

Egypt and Moses

A primary confession in the OT is that Yahweh delivered Israel's ancestors from slavery in Egypt and brought them into the land of

---

[59] C. S. Ehrlich, "The Text of Hosea 1:9," JBL 104 (1985): 13–19, supports the reading "I am not your God" in place of "I am not yours," but this substitution requires a textual change and breaks the double play on names.

[60] In Exod 6 the term bərît signifies a divine promise.

[61] Cf. Jer 31:33.

[62] R. Smend, "Die Bundesformel," Die Mitte des Alten Testaments (BET 99; Munich: C. Kaiser, 1986), 1–39. Smend's reading of Hos 1:9, however, is closer to that of Ehrlich.

[63] Knauf, Midian, 6–8, 31–43, demonstrates, for example, that the Midianites cannot be described as bedouin. Some of them were involved in agriculture and trade. Even the term nomad must include some aspects of sedentary existence.

Canaan. This is the act that tied Yahweh and Israel together and served as a prelude to their meeting at Sinai. Apart from this crucial event, the OT attributes little significance to Israel's stay in Egypt, even though the canonical version puts the period at centuries![64] One of the few enduring legacies from Egypt is the name "Moses" which is related to the Egyptian term for child bearing. The word forms part of the names of the Pharaohs Thutmoses and Ramses.[65] A second legacy comes indirectly from Egypt but is likely a historical element in the biblical tradition: Moses had a Cushite wife (Num 12:1).[66]

Moses has a decisive role in the Pentateuch as the figure whom Yahweh uses to lead Israel from slavery. He is also a mediator to Israel of divine instruction (tôrāh),[67] given at Mt. Sinai and renewed with a second generation through a covenant ceremony in the plains of Moab (see chapter 4). These accounts become central for later Israel's religious identity, especially the various tôrôt or instructions contained in the Pentateuch. In cultural terms the tôrôt provide the basis for the distinctive ethos of Israel and later Judaism. Scholars have made decisions about the historical origins of this material only with great difficulty,[68] preferring instead to discuss the dating and development of the literary sources included in the Pentateuch, which reaches its final form centuries later. Perhaps the stories of the exodus from Egypt and the wilderness wandering are best interpreted on analogy with the ancestral accounts in Genesis. They first concerned experiences of particular tribes and clans which later become part of the national heritage in the land of Canaan.

TRIBAL ISRAEL IN CANAAN

The "outsider" claim of the ancestral and Exodus accounts still influences the historical theories that treat the origins of Israel and its religious ethos. Recent studies, however, have questioned the historical

---

[64] Gen 15:13–16; Exod 12:40. Cf. S. Kreuzer, "430 Jahre, 400 Jahre oder 4 Generationen. Zu den Zeit-angaben über den Ägyptenaufenthalt der 'Israeliten,' " ZAW 98 (1986): 199–209.

[65] The Hebrew etymology given for his name in Exod 2:10 is a popular explanation.

[66] Cush is probably a region of Midian. Cf. Hab 3:7.

[67] The noun torah essentially means instruction in both singular and plural (tôrôt) forms.

[68] H. Engels, Die Vorfahren Israels in Ägypten. Forschungsgeschichtlicher Überblick über die Darstellungen seit Richard Lipsius [1849] (FTS 27; Frankfurt: J. Knecht, 1979); W. Schmidt, Exodus, Sinai und Moses (Darmstadt: Wissenschaftliche Buchgesellschaft, 1983). A treatment of the book of Exodus with attention to extrabiblical sources is that of N. Sarna, Exploring Exodus. The Heritage of Biblical Israel (New York: Schocken Books, 1986).

validity of this claim (not necessarily its symbolic value), and its validity seems now to be the minority view among scholars.[69] A major problem concerns the search for adequate sources and appropriate cultural models. A widely accepted proposal from earlier years used the model of a sacral confederation (an amphictyony) of tribes in Greece and Rome as a way to identify early Israel's social cohesion in Palestine.[70] According to this reconstruction, whatever unity the twelve tribes had came from their common veneration of Yahweh at a central shrine. More recent research has come to reject that proposal since several of the distinctive elements from the classical model have been forced on the OT texts; nonetheless, some scholars have maintained modified forms of the model in the absence of a better alternative.[71] The problem of historical interpretation does not exist for Israel alone. Essentially the same issue faces the interpreter of neighboring nation-states such as Ammon, Moab, or Edom, about whom even less is known than is known about Israel. Each of these entities maintained a nucleus of cohesion in the transitional period from tribal/regional associations to statehood in the Iron Age.

Defining Tribal Israel

The search for cultural and political analogies for tribal Israel has gone in several directions.[72] One model employs the analogy of pastoral-nomadic tribes of Middle Bronze Age (MBA) Syria known from the Mari texts.[73] These tribes, who were already partially intergrated into the

---

[69] N. Gottwald, *The Tribes of Yahweh. A Sociology of Religion of Liberated Israel (1250–1050 B.C.)* (Maryknoll: Orbis, 1979); N. P. Lemche, *Early Israel. Anthropological and Historical Studies on the Israelite Society Before the Monarchy* (Leiden: Brill, 1985); G. Ahlström, *Who Were the Israelites?* (Winona Lake: Eisenbrauns, 1986); R. Coote and K. Whitelam, *The Emergence of Israel in Historical Perspective* (Sheffield: Almond Press, 1987); J. A. Soggin, "Ancient Israel: An Attempt at a Social and Economic Analysis of the Available Data," *Text and Context. Old Testament and Semitic Studies for F. C. Fensham* (ed. W. Claassen; JSOTSS 48; Sheffield: JSOT Press, 1988), 201–8; Whitelam, "Israel's Traditions of Origin: Reclaiming the Land," *JSOT* 44 (1989): 19–42.

[70] M. Noth, *Das System der Zwölf Stämme Israels* (BWANT 1; Stuttgart: Kolhammer Verlag, 1930).

[71] O. Bächli, *Amphiktyonie im Alten Testament* (TZ 6; Basel: Friedrich Reinhardt, 1977), contains a good discussion of the issues.

[72] R. Neu, " 'Israel' vor der Entstehung des Königtums," *BZ* 30 (1986): 204–21, and "Die Bedeutung der Ethnologie für die Alttestamentliche Forschung," 11–26. His discussion is the best brief review of the proposals on the social identity of tribal Israel. Cf. also W. Thiel, *Die soziale Entwicklung Israels in vorstaatlicher Zeit* (Neukirchen-Vluyn: Neukirchener Verlag, 1985); and his "Vom revolutionären zum evolutionären Israel?" *TLZ* 113 (1988): 401–10.

[73] A. Malamat, "Pre-monarchical Social Institutions in Israel in the Light of Mari," *VT Sup* 40 (1988): 165–76; idem, *Mari and the Early Israelite Experience* (Oxford: Oxford University Press, 1989), 27–52.

urban culture of Mari, maintained social cohesion through kinship ties and conservative principles of tribal control of property. The OT preserves cognate terms for tribal organization and inheritance practices that are plausible indications of similar social structure in early Israel. Other proposals have looked to associations of pre-Islamic Arabian tribes[74] or to African tribal societies known as "segmented societies" for analogies.[75] The former shows the importance of religious ideology in binding tribes together, and the latter have models of political enforcement and social cohesion that do not depend on central administrative institutions for leadership. Again the parallels are helpful; in segmented societies genealogies serve as indicators of social relationships, deities are protectors of the clans and identified as the god(s) of the ancestors, and the tribes manage policies of judicial enforcement apart from hierarchical, centralized control.[76] However, one must take care in using models that are as far removed in time and geography as the African societies are from tribal Israel; otherwise one runs the risk of using a composite model to overinterpret the biblical evidence.

One must not consider various models of clan/tribal organization in isolation from one another but take them as heuristic devices which assist one in seeing patterns and connections in the OT material itself. For example, C. Schäfer-Lichtenberger's reconstruction of early Israel[77] combines elements from the segmented society model with elements from M. Weber's classic sociological study, *Das antike Judentum*,[78] where he proposed a type of oath-bound confederation dedicated to the worship of Yahweh, and she also includes modified elements of Noth's amphictyonic model. Nevertheless, probably the best analogies for the cultural development of Israel are not the anthropological parallels from different

---

[74] B. Lang, "The Yahweh-Alone Movement and the Making of Jewish Monotheism," in his *Monotheism and the Prophetic Minority* (SWBAS 1; Sheffield: Almond Press, 1983), 57–59.

[75] F. Crüsemann *Der Widerstand gegen das Königtum. Die antiköniglichen Texte des Alten Testaments und der Kamp um den frühen israelitischen Staat* (WMANT 49; Neukirchen-Vluyn: Neukirchener Verlag, 1978); C. Sigrist, *Regulierte Anarchie. Untersuchungen zum Fehlen und zur Enstehung politischer Herrschaft in segmentären Gesellschaften Africas* (Frankfurt: Syndikat Autoren und Verlagsgesellschaft, 1979); F. Kramer, C. Sigrist, *Gesellschaften ohne Staat* (vol. 1; Frankfurt: Syndikat Autoren und Verlagsgesellschaft, 1978). Malamat has also used African societies as parallels; cf. his "Tribal Societies: Biblical Genealogies and African Lineage Systems," *Archives Européennes de Sociologie* 14 (1973): 126–36.

[76] For elements in the OT narratives which are not characteristic of segmented societies, see J. Rogerson, "Was Early Israel A Segmentary Society?" *JSOT* 36 (1986): 17–26.

[77] C. Schäfer-Lichtenberger, *Stadt und Eidgenossenschaft im Alten Testament. Eine Auseinandersetzung mit Max Webers Studie 'Das antike Judentum'* (BZAW 156; Berlin: de Gruyter, 1983), esp. 323–67.

[78] Translated in English as *Ancient Judaism* (Glencoe: The Free Press, 1952).

cultures and time periods, but the development of the Transjordanian states of Ammon and Moab. Unfortunately even less information is preserved about their early history than about Israel's.

It must be admitted that no single historical model adequately explains the origins of Israel in the land of Canaan or holds the key to understanding early Israel's clan/tribal structure. A straightforward reading of Num 21 and Josh 1–11 suggests that several intense battles delivered most of the land into the hands of the invading tribes.[79] But other texts suggest a longer period of settlement and struggle took place with different tribes pursuing their own course of events.[80] Both models have had their supporters among historians, and common to both models is the assumption that Israel (or parts thereof) entered the land of Canaan from Transjordan or at least the fringes of settled existence. A third model has leaned more heavily on the depiction in the Amarna texts of fourteenth-century Palestine as a collection of small city-states under the oppressive rule of Egypt. A process of retribalization and resettlement took place among indigenous peoples as Egytian control declined and as they rejected the control of the urban officials in Palestine.[81] According to this view, Israel's origins are linked with the resettlement process of non-sedentary elements already in Canaan.[82]

Shifts in Settlement Patterns

Settlement patterns in Palestine and Transjordan do show significant demographic shifts taking place in the transitional period from the Late Bronze Age to the Iron Age (ca. 1200–1150 B.C.E.), and they provide the best starting point for discussing the emergence of Israel in Palestine.[83] This starting point does not require immediately a historical

---

[79] The best statement of this position appears in J. Bright, *A History of Israel* (Philadelphia: Westminster Press, 1981), 120–33. J. J. Bimson, *Redating the Exodus and Conquest* (Sheffield: Almond Press, 1981) has proposed dating the conquest of Canaan by Israel in the fifteenth century B.C.E. He provides a recent assessment of the archaeological evidence in "The Origins of Israel in Canaan: An Examination of Recent Theories," *Themelios* 15 (1989): 4–15.

[80] Judg 1 and its list of unconquered territory (cf. Josh 13:1b). The best statement of this position is M. Weippert, *The Settlement of the Israelite Tribes in Palestine: A Critical Survey of Recent Scholarly Debate* (SBT 21; London: SCM Press, 1971).

[81] G. Mendenhall, "The Hebrew Conquest of Palestine," *BA* 26 (1962): 66–87; and N. Gottwald, *The Tribes of Yahweh. A Sociology of Religion of Liberated Israel: 1250–1050 B.C.*; M. Chaney, "Ancient Palestinian Peasant Movements and the Formation of Premonarchic Israel," *Palestine in Transition. The Emergence of Ancient Israel* (SWBAS 2; ed. D. N. Freedman, D. F. Graf; Sheffield: JSOT Press), 39–94.

[82] A thorough treatment of these issues is that of J. Maxwell Miller, "The Israelite Occupation of Canaan," *Israelite and Judean History* (ed. J. Hayes, J. M. Miller; Philadelphia: Fortress, 1977), 213–84.

[83] B. Price, "Secondary State Formation: An Explanatory Model," *Origins of the State* (ed. R. Cohen, E. R. Service; Philadelphia: Institute for the Study of

judgment concerning the struggles described in Joshua and Judges or a verdict for or against the "outsider" status of Israel. The settlement patterns show a marked increase of new, mainly unfortified, settlements in the hill country of the West Bank and Galilee regions west of the Jordan and in the hills and plateaus of central Transjordan.[84] These settlements should be contrasted with the LBA patterns which show population concentration in urban sites in the lower valleys and on the coast, some of which were fortified.[85] Some of the larger sites such as Megiddo[86] or Beth Shan[87] show significant continuity in transition from the LBA to the IA, while others, like Hazor[88] or Lachish,[89] show wide

---

Human Issues, 1978), 165: "probably the most powerful class of data to use in socio-political explanation is settlement patterns in the arrangement of population upon a landscape."

[84] I. Finkelstein, The Archaeology of the Israelite Settlement (Jerusalem: IEJ, 1988) and R. Boling, The Early Biblical Community in Transjordan (Sheffield: The Almond Press, 1988) have the most comprehensive data on settlement patterns for the period in question. Cf. L. Stager, "The Archaeology of the Family," BASOR 260 (1985): 1–36; F. Frick, "Ecology, Agriculture and Patterns of Settlement," in Clements, ed., The World of Ancient Israel, 67–93. For a limited use of settlement patterns in the discussion of the Israelite occupation of the land, cf. V. Fritz, "Conquest or Settlement? The Early Iron Age in Palestine," BA 50 (1987): 84–100.

[85] R. Gonen, "Urban Canaan in the Late Bronze Period," BASOR 253 (1984): 61–73; G. London, "A Comparison of Two Contemporaneous Lifestyles of the Late Second Millennium B.C.," BASOR 273 (1989): 37–56.

[86] G. I. Davies, "Megiddo in the Period of the Judges," OTS 24 (1986): 34–53. For a recent treatment of the stratigraphical problems still associated with Megiddo, cf. G. J. Wightman, "Megiddo VIA-III: Associated Structures and Chronology," Levant 17 (1985): 117–29.

[87] Beth Shan was a major Egyptian garrison in Palestine in the LBA and perhaps into the early Iron Age. See F. James, The Iron Age at Beth Shan. A Study of Levels VI—IV (Philadelphia: University of Pennsylvania Museum, 1966); Y. Yadin, S. Geva, Investigations at Beth Shean. The Early Iron Age Strata (Qedem 23; Jerusalem: Hebrew University, 1986); cf. the summary in Y. Garfinkel, "The Early Iron Age Stratigraphy of Beth Shean Reconsidered," IEJ 37 (1987): 224–28. The work by Yadin and Geva suggests that stratum VI, the last Canaanite stratum with monumental architecture, was destroyed in the first half of the twelfth century.

[88] Y. Yadin, Hazor. The head of all those kingdoms (London: The British Academy, 1972), 67–109; and his "The Transition from a Semi–Nomadic to a Sedentary Society in the Twelfth Century B.C.E.," Symposia Celebrating the Seventy-Fifth Anniversary of the Founding of the American Schools of Oriental Research (1900–1975) (ed. F. M. Cross; Cambridge: ASOR, 1979), 57–68.

[89] D. Ussishkin, "Levels VII and VI at Tel Lachish and the End of the Late Bronze Age in Canaan," Palestine in the Bronze and Iron Ages: Papers in Honour of Olga Tufnell (ed. J. Tubbs; London: Institute of Archaeology, 1985), 213–28. Ussishkin proposes 1150 B.C.E. as an approximate date for the transition to the Iron Age. The destruction of Hazor, for example, would likely have been several decades earlier.

destruction followed by smaller, poorer, and unfortified settlements. We should not assume automatically an Israelite identity for the inhabitants of each new site or for the inhabitants of each resettled site after its demise at the end of the LBA. The conclusion that some of these settlers of the early IA are "Israelite" depends finally on the claims of the biblical text rather than on the results of field work or of the analysis of material culture. Nevertheless, the settlement patterns in the hill country and Galilee present a chronological and geographical profile that essentially fits an emerging tribal association named Israel. The coastal settlements of the period by and large belong to the Philistines[90] who, it might be added, are associated with a distinctive culture of the early IA primarily because of the biblical text. Ammon and Moab, and to a lesser extent Israel, would be primarily responsible for the central and northern Transjordanian settlements.

The Material Culture and Religion of Iron Age I

For all the difficulties in identifying early Israelite elements, we are fortunate in having recent works that mark a real advance not only in identifying settlement patterns but in analyzing the material culture as well.[91] In addition to noting the decline of the Canaanite city-state system in the transition to the IA, one also sees a marked decline in the number of temples. Approximately twenty temples are known from LBA Palestine, and only a few survive the transition period to the IA. Dever points out that the prominence of altars, benches, and votive vessels in the temples demonstrates an emphasis on sacrifices and gifts for the deities. The anthropomorphic figures, both male and female,[92] and the zoomorphic figures, demonstrate that an assortment of deities were venerated in the same city. Only rarely is there inscriptional evidence

---

[90] T. Dothan, *The Philistines* (New Haven: Yale University Press, 1982). Cf. idem, "The Arrival of the Sea Peoples: Cultural Diversity in Early Iron Age Canaan," *Recent Excavations in Israel: Studies in Iron Age Archaeology* (AASOR 49; ed. S. Gitin, W. Dever; Winona Lake: Eisenbrauns: 1989), 1–14. In the same volume, see M. Dothan, "Archaeological Evidence for the Movement of the Early 'Sea Peoples' in Canaan," 59–70.

[91] In addition to the works previously cited, the following articles by W. G. Dever provide bibliography and discussion of the pertinent issues relating to early Israel's material culture: "Material Remains and the Cult in Ancient Israel: An Essay in Archaeological Systematics," *The Word of the Lord Shall Go Forth. Essays in Honor of David Noel Freedman in Celebration of His Sixtieth Birthday* (ed. C. Meyers, M. O'Connor; Philadelphia: ASOR, 1983), 571–87; cf. his "The Contribution of Archaeology to the Study of Canaanite and Early Israelite Religion," in Miller, et al., eds., *Ancient Israelite Religion*, 209–47. See also the treatment by A. Mazar, *Archaeology of the Land of the Bible* (New York: Doubleday, 1990), 232–367.

[92] O. Negbi, *Canaanite Gods in Metal. An Archaeological Study of Ancient Syro-Palestinian Figurines* (Tel Aviv: Institute of Archaeology, 1976).

associated with the figures,[93] but comparative studies suggest representatives of Ba'al, who in anthropomorphic form typically stands and brandishes a club or weapon.[94] 'El is typically a seated male figure,[95] and either 'Anat, 'Asherah, or 'Ashtarte is represented by the female figure, who typically appears on clay plaques and jewelry in a frontal nude pose.[96] The zoomorphic figures include bovine and serpent models. Since a number of the figurines are discovered in domestic contexts, some of them likely reflect individual religious practices carried out in private homes or small chapels. The large cities of Hazor and Lachish had at least four different temples operating concurrently, and Dever proposes it is quite possible that a larger site could have a dozen or more temples.[97]

The "Ba'al" figures are powerful cultural symbols apparently representing mastery over the storm and other powers of chaos. The brandished club perhaps represents lightning and thunder as well as martial prowess. The seated "'El" figures, then, would represent beneficent rule in the cosmos associated with the father of the gods. Probably the "nude female" figurines represent other powerful cultural symbols of procreation and nurture. Such an interpretation satisfactorily accounts for the exposed breast and pubic triangle common to them. Some of these nude figures appear on jewelry, which also suggests the function of an amulet or charm.

Those worship sites known from the early IA suggest a continuation of the emphasis on sacrifice. Sheep and goat remains are the most

---

[93] Cf. E. Puech, "The Canaanite Inscriptions of Lachish and their Religious Background," *TA* 13–14 (1986–87): 13–25. In these difficult inscriptions he finds references to Ba'alat, 'Elat, Shemesh, Ba'al and 'El'ab. An Egyptian stele at Beth Shan refers to Mikal, who is the Ba'al of the city according to R. de Vaux, *The Early History of Israel* (Philadelphia: Westminster, 1978), 117. A seal was found at Bethel depicting two deities, one male and one female, with the reading 'Ashtarte. The masculine figure could represent Ba'al, but there is no epigraphical evidence. See J. L. Kelso, *The Excavation of Bethel [1934–1960]* (AASOR 39; Cambridge: ASOR, 1968), 86, and plate 43.

[94] A. Vanel, *L'iconographie des dieu de l'orage* (Paris: Gabalda, 1965).

[95] N. Wyatt, "The Stela of the Seated God from Ugarit," *UF* 15 (1983): 271–77.

[96] M. Tadmor, "Female Cult Figurines in Late Canaan and Early Israel: Archaeological Evidence," *Studies in the Period of David and Solomon and Other Essays* (ed. T. Ishida; Eisenbrauns, 1982), 139–74; U. Winter, *Frau und Göttin. Exegetische und ikonographische Studien zum weiblichen Gottesbild im Alten Israel und in dessen Umwelt* (OBO 53; Freiburg: Universitätsverlag, 1983); S. Schroer, "Die Göttin auf den Stempelsiegeln aus Palästina/Israel," *Studien zu den Stempelsiegeln aus Palästina/Israel* (vol. 2; OBO 88; ed. O. Keel, S. Schroer; Freiburg: Universitätsverlag, 1989), 89–212, have treatments of the subject.

[97] For sites with multiple temples see A. Rowe, *The Four Canaanite Temples of Beth Shan* (Vol. 1; Philadelphia: University of Pennsylvania Museum, 1940); Yadin, *Hazor*, 65–107; O. Tufnell, *Lachish II. The Fosse Temples* (London: Oxford University Press, 1940); D. Ussishkin, *Excavations at Tel Lachish, 1973–77. Preliminary Report* (Tel Aviv: Institute of Archaeology, 1978), 10–25.

prevalent. There are no clearly "Israelite" temples in the early IA at the former LBA urban sites. The best possibilities for Israelite shrines consist of only a few small rooms with typical cultic assemblies such as offering bowls and limestone altars.[98] The number of figurines and anthropomorphic representations from the excavated sites declines considerably, with their presence primarily limited to the urban areas. It is possible that some of these representations from the early IA depict Yahweh, but this cannot be confirmed or refuted without accompanying texts.[99] Such representations of Yahweh almost certainly existed among some circles; otherwise there would be no reason for the aniconic stipulations in the biblical text (see pp. 38–39).

Two early IA worship centers outside urban areas are a so-called "Bull Site" south of Ibleam[100] and a sacrificial area with a tower on the southern end of Mt. Ebal.[101] Both sites are possibly early Israelite. The Bull Site was an open air cult place, not a domestic area, with a stone wall enclosure measuring ca. 21 x 23 meters. A *maṣṣēbāh* and a few ceramic pieces of stand or pottery shrine were discovered there, but the most spectacular find was a bronze bull, 17.5 x 12.4 centimeters. This is the largest specimen of its type found in the Levant. The bull was a recognized symbol of power and fertility, and it was frequently used in the depiction of different deities.[102] In this case the bull might represent 'El, Ba'al or even Yahweh.[103]

The tower or platform at the site on Mt. Ebal, measuring ca. 9 x 7 meters, had walls more than a meter thick and no visible entrance or domestic floor. Associated with the structure were numerous jars and jugs, and large quantities of bones. The majority of the bones had been

---

[98] Cf. Judg 17–18 for shrines in houses.

[99] See G. Ahlström, "An Archaeological Picture of Iron Age Religions in Ancient Palestine," *Studia Orientalia* 55/3 (1984): 12–13; J. G. Taylor, "The Two Earliest Known Representations of Yahweh," *Ascribe to the Lord. Biblical and Other Studies in Memory of Peter C. Craigie* (JSOTSS 67; ed. L. Eslinger et al., Sheffield: JSOT Press, 1988), 557–65.

[100] A. Mazar, "The 'Bull Site'—An Iron Age I open Cult Place," *BASOR* 247 (1982): 27–42.

[101] A. Zertal, "An Early Iron Age Cultic Site on Mt. Ebal: Excavation Seasons 1982–87," *TA* 13–14 (1986–87): 105–65; "A Cultic Center with a Burnt Offering Altar from Early Iron I Period at Mt. Ebal," in Augustin, et al., eds., *Wünschet Jerusalem Frieden*, 137–53.

[102] M. Weippert, "Gott und Stier," *ZDPV* 77 (1961): 93–117; A. H. W. Curtis, "Some Observtions on 'Bull' Terminology in the Ugaritic Texts and the Old Testament," *OTS* 26 (1990): 17–31.

[103] See also R. Wenning, E., Zenger, "Ein bäuerliches Baal-Heiligtum im samarischen Gebirge aus der Zeit der Anfänge Israels," *ZDPV* 102 (1986): 75–86. These scholars describe the site as "a clan-shrine for farmers of pre-Yahwistic Israel (p. 81)." The presence of the bull figurine does not make the site pre-Yahwistic.

burned, suggesting the immediate area was used for sacrificial ritual. The bones came from sheep, goat, cattle, and deer. The excavator suggested the tower itself was a large, open air altar. While that is possible, it is also feasible that the structure represents a type of fortress/temple (*migdāl*) or a center with sacrificial ritual. Egyptian scarabs discovered at the site provide a dating at the end of the thirteenth century with a probable occupation of a century or more. There is no proof that this site on Ebal (or the "Bull Site" described above) was Israelite, though it is a plausible if not probable conclusion. If it is not an example of an early Israelite shrine, then the Ebal site (and the Bull Site) offers a helpful analogy to the types of worship sites used by the early tribes.

The excavations at *Seilun* in the hill country north of Jerusalem have not produced direct evidence of a sanctuary,[104] but as the probable location of biblical Shiloh, the site is a prominent candidate for an early Israelite pilgrimage center.[105] This presupposition should be kept in mind when assessing the material culture and its interpretation by the excavators. Area C to the west of the mound produced perhaps the finest examples of courtyard buildings with monoliths of any early IA site. Large storage jars (oil, wine?) and stone-lined silos for grain were discovered among the structures. The excavator proposed that the quality of the buildings and the storage facilities imply the presence of a worship center, especially since the heaviest concentration of new, early IA settlements are located around the area. Perhaps the shrine was on the top of the mound, which unfortunately has been cleared of earlier remains in the course of the centuries. Were it not for the claims of the biblical text, however, the excavators would have only the surprising fact of fine buildings and storage facilities located adjacent to a *tell* whose earlier remains had been removed. It is worth noting that the site suffered destruction at some point in the eleventh century B.C.E., which would fit with the account of Israelite defeat by the Philistines in 1 Sam 4.[106]

Domestic features in the early IA culture such as three and four-room houses, and collared rim storage jars have been understood by some scholars as distinctively Israelite. They are not distinctively Israelite, but taken in context with other matters they are possible indicators of early Israelite settlements. Overall, the continuity with material culture from the LBA far outweighs the differences in the transition to the IA. On the basis of material cultural analysis, early Israel is indistinguishable from the larger Canaanite world. The cultural indicators just mentioned help identify them with only limited probability. The material culture of the hill country suggests these early "Israelites" cultivated

---

[104] Finkelstein, *Israelite Settlement*, 211–28.

[105] Judg 18:31; 21:19; 1 Sam 1:3.

[106] The text does not state that the Philistines destroyed Shiloh at this time. Jer 7:12, 14 preserves the memory of some destruction at the site.

cereal crops, practiced animal husbandry, and were less socially strati-
fied than their LBA predecessors.

Finkelstein's own interpretation of the settlement patterns and
material culture is worth considering. He concludes most of the new
settlements suggest pastoralists in the process of establishing a more
sedentary and agrarian existence. They are *not* representative of nomadic settlers or of new inhabitants in Palestine but are part of a large,
essentially pastoral subculture that inhabited the fringes of sedentary
existence during the LBA. They left the more urban culture of the Middle
Bronze Age in the wake of the turmoil and destruction which brought
that period to an end. Significantly, Finkelstein calls them Israelite
because this is the name later used for inhabitants of the region, but he
suspects that this name was not prominently used until the rise of the
monarchy.

Early Tribal Israel: A Proposal

I would propose the following reconstruction in light of the preced-
ing analysis of the material culture and the biblical texts. As Egyptian
power declined, and with it the influence of the remaining urban
settlements in Palestine, those we call Israel were prominent among the
builders of new dwellings in the depopulated hill country. As with other
groups settling in Canaan (e.g., Philistines), the settlement process in
some urban areas involved struggles throughout several generations.
Other areas were resettled peacefully. Israel would be not an ethnic term
or primarily a territorial reference but the name of a tribal ancestor
which was used to designate a decentralized tribal association. We
cannot assume much cohesion among the tribes and clans,[107] but there
is no reason to doubt the importance of both religious ideology and
economic self-interest in defining earliest Israel. The best parallels come
from the emerging Transjordanian states, each of which defined itself
primarily as a people with a national deity (pp. 26–30).

For several generations Israel's ancestors had moved about from
Egypt to Syria, as had a number of similar groups. Some elements in
these mobile population groups were native to Palestine and some not.[108]
These early tribal groups, therefore, would define themselves in opposition to the city-state system that prevailed in Palestine during the LBA
although culturally they too were Canaanite. This would give an emerg-

---

[107] For example, we cannot assume the loose confederation had 12 tribes.
The number is an ideal figure. See the discussion in J. Gray, "Israel in the Song of
Deborah," *Ascribe to the Lord*, 421–55.

[108] The *'Apiru, Shasu, Sutu, Amurru*, are names of mobile groups known from
the Egyptian and Mesopotamian sources. Some elements from these known
population groups probably comprised parts of earliest Israel just as they did for
the newly emerging Transjordanian peoples.

ing tribal association (Israel) sufficient means of identification. There would be opposition to the social policies that had prevailed in LBA Canaan and enough cohesion to form a loose coalition of tribes and clans related to one another through lines of kinship and obligations of mutual support. The emergence of an early tribal association known as Israel would illustrate the process known among anthropologists as secondary state formation.

Analogies derived from sociology and anthropology suggest a loose type of pan-tribal identity for Israel, with individual clans and tribes moving in and out of active participation in any confederation. The new fact of sedentary existence on Israel's part, i.e., the possession of family and clan property in Canaan, would be affirmed as the fulfillment of promises made by the ancestral God(s). If Israel was the name of an ancestor whose name came to signify the whole coalition, so Yahweh, the God who had delivered one group of slaves from Egypt and brought them to Canaan, became the God of the larger confederation of Israel.[109] From its beginnings, therefore, one can see the identity of Israel being formulated in cultural and theological terms.

YAHWEH AND THE GODS OF CANAAN: POLYTHEISM AND SYNCRETISM

One reflection of the outsider status of Israel is the scriptural acknowledgment (Josh 24:2) that their ancestors once honored foreign gods elsewhere.[110] It is a strange acknowledgment but not inconsistent with the more prevalent claim of problems for Israel in the land of Canaan. The comment of Josh 24:2 comes in the literary context of tribal settlement in Canaan and the call to renew the covenant vows with Yahweh; it is part of the great literary work known as the Deuteronomistic History (Dtr H) stretching from Deuteronomy to 2 Kings. Indeed, the period from the Israelite occupation to the period of kingship is treated in narrative form only in the Dtr H, so that in concentrating on the issue of Yahweh over against the gods of Canaan in this period, we follow a theme especially emphasized in the only surviving narrative accounts.

We have already noted one major element in the religion of early Israel, specifically the affirmation that the ancestors worshipped mani-

---

[109] In his survey of recent research A. Lemaire has made a similar proposal for an early coalition based on the worship of Yahweh; "Reserches actuelles sur les origines de l'ancien Israël," *Journal asiatique* 270 (1982): 5–24; and "La Haute Mésoptamie et l'origine des Benê Jacob," *VT* 34 (1984): 95–101.

[110] See Smith, *The Early History of God*; J. C. De Moor, *The Rise of Yahwism*; T. Mettinger, "The Elusive Essence," for recent and detailed discussions of early Israelite religion.

festations of 'El, a generic term for God in Canaan that was also used as the name of the high god (pp. 16–18). Yahweh is identified with 'El, or as some scholars would have it, Yahweh supplants 'El as the high deity and assumes many of 'El's characteristics. In either case, there is no polemic against 'El in the Dtr H, whereas the polemic against other deities and Israel's defection from Yahweh to serve them are major themes in the work.

Polytheism, Monolatry, and Syncretism

Early Israelite religion in Canaan is often discussed under the question of monotheism or polytheism.[111] There is general agreement among scholars, however, that early Israel does not conform to the modern definition of monotheism, which formally denies the existence of all deities except one. Perhaps the term monolatry better applies to the religion of early Israel, or at least to dominant segments within the tribal association, since the term emphasizes a devotion to one deity without denying the existence or activity of other divine beings. But even the term monolatry requires comment. The identification of 'El and Yahweh might be described as an integrating or unpolemical monolatry, while the opposition to the veneration of other deities might be described as an intolerant, exclusive, or polemical monolatry. Some insist that there is a close enough relationship between the religion of early Israel and the later affirmation of Yahweh's exclusivity in Second Isaiah to describe the religion of the former period as "practical monotheism." Less plausibly others would insist that Israel was essentially polytheistic until the emergence of "Yahweh-alone" minority-movements in the ninth and eighth centuries which later gave rise to an affirmation of Yahweh as the only God in the post-exilic period.

The struggle for adequate terminology, however, is but one of the problems in defining early Yahwism. One cannot assume early Israel had

---

[111] H. P. Müller, "Gott und die Götter in den Anfangen der biblischen Religion. Zur Vorgeschichte des Monotheismus," *Monotheismus in Alten Israel und seiner Umwelt* (BB 14; ed. O. Keel; Fribourg: Schweizerisches Katholisches Bibelwerk, 1980), 99–142; same volume, F. Stolz, "Monotheism in Israel," 143–84; H. Vörlander, "Der Monotheismus Israels als Antwort auf die Krise des Exils," *Der einzige Gott. Die Geburt des biblischen Monotheismus* (ed. B. Lang; Munich: Körel, 1981), 84–213; B. Lang, "The Yahweh-Alone Movement and the Making of Jewish Monotheism," in his *Monotheism and the Prophetic Minority* (SWBAS 1; Sheffield: Almond Press, 1983), 13–59; B. Halpern, " 'Brisker Pipes than Poetry:' The Development of Israelite Monotheism," *Judaic Perspectives on Ancient Israel* (ed. J. Neusner et al., Philadelphia: Fortress Press, 1987), 77–116; D. Petersen, "Israel and Monotheism: The Unfinished Agenda," *Canon, Theology, and Old Testament Interpretation* (ed. G. Tucker et al.; Philadelphia: Fortress, 1988), 92–107; W. H. Schmidt, " 'Jahwe und . . . ' Anmerkungen zur sog. Monotheismus-Debatte," *Die Hebräische Bibel* (ed. E. Blum), 435–47.

only a single viewpoint (or practice) concerning polytheism, nor can one view all forms of polytheism in a single light. The ancient world produced a variety of religious experiences including those of polytheists whose devotion to and communion with one deity can hardly be distinguished from monolatry. If one asks about Yahwism from the perspective of Israel's social identity, then the affirmation of the OT is deceptively simple: Yahweh is the god of Israel, just as Kemosh is recognized as the god of Moab and Milcom as the god of Ammon (Num 21:29; 2 Kings 23:13).[112] No matter how this simple answer is modified by historical analysis (e.g., a diverging polytheism or syncretism among some tribal elements), it remains the best explanation of the driving force behind early Israel's identity and of the affirmation of monotheism on the part of later biblical writers. The typically pointed comments of Wellhausen are relevant here: "Yahweh the God of Israel, Israel, the people of Yahweh; that is the beginning and the enduring principle of the following political and religious history [of Israel]. Before Israel was, Yahweh was not" . . . and Yahweh was "from the beginning ('von Haus aus') the God of Israel and then very much later became the universal God."[113]

Yahweh is the vigorous God who gains the promised land for Israel. Whether in earlier poetry or later prose, the affirmation is the same. It is this confession that must have been the dominant voice in early Israel, refracting the experience of several generations and perhaps different tribes. Yahweh had come into the land from the south, having gained the upper hand against Egypt and any who would thwart his people's settlement in the promised land. Of course, the historical process underlying the settlement period and the martial language associated with it were more complex than the biblical accounts reveal. As noted above (pp. 25–30), current biblical scholarship has downplayed the historical element in both the outsider and the conquest models of Israel's origins; yet with proper caution, these elements should not be denied their role in the formation of early Israel. Yahweh was a warrior, Israel was the people of Yahweh.[114] In this relationship reside Israel's identity and the basis for the later polemic against other deities.

---

[112] There is remarkably little evidence for a polytheistic state cult in Ammon or Moab during the IA. Admittedly very little is known about the religion of early Ammon or Moab, but the fact remains that a good case can be made for a monolatrous cult in both states. Cf. F. M. Cross, "The Epic Traditions of Early Israel," 36–38; and for comments on Ammon see J. Tigay, *You Shall Have No Other Gods. Israelite Religion in the Light of Hebrew Inscriptions* (HSS 31; Atlanta: Scholars Press, 1986), 19–20.

[113] J. Wellhausen, *Israelitische und jüdische Geschichte* (8th edition; Berlin: G. Reimar, 1921), 23, 32.

[114] Exod 15:3: "Yahweh is a warrior (*'iš milḥāmāh*), Yahweh is his name!" On the early designation of Israel as the people (*'am*) of Yahweh in Judg 5:14 (13H), see N. Lohfink, "Beobachtungen zur Geschichte des Ausdrucks יהוה עַם," *Probleme*

The OT has a number of ways to describe the exclusivity of the relationship between Yahweh and Israel. The difficulty comes in knowing how much of this claim goes back to earliest Israel in the land of Canaan. According to the Exod 20:3 and Deut 5:7, the initial commandment of the Decalogue seeks to preserve the relationship with the prohibition "You shall not have other gods (*'elōhîm 'aḥērîm*) besides me (*'al pānay*)." Recent scholars have been inclined to date the completed Decalogue to the exilic period[115] with its formulation first in Deuteronomy. This raises the question whether a form of the prohibition belongs to the early period of Israel's settlement in Canaan. Most probably, the answer is yes.[116] Israel was defined from the beginning in both theological and social categories. The confession of Yahweh as the God of Israel provided the essential cultural identity for the early tribal association. In any case, none of the hypothetical early sources of the Pentateuch demonstrate an acceptance of polytheism,[117] nor is there any evidence for Yahweh as a member of a pantheon elsewhere in the ANE.

The material culture of the early IA (1200–1000 B.C.E.) in Palestine makes a constructive parallel for the discussion of polytheism and syncretism in early Israel. Already noted (pp. 30–34) is the sharp decline in the number of temples from the LBA and a corresponding decline in the number and types of figurines clearly depicting deities. These two elements should be viewed together and are plausibly explained as a reflection of a dominant strain in early Yahwism; both elements have socio-economic as well as theological implications. Both elements presuppose that the Canaanite ethos of early Israelite religion did not require (or want) the tangible representations of cultic practice that were so capable of manipulation and abuse. Temple and divine image were associated with the oppressive practices of the former city-states.[118] And

---

Biblischer Theologie. Gerhard von Rad zum 70. Geburtstag (ed. H. W. Wolff; Munich: Kaiser, 1971), 281–83.

[115] F. Hossfeld, *Der Dekalog. Seine späteren Fassungen, die originale Komposition und seine Vorstufen* (OBO 45; Freiburg: Vandenhoeck & Ruprecht, 1982); F. Crüsemann, *Bewahrung der Freiheit. Das Thema des Dekalogs in sozialgeschichlicher Perspektive* (Munich: Kaiser, 1983), 26.

[116] See the discussions in F. Stolz, "Monotheism in Israel," 154–65 and H. P. Müller, "Gott und die Götter in den Anfangen der biblischen Religion. Zur Vorgeschichte des Monotheismus," in Keel, ed., *Monotheismus in Alten Israel und seiner Umwelt*, 132–37; H. J. Zobel, "Der frühe Jahwe-Glaube in de Spannung von Wüste und Kulturland," *ZAW* 101 (1989): 342–65.

[117] See E. Zenger, "Das jahwistische Werk—ein Wegbereiter des jahwistischen Monotheismus?", 26–53; and J. Scharbert, "Jahwe im frühisraelitischen Recht," 160–83, in *Gott, der einzige. Zur Entstehung des Monotheismus in Israel* (ed. H. Haag; Freiburg: Herder, 1985).

[118] C. Dohmen, *Das Bilderverbot. Seine Entstehung und seine Entwicklung im Alten Testament* (BBB 62; Frankfurt: Athenäum, 1986) follows the literary judgment that the Decalogue is exilic in date. But in a complicated reconstruction he proposes

because temple and image were symbols of imperial control, many pastoralists and small landowners would oppose them. Perhaps it is better to think in terms of early Yahwistic *independence* from these two elements of the typical religious patterns in Canaan rather than a carefully thought out rejection of Canaanite religion and images of the divine. From a socio-cultural viewpoint Yahwism too is a Canaanite religion.[119]

The Book of Judges

Israel's early existence in Canaan is described in the book of Judges, so named for the assortment of characters among the tribes who delivered Israel from the hand of oppressors. These individual accounts of "judges" originally described regional conflicts and have been expanded as episodes in a national history by later editors. The book portrays an Israel that did not live up to its responsibilities before Yahweh and which suffered the consequences. This depiction makes it difficult to understand how the tribes related to one another in administrative and political matters. Judges expands on the comment in Joshua 13:1—"there remained much land to be possessed"—and portrays the difficulties faced by the generations after Joshua who struggled to establish themselves in Canaan.[120]

An introductory statement of life in Canaan succinctly summarizes the view of the Deuteronomistic Historian(s) regarding the relationship of early Israel to the deities and cultural life in Canaan. The generation

---

the prohibition against divine images in the second commandment has antecedents in early Israel. On the relationship between divine images and Israel's socio-cultural context, see J. M. Kennedy, "The Social Background of Early Israel's Rejection of Cultic Images: A Proposal," *BTB* 17 (1987): 138–44; R. Hendel, "The Social Origins of the Aniconic Tradition in Early Israel," *CBQ* 50 (1988): 365–82. For a discussion of these issues in the broader context of the ANE see W. Hallo, "Texts, Statues and the cult of the divine king," *VT Sup* 40 (1986): 54–66.

[119] See the perceptive comments by M. D. Coogan, "Canaanite Origins and Lineage: Reflections on the Religion of Ancient Israel," in Miller, et al., eds., 115–24; and the succinct comment of B. Halpern, *The Emergence of Israel in Canaan* (SBLMS 29; Chico: Scholars Press, 1983), 246: "Israel's religion was a Canaanite religion."

[120] Cf. R. Boling, "In Those Days There was no King in Israel," *A Light Unto My Path: Old Testament Studies in Honor of Jacob M. Myers* (ed. H. N. Bream et al.; Philadelphia: Temple University Press, 1974), 33–48; W. Dumbrell, " 'In those days there was no King in Israel; every man did what was right in his own eyes.' The Purpose of the book of Judges Reconsidered," *JSOT* 25 (1983): 23–33; and B. W. Webb, *The Book of Judges. An Integrated Reading* (JSOTSS 46; Sheffield: JSOT, 1987); M. Brettler, "The Book of Judges: Literature as Politics," *JBL* 108 (1989): 395–418. Brettler dismisses the work of Dumbrell too quickly (p. 413, footnote 103) and overemphasizes the pro-Judean monarchy view in the book.

that followed the death of Joshua enacted a pattern that would repeat itself in Israel's history (Judg 2:11–13):

> The children of Israel then acted wickedly in the eyes of Yahweh and served the baals (ba'alîm). They rejected the God of their fathers, who brought them out of the land of Egypt, and they followed after other gods ('elōhîm 'aḥērîm) from the gods of the peoples living around them. They worshipped them and thus provoked the anger of Yahweh. They rejected Yahweh and served Ba'al and the goddesses ('aštārôt).

The passage continues with statements of Yahweh's anger at Israel's apostasy, the giving over ("selling") of Israel into the hands of their enemies, the groaning of Israel under oppression, Yahweh's raising up of a judge to deliver them, and the subsequent failure of Israel after the death of the judge (Judg 2:14–19). Then the cycle would repeat itself. The relationship between Israel and its cultural environment is assessed as a series of seductions by the Canaanite gods and capitulations by Israel. Defection from Yahweh is symbolically described as "harlotry."[121] The passage is really a compressed statement that depicts the Canaanite deities in a negative fashion with little individuality. For all its polemic, the book of Judges provides only a few specific examples of polytheism and syncretism.

There are parallels to 2:11–13 in Judg 3:7 and 10:6, each of which has similar, Deuteronomistic vocabulary.[122] The term "other gods" is used frequently in the Dtr H and is nothing more than a collective term for the deities involved in the forms of apostasy and syncretism opposed by the writers. This is clear from the parallel passage in 10:6 which reports the worship of the gods of the Arameans, Sidonians,[123] Moabites, Ammonites, and Philistines. Ba'al is a common semitic term meaning "Lord" or "owner" and is used as a title for a variety of male (ba'al) and female (ba'alāh) deities in IA texts.[124] Thus the plural form in 2:11 can refer collectively to various, locally revealed deities as well as various manifestations of a cosmic Ba'al. There is an analogy with the references to the god(s) known as 'El, where the term 'ēl serves as the name for the high god of Canaan or as a generic reference to a (local) deity. This pattern of the one and the many is reflected in the two references of vv. 11 and 13, the first in the plural and the second in the singular.

The plural reference translated "goddesses" in 2:13 is literally rendered 'Ashtartes, which in singular form refers to the widely known

---

[121] 2:17 reads literally "whoring after other gods" (zanū 'aḥare 'elōhîm 'aḥērîm), unlike the ancestors who had followed Yahweh's commands. V. 20 understands the defections as the breaking of the covenant (bǝrît) Yahweh instituted with Israel's ancestors. Cf. Deut 4:44; 5:1–22.

[122] Cf. also 1 Sam 7:3 and 12:10.

[123] Probably a summary term for the Phoenicians.

[124] J. De Moor, M. Mulder, "בעל," TDOT, 2.181–201. This standard treatment assumes too much uniformity in the OT references to Ba'al.

goddess 'Ashtarte.[125] She is identified with Hathor in Egypt and as 'Ishtar in the Mesopotamian realm. An interpreter faces similar problems in the interpretation of the plural form 'Ashtartes as with the plural form ba'als. Comparative evidence shows that the Mesopotamian 'Ishtar had a number of regional manifestations so that she was known variously as 'Ishtar of Arbela, Nineveh, Bit Kimori, etc. 'Ashtarte is not a title in the sense of ba'al(āh), but the tendency of the various Syro-Palestinian goddesses to merge and exchange functions makes her identification difficult. The parallel passage of Judg 3:7 has a different reading, the plural form 'ašērôt. The singular form is 'Asherah, a well-known goddess in the Semitic world.[126] This variety could well mean that the writer simply used collective terms that were better known than the generic, feminine plural for god ('elôt) or the feminine plural for ba'al (ba'alôt), neither of which occurs in the OT as a designation for goddesses. Possibly the plural term is simply a corruption of the singular form.[127] One should assume that the references to any of the "other gods" in the Dtr H are typically general and polemical rather than specific. This does not mean they are necessarily tendentious, only that the references are a type of shorthand to indicate religious practices the writers opposed.

Extrabiblical Texts

Another hindrance to a completely satisfactory interpretation of the references in the biblical record comes in the nature of the comparative evidence. Scant textual evidence exists for the period of Israel's settlement in the land, although there are many references to Ba'al, 'Ashtarte and 'Asherah in sources from earlier and later periods. Each Canaanite deity maintains a rather fluid identity in the course of time and in transition between population groups. Therefore, without accompanying texts, the considerable number of figurines and drawings in masculine, feminine, and zoomorphic forms remain mute evidence. Consequently scholars have depended on such discoveries as the LBA city of Ugarit, modern *Ras Shamra*, in northern Syria, whose rich material culture preserves texts about the deities 'El, 'Asherah, Ba'al, his sister and consort 'Anat, Mot, 'Ashtarte, and others, administrative documents, temples, art work, etc. Particularly important are the depictions of 'El, the father of the gods, and his spouse 'Asherah,[128] and above all,

---

[125] The name of the goddess in the Old Testament has perhaps been corrupted to read Ashtoreth, inserting the vowels of the word *bōšet*, shame, in the consonants 'štrt. On the goddess cf. J. Leclant, "Astarté à cheval d'après les représentations égyptiennes," *Syria* 37 (1960): 1–67.

[126] W. Maier, *'Ašerah: Extra biblical Evidence* (HSM 37: Atlanta: Scholars Press, 1986). See also pp. 79–80.

[127] The singular form 'Asherah is used in Judg 6:25–26, 28, 30.

[128] 'trt in the Ugaritic consonantal script.

the vigorous god named Hadad, the chief deity of Ugarit, though he is far more often called by his title Baʻal. This Baʻal is also known as the son of Dagan and as Baʻal Ṣaphon, i.e., the Baʻal of/at Ṣaphon, the imposing mountain north of *Ras Shamra* known today as *Jebel el Aqraʻ*. The Ugaritic Baʻal is no mere local deity or limited to the fertility cycle; Baʻal is a cosmic lord.[129]

The Ugaritic materials are obviously vital in the reconstruction of Syro-Palestinian religion and in the interpretation of the OT references to Canaanite deities. But with such a reconstruction there is inherently a problem in moving from the better known to the lesser known. For all the splendor of the Ugaritic discoveries, they must be interpreted first of all as the material culture of an LBA city-state not as the model of a general religion of Syria.[130] Scholars have noted, for example, that the procedures of the administrative-cultic texts do not necessarily agree with the information contained in the mythic texts,[131] suggesting greater plurality in religious practices at Ugarit than depicted by the more selective mythic texts of the scribes. Such a pattern would apply as well to Israelite cultic practices described in the OT when compared with the greater variety of practices among the general populace. One cannot assume, furthermore, that the description of Ugarit as "Canaanite"[132] means a homogenous culture, or that the dominance of Baʻal Hadad, as known in the Ugaritic texts, held sway in the hill country cults of Palestine during the LBA.

The best sources for comparison with the OT are the Phoenician, Punic, and Aramaic texts from the IA. Those that are extant, however, mostly date from IA 2 and later, and they refer to several different pantheons which cover an area from the Euphrates west to North Africa and Spain. The Phoenician cults were particularly popular and spread aggressively throughout the Mediterranean world (pp. 73–99), but they are by no means identical with the religion(s) of Ugarit. These later cults have left their mark on the OT. A discovery of archival and mythic texts

---

[129] The literature is enormous; cf. A. Kapelrud, *Baal in the Ras Shamra Texts* (Copenhagen: Gad, 1952); P. J. van Zijl, *Baal. A Study of Texts in connexion with Baal in the Ugaritic Epics* (AOAT 10; Neukirchen-Vluyn: Kevelaer, 1972); L. Toombs, "Baʻal, Lord of the Earth: The Ugaritic Baal Epic," *The Word of the Lord Shall Go Forth. Essays in Honor of David Noel Freedman in Celebration of His Sixtieth Birthday* (ed. C. Meyers, M. O'Connor; Philadelphia: ASOR, 1983), 613–23.

[130] A. Caquot, M. Sznyer, *Ugaritic Religion* (Iconography of Religions 15, 8; Leiden: Brill, 1980), 7.

[131] J. M. Tarragon, *Le culte à Ugarit. D'après les textes de la pratique en cunéiformes alphabetiques* (Cahiers de la Revue Biblique 19; Paris: Gabalda, 1980), esp. 183–84.

[132] A. Rainey, "The Kingdom of Ugarit," *BA* 28 (1965): 105–6, points out that "Canaanite" is but one of several ethnic groups listed in the Ugaritic administrative texts.

from either Tyre or Sidon would likely afford more explicit parallels for the early religion of Israel than the Ugaritic texts.

As noted above (pp. 28–34), Israel's emergence in the land of Canaan is best placed historically in that transitional period between the LBA and the IA. Not only did political realities undertake significant shifts, but we should suppose correspondingly that religion and culture in Palestine underwent substantial changes as well. Just as Yahweh, the "One of Sinai" (Judg 5:4[5H]), emerged as the god of Israel, so relatively newer forms of Ba'alism apparently emerged in Canaan at the same time. In the Amarna correspondence, for example, there are personal names formed with the theophoric elements Ba'al, Adad, and 'Adon, which suggest deities with these names or titles were venerated in the city-states of Syria-Palestine.[133] What is missing from the Amarna texts and from Egyptian topographical lists of the LBA and early IA are any place names in Palestine with the theophoric element Ba'al.[134] Names such as Ba'al Gad,[135] Ba'al Ḥamon,[136] Ba'al Ḥaṣor,[137] Ba'al Ḥermon,[138] Ba'al Me'on,[139] Ba'al Pe'or,[140] Ba'al Peraṣim,[141] Ba'al Ṣaphon,[142] Ba'al Shalishah,[143] Ba'al Tamar,[144] Ba'alat Judah,[145] Ba'alah,[146] "Mount" Ba'alah,[147] Ba'alat,[148] Ba'alat Be'er,[149] Ba'alot,[150] and Bamoth Ba'al[151] first occur in the OT and likely refer to cultic sites and places associated with a theophany.

---

[133] E.g., Ba'al-meḫir, EA 245:44; 257:3; 258:2; 259:2; Šipi–ba'lu, EA 330:3; 331:4; 332:3; and a plural form Ba'alūma, EA 162:76; Adda-danu, EA 292:3; 293:3; 294:3; Aduna, EA 75:25; 140:10.

[134] W. Borée, Die alten Ortsnamen Palästinas (Leipzig: E. Pfeiffer, 1930), esp. 95–97; B. Isserlin, "Israelite and Pre-Israelite Place-Names in Palestine: A Historical and Geographical Sketch," PEQ 89 (1957): 135; A. Rainey, "The Toponymics of Ancient Israel," BASOR 231 (1978): 3–4; B. Rosen, "Early Israelite Cultic Centres in the Hill Country," VT 38 (1988): 114–17.

[135] Josh 11:17; 12:7; 13:5.

[136] Song Sol 8:11.

[137] 2 Sam 13:23.

[138] Judg 3:3; 1 Chron 5:23.

[139] Num 32:38; Josh 13:17; Jer 48:23; Ezek 25:9; 1 Chron 5:8; cf. the Mesha Inscription, lines 9, 30.

[140] Num 25:18; 31:16; Deut 3:29; Hos 9:10.

[141] 2 Sam 5:20; 1 Chron 14:11.

[142] Located in Egypt; Exod 14:2, 9; Num 33:7.

[143] 2 Kings 4:42.

[144] Judg 20:33.

[145] 2 Sam 6:2; cf Josh 15:9.

[146] Josh 15:9; cf. 15:29 and 15:60.

[147] Josh 15:11.

[148] Josh 19:44.

[149] Josh 19:8; cf. 1 Chron 4:33.

[150] Josh 15:24.

[151] Josh 13:17; cf. line 27 of the Mesha Inscription.

Ba'al place names are also absent from the ancestral accounts in Genesis. One finds, for example, several references to Bethel, including its older (?) name Luz, as well as a reference to 'El Bethel (Gen 12:8; 28:19). There is the place of Jacob's nocturnal struggle, named Penuel or Peniel (Gen 32:31–32). In both cases the theophoric element of the place name is 'ēl, just as it is with the personal name Israel. It is probable, therefore, that some of the Ba'al place names are associated with early Israel. The Ba'al element in Israelite place-names would be an appellative or title representing Yahweh, or perhaps in certain instances, a reflection of the fact that some early Israelites worshipped another deity besides Yahweh.

Other Egyptian texts may provide a clue to the type of developments in this transitional period that led to new forms of Ba'al veneration in Canaan. Beginning with the nineteenth dynasty, the Egyptian deity Seth rose to prominence as the royal or dynastic god. He was also identified with the Canaanite title Ba'al, and as a result the Egyptian signs for both names were interchangeable. It also meant Seth assumed some of the characteristics of Hadad, exhibiting martial characteristics as a heavenly warrior in assisting Ramses II and III in their victories. The language and martial characteristics are most clear in the twelfth century Medinet Habu inscriptions of Ramses III. These affirmations of Seth/Ba'al were not widely shared among the Egyptian populace, and Seth suffered at the hands of later Egyptian reformists who rejected his syncretistic form as "foreign."[152]

The Ba'al place names in Palestine reflect Canaanite and Israelite adaptations of emerging forms of Ba'alism that, like Yahwism, partook of the dynamic cultural and political shifts of the transitional period. They offer a chronological point for these developments and evidence for a characteristic of early Israelite religion: rivalry between Yahweh and Baalism. In the identification of Yahweh with 'El, the chief deity of the Palestinian region through most of the second millennium, early Israel showed itself to be culturally Canaanite. But the relationship between Yahweh and Baalism was double-sided; on the one hand, Yahweh had elements in common with Baalism, sharing the title of Lord (Ba'al), if not the same identity with other deities (e.g., Hadad). Even if Yahweh's origins are located south of Canaan, Yahweh may well have possessed many of the characteristics of a Canaanite Ba'al (e.g., martial prowess, control of atmospheric phenomena). For example, after David defeated the Philistines he named the place of victory Ba'al Pərāṣîm, because Yahweh (the "Lord" or the Ba'al) had broken through (prṣ) the powers of the enemy.[153] Yahweh was the divine warrior who had gained the land

---

[152] S. M. Kang, *Divine War in the Old Testament and in the Ancient Near East* (BZAW 177; Berlin: de Gruyter, 1989), 78, 96–97.

[153] 2 Sam 5:20. In 1 Chron 14:7 one of David's sons is named Bə'alyada' = Ba'al knows. 2 Sam 5:16 records the name as 'Elyada' = God knows.

for Israel.[154] On the other hand, Yahweh was not to be identified as just another Canaanite Ba'al. By the ninth century intense rivalry between Yahwism and the Ba'alism of Phoenicia would develop and eventually lead to struggles (pp. 73–78). Some aspects of an earlier rivalry in Israel also make sense if certain forms of Ba'alism emerged in Palestine approximately the same time as Yahwism.

SACRIFICE IN ISRAEL

Early Israel offered sacrifices at various sanctuaries in the land. That is the testimony of the biblical text, and it is consistent with what is known about the material culture of early IA sites in Palestine (see pp. 73–78). Early Israel had a cultic calendar with sacrificial prescriptions as would any sedentary Canaanite population oriented to the changing seasons of the year. One of the earliest "Hebrew" inscriptions (eleventh/tenth century B.C.E.) is the so-called Gezer calendar, which can be coordinated with the cultic calendars of the Pentateuch.[155] A passage in the Book of the Covenant (Exod 23:14–19a) stipulates that Israel should assemble before Yahweh three times a year, and this requirement is developed in more detail in Deuteronomy and Leviticus. The seasonal calendar of the completed Pentateuch combines cyclical elements associated with agriculture and animal husbandry with annual celebrations of Yahweh's great acts in Israel's history.

The Pentateuch contains extensive sections concerning sacrificial ritual,[156] including instructions for the priests that contrast markedly with the brief reports of sacrificial activity by the patriarchs in the ancestral accounts. Many of these lists and instructional codes were not compiled originally for liturgical reading; instead, they preserve material necessary for priestly roles in sacrificial rites at a central sanctuary, combining both descriptive and prescriptive or procedural elements.[157]

---

[154] P. D. Miller, Jr., "El the Warrior," *HTR* 60 (1967): 411–31; and his *The Divine Warrior in Early Israel* (HSM 5; Cambridge: Harvard University Press, 1973). The poetic descriptions of Yahweh as a warrior have parallels with descriptions of both 'El and Ba'al.

[155] S. Talmon, "The Gezer Calendar and the Seasonal Cycle of Ancient Canaan," *JAOS* 83 (1963): 177–87.

[156] "Ritual . . . refers to a complex performance of symbolic acts, characterized by its formality, order, and sequence, which tends to take place in specific situations, and has as one of its central goals the regulation of the social order"; F. H. Gorman, *The Ideology of Ritual. Space, Time and Status in the Priestly Theology* (JSOTSS 91; Sheffield: JSOT Press, 1990), 19.

[157] A. Rainey, "The Order of Sacrifices in Old Testament Ritual Texts," *Bib* 51 (1970): 485–98. Cf. D. W. Baker, "Leviticus 1–7 and the Punic Tariffs: A Form Critical Comparison," *ZAW* 99 (1987): 188–97.

The Pentateuchal figures of the tabernacle and the high priest Aaron serve as models for the Jerusalem temple and its priests respectively. The texts concerning sacrifice find their present place in the Pentateuch as a result of the Babylonian exile and the subsequent rise of priests to positions of official leadership in the post-exilic period, a time in history far removed from the initial settlement of the tribes in the land and the sacrificial rites associated with local shrines. The post-exilic period is the time of the Pentateuch's final composition, which reflects priestly concerns with holiness (*qādôš*) and the means of atonement (*kpr*).[158] One should not assume, however, that Israel's sacrificial system had a strictly evolutionary development from the simple ritual of the clan to the complex ritual of the state and finally that of the post-exilic community. Late Bronze Canaan already had many temples with accompanying rituals that early Israel did not take over indiscriminately.[159]

Old Testament sacrificial texts share many characteristics with what is known of west-Semitic sacrificial ritual.[160] This not only includes terminology, but probably extends to common forms of certain ritual activities. Unfortunately for modern interpretation, all the attention to ritual detail in the biblical text does not result in extensive discussion of the reasons for sacrificial activity. In terms of a cultural analysis,[161] sacrifice in Israel has integrative and maintainance functions as part of a larger world view that understands social relationships defined by sacred and profane spheres. "Holiness" defines the character of God and, in derivative fashion, what is properly sacred or complete and whole.[162] Profane refers to what is neutral (with regard to holiness) or incomplete or broken. Sacrifice is a means of communication between the two spheres which maintains or restores parties in the correct order of social relationships. The cultic calendar of the Pentateuch illustrates this with its coordination of ritual for daily sacrifice, sabbath cycles, and pilgrim-

---

[158] N. Kiuchi, *The Purification Offering in the Priestly Literature, Its Meaning and Function* (JSOTSS 56; Sheffield: JSOT Press, 1987); Gorman, *The Ideology of Ritual,* 39–60.

[159] Most of the material in the sacrificial codes probably comes from the Solomonic temple with updates from the early post-exilic temple in Jerusalem.

[160] R. Dussaud, *Les origines cananéennes du sacrifice israélite* (2d ed.; Paris: Leroux, 1941); D. M. L. Urie, "Sacrifice among the Western Semites," *PEQ* 81 (1949): 67–82; B. Janowski, "Erwägungen zur Vorgeschichte des israelitischen šelamim-opfers," *UF* 12 (1980): 231–59. Janowski contains an extensive bibliography on Israelite sacrifice in its ANE context. Cf. G. A. Anderson, *Sacrifices and Offerings in Ancient Israel: Studies in their Social and Political Importance* (HSM 41; Atlanta: Scholars Press, 1987).

[161] Cf. D. Davies, "An Interpretation of Sacrifice in Leviticus," *ZAW* 89 (1977): 387–99.

[162] P. J. Budd, "Holiness and Cult," in Clements, ed., *The World of Ancient Israel,* 275–98.

age festivals. Within this framework are additional measures for individuals with specific needs. Peace or communion sacrifices foster well-being (*šālôm*) between parties; thank or praise offerings foster the relationship between God and worshippers; expiatory rites "clean" and restore parties separated by one partner's defiling activity. In theological terms, the Pentateuch represents the sacrificial system as a gift of God and as appointed by God to make efficacious the particular goal of a sacrificial rite (communion, cleansing, forgiveness, praise of the deity, etc.). Leviticus 17:11, a text from the Holiness Code, succinctly expresses this understanding of gift given and its effects defined.

> For the life (*nepeš*) of a living entity (*bāśār*) is in the blood, and I have given it to you [for use] on the altar to make atonement for your lives (*nepeš*), for the blood with the life shall make atonement.

Much discussion of this verse has concentrated on the meaning of the verb "to make atonement" (*kpr*), or the noun "life," with the intention of drawing some broader conclusions about the nature of Israelite sacrificial practice.[163] How, for example, does it work? But one should not ignore either how much of a working definition of sacrifice and ritual is simply assumed by the declarative statement: "I have given it [blood] to you . . . to make atonement." These activities are a "given" part of a larger world view in Israel, elements of which were widely shared in the ancient world. Blood was the symbol of life, life that a deity could grant or take. The altar was the symbol of the meeting place between deity and worshipper where gifts were exchanged and communion restored between the two parties. There was likely no more agreement (or understanding) regarding sacrifice in ancient Israel than among modern interpreters. Or stated differently, there was likely a broad variety in Israelite sacrificial practice and understanding.

Several points are crucial in order to appreciate sacrificial ritual. Sacrifice was not an activity done in isolation from other customary and ritual activity. Prayers, vows, singing, dancing, religious instruction, etc., were associated with sacrifice and provided a meaningful context for it. According to Pentateuchal texts there is a procedural pattern to sacrifice: expiation (cleansing), consecration (setting apart, a dedication), and communion (restoration).[164] Sacrifice was intended to be a means to these ends, not an end in and of itself. Sacrificial acts, therefore, like other elements of public worship, were intimately related to piety before God. But they also helped define the boundaries of a proper social order by mediating between sacred and profane spheres. Sacrificial worship

---

[163] Cf. Kiuchi, *The Purification Offering*, 101–9; Gorman, *The Ideology of Ritual*, 181–90.

[164] Rainey, "The Order of Sacrifices," 498.

was intended to foster a proper social ethic among participants, not to substitute for it. Moreover, one should not underestimate the voluntary nature of much sacrificial activity. Free-will and discretionary offerings likely played a large role among families who regularly participated in public ritual, since births, deaths, sickness, marriage, etc. came at regular intervals in the life cycle apart from the stipulations of a cultic calendar or prescribed activity of a larger temple. And for many families, especially those in rural areas or settings of some distance from a larger center, sacrificial ritual was an indispensable part of popular religion, habitually carried out by the family at local shrines or regional centers throughout the pre-exilic period.

Two accounts of sacrifice in the Pentateuch portray the importance of sacrifice in binding Yahweh and Israel to each other. In Gen 15 the sacrificial ritual is the performance of a self-binding oath by Yahweh in the promise of land and posterity to Abram (see pp. 19–20). The ritual slaying of the animals is a symbol of Yahweh's resolve in oath-making and implies a fate for the oath-maker like that of the animals in the case of non-compliance.[165] In Exod 24:3–8 Moses commissions sacrifices and sprinkles half the blood on the altar and half on the assembled people, who affirm that "all Yahweh has spoken we will do (and obey)." The blood serves symbolically as a seal or a bond of the relationship between Yahweh and people, also underscoring the solemnity of the people's oath and illustrating the fate of non-compliance.[166]

These two accounts are the product of lengthy reflection and serve theological purposes for later Israel, but the ritual activity described is not out of place in early Israel. The activity can be compared with the narrative account in 1 Sam 11:1–11, namely, the account of Saul's muster of Israel for battle against the Ammonites. Even though his slaying of a yoke of oxen is itself not described as a sacrificial act, the shed blood represents a powerful symbol. Saul divides the slain animals into twelve portions, sending a portion to each tribal representative with the call to muster for battle. The pieces of the oxen are a graphic reminder that the social order has broken down (the Ammonites have oppressed Jabesh Gilead) and a reminder of the consequences of non-compliance with the call to muster. Saul's method of "call-to-arms" is a reminder of the tribes' solemn obligation for self-defense that was a part of his accession to the monarchy.

---

[165] On the antiquity of the sacrificial rite and its meaning, cf. Hasel, "The Meaning of the Animal Rite in Gen. 15," 61–78. He dismisses the self-curse element in the sacrifice because it seems unlikely that Yahweh would take up such an oath against himself. On the contrary, this element underscores the radical nature of divine commitment.

[166] See R. S. Hendel, "Sacrifice as a Cultural System: The Ritual Symbolism of Exodus 24, 3–8," ZAW 101 (1989): 366–90, for a discussion of the text.

The OT contains more than one attempt to cut down on perceived abuse of sacrificial practice among the Israelites. For example, the prescription of Deuteronomy that sacrificial *worship* should be limited to the one place among Israel's tribes clearly presupposes disagreement with the manipulation of blood in sacrificial rites (see pp. 142–48). And the frequent polemic against sacrifice among the prophets is further testimony to the perceived abuse of sacrifice as a magical or coercive act (see pp. 170–85). Neither Deuteronomic reform nor prophetic polemic, however, should be understood only as a critique of sacrificial rites in popular religion. Their negative assessments presuppose that ritual abuse existed at every level of society including rites at state temples (official religion). And both priestly texts and prophetic accusations assume that the efficacy of the sacrifice finally depends on God and not on human manipulation.

Conclusion

According to the OT narratives, tribal Israel emerged as descendants of a wandering family, who became slaves in Egypt and later were given the land of Canaan by Yahweh, Israel's deity. In cultural and historical terms, the origins of tribal Israel were undoubtedly more complex than the depiction in the OT; however, it must be noted that the OT narratives themselves have significant symbolic value as the scriptural foundation of Israelite self-understanding regardless of the reconstructions of Israel's origins by modern research.

Much of current biblical scholarship has limited the claim of Israel's "outsider status" (e.g., ancestors as a wandering family, slaves in Egypt) to its symbolic value. Apart from the OT itself, there is no extant evidence for tribal Israel (or its ancestors) outside of Canaan. The material culture of Palestine in IA I, broadly defined, is Canaanite, and this cultural and historical period in Palestine is the best starting point for defining tribal Israel. Israel emerged as part of the Canaanite world, whatever additional factors contributed to the tribal association's political cohesion and to its self-understanding over against its neighbors.

The conclusion that tribal Israel was indigenous to Canaan from its origins, no matter how widespread in current research, is probably an overreaction to earlier theories that identified tribal Israel too closely with a romanticized notion of nomadic outsiders. Granted that Israel was culturally "Canaanite," there is still much to be said for the influences on it of (1) the non-urban, pastoral and agrarian strata in and around Canaan, including those non-sedentary groups who moved seasonally and periodically; (2) those opposed to the societal model of competing city-states (as reflected in the Amarna correspondence) and Egyptian hegemony; (3) above all, the religion of Yahweh, whose mountain south of Canaan distinguishes him and his followers among the inhabitants of Canaan. None of these influences necessarily diverge from Canaanite culture, but all of them contribute to a self-understanding of tribal Israel, and they provide it with an identity to distinguish itself from other Canaanites.

Israel as a State with Monarchy   2

THE TRANSITION TO MONARCHY AMONG THE ISRAELITE TRIBES followed the
common pattern for most states in the ANE. Hierarchical patterns of
leadership gradually arose, probably developing from earlier clan/village
practices, and eventually resulted in monarchy. Typically monarchy
included hereditary succession for the ruler and the control of other key
offices by influential families.[1] No single reason suffices to explain the
growth of this pattern, but a mixture of internal developments and external
pressures led most sedentary societies to adopt it. For all that kingship
had in common in the ANE, local custom and circumstances saw to it
that the duties and perception of the monarch differed from state to state.

Biblical texts record both enthusiasm for and opposition to the rise
of monarchy in Israel. One approach accounts for this fact by positing
multiple sources in 1–2 Samuel, the work which preserves the details of
monarchical development in Israel. According to this view, one of the
sources is regarded as early and more reliable historically because it
affirmed the rise of monarchy (1 Sam 9:1–10:16); another source is
regarded as late and reflecting disillusionment because of a negative
experience of monarchy in Israel (1 Sam 8:1–22). If the analysis of early
Israel in the previous chapter is accurate, the loosely associated clan and
tribal structures would not lead automatically to monarchy. Any transition from tribal authority to chiefdom[2] to monarchy would have

---

[1] T. Ishida, *The Royal Dynasties in Ancient Israel* (BZAW 142; Berlin: de
Gruyter, 1977).

[2] J. Flanagan, "Chiefs in Israel," *JSOT* 20 (1981): 47–73.

engendered some opposition among elements resistant to change. Particularly in the case of early Israel, a significant percentage of its population would be wary of centralized control along the model of the Amarna period with its examples of economic exploitation among the city-states. In the case of 1–2 Samuel, this means that the "later" source preserves some historically reliable traditions.

Other interpreters have proposed that the tribal influence in early Israel was so strong and the experience of exploitation in the LBA city-states so bitter, that the monarchy in Israel was essentially an alien institution,[3] the most radical revolution in Israel,[4] or an example of the paganization of Israel.[5] These assessments are too extreme in their assumption that early Israel's political organization and social identity were fixed norms. The book of Judges does not depict pre-monarchic Israel as the ideal model of social organization or of anything else! In its canonical form Judges is designed to instruct a later Israel how an earlier Israel survived in spite of its failures to maintain its theological integrity before Yahweh. Therefore, neither a purely source-critical approach to the traditions nor dependence on a general sociological model suffice to account for the development of monarchy in Israel, although both approaches have made important contributions for historical reconstruction. As with any particular context, there are variables peculiar to time and place that influence cultural development.

Attention to settlement patterns again provides some clues for understanding the rise of monarchy in Israel. Finkelstein has pointed out that most of the early IA settlements were located in the east or central regions of the hill country.[6] By the period of the tenth century and later, the beginning of IA II, there was an increase of settlements in those areas further to the west as well as an overall increase in population density. That settlement growth is plausibly explained by factors such as a general population growth, increasing economic specialization and production, emerging trading relations, even technological advancement which made the difficult western hills more accessible for use. The settlement patterns also brought the Israelites into closer contact with the Philistines, who themselves wished to expand eastward from the coastal regions.

These socio-cultural factors promoted the need for more centralized administration among the tribes, and in retrospect, make the develop-

---

[3] Gottwald, *The Tribes of Yahweh*.

[4] E. Neufeld, "The Emergence of a Royal-Urban Society in Ancient Israel," *HUCA* 31 (1960): 31–53.

[5] G. E. Mendenhall, "The Monarchy," *Int* 29 (1975): 155–70.

[6] I. Finkelstein, "The Emergence of the Monarchy in Israel: The Environmental and Socio-Economic Aspects," *JSOT* 44 (1989): 43–74. See also Mazar, *Archaeology of the Land of the Bible*, 368–402.

ment toward political stratification and institutional authority appear inevitable. It is no coincidence that Saul, the first "king" of Israel, was from the central hill country. He was anointed ruler (nāgîd)[7] over Israel which, in essence, meant the tribes of the central hill country and elements in Transjordan. He was a military leader and developed some new institutions for the administration of the tribal association he ruled. Historically, however, his successor David is responsible for the development of an Israelite state[8] and the classical dynastic model of monarchy.

MONARCHY AND ITS SPHERES OF INFLUENCE

The importance of the monarchy in the OT traditions can hardly be overestimated.[9] It is a central symbol for the political and religious identity of Israel. Recent studies have given somewhat less attention to the status and function of the monarch in Israel, but in the quarter century after World War II these roles were at the center of discussion.[10] In comparison with other cultures of the ANE, Israel's understanding of monarchy has been portrayed as representative of "divine kingship," where the monarch is considered a divine or semi-divine being. Others interpret Israel's understanding of the monarch as completely mortal but raised to a special relationship with Yahweh by virtue of the royal office.

---

[7] Lohfink, "Beobachtungen zur Geschichte des Ausdrucks עם יהוה," in Wolff, ed., *Probleme Biblischer Theologie*, 281–90; T. Mettinger, *King and Messiah. The Civil and Sacral Legitimation of the Israelite Kings* (CB/OTS 8; Lund: CWK Gleerup, 1976), 151–84; B. Halpern, *The Constitution of the Monarchy in Israel* (HSM 25; Chico: Scholars Press, 1981), 1–13.

[8] S. Herrmann, "King David's State," *In the Shelter of Elyon. Essays on Ancient Palestinian Life and Literature in Honor of G. W. Ahlström* (JSOTSS 31; ed. W. B. Barrick, J. R. Spencer; Sheffield: JSOT Press, 1984), 261–75.

[9] J. J. M. Roberts, "In Defense of the Monarchy: The Contributions of Israelite Kingship to Biblical Theology," in Miller, et al., eds., *Ancient Israelite Religion*, 377–96; K. W. Whitelam, "Israelite Kingship. The royal ideology and its opponents," in Clements, ed., *The World of Ancient Israel*, 119–39.

[10] H. Frankfort, *Kingship and the Gods* (Chicago: University of Chicago, 1948); A. R. Johnson, *Kingship in Ancient Israel* (2d edition; Cardiff: Univ. of Wales, 1967). One should compare the reconstruction of H. Ringgren, *Israelite Religion*, 220–238, with that of G. Fohrer, *History of Israelite Religion* (Nashville: Abingdon, 1972), 140–50. More recent reviews of this issue are that of W. Zimmerli, "The History of Israelite Religion," *Tradition and Interpretation* (ed. G. W. Anderson; Oxford: Clarendon Press, 1979), 352–59; P. D. Miller, Jr., "Israelite Religion," in Knight and Tucker, eds., *The Hebrew Bible and its Modern Interpreters*, 218–32; and Whitelam, "Israelite Kingship," 128–36.

The latter perspective is the better interpretation overall, although there can be no doubt that the monarchy played a dominant role in Israelite society during its existence and "embodied" many elements vital for Israel's cultural self-understanding. Furthermore, the monarch as a person was a "focal point" for the relationship between Yahweh and the people, as 1–2 Kings, 1–2 Chronicles, and the royal psalms make clear in their various depictions.[11]

The accounts of the rise of kingship in Israel are dominated by interest in the figure of David, historically the second king of Israel and founder of a dynasty with its capital located at Jerusalem. Even those accounts which are either anti–David or at least note some of his failings still reflect his importance for the understanding of kingship. A number of the elements preserved about the first king Saul really function to introduce David.[12] For example, even though Saul ends up as a tragic failure, David is related to Saul's house through marriage and a personal relationship with Jonathan, Saul's son and heir to the throne, so that his accession to the throne is prepared for upon their deaths. Saul's failure as the king stands as a sign that Israel cannot have a king "like the other nations" on its own terms.[13] Yahweh is the true king of Israel and has the right to judge and define who will take positions of leadership in Israel. One function of the accounts of Saul's pursuit of David, where David gains the upper hand against Saul but refuses to take his life, is to depict the significance of the king as Yahweh's anointed or "messiah" (māšiaḥ)[14] and to indicate David's acceptance of that definition of kingship as sacrosanct even before his own occupation of the throne. Hence any king duly anointed as a sign of divine approval could be called Yahweh's messiah.

Anointed Leader and Dynasty

Anointing with oil was a ritual act that conferred a blessing or status. It was a symbol of divine designation. Priests (Exod 29:7) and prophets[15] could be anointed as well as kings. In the case of kings the

---

[11] B. Lang has reasserted the theory of divine kingship in Israel, proposing that monotheistic editing of the canon has left only isolated hints, "Der ver-göttlichte König im polytheistischen Israel," *Menschwerdung Gottes* (NTOA 7; ed. D. Zeller; Freiburg: Universitätsverlag, 1988), 37–59. His approach has virtually no control since where he lacks specific evidence he can claim editors have removed or obscured it.

[12] Even a chronology for Saul's reign has not been preserved accurately in the OT. Cf. 1 Sam 13:1.

[13] D. Gunn, *The Fate of King Saul* (JSOTSS 14; Sheffield: JSOT Press, 1980).

[14] E. Kutsch, *Salbung als Rechtsakt im Alten Testament und im Alten Orient* (BZAW 87; Berlin: A. Töpelmann, 1963); Mettinger, *King and Messiah*, 185–253.

[15] 1 Kings 19:16–21. According to the text, however, Elisha was not anointed with oil but covered with Elijah's mantle as a sign that he would take up the

ritual act was associated with the reception of Yahweh's spirit (*rûaḥ*) and divine approval of their institutional roles. There is a connection between the activity of the judges from the tribal period and those people of various functions anointed in the monarchical period. The judge was raised up by Yahweh for a specific task. He or she typically had no other credentials except that Yahweh's spirit came upon them. Thus the sociological term "charisma" was attached to their activity.[16] Yahweh was the true Judge of Israel; individuals judged Israel as Yahweh induced them to act.[17] When Samuel anointed Saul as ruler (*nāgîd*) over Israel, the spirit of Yahweh rushes upon Saul, just as it would come upon him in the context of preparing for battle against the Ammonites.[18] With the aid of the Greek translation, 1 Sam 10:1, 6f., demonstrate the connection between anointing, new status, and the reception of the spirit of Yahweh:[19]

> [1] Has not Yahweh anointed you ruler (*nāgîd*) over his people Israel? You shall judge (or muster)[20] the people of Yahweh and save them from the hand of their enemies roundabout. And this will be the sign that Yahweh has anointed you ruler (*nāgîd*) over his inheritance . . . [6] and the spirit of Yahweh shall come upon you . . .

This account and that of the Ammonite battle in 1 Sam 11:1–11 are noteworthy for two reasons. First, they illustrate the continuity between the judges and the development of a more permanent and institutionally secure leadership. Second, they show the connection between the leadership of an army and the development of kingship.[21] David's own success as a warrior played no small role in the subsequent development of his reputation.[22]

---

prophetic office. Subsequently Elisha took Elijah's mantle and received Elijah's spirit (2 Kings 2:9–15).

[16] A. Malamat, "Charismatische Führung im Buch der Richter," *Max Webers Studie über das antike Judentum: Interpretation und Kritik* (ed. W. Schluchter; Frankfurt: Suhrkampf, 1981), 110–33.

[17] Othniel, Judg 3:10; Gideon, Judg 6:34; Jepthath, Judg 11:29; Samson, Judg 14:6, 19, 15:14.

[18] 1 Sam 10:1–16; 1 Sam 11:1–15. This second passage may preserve elements from another source that also detailed Saul's rise to kingship.

[19] The LXX preserves a better reading in 10:1 since it is probable that double references in the Hebrew text to "Yahweh anointing you" resulted in a scribal haplography and the omission of the words in between the two phrases. Cf. P. K. McCarter, *I Samuel* (AB 8; Garden City: Doubleday, 1980), 171.

[20] McCarter would restore *t'ṣr* as in 1 Sam 9:17 instead of *tšpṭ*.

[21] Cf. 1 Sam 8:19b–20: "a king (*melek*) should be over us so that we might be like all the nations; our king should judge (*špṭ*) us, and go out before us and fight our battles."

[22] J. M. Miller, "Saul's Rise to Power: Some Observations Concerning 1 Sam 9:1–10:16; 10:26–11:15," *CBQ* 36 (1974): 165–74, has pointed out that in addition to the so-called charismatic judges, rulers such as Abimelech, Jepthah, Saul and the

In the OT the person of David and his dynasty are intimately bound up with the understanding of the king as Yahweh's messiah. Over the course of centuries the Davidic dynasty became the institutional vehicle which bore this title and provided opportunity for its rich theological development. According to Psa 89:3–4 Yahweh speaks:

I made a covenant (bərît)[23] with my chosen one; I swore to David my servant, "I will establish your seed forever, and I will build your throne for all generations."

The saying is reminiscent of the prophet Nathan's reply to David's proposal to build a *house* (i.e., temple) for Yahweh in Jerusalem (2 Sam 7:1–16).[24] Nathan prophesies that instead Yahweh will build David a *house* (i.e., a dynasty). Unlike with Saul, Yahweh will not remove his favor from David's *house*.[25] His throne will be forever.[26] David's seed will build the *house* for Yahweh in Jerusalem. The relationship between Yahweh and David's seed will be that of Father and son.[27] The two contexts share much in vocabulary except the term covenant, which in the psalm reference stands for Yahweh's oath of promise to David. There is also a parallel with the relationship between Abram and Yahweh. The initial call of Yahweh to Abram included the promise to make his name great, but the oath and covenant ceremony came later.[28] And as with the oath to Abram, Yahweh obligates himself to David's line.

The City of David and the Temple

No less crucial for the development of Israelite religion is the role of Jerusalem. Historically the former Jebusite city passed into the control of David and even bore his name (2 Sam 5:6–12). When Jerusalem or Zion expanded to become the capital of the kingdom, first of the confederated tribes and later of Judah, much of it remained the property of the dynasty. The first expansions came with David's own building projects and purchase of additional property. Among his most notable acts was

---

fugitive David gathered fighters around them. These bands were the forerunners of the standing army or personal army of the later kings. Miller's point should be supplemented by the treatment of chieftains in Flanagan, "Chiefs in Israel," 47–73.

[23] Cf. 89:28, 34 and 38–39. The lament of Psa 89 accuses Yahweh of rejecting his anointed servant from David's line and the covenant made with David's seed.

[24] Cf. D. J. McCarthy, "II Samuel 7 and the Structure of the Deuteronomistic History," *JBL* 84 (1965): 131–38.

[25] Cf. Psa. 89:30–37 with 38–45.

[26] Cf. Psa 89:29, 36, 44.

[27] Cf. 89:26–27; Psa 2:7.

[28] Cf. Gen 12:2 and 15:1–21 with 2 Sam 7:9 and 2 Sam 23:1–7. David's so-called last words contain a reference in 23:5 to God's dynastic promise as an "everlasting covenant" (berît 'ôlām).

the bringing of the ark into Jerusalem, for it was the primary symbol of Yahweh's presence with the tribal association. With the completion of the building projects of Solomon, Jerusalem expanded to more than twice the size of the city taken by David. With its royal palace and national temple, Jerusalem became the focal point for the state-sponsored worship of Yahweh. By the end of the eighth century, the city expanded again under the reign of Hezekiah. Precise details are disputed, but by the reign of Hezekiah the city had grown to ten times the size of the city taken by David.[29] It was far and away the largest city in either Israel or Judah.

In the OT the language of election for the city is as pronounced as that for Israel and the Davidic line. Yahweh "chose (*bḥr*) Mt. Zion, which He loves."[30] It is Yahweh's "holy mountain," or "the mountain of his holiness,"[31] the "city of God," or the "city of the great king."[32] Jerusalem has an elect status and security. God is in its midst, it will not be moved;[33] the Lord of Hosts is with Jerusalem, the God of Jacob is a "stronghold."[34] The psalmist bids an inquirer to walk around Zion and observe her buildings and fortifications; "this is God" adds the writer (Psa 48:14). Jerusalem, therefore, becomes a symbol of Yahweh's kingship and mastery over the forces of chaos whether they be human enemies or unruly forces in the cosmos.[35]

The temple in Jerusalem plays a decisive role in the exaltation of the royal city. It is a "holy place" (*māqôm*), or "holy temple" (*hêkāl*), the "house of God" or the "house of Yahweh" with the "tent of your glory."[36] When the psalmist affirms that Yahweh of Hosts is with Zion, the spatial context is first of all the city itself; God dwells in Zion (Pss 9:11; 132:13–14). We miss crucial elements of the affirmation if we think abstractly of Yahweh's dwelling. In material terms Zion and the temple

---

[29] Y. Shiloh, "Judah and Jerusalem in the Eighth-Sixth Centuries B.C.E.," *Recent Excavations in Israel: Studies in Iron Age Archaeology* (AASOR 49; ed. S. Gitin, W. Dever; Winona Lake: Eisenbrauns: 1989), 71–96. He estimates a size of 600 dunams for the city and immediate suburbs and a population of between 25,000 and 40,000 persons.

[30] Pss 78:68; 132:13.

[31] Psa 2:6, *har qodšî*; Psa 48:1, *har qodšō*.

[32] Psa 48:2.

[33] Psa 125:1–2.

[34] The word for stronghold is *miśgāb*. Cf. Pss 46:7, 11; 48:3. It is also used in the Psalms as an individual's affirmation of God. Cf. 9:9; 18:2; 59:9, 17; 62:2, 6.

[35] J. Jeremias, *Das Königtum Gottes in den Psalmen. Israel's Begegnung mit dem kanaanäischen Mythos in den Yahwe König-Psalmen* (FRLANT 141; Göttingen: Vandenhoeck & Ruprecht, 1987); B. C. Ollenburger, *Zion, The City of the Great King* (JSOTSS 41; Sheffield: JSOT Press, 1987).

[36] Pss 24:3; 26:8; 42:4; 65:4. The reference to the "tent" (*'ōhel, miškān*) may refer to a model of the tabernacle or the tent of meeting from the pre-monarchical period. Cf. R. E. Friedman, "The Tabernacle in the Temple," *BA* 43 (1980): 241–48.

are symbols of Yahweh's identity: strength, security, permanence, holiness, and beauty. Together Zion and temple represent Yahweh and symbolically communicate a divine presence when people come to them to seek God.[37] In the "holy of holies" of the temple Yahweh is invisibly "seated" or "enthroned" over the cherubim,[38] so that the temple takes on the symbolic role of the ark which it housed. As other traditions would put it, Yahweh's name,[39] or glory[40] or face[41] dwells in the temple. Yahweh's presence in Zion, however it was affirmed, was but an aspect of Yahweh's rule over creation. Other liturgical texts clearly relate that Yahweh dwells in "heaven."[42] This seeming dichotomy is not to be explained as a logical contradiction or as an example of confusion. The double affirmation of Yahweh's presence in Zion and in heaven is a way of grappling with the age-old problem of divine transcendence and immanence. Yahweh's immanence is mediated to Israel through the central institutions of temple and dynasty.

The close relationship between the Davidic dynasty, Zion, and the temple is depicted succinctly in Psa 132, which portrays David as anxious to find a suitable place for Yahweh to dwell. He brings the ark to Zion, which is the resting place (menûḥāh) where Yahweh desires to dwell forever. A temple is not explicitly named, but the psalm assumes one to be the resting place of the ark in Jerusalem. Yahweh's oath to David's line fits naturally in the context, but the promise of the dynasty's continuance is formulated conditionally on the obedience of the Davidic king to Yahweh's covenant (bərît) and testimony (Psa 132:11–12).

An equally remarkable passage describes Yahweh as the victorious warrior who has made his own dwelling and brings Israel to it.

> You will bring them[43] and plant them in the mountain of your inheritance (naḥalāh), the place you have fashioned for your dwelling, O Yahweh, a sanctuary (miqqədāš), O Lord which you have made! Yahweh shall rule (yimlōk) for forever! (Exod 15:17–18).

---

[37] Pss 27:4; 42:2; 63:2; 84:7; 96:6.

[38] Psa 99:1; cf. 2 Sam 6:2 and T. Mettinger, "YHWH SABAOTH—the Heavenly King on the Cherubim Throne," *Studies in the Period of David and Solomon and Other Essays* (ed. T. Ishida; Winona Lake: Eisenbrauns, 1982), 109–38.

[39] An important phrase for the Dtr H. Cf. Deut 12:5; 1 Kings 8:20.

[40] Important in priestly circles. Cf. Exod 40:34–5; 1 Kings 8:10–13; Ezek 8:4, 11:23.

[41] Pss 24:6; 27:4, 8; 95:2; 102:2; 105:4.

[42] Pss 2:4; 33:13–14; 53:2. M. Metzger, "Himmelische und irdische Wohnstatt Jahwes," *UF* 2 (1970): 139–58.

[43] Literally "him," a reference to the people of verse 16 whom Yahweh had purchased or acquired (qnh). Cf. 15:13 and the reference to the people you "have redeemed" (g'l) and brought to your "holy habitation" (nəwēh qōdeš).

In the old hymn of Exod 15:1–18, which celebrates Yahweh as the redeemer of Israel from Egypt, the language of divine dwelling is similar to that of Psa 132 and many other references in the Psalms, but the movement is reversed. Whereas David brought the ark (i.e., Yahweh) to Jerusalem for a proper dwelling place, Yahweh brings the redeemed people to his sanctuary and plants (*nṭ'*) them that they will have a proper dwelling place! Zion, of course, is not named, but the similarity of language shows how the temple in Jerusalem was able to gather and reinterpret various traditions of God's dwelling. In the context of the book of Exodus, the references to Yahweh's dwelling in 15:17 point toward Sinai or Horeb, the mountain of God.[44] The same language heard in Jerusalem reminds the hearer of the temple on Mt. Zion. The similarity of language leads to yet another meaningful connection for understanding the symbol of Zion as the seat of the temple and the location of the Davidic dynasty: temple and dynasty are aspects of Yahweh's rule (*mlk*) as divine king.

CITY, TEMPLE, AND DYNASTY IN CULTURAL ANALYSIS

The development from tribal association to national state carries with it a number of socio-cultural changes. Even though the books of Samuel and Kings are preserved by those circles supportive of Jerusalem, temple, and Davidic dynasty, they still contain elements which portray these fundamental institutions in various ways. David apparently held the various tribes together by a combination of personality and political will, backed by strong military forces which included troops personally loyal to him. But already in David's reign there are unmistakable signs of political discontent, and upon the death of Solomon the political union of tribes and territory dissolved. In hindsight, the relatively rapid development of the state and the number of inevitable socio-cultural changes present a classic model for unease and dissent.[45]

The triad of king, capital city, and temple was a legacy that David and Solomon passed on to Israel. Of course the triadic model was much older than the IA, having existed for centuries in the ANE before its development in Israel. It promoted an understanding of a state society

---

[44] Exod 3:1 already named Horeb as the mountain of God. Exod 19:3 refers to "the mountain" in the wilderness of Sinai where Moses ascends to meet God (cf. textual notes BHS). One account of the march to Canaan has the people depart from the "mountain of Yahweh" (Num 10:33). On Zion and the transfer of traditions to it, see R. Clifford, *The Cosmic Mountain in Canaan and in the Old Testament* (HSM 4; Cambridge: Harvard, 1971), 131–77.

[45] J. R. Rosenbloom, "Social Science Concepts of Modernization and Biblical History: The Development of the Israelite Monarchy," *JAAR* 40 (1972): 437–44.

and character in Israel in which the will of God was made manifest through these central institutions. And the model presupposed a hierarchical pattern of social order with society organized under the authority of monarch and national cult. In affairs of the state, there was no separation of religion from political structures, since the very basis for the state resided in the confession that Yahweh had raised the Davidic dynasty to its place of rule and had elected Jerusalem as the place where his name would dwell in the temple. On the one hand, such an order promoted political and religious stability; on the other hand, it could become too authoritarian and even idolatrous.

The books of Samuel and Kings concentrate on the responsibility of the kings for the cultic life of the nation (official religion). David's dynasty is divinely willed; this is a given for the evaluators who preserved the accounts. Thus it is all the more remarkable that elements unflattering to David are preserved along with explicit condemnation of some of Solomon's activities (see pp. 63–64). As a result of Solomon's failures, even Jeroboam, the first king of the separatist northern kingdom, is initially supported by Yahweh (1 Kings 11:37–38); he is condemned subsequently only because of his cultic policies. Throughout 1–2 Kings monarchical rule is evaluated in terms of the ruler's fidelity to Yahweh's commands for exclusive worship and cultic purity. The course of history is understood in light of the tension between Yahweh's own fidelity to the promises made to David and the repeated failure of the rulers to comply with their obligations. Even official religion was corrupted over the centuries, according to the Dtr H. Behind the accounts as we now have them are the facts of Israelite and Judean defeats at the hands of Assyria and Babylon respectively, and the exile of elements of both populations from their homelands. How to understand those catastrophes as divine judgments is a major theme of the accounts, and, with few exceptions, primary blame is laid against the kings of Israel and Judah, who are depicted as rejecting Yahweh in favor of the gods and customs of Canaan.

The Reigns of David and Solomon: Cultural Development and Syncretism

Settlement patterns from the tenth century B.C.E. demonstrate quite an increase in terms of numbers and sizes of settlements from the early IA (1200–1000). In addition to expanding and developing Jerusalem, David and Solomon (re)built key cities for the administration of the realm. The principal sites are Hazor, Megiddo, Gezer, and Lachish, but these are only the biggest examples of a number of changes. It is not necessary to decide whether it was David or Solomon who sponsored the building projects at individual cities, since the contrast between the settlement patterns of the twelfth and tenth centuries is obvious enough. These key cities had extensive gate and fortification systems and a variety of substantial public buildings.[46] Culturally these royal cities symbolize the power and authority of the central administration, and along with the temple in Jerusalem, they demonstrate the extent of cultural changes from the earlier period.[47] Two trends from the earlier period hold for the period of the united monarchy as well: apart from the royally sponsored temple in Jerusalem, there is no emphasis on temple building, and the percentage of "cultic figurines" found is still less than that from the LBA period.[48]

Although the judgment that the whole development of the monarchy and the subsequent social stratification were a radical departure from the tribal life of early Israel is too extreme, the cultural record does confirm that substantial socio-economic development took place. If these changes imply radical syncretism between indigenous Canaanite elements and Israel, then these ought to be most obvious in Jerusalem of the united monarchy. And according to some scholars, that is exactly the case. We should begin an analysis with the observation that the designation of Jerusalem as the national capital is a political and cultural compromise. Since Jerusalem was outside the functioning jurisdiction of the Israelite tribes when David conquered it, the city became an extra-territorial entity belonging to him. This made it a neutral place among the tribes initially, though as a capital the city's fortunes were quickly bound up with those of the ruling dynasty. The temple constructed by Solomon was also a compromise; on the one hand, it was a Canaanite structure built by Phoenician craftsmen. On the other hand, it housed the ark of the covenant in the holy of holies, preserving the significance of the central symbol of Yahweh's presence among the tribes. Moreover, even with its architectural symbolism, the temple still preserved the aniconic tradition associated with the ark: Yahweh is not graphically depicted in stone, wood, or metal. Unfortunately, we are limited to the biblical texts themselves in discussing the status of Jerusalem during this period, because very few remains of the Davidic-Solomonic building projects have survived.

Jebusite Inheritance and the Temple

Three elements are decisive for the syncretism represented at Jerusalem.[49] The first concerns the account of David's purchase of a threshing

---

[46] Dever, "Monumental Architecture in Ancient Israel in the Period of the United Monarchy," *Studies in the Period of David and Solomon and Other Essays* (ed. T. Ishida), 269–308; idem, *Recent Archaeological Discoveries and Biblical Research,* 85–117.

[47] K. W. Whitelam, "The Symbols of Power: Aspects of Royal Propaganda in the United Monarchy," *BA* 49 (1986): 166–73.

[48] Particularly scarce are male figurines.

[49] F. Stolz, *Strukturen und Figuren im Kult von Jerusalem. Studien zur altorientalischen, vor- und frühisraelitischen Religion* (BZAW 118; Berlin: de Gruyter,

floor for the future location of the temple and its subsequent construction under Solomon. Behind the OT accounts of the purchase, some discern a taking over of a Jebusite cult place if not an existing temple.[50] Perhaps the threshing floor had served a cultic function, but whether the site already had a modest temple on it is uncertain at best. Jerusalem would certainly have possessed cult places if not temples, and it would not be unusual for David to acquire a preexisting shrine or to build one in his capital. Indeed, not to have made some provision for a royally sponsored cult would be unusual. According to the account of the bringing of the ark into Jerusalem, David had erected a tent for the ark's home (2 Sam 6:17). According to another account, however, there is already a house of Yahweh in Jerusalem during his reign (2 Sam 12:20). In either case, one of the constant elements in the history of religion is the continuity of cultic sites regardless of the cult celebrated at the site. The history of Jerusalem from David's time until today is a perfect example. Thus it would not be surprising if the temple of Solomon was constructed on the site of a Jebusite cult place—but if that was so, the biblical texts themselves make no mention of it.

On the one hand, the plans of the Solomonic temple fit architecturally in the Syro-Phoenician world, as do the descriptions of Solomon's palace and other public buildings.[51] In essence, the house of Yahweh is a Canaanite temple in the land of Canaan, and the particulars of its cult are developed in the context of a Canaanite ritual heritage. On the other hand, it runs beyond the evidence or the balance of probability to see the Solomonic temple as a specifically Jebusite inheritance. Some Jebusite contributions to the temple cult are possible if not probable, but they are difficult to identify.

1970); H. H. Schmid, "Jahweglaube und altorientalisches Weltordnungsdenken," in his *Altorientalische Welt in der alttestamentlichen Theologie* (Zürich; Theologischer Verlag, 1974), 31–63; J. Soggin, "Der offiziell geförderte Synkretismus in Israel während des 10. Jahrhunderts," *ZAW* 78 (1966): 179–204; idem, "Der Beitrag des Königtums zur israelitischen Religion," *VT Sup* 23 (1972): 9–26.

[50] 2 Sam 24:18–25; 1 Chron 21:18–29; cf. K. Rupprecht, *Der Temple von Jerusalem. Grundung Salomos oder jebusitisches Erbe?* (BZAW 144; Berlin: de Gruyter, 1977).

[51] D. Ussishkin, "Building IV in Hamath and the Temples of Solomon and Tell Tayanat," *IEJ* 16 (1966): 104–10; cf. his "King Solomon's Palace and Building 1723 in Megiddo," *IEJ* 16 (1966): 174–86; T. Busink, *Der Tempel von Jerusalem, von Salomo bis Herodes; eine archäologisch-historische Studie unter Berucksichtigung des westsemitischen Tempelbaus* (Leiden: E. J. Brill, 1970); W. G. Dever, "The MB IIC Stratification in the Northwest Gate Area at Shechem," *BASOR* 216 (1974): 31–43; J. Ouellete, "The Basic Structure of Solomon's Temple and Archaeological Research," *The Temple of Solomon* (ed. J. Gutmann; Missoula: Scholars Press, 1976), 1–20; C. J. Davey, "Temples of the Levant and the Buildings of Solomon," *Tyndale Bulletin* 31 (1980): 107–46; Mazar, *Archaeology of the Land of the Bible*, 375–80.

The big change in the royal cult of Jerusalem is actually an inner-Canaanite development from a mobile tent to a permanent house. Culturally speaking, a tent for a deity is no less at home in the larger Canaanite world than a temple. The mythic texts from Ugarit have the high god 'El residing in a tent, and it is quite possible that similar motifs influenced the accounts of the earlier tabernacle.[52] But there is a vast cultural difference between a temple built by the king in the capital and the theology of the mobile deity invisibly present among the people in their own movement. The priests' placing the ark (= the symbol of Yahweh's presence among the tribes) in the inner sanctum of the temple joined the identity of tribal Israel with that of the monarchical state. The temple is the symbol in Solomon's building projects that brings to expression a state theology (official religion) and administrative centralization in cultic affairs.

A Canaanite Pantheon in Israelite Jerusalem?

A second indication of syncretism comes in the religious terminology associated with Jerusalem which is said to reflect a Canaanite pantheon.[53] Schmid points to the names of David's children as examples. Names such as Absalom or Solomon are said to represent the Canaanite deity Shalem, a name also presupposed in the place names of Salem and Jerusalem (2 Sam 3:3; 5:14). Absalom was born at Hebron, so it is difficult to see any particular connection with Jerusalem. Solomon is but one of two names given to the second son of David and Bathsheba, the other being Jedidiah, a good Yahwistic name (2 Sam 12:25). The concept of šālôm as a part of Yahweh's rule does not suggest a divine partner or underling elsewhere in the OT, but, as implied in the double name of Solomon/Jedediah, it is an attribute or characteristic of Yahweh.

Both Stolz and Schmid resort to extrabiblical texts to demonstrate that Shalem was a deity worshipped in Jerusalem and integrated into the royal cult sponsored by David and Solomon. According to them, Shalem is really a type of 'Aštar deity, and they draw parallels with gods and goddesses from Ugarit (Šalem, Šahar, 'Aštar), Phoenicia ('Attart, Milk-'Attart, Melqart), Arabia ('Attar), Mesopotamia ('Ištar), Moab and Ammon ('Aštar-Kemosh, Milcom), etc. These extrabiblical parallels are then placed beside the suggested biblical evidence for the official worship of Shalem

---

[52] R. J. Clifford, "The Tent of El and the Israelite Tent of Meeting," CBQ 33 (1971): 221–27; F. M. Cross, "The Priestly Tabernacle in the Light of Recent Research," Temples and High Places in Biblical Times (ed. A. Biran; Jerusalem: HUCA, 1981), 169–80.

[53] For what follows cf. Stolz, Strukturen und Figuren im Kult von Jerusalem, 179–218; H. H. Schmid, "Jahweglaube und altorientalisches Weltordnungsdenken," 42–43; H. Vorländer, "Der Monotheismus Israels als Antwort auf die Krise des Exils," in Lang, ed., Der einzige Gott, 84–113.

in Jerusalem, namely, that Solomon built "high places" for 'Ashtarte, Kemosh, and others according to 1 Kings 11:1–8. How one gets from the name Jerusalem to a deity Shalem—who is really not named in 1 Kings 11:1–8—remains unclear. The deities in 1 Kings 11:1–8 are mentioned as a result of Solomon's marriages to foreign women (and perhaps his attempted inculturation of various elements now under his political control). Political marriages required a delicate kind of diplomacy, and particularly in state-arranged marriages between royal families, the honoring of the national god(s) was essential. One should not assume that the Deuteronomistic interpretation in 11:5 depicts Solomon building "high places" for already existing cults in Jerusalem (and thereby incorporating them into the official cult of the state), while 11:8 simply describes what he did for his wives.[54] Contextually 1 Kings 11:1–8 should be understood as a polemic against both Solomon's harem as the focal point for his "apostasy" and its effects upon his Yahwistic orthodoxy.[55] One would be justified in speaking of an official pantheon in Jerusalem if these deities were honored at the temple Solomon built next to his own palace, but this is not stated in the text, and it is unlikely (see p. 84–88).

In the name of David's son Adonijah, a name which means "my Lord is Yahweh," some would see another example of syncretism with the Canaanite deity 'Adon or 'Adonay.[56] Again there is no particular connection with Jerusalem since Adonijah too was born in Hebron. One son's name, Bə'alyada', has the theophoric element ba'al, though parallel texts preserve 'Elyada'.[57] The parallel names most likely reveal that Ba'al was nothing more than a title for 'El or Yahweh. We should interpet the name Adonijah by analogy; 'Adon or 'Adonay are titles for Yahweh or 'El, and probably do not represent an incorporation of a pre-Israelite Canaanite deity into the royal cult of Jerusalem any more than the naming of Absalom or Solomon represent veneration of Shalem.

Several sons have theophoric names formed with 'ēl. These are particularly important since 'El 'Elyon, creator of heaven and earth, was probably worshipped by the pre-Israelite inhabitants of Jerusalem as a manifestation of the high god 'El.[58] The identification of 'El 'Elyon with

---

[54] Stolz, *Strukturen und Figuren im Kult von Jerusalem*, 204, makes this division between the native cults in 11:5 and the activities Solomon undertook for his wives.

[55] If one follows the LXX and puts 11:6 after 11:8, then the connection between 11:5 and the building projects for the foreign wives is even closer.

[56] H. W. Jüngling, "Der Heilige Israels. Der erste Jesaja zum Thema 'Gott,' " *Gott, der einzige. Zur Entstehung des Monotheismus in Israel* (ed. H. Haag; Freiburg: Herder, 1985), 103.

[57] Bə'alyada' = 1 Chron 14:7; 2 Sam 5:16; 1 Chron 3:8 = 'Elyada'.

[58] Gen 14:18–20. Cf. the ostracon discovered in Jerusalem, dating to the seventh century, which reads in its third line: [*'el*] *qn'rṣ*, "'El, creator of the land." The second line has a good Yahwistic personal name *mkyhw*, Michaiah. See N. Avigad, "Excavations in the Jewish Quarter of the Old City of Jerusalem, 1971,"

Yahweh, however, is likely as old as David's conquest of Jerusalem if not older; indeed, the name Yahweh may have originated as an epithet of 'El, and the continued use of 'El in the OT assumes an identity with Yahweh (pp. 13–21). Some scholars have proposed that the poem in Deut 32 reflects a time when ('El) 'Elyon was considered the head of the Jerusalem pantheon and Yahweh played a subordinate role, albeit a meaningful one, as Israel's national god.[59] The text of the larger poem and its dating are complex and sharply debated. The crucial lines of 32:8–9 should be translated:

> When the Most High ('elyôn) apportioned the nations, when He divided the human species, He established the peoples' boundaries according to the number of the sons of God (banê 'elōhîm).[60] But Yahweh's portion is his people, Jacob is his inheritance.

Whatever the pre-history of the text and date of the poem, the best interpretation is that 'Elyon is simply an epithet of Yahweh as it was for 'El (cf. Pss 7:18; 18:14; 21:8; 47:3; 92:2). The poem celebrates the fact that Yahweh, who rules the divine and human worlds, assigned guardians or watchers over the nations, but reserved Israel as his own. This interpretation is the most natural one in the context of the poem, and it is certainly the presupposition of the larger book of Deuteronomy.[61]

The supposition of an official pantheon in Jerusalem during the reigns of David and Solomon actually rests on quite fragmentary evidence, as Schmid essentially admits:

> In good Canaanite form a series of different, subordinated deities were venerated [in Davidic-Solomonic Jerusalem], and it is to be presumed that this played a greater role in early Israelite religion than results from the present Old Testament.[62]

IEJ 22 (1972): 195–96; P. D. Miller, Jr., "El, the Creator of Earth," BASOR 239 (1980): 43–46.

[59] O. Eissfeldt, "El and Yahweh," JSS 1 (1956): 28–30. He is followed by H. Vorländer who observes that Yahweh may well have been the god of the land or had special care of Israel without being the High God; cf. his "Der Monotheismus Israels," in Lang, ed., Der einzige Gott, 100: "Judah valued Yahweh as its chief God but not as the only god or necessarily the highest god. As with the whole Syro-Palestinian realm, El occupied the place of highest god over deities and human beings, as is well known from Ugarit." He points approvingly to Deut 32:8f.

[60] This follows the reading of the LXX which has "angels of God." Cf. P. W. Skehan, "A Fragment of the 'Song of Moses' (Deut 32) from Qumran," BASOR 136 (1954): 12–15, who notes that banê 'elōhîm is the reading of a Hebrew fragment of Deuteronomy discovered at Qumran.

[61] G. Braulik, "Das Deuteronomium und die Geburt des Monotheismus," in H. Haag, ed., Gott, der einzige, 154–59.

[62] Schmid, "Jahweglaube und altorientalisches Weltordnungsdenken," in Schmid, ed., Altorientalische Welt: Zur Entstehung des Monotheismus in Israel, 42.

Schmid's point about Canaanite influence is sound, however, once we recognize that David and Solomon assimilated a number of the urban Canaanite traditions in their rise to political power. They subordinated other traditions in establishing their rule. Nevertheless, the evidence is insufficient for an official pantheon in Jerusalem served by the state cult. Yahweh's kingship or rule over other deities, angels, seraphim, etc. is a divine pattern that had a parallel in David and Solomon's political administration over a variety of entities in the national state. It is quite doubtful that a "Canaanite" deity other than Yahweh had much more support in Jerusalem after David's rise to power than the authority a former Jebusite king might have in the city. Yahweh would have no more divine rivals in Jerusalem than David or Solomon would have political rivals. But just as David or Solomon must have officials who do their bidding, so Yahweh could stand in a divine council and rule.[63]

The Zadokite Priesthood

The third indication of syncretism comes in the incorporation of Zadok as priest in Jerusalem. He is named as a priest under David's reign when Solomon removes Abiathar from his priestly duties (2 Sam 20:25; 1 Kings 2:35). Evidence for Zadok's levitical ancestry is not strong,[64] and some find the significance of his name indicated in the names of two pre-Israelite kings of Jerusalem, Melchizedek and Adonizedek.[65] With these references one should compare Psa 110, which portrays the priestly duties of the Davidic monarch on analogy with Melchizedek, the priest-king of Salem. Comparatively little is known about the priestly duties of the Davidic line, but the reference to Melchizedek in the context of the royal cult probably depends more on his association with 'El 'Elyon in Gen 14:18–20, the only other reference to Melchizedek in the OT, than any other factor. And as we have seen, that is not the kind of syncretism (Yahweh='El) opposed by the biblical writers. Just as the king inherited certain privileges patterned after Melchizedek, so the priesthood in the new temple could borrow or transfer elements appropriate for the cult of the national state. If Zadok is an incorporation from the Jebusite cult into the Israelite cult of Jerusalem, his transfer to Yahwistic service

---

[63] On the concept of the divine council and Yahweh's rule, see P. D. Miller, Jr., "Cosmology and World Order in the Old Testament: The Divine Council as Cosmic-Political Symbol," *Horizons in Biblical Theology* 9 (1987): 53–78.

[64] 2 Sam 8:17 and 1 Chron 6:38 (53E).

[65] Gen 14:18; Josh 10:1, 3. Cross, *Canaanite Myth and Hebrew Epic*, 195–215, has shown that the name itself does not presuppose the Canaanite deity Ṣidqu or Ṣedeq, and has sought to defend his levitical origins. With modifications this thesis is developed in S. Olyan, "Zadok's Origins and the Tribal Politics of David," *JBL* 101 (1982): 177–93.

should be understood similarly as further incorporation of 'El veneration, which for the city of Jerusalem meant 'El 'Elyon.

The Pattern of Kingship in Jerusalem

Stolz, Schmid, and others make their strongest point in the claim that the perception of Yahweh's kingship or cosmic rule played an influential role in the developing Jerusalem cult.[66] Yahweh took his place at the head of the divine council, a better term to use than pantheon. Cosmic rule through a divine council is assumed in Deut 32, Psa 82, and 1 Kings 22:19–22.[67] The various "deities" known in southern Canaan were functionally no different than the cherubim or seraphim, since they too were subject to Yahweh's command. Also, integral to Yahweh's cosmic rule were the concepts of blessing, creation, and order. The linking of rule with concepts of creation and order was widespread in the ANE, and the presence of a divine council would be natural in the official Yahwistic cult sponsored by the state.[68]

Two of the strongest symbols of royalty and rule come in the respective "seats" of Solomon and Yahweh. It is no coincidence that the two seats are described with shared characteristics. In the royal ideology the king was understood as the "son" or viceregent of Yahweh. Their thrones and the footstools, wings, cherubs, etc. have a number of iconographic parallels in the ANE, particularly in Canaanite ivory and stone carvings.[69] Yahweh was understood as invisibly enthroned above the cherubim in the temple. Solomon's throne description apparently has its closest parallels from Egypt's royal and temple furniture.

Thus one can characterize the Jerusalem cult of Yahweh as Canaanite and can assume that several of the concepts used in its propaga-

---

[66] W. H. Schmidt, *Königtum Gottes in Ugarit und Israel* (BZAW 80; Berlin: Töpelmann, 1966). He sees the influence of both 'El and Ba'al traditions in the understanding of Yahweh's cosmic rule. Cf. also the important reconstruction by Ollenburger, *Zion, City of the Great King*; and N. Lohfink, "Der Begriff des Gottesreichs vom Alten Testament her gesehen," *Unterwegs zur Kirche. Alttestamentliche Konzeptionen* (ed. J. Schreiner; Freiburg: Herder, 1987), 33–86. In his wide-ranging essay, Lohfink proposes that pre-monarchical Israel understood the concept of Yahweh as king but didn't use it for fear that it would legitimate the assumption of monarchy by one of its own. With the development of the monarchy, the term was used, but it then could serve the function of critique over against human pretension.

[67] Cf. Mullen, *The Assembly of the Gods*, 202–5, 226–44; Miller, "Cosmology and World Order in the Old Testament," 53–78.

[68] This viewpoint is argued in some detail by Schmid, "Jahweglaube und altorientalisches Weltordnungsdenken," in Schmid, ed., *Altorientalische Welt*, against the view of some that creation as an article of faith was a later development in Yahwism.

[69] See the profusely illustrated, two-volume work by M. Metzger, *Königsthron und Gottesthron* (AOAT 15/1–2; Neukirchen-Vluyn: Kevelaer, 1985).

tion were not derived from the earlier tribal spheres of existence, or if they were so derived, they existed only in incipient forms in the pre-monarchical era. With regard to cultural development, one must be careful with the value judgments assumed for the term syncretism. M. Rose has quite correctly pointed out that no great religion is without contributions from a number of sources.[70] Some of these sources might be classified as "positive" contributions which assist a cult in presenting more effectively its own self-understanding. Other borrowed elements might be classified as "neutral." They have their role, but perhaps they could be replaced or reassessed without essential loss. And still others will be assessed as "negative" and opposed by some adherents of the religion because they are perceived as detrimental, even if they are popular and employed by other adherents of the religion.

A profound cultural factor for Israelite religion comes in the traditions of Solomon's great wisdom (see pp. 219–21). In the ANE, the royal patronage of wisdom was widespread and far older than Solomon, but the emergence of monarchical institutions provides an appropriate cultural setting for the development of the wisdom movement in Israel.[71] This is not to deny the presence of earlier wisdom movements associated with villages or clans or that significant developments came later than the united monarchy. Solomon is depicted as personally interested in an early form of scientific classification and as the recipient of wisdom from Yahweh.[72] Many would insist, however, that schools for formal instruction, the development of a class of scribes, and the rise of literacy among the general populace were also keys to an indigenous wisdom movement in Israel.[73]

The search for wisdom was an international movement with cultural borrowing (syncretism) assumed among the sages. It is easy to understand why Solomon was associated with it, and why, in spite of

---

[70] M. Rose, *Der Ausschliesslichkeitanspruch Jahwes. Deuteronomische Schultheologie und die Volksfrömmigkeit in der späten Königszeit* (BWANT 106; Stuttgart: Kohlhammer, 1975), 266.

[71] K. Kitchen, "Egypt and Israel During the First Millennium B.C.," *VTSup* 40 (1986): 119–23, compares the biblical references to Solomon in light of Egyptian analogies. Cf. R. N. Whybray, "Wisdom Literature in the Reigns of David and Solomon," in Ishida, ed., *Studies in the Period of David and Solomon and Other Essays*, 13–26.

[72] L. Kalugila, *The Wise King. Studies in Royal Wisdom as Divine Revelation in the Old Testament and Its Environment* (CB/OT 15; Lund: Gleerup, 1980).

[73] B. Lang, "Schule und Unterricht im alten Israel," *La Sagesse de l'Ancient Testament* (BETL 51; ed. M. Gilbert; Leuven: University Press, 1979), 186–201; A. Lemaire, *Les écoles et la formation de la Bible dans l'ancien Israël* (OBO 39; Göttingen: Vandenhoeck & Ruprecht, 1981); idem, "Sagesse et Ecoles," *VT* 34 (1984): 270–81; E. Puech, "Les écoles dans l'Israël préexilique: données épigraphiques," *VTSup* 40 (1986): 189–203; E. Lipiński, "Royal and State Scribes in Ancient Israel," *VTSup* 40 (1986): 157–64.

the openness to experience on the part of the sages, Yahwism still defined the orientation to the wisdom movement in Jerusalem.

THE DIVISION OF THE KINGDOM IN 1–2 KINGS AND THE PROBLEM OF SYNCRETISM

Jeroboam I

If Solomon received criticism in the Dtr H for his openness to the religions and cultures represented in his harem, then Jeroboam I, the initial king of the northern kingdom, is vilified in the sources. In uncompromising language he becomes the one who made Israel to sin. His cultic measures are described in 1 Kings 12:28–33 as rank idolatry and polytheism. Both charges are unmistakable in the description of the two golden calves he made and the phrase of v. 28: "Here are your gods,[74] Israel, who brought you up from the land of Egypt," essentially a quote from the account of the golden calf in Exod 32.[75] Clearly the Dtr H depicts the calves as idols and a violation of the first and second commandments of the Decalogue. Cultural parallels abound for the bull or calf as a symbol of divine strength and virility, and as a pedestal for a deity (see pp. 32–33). But it is not clear that Jeroboam intended the calves themselves as divine images. Perhaps he intended these calves as pedestals for Yahweh in a manner similar to the Jerusalemite cherubim, one calf in Dan and one in Bethel.

The plural terminology and the two sanctuaries, however, point to an influential perception in some Yahwistic circles and in other types of Canaanite religion. Different pedestals in different cities implied multiple forms of Yahwism, or perhaps better said, different forms of Yahweh, each taking root at a particular site and developing in accord with local traditions. There are cultural parallels in Canaan with the many forms of Ba'al and the incredible mixing and merging on the part of the popular goddesses. For example, the Israelite king Ahaziah would send an inquiry to Ba'al Zebub in Ekron. Elijah castigates him for lack of faith in the God of Israel, but one should note that there was also a shrine for Ba'al in Samaria (2 Kings 1; 1 Kings 16:32). The account presupposes a perception on the part of Ahaziah and others that localized expressions of deity often developed special traits. After all, Ekron is a Philistine city, and it

---

[74] The plural is clear from the verb which follows. Cf. H. Donner, "Hier sind deine Götter, Israel," *Wort und Geschichte. Festschrift für Karl Elliger zum 70. Geburtstag* (ed. H. Gese & H. P. Rüger; AOAT 18; Neukirchen-Vluyn: Neukirchener Verlag, 1973), 45–50.

[75] Exod 32:1, 4; cf. J. Hahn, *Das Goldene Kalb. Die Jahwe-Verehrung bei Stierbildern in Geschichte Israels* (Frankfurt: Lang, 1981).

is unlikely that an Israelite king would inquire of Ekron's deity apart from the assumption of that Ba'al's special powers.[76] The importance and individuality of these multiple forms of Yahwism are reflected in the comment of Absalom that to fulfil a vow he wished to go and sacrifice to Yahweh-in-Hebron (2 Sam 15:7). Certainly Absalom could offer a sacrifice to Yahweh in Jerusalem! The critique of Jeroboam's calves is noteworthy because it is a severe criticism of a type of cultic practice with longstanding precedent in Canaan. That this critique is mixed up with accusations of deviation from Jerusalem on other matters should not obscure the fact that some forms of Yahwism fall under the charge directed at Jeroboam.

Jeroboam's two sanctuaries in Bethel and Dan represent the royal cult and state religion.[77] Unfortunately, the excavations at *Beitin*, the Bethel of the OT period, did not produce any architectural evidence for a temple. Probably the temple was located on the hill between *Beitin* and *et Tell*. At Dan (*T. Qadi*), however, a sacred area was discovered which affords some idea of the official cultic activities in the northern kingdom.[78] A large, stone platform was built near the spring that feeds the river Jordan. The earliest phase of the stone platform dates to the tenth century and measured ca. 18.5 by 9 meters. This is likely the cult center constructed by Jeroboam I, which was destroyed by an intense fire. It was quickly rebuilt to an expanded size, ca. 18 x 19 meters, with a distinctive ashlar masonry known from the contemporary period at Samaria. A courtyard of crushed limestone was added to this second phase. The ashlar masonry in particular helps fix the date of the expansion to the period of Ahab, who constructed the city wall at Samaria out of similar masonry. A final phase dates to the first half of the eighth century with the addition of monumental steps rising to the top of the platform.

If the platform supported a permanent structure, the evidence for it has not survived. Perhaps the platform was the foundation of an open air shrine or supported a semi–permanent tent along the model of the tabernacle or the tent David pitched in Jerusalem for the ark. Three male-faience figurines were discovered along with a fragment of a horn from a monumental altar. The altar fragment essentially confirms what one suspects from the other elements of the sacred area: ritual worship at the site included the offering of animal sacrifice along with votive

---

[76] There is a parallel to this phenomenon in a reference to two Ishtars, one in Arbela and one in Nineveh. See R. Borger, *Die Inschriften Asarhaddons, Königs von Assyrien* (BAFO 9; Graz, by the author, 1956), Assur 5, paragraph IV.

[77] Amos 7:13 describes Bethel as a "temple of the king (*miqdaš melek*) and a royal sanctuary (*bêt mamlākāh*)."

[78] A. Biran "Tel Dan," *BA* 37 (1974): 40–43; "An Israelite Horned Altar at Dan," *BA* 37 (1974): 106–7; "Tel Dan Five Years Later," *BA* 43 (1980): 175–76; "Two Discoveries at Tel Dan," *IEJ* 30 (1980): 91–92.

offerings of various kinds. Smaller altars have been discovered around the platform and in a broad room next to the sacred area. The altar in the broad room was an incense altar, and with it were several small shovels for cultic use.[79]

The sacred area was also used for commercial purposes; at least that is the best interpretation of the stone vat and drainage system in the sacred area.[80] Olive oil was apparently processed there under the shadow of the sacred platform, perhaps under royal patronage. A large industrial area at *Kh. Muqanna*, the site of biblical Ekron, where the largest olive oil processing center known from the IA has been discovered, appears to confirm a link in the region between industry and cult. Within the industrial area were several limestone incense altars in smaller rooms or chapels.[81]

Dan also had an installation on the right hand side of the gate that is probably connected with the sanctuary on the summit. A small raised platform consisting of finely worked masonry occupied a prominent place within the gate. It must have functioned as a footstool or podium, a role that is confirmed by ornamental stone column bases around it for an awning of some kind.[82] Nearby a *maṣṣēbāh* was found, which, if associated with the small platform, suggests the latter displayed a divine statue or cult symbol.[83] Another possibility is that the king or city governor used the "seat" as a reviewing stand or place to hold court.

Other Centers of Worship in Israel and Judah

The sacred area at Dan should be compared with that of Arad in the Negev. Arad was a border fortress and administrative center of Judah, whose IA strata the excavators date from the united monarchy to the defeat of Judah by the Babylonians in 587.[84] The date of the small, broad-room temple at Arad is not clear; the excavators concluded it goes back to Solomon (i.e., tenth century), but it may be no earlier than the

---

[79] A. Biran, "The Dancer from Dan, the Empty Tomb and the Altar Room," *IEJ* 36 (1986): 168–87.

[80] L. Stager and S. R. Wolff, "Production and Commerce in Temple Courtyards: An Olive Press in the Sacred Precinct at Tel Dan," *BASOR* 243 (1981): 95–102.

[81] S. Gitin, "Tel Miqne-Ekron: A Type-Site for the Inner Coastal Plain in the Iron Age II Period," *Recent Excavations in Israel: Studies in Iron Age Archaeology* (AASOR 49; ed. S. Gitin, W. Dever; Winona Lake: Eisenbrauns: 1989), 23–58.

[82] Biran, "Dan Five Years Later," 176–78.

[83] Y. Shiloh, "Iron Age Sanctuaries and Cult Elements in Palestine," in Cross, ed., *Symposia Celebrating the Seventy-Fifth Anniversary of the Founding of the American Schools of Oriental Research (1900–1975)*, 149–53.

[84] Y. Aharoni, "Arad, Its Inscriptions and Temple," *BA* 31 (1968): 2–31; Z. Herzog, M. Aharoni et al., "The Israelite Fortress of Arad," *BASOR* 254 (1984): 1–34. Others would lower the dates for the beginning of the fortress to the ninth or even eighth century. See pp. 88–89.

eighth century. While the precise relationship between the temple at Arad and Jerusalem is unclear, the best conclusion is that the relationship was a close one. Ostraca discovered in rooms beside the sacred area contain the names of the priestly families of Pashhur and Meremoth and the phrase "the house of Yahweh," which is probably a reference to the Jerusalem temple.[85] Incised on offering bowls were references to the sons of Korah (*bny qrḥ*), and on others, the two letters *qōph* and *kaph*, which probably represent the phrase "holy to the priests."[86] The broad room of the temple itself measured only 9 x 2.7 meters, with a small 1.5 x 1.5 meter recess in its western wall approached by steps. At the entrance to this recess or "holy of holies" were two small, limestone incense altars, and inside was a *maṣṣēbāh* which had been buried. The courtyard, which was ca. 10 x 10 meters, had a sacrificial altar built of unhewn stones, and room nearby preserved a ceramic incense stand.[87]

A small cult room or chapel was discovered at Lachish which dates to the period of the united monarchy or a little later.[88] It was only 2.3 by 3.3 meters with low benches along the walls. One end had a raised area which may have supported an altar or statue. The room itself had several cultic elements including incense stands and altars, chalices, and a small *maṣṣēbāh*. A much larger limestone *maṣṣēbāh* was discovered near the room. A room this small was probably not intended for public use. Its exact purpose is not clear, but the combination of storeroom and private chapel is perhaps the best conclusion.

Recently D. Ussishkin has reexamined the reports of the excavations at Megiddo (*T. el Mutesellim*) and has proposed a cult center on the eastern high-point of the mound which also dates from the period of the united monarchy or perhaps slightly later.[89] He describes it as "the finest shrine from the First Temple period known today." The main room (9.1 x 4 meters) had cultic objects such as limestone tables, model "house shrines," burnt debris with animal remains, and two large *maṣṣēbôt*, and was associated with courtyards and adjoining rooms.[90] At some point in

---

[85] Ostraca 18, 50–51.

[86] Cf. the ivory pomegranate with a similar inscription that may have belonged in the Jerusalem temple; see A. Lemaire, "Une inscription paléo-hebraïques sur grenade en ivoire," *RB* 88 (1981): 236–39.

[87] Aharoni, "The Solomonic Temple, the Tabernacle and the Arad Sanctuary," *Orient and Occident. Essays presented to Cyrus H. Gordon on the Occasion of his Sixty-fifth Birthday* (AOAT 22; ed. H. Hoffner; Neukirchen-Vluyn: Neukircherner Verlag, 1973), 1–8.

[88] Y. Aharoni, *Lachish V. The Sanctuary and the Residency* (Tel Aviv: Gateway, 1975), 26–32.

[89] D. Ussishkin, "Schumacher's Shrine in Building 338 at Megiddo," *IEJ* 39 (1989): 149–72.

[90] The *maṣṣēbôt* were both more than two meters in height. The room also contained four smaller "pillars," one of which preserved a carved male figure on

the pre-exilic period the proposed shrine was buried, although no one built over the site for centuries after that. Perhaps the "shrine" dates to stratum IV-A (normally assigned to the Solomonic period), but the complex is quite unlike the description of the Solomonic temple in Jerusalem. If it is so dated, it would further illustrate the cultic diversity of the period. One wonders, for example, if this cult shrine would be similar to those Solomon had built for his foreign-born wives? It is also possible that the "shrine" represents the work of Omri or Ahab, or even that it is part of a public building but misidentified as an actual shrine.[91] In any case, these cult-rooms of Megiddo and Lachish reveal the role of the large cities and their cultic influence in the early monarchical period.

THE OMRIDE DYNASTY AND THE INFLUENCE OF PHOENICIAN CULTURE

The rise of the Omride dynasty in Israel brought with it continued cultural development for the northern kingdom. Omri and Ahab built a new capital named Samaria which, on the one hand, was crown property and a rival to Jerusalem, and on the other hand, was well located for the development of their international policies. The marriage between Ahab and the Phoenician princess Jezebel depicts one feature of dynastic policy, which was to establish closer ties with the coastal cities of Tyre and Sidon for trading purposes. Another element of their policies included a defensive alliance with Damascus against the encroaching Assyrians. Whatever should be said of Elijah and Jehu's motives, their opposition to the Omride dynasty[92] came at a time when the northern kingdom was culturally more urbanized than ever before with the development of several fortified and administrative centers in the land.[93] Samaria, for example, was an international city with superb examples of stone masonry and ivory carving.[94] It was also an administrative center built

---

top of it. In adjoining rooms were found proto-aeolic capitals, small, limestone altars and offering stands.

[91] See E. Stern, "Schumacher's Shrine in Building 338 at Megiddo: A Rejoinder," *IEJ* 40 (1990): 102–7.

[92] G. Hentschel, "Elija und der Kult des Baal," in Hagg, ed., *Gott, der einzige,* 54–90.

[93] K. Kenyon, *Royal Cities of the Old Testament* (London: Barrie and Jenkins, 1971), 71–110; D. N. Pienaar, "The Role of Fortified Cities in the Northern Kingdom During the Reign of the Omride Dynasty," *JNWSL* 9 (1981): 51–57; C. H. J. de Geus, "Die Gesellschaftskritik der Propheten und die Archäologie," *ZDPV* 98 (1982): 54; E. Stern, "Hazor, Dor and Megiddo in the Time of Ahab and Under Assyrian Rule," *IEJ* 40 (1990): 1–11.

[94] M. Mallowan, "Samaria and Calah-Nimrud: Conjunctions in History and Archaeology," *Archaeology in the Levant. Essays for Kathleen Kenyon* (ed. R. Moorey,

and ruled by the royal house. The domestic areas for the common people were located elsewhere, probably under the present village of *Sebestiyeh*, east of Samaria's acropolis.[95] Hazor, Megiddo, Dan, Yokneam, and other cities preserve remains of urban development and official buildings.

Just as Ahab and Jezebel represent the epitome of the northern kingdom's apostasy and failure in 1–2 Kings,[96] so their nemesis Elijah embodies the Yahwism favored in the Dtr H. His very name ("my God is Yahweh") depicts his program.[97] The theme of his opposition is given succinctly in the contest on Mt. Carmel: "If Yahweh is God, then follow him; if (the) Ba'al [is God], then follow him."[98] It was a question that was theological and cultural at the same time, for it was directed to Israel in terms of national policy and the integrity of its identity as the people of Yahweh. The account of the contest on Mt. Carmel is designed to demonstrate that Yahweh is the God of Israel and that Ba'al is, if anything, an object to be satirized.[99] Behind the literary accounts, however, stand intense struggles between Yahwism and forms of Phoenician Ba'alism. Not only does that intensity come through in the testimony of persecution and mass executions, but it is reflected in the comment that the altars of Yahweh have been torn down by the Israelites (1 Kings 19:10, 14)! Elijah even had to repair the altar of Yahweh before offering sacrifice.

The Ba'alism of the Omrides was not a denial of Yahweh as a god in Israel but a denial of Yahweh as the only God for Israel. For example, Ahab's two sons had Yahwistic names,[100] and even the negative stance taken by the historians toward Ahab does not deny the king's acceptance of Yahweh as a god in Israel (1 Kings 21:17–29). To some degree the Omride policies were like that of Solomon. The dynasty's international outlook meant the incorporation of a number of cultural elements from neighbors, particularly from the Phoenicians represented by queen Jezebel. Ahab and Jezebel are singled out in the Dtr H as the two primarily responsible for the introduction of Ba'alism in Israel, but Phoenician cults spread widely by colonization and trade from the tenth century

---

P. Parr; Warminster: Aris and Phillips, 1978), 155–63. Most of the ivories discovered at Samaria come from a period later than Ahab, but he is the one credited with a house of ivory in 1 Kings 22:39.

[95] So Kenyon, *Royal Cities*, 82.

[96] An extremely large amount of space in the Dtr H is devoted to the Omride dynasty (1 Kings 16:21 to 2 Kings 10:11). See further, 2 Kings 21:3, 13; Mic 6:16.

[97] C. Dohmen, *Das Bilderverbot*, 256.

[98] 1 Kings 18:21. "(The) Ba'al" is part of the text, but the definite article usually is not translated in English. All references in the OT to a deity Ba'al in the singular have the definite article with it.

[99] L. Bronner, *The Stories of Elijah and Elisha as Polemics against Baal Worship* (POS 6; Leiden: Brill, 1968).

[100] 'Ahaziah, 1 Kings 22:52; Jehoram, 2 Kings 3:1.

on,[101] and it was inevitable that their popularity would have an impact on Israel. The Phoenician upsurge of the ninth century was of larger magnitude than the more general cosmopolitan period fostered by Solomon.

Some scholars understand Omride political and social policies in light of a cultural dualism, one political system for the Canaanite population (with Samaria as the administrative seat) and one for the Israelite population (with Jezreel as the administrative seat).[102] There is no convincing evidence, however, for two political systems and two social policies in Israel. The proposed dualism overestimates the cultural distinctions between Israel and Phoenicia, and it underestimates the variety of expression that results when popular socio-cultural movements take root and expand in a host culture. The Phoenician religion represented by Jezebel would have had official support from Ahab just as Solomon built temples for the deities of certain wives. When combined with the expanding popularity of the Phoenician cults and commerce, royal support would produce a variety of syncretistic developments in Israelite society, ranging from outright rejection of Yahweh as the God of Israel in favor of a Phoenician Ba'al to an identification of Yahweh as a Phoenician Ba'al. After all, the use of the title Ba'al for Yahweh had a place in Israel from an early period (see pp. 43–45).

Unfortunately, nothing remains in the archaeological record of the house of Ba'al in Samaria referred to in 1 Kings 16:32 or of any IA structures on Mt. Carmel.[103] Indeed, with all the inscriptional and architectural remains which witness to the popularity of Phoenician religion, there is very little in the material culture of Israel that can be associated directly with Ba'al. This problem is well illustrated by the inability to answer the question: which Ba'al did Elijah oppose on Mt. Carmel? Some would answer that the account originally has to do with a local god of Carmel whose place of worship becomes a pawn in the struggle between Yahwism and Ba'alism.[104] The location of Mt. Carmel

---

[101] P. Xella, "Le polytheisme phenicien," *Religio Phoenicia* (Studia Phoenicia 4., ed. C. Bonnet; Lipinski; Marchetti; Namur: Societé des études classiques, 1986), 29–39; see also the collected essays in S. Moscati, *The Phoenicians* (New York: Abbeville Press, 1988); and R. Clifford, "Phoenician Religion," *BASOR* 279 (1990): 55–64.

[102] A. Alt, "Der Stadtstaat Samaria," *Kleine Schriften* 3.258–302, esp. 265–70; H. Donner, "The Separate States of Israel and Judah," in *Israelite and Judaean History* (ed. J. H. Hayes, J. M. Miller; Philadelphia: Trinity Press International, 1990), 399–408.

[103] Y. Yadin, "The House of Ba'al of Ahab and Jezebel in Samaria, and that of Athalia in Judah," in Moorey and Parr, eds., *Archaeology in the Levant. Essays for Kathleen Kenyon*, 127–29, proposes the comment in 16:32 is a gloss and that the house Ahab built for Ba'al is not in the city of Samaria but upon Mt. Carmel.

[104] A. Alt, "Das Gottesurteil auf dem Karmel," *Festschrift Georg Beer zum 70. Geburtstag* (ed. A. Weiser; Stuttgart: W. Kohlhammer, 1935), 1–18.

as a border sanctuary between Israel and Phoenicia lends itself to this geographic interpretation, even if the Ba'al of Carmel was originally more than a local deity. The mountain is a good candidate for the site of *baali–rasi*, mentioned in the campaign annals of Shalmaneser III.[105]

The local Ba'al theory has lost many of its supporters in light of the discoveries at Ugarit which have an exalted place for Ba'al (Hadad), a cosmic storm deity. Possibly, therefore, the imposing figure of Hadad stands behind the Ba'al at Carmel.[106] Others stress the supposed Tyrian connection of Jezebel as the decisive clue, assuming that she was the daughter of the Tyrian King Ittobaal,[107] and holding that the Ba'al of Carmel was identical with the Tyrian Ba'al she worshiped. But reconstructing the Tyrian pantheon is no simple task! A seventh-century treaty between Tyrian and Assyrian kings lists the respective deities for Tyre,[108] three of whom have been proposed as the Ba'al of Carmel. The Tyrian deities are led by Baal-sameme, or Ba'al Shamēm as he is known in the Syro-Phoenician world,[109] followed by *Baal-malage* and *Baal-ṣapunu*.[110] After these three appears *Milqartu*, or Melqart as he is better known, who is explicitly called the Ba'al of Tyre and identified with Hercules in a later inscription from Malta.[111] The obscure *Baal-malage* is the only one of the four not proposed as the Ba'al at Carmel.

---

[105] E. Michel, "Die Assur-Texte Salmanassars III (858–824)," *WO* 2 (1954): 38–39; Y. Aharoni, "Mount Carmel as Border," *Archäologie und Altes Testament* (Fest. K. Galling; ed. A. Kuschke, E. Kutsch; Tübingen: Mohr, 1970), 1–7. Aharoni supports this identification and suggests that Mt. Carmel was known by different names in Egyptian sources. Cf. S. Aḥituv, *Canaanite Toponyms in Ancient Egyptian Documents* (Jerusalem: Magnes Press, 1984), 124–25. The changing of the name is a good illustration of the development proposed above (pp. 43–45) for the origin of Ba'al place names in Palestine.

[106] So M. Avi Yonah, "Mount Carmel and the God of Baalbek," *IEJ* 2 (1952): 118–24.

[107] Josephus (*Ant.* 8.13.2) is the one who provides this information. According to 1 Kings 16:31 Jezebel is the daughter of the king of the Sidonians, but most have interpreted this term as synonymous with Phoenician.

[108] R. Borger, *Die Inschriften Asarhaddons, Königs von Assyrien*, para. 69, IV, 10–14.

[109] Perhaps this "Lord of Heaven" is the best known Ba'al of the first millennium, but how he might be related to the Ugaritic Ba'al Hadad is not clear. Ba'al Shamēm is not explicitly attested before the tenth century, though he becomes extremely popular in the following centuries. Cf. O. Eissfeldt, "Ba'alšamēm und Jahwe," *Kleine Schriften* (vol. 2; Tübingen: Mohr, 1963), 171–98. He proposes Ba'al Shamēm as the Ba'al of Carmel.

[110] Baal-malage remains obscure but Baal-ṣapunu or Ba'al Ṣaphon is attested elsewhere at Ugarit and in Egypt. Clifford, *The Cosmic Mountain*, 134, has suggested Ba'al Ṣaphon as the Ba'al of Carmel.

[111] KAI 47. R. de Vaux, "Les prophètes de Baal sur le mont Carmel," *Bible et Orient* (Paris: CERF, 1967), 485–97, has proposed Melqart as the Ba'al of Tyre who is worshiped at Carmel.

On the one hand, that each of these three deities is linked explicitly with Tyre, that they were popular during the IA, and that their respective cults were not limited to the Phoenician coast, a case can be made for the veneration of any one of them as the Ba'al of Carmel. On the other hand, what if Jezebel is really from Sidon and not Tyre?[112] Less is known about the pantheon in Sidon from this period, though later in the IA Ešmun is the city's chief deity.[113] There is also a reference to the Ba'al of Sidon and his temple, but the deity is not further identified.[114]

A later Greek dedicatory inscription from the monastery at Mt. Carmel preserves a fragmentary dedication "to the heliopolitan Zeus Carmel."[115] Since the name Zeus could substitute for Semitic Ba'al in the classical period, the inscription is probably no more than a reference to the (local) Ba'al of Carmel. This inscription might be compared with a bilingual inscription from the site of Dan which reads: "to the god who is in Dan (or among the Danites)."[116] Surprisingly the god is not named, though Dan was earlier the site of a national temple dedicated to the worship of Yahweh. Taken together these two inscriptions show the persistence and popularity of the "local cult" of regional deities who are defined geographically. We are likely faced with a complex fluidity in which the deity of a regional center like Carmel or Dan has some properties which are old and linked with a specific holy site. If a Ba'al or Yahweh is imported to the site, then the imported god is identified with the local deity. But it can be very difficult to identify which deity is intended with the appellative Ba'al or the generic term 'ēl when the terms are joined with a geographical name. This is particularly true of the Phoenician cults where one cannot always trace names and titles back to the Bronze Age.[117]

---

[112] S. Timm, *Die Dynastie Omri* (FRLANT 124; Göttingen: Vandenhoeck & Ruprecht, 1982), 87–101. He proposes that Jezebel is from Sidon and that there is not enough information to decide the identity of the Ba'al at Carmel.

[113] KAI 14:1, 17; 16:1. He is first mentioned in the treaty text between Tyre and Assyria; cf. Borger, *Die Inschriften Asarhaddons, Königs von Assyrien*, para. 69, IV, 14.

[114] KAI 14:18. And there is also a Ba'al of Lebanon who may or may not be identified with one of the deities already mentioned. See KAI 31.

[115] Avi Yonah, "Mount Carmel and the God of Baalbek," published the inscription. The translation offered above is that of K. Galling, "Der Gott Karmel und die Achtung der fremden Götter," *Geschichte und Altes Testament* (ed. G. Ebeling; Tübingen: J. C. B. Mohr, 1953), 105–26, which differs from that of Avi Yonah.

[116] A. Biran, "To the God who is in Dan," *Temples and High Places in Biblical Times* (ed. A. Biran; Jerusalem: HUCA, 1981): 142–51.

[117] See P. Xella, "Aspekte religioser Vorstellungen in Syrien nach den Ebla-und Ugarit-Texten," *UF* 15 (1983): 279–90; idem, "D'Ugarit à la Phenicie: Sur les traces de Rashap, Horon, Eshmun," *WO* 19 (1988): 45–64; and note 101 above for further references to this issue.

In the final analysis, therefore, the Ba'al on Mt. Carmel cannot be identified conclusively. The accounts of the Omride policies in 1 Kings 17–19 prefer to emphasize the majesty of Yahweh, the God of Israel, who has raised up a prophet like Moses (Elijah) to turn Israel from its ties to Ba'alism.[118] First Kings 18:18 signals the reader that Ba'alism includes more than one form of defection from Yahweh with the use of the plural form ba'alîm (the baals). Indeed, two different Ba'als are mentioned in the accounts of the Omride dynasty, the Ba'al on Mt. Carmel (Ba'al Shamem or Melqart?) and Ba'al Zebub, the deity of Ekron, who was sought by the Omride Ahaziah (2 Kings 1:1–3). The latter deity cannot be identified with certainty either. Zebub is likely a corruption of the phoneme z-b-l ("prince"), an element of the name Jezebel. If the reference to a Ba'al at Ekron is accurate, it illustrates the assimilation of the popular appellative among the Philistines. Ekron is recognized as a Philistine city in 1 Sam 5:10.

In 1–2 Kings Elijah and his successor Elisha are the best known prophets of the northern kingdom. And in conjunction with them are several references to prophetic bands or associations (e.g., 2 Kings 2). These bands are groups who likely represented a traditional and reformist Yahwism, and they can be compared to the Rechabites or the Nazirites as "witnesses" of their faith in the larger society (see pp. 156–57). This role in the culture of Israel is more important to understanding Elijah than the supposition that his eastern origins reflect a less Canaanized form of Yahwism than that of many of his Israelite contemporaries.[119] Prominent in the portrait of these two prophets is the view that an exclusive relationship existed between Yahweh and Israel, a relationship compromised and threatened with extinction in the Omride period. From Israel's side this meant an emphasis on the first commandment, "You shall have no other gods besides me."

THE LATE NINTH AND EIGHTH CENTURIES

Jehu's coup against the Omride dynasty (2 Kings 9:1–10:28) was as much a political act which rejected Phoenician political and economic influence in Israel as it was a hostile reaction to Phoenician religion. The overthrow of the Omride dynasty was followed by the successful Assyrian penetration of southern Syria and by the rise of the powerful Hazael in Damascus, both of which contributed to a difficult period in Israel and

---

[118] R. L. Cohn, "The Literary Logic of 1 Kings 17–19," *JBL* 101 (1982): 333–50.

[119] G. Hentschel, "Elija und der Kult des Baal," in Haag, ed., *Gott, der einzige*, 85. Hentschel may be correct that Elijah is from Transjordan, an area less "Canaanized" than Samaria, but the association with the prophetic bands is still a more important indication of his social setting.

Judah in the second half of the ninth century. By the middle of the eighth century, however, both kingdoms had regained a measure of stability and independence. Assyria and Damascus too were in the process of recovering their strength and would play a prominent role in the last half of the century. By the end of the eighth century Israel and Damascus had been defeated and incorporated into the expanding Assyrian Empire. Judah was isolated and devastated by an Assyrian invasion; nevertheless, the Davidic dynasty and Jerusalem survived, and the Judean state managed to outlive the Assyrian Empire by a few years.

The Material Culture of the Period and Religion

The material culture of the period preserves several useful illustrations of the relationship between religion and culture. The first comes in the form of the Samaria ostraca, which were receipts for goods shipped to the Israelite capital from nearby villages. Their precise function is debated, but the shipments they record were probably a form of tax used to support the king's servants in the capital city. Of the ca. 100 ostraca and fragments, there are eleven names with the theophoric element Ba'al.[120] This fact is interpreted by many as an illustration of the Ba'al cult and its penetration in Israel. More than a thousand Israelite and Judean personal names are preserved in extrabiblical sources, and the Samaria ostraca are the *only* collection with even a sizable minority of theophoric names with ba'al.[121] The clan names preserved in the ostraca also demonstrate that the older system of clan and family property still survived somewhat intact over against the development of the monarchy and the administrative power of the capital.[122]

From the northern Sinai site of *Kuntillet 'Ajrud* come inscriptions and drawings from the late ninth or early eighth century.[123] The site is a caravanserei where travelers stopped for rest. Fragmentary inscriptions preserve references to Ba'al, 'El, Yahweh, and 'Asherah. The most intriguing of the inscriptions are the references to "Yahweh ("of Samaria" and "of Teman") and his/its 'Asherah," in formulas of blessing,

---

[120] 1:7; 2:4, 7; 12:2–3; 27:3; 31:3; 37:3; 43:2; 45:2; 46:2–3; 47:1. Cf. J. Fowler, *Theophoric Personal Names in Ancient Hebrew. A Comparative Study* (JSOTSS 49; Sheffield, 1988), 54–63.

[121] J. Tigay, *You Shall Have No Other Gods. Israelite Religion in the Light of Hebrew Inscriptions,* 5–20. Tigay suggests the Ba'al names in the Samaria Ostraca were Phoenician not Israelite (p. 16), and concludes that Hebrew inscriptional evidence from the pre-exilic period does not support a view of widespread apostasy from Yahweh in Israel or Judah.

[122] A. Lemaire, *Inscriptions hebraïques 1. Les ostraca* (Paris: Cerf, 1977), 55–65.

[123] Z. Meshel, *Kuntillet 'Ajrud: A Religious Centre From the Time of the Judaean Monarchy on the Border of Sinai* (no. 175; Jerusalem: Israel Museum, 1978); M. Weinfeld, "Kuntillet 'Ajrud Inscriptions and Their Significance," *Studi epigrafici e linguistici* 1 (1984): 121–30.

especially in the context of crude drawings which depict two standing, Egyptianized Bes figures and a seated female figure playing a lyre. One of the standing figures has a bovine face and hooves; the other is less bovine in appearance and has stylized, feminine breasts. The seated female lyre player has exposed breasts, though she wears a skirt. Grammatically the phrase Yahweh and his 'Asherah presents a problem if the pronominal suffix "his" is attached to a personal name; if, however, 'Asherah is a cult object and not a proper name, then the blessing makes grammatical sense. The interpretation of 'Asherah as a cult object also assists with another problem. There are three figures to identify in the drawing but only two are named.[124] We are better off interpreting the blessing formula independently of the drawings. That would mean none of the three figures necessarily represents 'Asherah or Yahweh, though another drawing at *Kuntillet 'Ajrud*, which depicts a stylized tree over a lion and is flanked by two ibexes, probably is an 'Asherah symbol.[125] Finally, the blessings formulae support this interpretation of 'Asherah since only Yahweh is named as acting agent.[126] Thus the 'Asherah at *Kuntillet 'Ajrud* is a cult symbol of the goddess or a principal of fertility under the aegis of Yahweh and not in the first instance the personal name of the goddess herself.[127]

Two epithets of Yahweh from the inscriptions are also extremely significant for the interpretation of Israelite religion. They are the phrases *yhwh šmrn*, "Yahweh (of) Samaria," and *yhwh t[y]mn*, "Yahweh (of) Teman."[128] Each epithet has the divine name in construct to a place name which serves as a particular means to identify Yahweh: the Yahweh who dwells in Samaria or Teman and embodies characteristics associated with each place. They reveal the power of local cults to identify even a national deity by regional characteristics (see pp. 145, 170–82). In the case of Samaria, the reference is to the capital city which, in turn, defines

---

[124] J. Hadley, "Some Drawings and Inscriptions on two pithoi from Kuntillet 'Ajrud," *VT* 37 (1987): 180–213, has a recent discussion of the inscriptions and drawings along with the important bibliography.

[125] This view is presented by Hadley and supported by the observations of R. Hestrin, "The Lachish Ewer and the 'Asherah," *IEJ* 37 (1987): 212–23; idem, "Understanding Asherah—Exploring Semitic Iconography," *BAR* 17 (1991): 50–59.

[126] Cf the blessing formula: *brktk lyhwh tmn w'šrth ybrk wyšmrk wyhy 'm 'd[n]y* = "I bless you to Yahweh of Teman and his 'Asherah; may he (*Yahweh*; 3rd masculine singular) bless you and may he watch you and may he be with my lord." See also the parallel from Jewish liturgy suggested by J. Tigay, "A Second Temple Parallel to the Blessings from Kuntillet Ajrud," *IEJ* 40 (1990): 218.

[127] For the viewpoint that the standing male figure represents Yahweh and the standing female figure 'Asherah, see B. Margalit, "The Meaning and Significance of Asherah," *VT* 40 (1990): 274–77.

[128] On the translation of the divine name in construct with a place name see J. Emerton, "New Light on Israelite Religion," *ZAW* 94 (1982): 3–8.

the northern kingdom. In the case of Teman, the reference is first to a region south(east) of Palestine long associated with Yahweh's dwelling.[129] Recent excavations at Jerusalem and Lachish (*T. ed Duweir*) provide insight into the kingdom of Judah at the end of the eighth century. These were the two largest cities in the kingdom, and they illustrate the power of the monarchical state in shaping the affairs of Judah. In the case of Hezekiah, the expansion and fortifications of the two cities reflect his preparation for war with Assyria. The Lachish excavations have confirmed the date of a common find in the material culture of this period: stamped jar handles with winged symbols and inscriptions reading *lmlk*, "belonging to the king," usually accompanied with one of four place names. These stamped handles probably marked the contents of produce (wine, oil) collected for the king and used to supply his army and administrators in the regional cities.[130] Lachish had a massive palace-fortress and defensive gate system, both of which are the largest known from the Israelite period in Palestine.[131] The siege and destruction of Lachish are depicted in the gypsum palace carvings of Sennacherib and reflected in the grim destruction of stratum III of the city. The OT portrays the survival of Jerusalem as Yahweh's miraculous intervention, and no doubt its preservation contributed significantly to the view that Yahweh would always intervene to deliver the seat of the temple from assault (2 Kings 18–19; Isa 36–39).

Hezekiah's Reform

According to both Kings and Chronicles, Hezekiah instituted a religious reform in Judah. Much of the account in 2 Kings 18:4–6 is cast in the typical Deuteronomic style. He removed the "high places" (*bāmôt*)—something his predecessors had not done even if they receive approval from the writers. A "high place" (*bāmāh*) is the site of cultic activity associated with public ritual.[132] He broke the standing stones

---

[129] Hab 3:3; cf. R. de Vaux, "Téman, ville ou région d'Edom?" *RB* 76 (1969): 379–85; L. E. Axelsson, "God Still Dwells in the Desert. A Conception characteristic for North Israelite Yahwism," in Augustin, et al., eds., *Wünschet Jerusalem Frieden*, 17–20.

[130] D. Ussishkin, "The Destruction of Lachish by Sennacherib and the Dating of the Royal Judean Storage Jars," *TA* (1977): 28–60; P. Welten, *Die Königs-Stempel. Ein Beitrag zur militärpolitik Judas unter Hiskia und Josia* (Wiesbaden: O. Harrassowitz, 1969); N. Na'aman, "Hezekiah's Fortified Cities and the LMLK Stamps," *BASOR* 261 (1986): 5–21.

[131] D. Ussishkin, *The Conquest of Lachish by Sennacherib* (Tel Aviv: Institute of Archaeology, 1982), 30–42.

[132] Cf. K. D. Schunck, "Zentralheiligtum, Grenzeheiligtum und 'Höhenheiligtum' in Israel," *Numen* 18 (1971): 131–39; P. Welten, "Kulthöre und Yahwetempel," *ZDPV* 88 (1972): 19–37; P. Vaughn, *The Meaning of "bama" in the Old Testament. A Study of etymological, textual and archaeological evidence* (SOTSMS 3;

they contained, and according to another text, he removed the altars at the high places (2 Kings 18:22).[133] He cut down the 'Asherah, and shattered a bronze serpent that Moses had made, to which the people had offered sacrificial worship. The last two activities presumably concern measures carried out in the temple of Jerusalem. "The 'Asherah" was a cult symbol, as was the bronze serpent. That Moses had made the serpent marks it out as a completely legitimate symbol (cf. Num 21:4–9) whose use had become perverted. Nehushtan had developed an identity of its own instead of serving as a symbol of Yahweh's presence in judgment and healing. The verb used to describe the sacrificial activity (*qṭr*) includes the use of incense and implies a propitiatory act to the snake. This reverses the role of the bronze serpent in the Pentateuchal account, where the serpent is made for an apotropaic symbol to ward off the effects of snakebite.

It makes sense to understand "the 'Asherah" removed by Hezekiah as a cult symbol too. Just as the tree represented fertility and blessing, so an 'Asherah symbol in the temple courtyard or the temple itself might have meant nothing more than that.[134] "Yahweh's 'Asherah" symbolized his role in the life cycle and fertility, but for some the feminine symbol took on an identity of its own and was identified as a goddess in her own right. Or perhaps the symbol even merged in syncretistic fashion with the identity of another goddess such as 'Ashtarte or 'Anat. When understood as a deity in her own right, 'Asherah could then be identified as the consort of Yahweh. There are good parallels at Ugarit for the role of a consort as demonstrated by 'Athirat (='Asherah, who was the consort of 'El) and 'Anat (sister and paramour of Ba'al). We lack enough information to reconstruct the growth of these views in Israel or Judah, but such differing perceptions would help explain important characteristics about the term 'Asherah and its use in the OT. The term is used in the singular and plural to refer to a deity[135] *and* to cult objects.[136] Deuteronomy 16:21–22 is important in this regard:

> You shall not plant for yourself an 'Asherah, any tree (*kol ēṣ*), beside the altar of Yahweh your God which you shall make for yourself; nor shall you erect a standing stone (*maṣṣēbāh*) which the Lord your God hates.

Apparently a tree, any tree or even a fashioned wood implement, was capable of developing its own identity for some worshippers rather than remaining a symbol for divine activity, especially when associated with

---

Cambridge: University of Cambridge, 1974); W. Boyd Barrick, "What do we really know about 'high places'?" *SEA* 45 (1980): 50–57.

[133] This text assumes that the altars were used for Yahwistic sacrifices.

[134] Abram planted a tree in Beersheba; see Gen 21:33.

[135] E.g., 2 Kings 23:4 = singular; Judg 3:7 = plural.

[136] E.g., Deut 16:21–22 = singular; Exod 34:13 = plural.

a *maṣṣēbāh*, the male symbol of fertility. But such pairing of male and female fertility symbols in standing stone and a tree (or wooden pole) is not self-evident. A *maṣṣēbāh* might be a stone of witness or simply an indicator of an invisibly enthroned deity for others (Gen 28:10–19; 35:6–15). The polemic against the 'Asherah, no less than that against Nehushtan and the *maṣṣēbôt*, is a reaction against developments within the cult of Yahweh. In every case these cultic symbols had been associated with Yahweh for some time.

The association in the OT of 'Asherah with Ba'al and apparently with Yahweh suggests first of all that she/it was an Israelite fertility symbol, and developed as an independent deity only in certain circles. This conclusion would help to explain how she can be associated with Ba'al and Yahweh rather than with 'El as portrayed at Ugarit. Also it would explain why the prophets of 'Asherah are mentioned just in passing in 1 Kings 18:19 and why there is little, if any, polemic directed against the goddess 'Asherah by the eighth-century prophets.[137] There is another parallel to this phenomenon in the references to the worship of the "host of heaven." The phrase is used of the celestial court around Yahweh in an early and unpolemical context in 1 Kings 22:19; the same term is also used in 2 Kings 21:3 for deities worshipped by Manasseh, Hezekiah's son. In the latter reference one may discern elements of divination rites and perhaps Assyrian influence as well (see pp. 97–98).

The role of 'Asherah in Israelite religion can be understood differently. Since virtually all the references to her in the OT are Deuteronomistic and negative, perhaps they provide no accurate guide to her status in the variety of Israelite religion except by polemic. On the assumption, however, that polemic presupposes popularity or at least official sanction as a goddess, 'Asherah has been understood as Yahweh's spouse (consort) in the official cult in Jerusalem whose role was eliminated by the measures of Hezekiah and Josiah, and who was falsely described as the consort of Ba'al in the Dtr H.[138] Some of this ingenious reconstruction is plausible except for the claim that 'Asherah was falsely described as a consort of Ba'al.[139] Her role as both cult symbol and goddess would link her with more than one deity or cultic practice. As noted above, it would be unwise to take the graffiti from *Kuntillet 'Ajrud* as a guide to official policy in either Israel or Judah,[140] or to assume a clearly defined goddess

---

[137] See Mic 5:14(13H) and the plural form 'Asherim, probably a reference to the wooden cult symbols.

[138] S. Olyan, *Asherah and the Cult of Yahweh in Israel* (SBLMS 34; Atlanta: Scholars Press, 1988).

[139] The Dtr H does not actually describe 'Asherah as a consort of Ba'al. She, like 'Ashtarte (singular or plural), is simply listed with Ba'al (singular or plural) as a snare to Israel.

[140] As does Olyan, *Asherah and the Cult of Yahweh*, 23–37. Cf. the similar

in the graffiti's references to "Yahweh's 'Asherah." On the basis of the Deuteonomistic polemic, it is difficult to derive a precise chronology of the development from 'Asherah as a Yahwistic symbol to veneration as a goddess in her own right. And although it is surprising that Jehu massacres Ba'al worshippers but does nothing against the 'Asherah,[141] the lack of action is plausibly explained by analogy with the bronze serpent, *maṣṣēbôt*, and the host of heaven, each of whom had a recognized place in Yahwism until their respective roles developed in ways opposed in the Dtr H.

Plural forms are an important element for the interpretation of 'Asherah as a deity and as a cult symbol. There were a number of local manifestions of 'Asherah in Israel and Judah, some of which were associated with the cults of the state sanctuaries and some which were not. "Official" religion under the monarchy is that which was practiced in the state sanctuaries and sponsored by the royal house, not what is written in the Dtr H or the pre-exilic prophets. The protests by the biblical writers presuppose that the *veneration* of 'Asherah is not compatible with Yahwism. That conclusion very likely had its supporters as well as its opponents among representatives of official religion in Israel.

JUDAH IN THE SEVENTH AND EARLY SIXTH CENTURIES AND JOSIAH'S REFORM

With the defeat of Israel and the exile of its leading citizens by the Assyrians (2 Kings 17:1–6), Judah was left alone between the great power from the east and the Egyptians to the south and west. Already in the eighth century Ahaz had accepted vassalage under the Assyrian ruler Tiglath Pileser III, and his grandson, Manasseh, found himself in the same position as Assyia reached the maximum extent of its empire under Esarhaddon. The assessment of Judean material culture and religion faces a complicated question in the extent to which Assyrian culture and religion influenced Judah or was even forced upon it. Three thorough studies have come to differing conclusions. Both McKay[142] and Cogan[143] have argued that the claim of Assyrian-imposed religion is false, while

---

assumption by G. Ahlström, *Royal Administration and National Religion in Ancient Palestine* (SHANE 1; Leiden: E. J. Brill, 1982), 42; and his "An Archaeological Picture of Iron Age Religions in Ancient Palestine," *SO* 55/3 (1984): 19.

[141] 2 Kings 9–10. Many scholars propose the reference to the prophets of 'Asherah in 1 Kings 18:19 is a later gloss.

[142] J. McKay, *Religion in Judah under the Assyrians* (SBT 26; London: SCM Press, 1973).

[143] M. Cogan, *Imperialism and Religion: Assyria, Judah and Israel in the Eighth and Seventh Centuries* B.C.E. (Missoula: Scholars Press, 1974).

Spieckermann has attempted to show that developments in late Assyrian religion are reflected in Judah in a number of ways including some measures enforced on the state cult.[144]

The question of cultural influence and syncretism is bound up with the equally complicated question of the nature and intent of the reform measures enacted by Josiah. In the Dtr H, Josiah represents the ideal of a king faithful to Yahweh who reforms the state cult (official religion) according to the Mosaic principles set out in Deuteronomy.[145] Both 2 Kings 23 and 2 Chron 34 record reform measures undertaken by Josiah, though the chronology and emphasis differ between them. The actual description of the practices opposed is much shorter in Chronicles than 2 Kings.[146] A listing of the reform measures in 2 Kings 23 is as follows.

1. Removal from the Solomonic temple of vessels for Ba'al, 'Asherah, and the host of heaven (ṣəbā' haššāmayim); their destruction and ashes spread in Bethel: 23:4.[147]

2. Removal of foreign priests (kəmārîm)[148] given by former kings, and those who sacrificed with incense (qṭr) to Ba'al, the Sun (šemeš), the Moon (yārēaḥ), the constellations (mazzālôt),[149] and to all the host of heaven: 23:5.

---

[144] H. Spieckermann, *Juda unter Assur in der Sargonidenzeit* (FRLANT 129; Göttingen: Vandenhoeck & Ruprecht, 1982).

[145] H. D. Hoffmann, *Reform und Reformen. Untersuchungen zu einem Grundthema der deuteronomistischen Geschichtsschreibung* (AThANT 66; Zürich: Theologischer Verlag, 1980), has proposed that the accounts of reforms and apostasy in 1–2 Kings are literary creations from the perspective of an exilic, Deuteronomistic writer who wanted to show how the reform of Josiah removed all the apostasies that accumulated in Judah. His purely literary approach is one-sided and ignores the cultural contexts of the apostasies described.

[146] Also, the Chronicler has Josiah enact reform measures over a period of several years, while virtually all of the king's reforming measures in Kings come as a result of the law book's discovery.

[147] 2 Chron 34:4 also refers to the altars of the ba'als which had upon them incense stands or smaller altars (ḥammānîm).

[148] The Aramaic cognate term is used for priests in KAI 225:1; 226:1. These two inscriptions reflect Neo-Assyrian influence and contain references to astral deities. The kəmārîm priests in 23:5 should be contrasted with the Yahwistic priests mentioned in 23:8–9.

[149] A hapax legomenon. Cf. *mazzārôt* in Job 38:32. Spieckermann, *Juda unter Assur*, 271–73, notes the close parallel with Neo-Assyrian *manzalatu*. See also M. Delcor, "Les cultes étrangers en Israel au moment de la réforme de Josias d'après 2 R 23: Etude de religions sémitiques comparées" *Mélanges bibliques et orientaux en l'honneur de M. Henri Cazelles* (AOAT 212; ed. A. Caquot, M. Delcor; Neukirchen-Vluyn: Kevelaer, 1981), 95–100; and I. Zatelli, "Astrology and the Worship of the Stars in the Bible," *ZAW* 103 (1991): 94–95. Both scholars think the term refers to the signs of the Zodiac or stations of the sun along its yearly journey. Whatever the precise meaning, the constellations were important for divination and as a form of science.

3. Destruction of the 'Asherah located in the temple and the "buildings of the dedicated ones" (bāttê haqqədēšîm)[150] where women wove garments or clothes (bāttîm)[151] for 'Asherah: 23:6–7.

4. Brought priests to Jerusalem from the "high places" (bāmôt) of Judah[152] and defiled the high places.[153] Broke down the "gate high places" (bāmôt šə'ārîm)[154] in the gate of the city: 23:8.

5. Defiled the tophet in the valley of Hinnom where people caused sons and daughters to pass through the fire for Molek (mōlek): 23:10.

6. Removed the horses given by former kings to the Sun and burned chariots (markəbôt) of the Sun[155] stored in "sacred quarters" (par-wārîm):[156] 23:11.

7. Destroyed the altars on the "roof of the upper chamber" ('al haggāg 'aliyyat) of Ahaz and those of Manasseh in the temple courtyards: 23:12.

8. Defiled the high places built by Solomon for 'Ashtarte, Kemosh, and Milcom and shattered maṣṣēbôt and cut down 'Asherim: 23:13–14.

9. Destroyed the high place at Bethel with its altar and 'Asherah and defiled the area around it: 23:15–16.

10. Removed the implements for divination and communicating with the dead ('ōbôt, yiddə'ōnîm),[157] and assorted divine images in the land:[158] 23:24.

---

[150] It is not necessary to read cult prostitutes for qədēšîm.

[151] Delcor, "Les cultes étrangers en Israel au moment de la réforme de Josias," 117–21.

[152] This text assumes some Yahwistic priests officiated at the high places. Cf. 2 Kings 18:22.

[153] 2 Chron 34:7 also refers to the cutting down of the incense altars (ḥammānîm) at the high places in the land.

[154] The phrase is commonly amended, but the MT is best understood as a reference to small chambers or recesses in the gate with sacrificial altars. Cf. Y. Shiloh, "Iron Age Sanctuaries and Cult Elements in Palestine," in Cross, ed., Symposia Celebrating the Seventy-Fifth Anniversary of the Founding of the American Schools of Oriental Research [1900–1975], 151–53.

[155] See Delcor, "Les cultes étrangers en Israel au moment de la réforme de Josias," 100–104.

[156] Another hapax legomenon. For the possibilities see McKay, Religion in Judah, 35–36; H. P. Stähli, Solare Elemente im Jahweglauben des Alten Testaments (OBO 66; Freiburg: Universitätsverlag, 1985), 5; and D. Runnalls, "The Parwār: A Place of Ritual Separation?" VT 41 (1991): 324–31.

[157] H. Rouillard, J. Tropper, "Vom kanaanäischen Ahnenkult zur Zauberei. Eine Auslegungsgeschichte zu den hebräischen Begriffen 'WB und YD'NY," UF 19 (1987): 235–54; T. J. Lewis, Cults of the Dead in Ancient Israel and Ugarit (HSM 39; Atlanta: Scholars Press, 1989), 99–170.

[158] 2 Chron 34:3–4 describes the idols as carved, pəselîm, and molten, massēkôt; 34:33 uses the term abominations, tô'ēbôt. 2 Kings 23:24 describes them polemically as dung balls, gillulîm, and filth, šiqquṣîm. The teraphim named in the same verse are perhaps statues of ancestors; see K. van der Toorn, "The Nature of the Biblical Teraphim in the Light of Cuneiform Evidence," CBQ 52 (1990): 203–22.

The 2 Kings 23 account reads very much like a summary of all the problems previously listed in the evaluation of the various kings, and it represents the most sustained polemic against the religious practices opposed by the Deuternomistic Historians. With few exceptions the vocabulary is that used elsewhere in Deut—2 Kings. Even so, there are several emphases to be observed. First, many of the practices named are associated with the temple built by Solomon. Solomon himself had constructed separate temples for the worship of certain deities, but here similar practices are located in the precincts of the Yahwistic temple. Second, there is an emphasis on astronomical phenomena in the references of the first two verses to the host of heaven (twice), Ba'al (twice), the foreign priests who sacrifice (twice)[159] with incense, 'Asherah, the sun, moon, and constellations. The horses and chariots associated with the sun in 23:11 imply solar worship as a particular element. Third, in distinction from the Chronicler, who uses only the plural form, Dtr H refers to the 'Asherah in the temple as well as to the 'Asherim at the high places. The Jerusalem 'Asherah is the object of special attention in that she/it is burned and the ashes spread on graves. Apparently the "houses" in 23:7 are booths or stalls in the temple precincts and associated with the veneration of the Jerusalem 'Asherah. Fourth, a number of altars are mentioned, some in the temple courtyard, some on the roof of an upper chamber, and apparently some with city gates. It is unlikely that these are for animal sacrifice, or in the case of the bāmôt in the gates, that they are part of the royally sponsored cult.

The shorter account in the Chronicler twice mentions the incense altars (34:4, 7), which is an indication of the kind of sacrificial practice opposed. By the late pre-exilic period there were established links between Jerusalem and the Arabian incense trade,[160] and that led undoubtedly to an increased use of incense in sacrificial ritual in the official temple cult and among privately supported bāmôt. Incense was used in the temple cult and its effects were propitiatory, apotropaic, and mediatory. Its availability and ease of use with ceramic stands, model shrines, and small altars made it popular. The priestly material in the Pentateuch has two accounts of the misuse of incense (Lev 10:1–7; Num 16:1–50), and behind them is an attempt on the part of the priestly traditions to limit the personnel and the practices associated with it.

---

[159] The first verb, qṭr bə in the piel, has kemarîm as its subject and bāmôt as its object; the second verb is also qṭr lə in hiphil participle with Ba'al and the heavenly bodies as objects.

[160] Y. Shiloh, "South Arabian Inscriptions from the City of David, Jerusalem," PEQ 119 (1987): 9–18; K. Nielsen, Incense in Ancient Israel (VT Sup 38; Leiden: Brill, 1986) demonstrates that incense was available and played an important role throughout the period of monarchy.

The Material Culture of the Period and Religion

There are illustrations of cultic practices from the material culture of the period. According to 2 Kings 23:8-9, Josiah removed the priests from the outlying high places, brought them to Jerusalem, and then defiled the cultic places. A similar claim of centralization is made earlier for Hezekiah in 2 Kings 18:22, though without any reference to priests. The cultural remains at Arad and Beersheba suggested to the excavators that Hezekiah did, in fact, remove or disable the altars for animal sacrifice at both sites. At the Arad sanctuary, the altar was covered in stratum VIII, but the sacred area continued in use until stratum VI when it was deliberately put out of business. The proposed date for the end of stratum VIII is the end of the eighth century, which coincides with the Hezekian reforms.[161] At Beersheba, pieces of a monumental altar were found dismantled and reused in a building in stratum II,[162] which, according to the excavators, came to an end at the same time as Arad stratum VIII. Unfortunately, the sacred area itself has not survived the years, and the excavators can only speculate on its location.[163] The end of stratum VIII at Arad and of stratum II at Beersheba are attributed to the destruction of the Assyrian king Sennacherib, who boasts that he shut Hezekiah up in Jerusalem like a bird in a cage and destroyed forty-six walled cities and numerous villages.[164]

The variety of finds from the material culture of Judah makes for an illuminating comparison with the accounts of reform in the Dtr H. At Arad, for example, the sanctuary gives every indication it represents the cult of Yahweh (see pp. 71–72). The ostraca preserve priestly names known from the OT, and correspondence demonstrates that the site had Judean governmental personnel. Yet the "holy of holies" contained a *maṣṣēbāh*, something polemicized against in the Dtr H. Apparently the sanctuary personnel followed the pattern set by the

---

[161] Z. Herzog et al., "The Israelite Fortress of Arad," *BASOR* 254 (1984): 19–26. The proposed dating of the strata is disputed; cf. A. Mazar and E. Netzer, "On the Israelite Fortress at Arad," *BASOR* 263 (1986): 87–91, with a reply by Z. Herzog, "The Stratigraphy of Israelite Arad: A Rejoinder," *BASOR* 267 (1987): 77–79. It should be noted that the evidence proposed for the cultic reforms is not excluded by the proposed changes of Mazar and Netzer (p. 89). D. Ussishkin proposes, however, not only to follow the lower dating of Mazar and Netzer, but also that the sanctuary was not built until stratum VII, some time in the later seventh century. Cf. his "The Date of the Judaean Shrine at Arad," *IEJ* 38 (1988): 142–57. The later chronology for the strata X–VIII at Arad is likely, but it is unlikely from a historical or archaeological viewpoint that the sanctuary was first built in stratum VII.

[162] Y. Aharoni, "The Horned Altar of Beer-sheba," *BA* 37 (1974): 2–6.

[163] Z. Herzog, A. F. Rainey, Sh. Moshkovitz, "The Stratigraphy at Beer-sheba and the Location of the Sanctuary," *BASOR* 225 (1977): 49–58.

[164] *ANET*, 286–88.

ancestral accounts and understood the *maṣṣēbāh* as compatible with official Yahwism. Whether the excavators are correct or not in their assumption that the reform movement of Hezekiah put the *maṣṣēbāh* and altar out of commission, the sanctuary continued in some form without these elements until the sacred area itself was subsequently covered over.

The monumental altar from Beersheba is another surprise. According to Exod 20:25, a Yahwistic altar should be constructed of unhewn stones. This was the case with the altar in Arad, but not so with the one from Beersheba. The ashlar limestone blocks were carefully shaped to form the altar, which included horns, i.e., points on the corners of the upper blocks, and what appears to be a crude snake etched in a lower block. Beersheba itself was a settlement with public buildings and fortifications which marked it out as a Judean regional center. Several cultic and zoomorphic vessels, an incense altar, and a number of female figurines were also discovered there.[165]

Jerusalem itself has furnished a considerable number of female figures from the eighth and seventh centuries, most of which are the terra-cotta "pillar figurine" model. In secondary literature they are often called Ashtarte/Ashtoreth or 'Asherah figurines, on the assumption that they are symbols of a goddess. They are common to many Judean sites in IA II, especially in the eighth and seventh centuries. Typically the body of the pillar is made out of one piece and the head from another. Often the breasts are enlarged and displayed, apparently as a sign of fertility. Whether these were intended as depictions of goddesses or as amulets/statues is disputed. In either case, the sheer frequency of the female figurines in the material culture of Judah, especially in the eighth and seventh centuries, reflects a society deeply concerned about human fertility and the fruitfulness of the land, if not deeply interested in the feminine aspects of the divine world.[166]

A cave and small cult room dating to the (early) seventh century and containing a large cache of pottery and figurines were discovered in

---

[165] Y. Aharoni, *Beer-sheba 1. Excavations at Tel Beer-sheba 1969–71 Seasons* (Tel Aviv: Institute of Archaeology, 1973) plates 27–29.

[166] How these figurines might relate to the Queen of Heaven (Jer 7:16–20; 44:15–19, 25) is not clear. The "name" of the queen is not given, nor is she explicitly related to either 'Asherah or Ashtarte. She is likely a developed form of 'Ashtarte with a number of elements adapted from the east Semitic (neo-Assyrian) Ishtar; see M. Delcor, "Le culte de la 'Reine du Ciel' selon Jer 7, 18; 44, 17–19. 25 et ses survivances," *Von Kanaan bis Kerala. Festschrift für Prof. Mag. Dr. Dr. J. M. P. van der Ploeg O. P.* (AOAT 211; ed. Delsman, Nelis, Peters, Römer, and van der Woude; Neukirchen-Vluyn: Kevelaer, 1982), 101–22; S. Ackerman, " 'And the Women Knead Dough': The Worship of the Queen of Heaven in Sixth-Century Judah," *Gender and Difference in Ancient Israel* (ed. P. Day; Minneapolis: Fortress Press, 1989), 109–24.

Jerusalem.[167] Among other finds were miniature furniture, a ceramic incense stand, offering bowls, two maṣṣēbôt,[168] and miniature terra cotta horses with small discs between their ears. Neither the purpose of the cave nor the meaning of its contents are obvious, but the horses with the discs find their best parallels with symbolic depictions of the sun. Perhaps the miniatures should be compared with 2 Kings 23:11 and the account of the horses and chariots for the sun which were removed from the temple and burned. These small, terra cotta figures from the cult room may well have been votive vessels for those who participated in a solar cult (see p. 96). The very setting of the cave may be a clue to its function. It was small and hidden from view, and many of the vessels at its entrance had organic remains in them. Possibly it was a place of prayer and private cultic practices, a peripheral cult to the official activity at the Jerusalem temple located only a few hundred meters away.

Human Sacrifice

Perhaps the most disputed point of the reform account is the reference in 23:10 to the Tophet in the valley of Hinnom.[169] Most interpreters have seen a reference to child sacrifice in the phrase "to pass through the fire" (h'br b'š) "to" or "for the [divine] king" (lammelek). Molek is an intentionally corrupted form of the Hebrew word melek, "king," with the substitution of the vowels from bōšet ("shame"). Ahaz and Manasseh are accused of these practices, and there are references to similar customs in Jeremiah.[170] The question is not whether there was human sacrifice in the ANE and the Mediterranean world. That is beyond doubt.[171] The question is whether the biblical writers have accurately preserved references to these sacrificial activities in Judah.

It is possible, for example, that the phrase "pass through the fire" refers not to human sacrifice but to a ritual of divination. And even if it refers to a ritual of human sacrifice, perhaps the term Molek is not a corrupted reference to a deity called "the king" but a sacrificial term (Molk or Mulk), a common noun known from many examples in the

---

[167] K. Kenyon, Digging Up Jerusalem (London: E. Benn, 1974), 135–43, and plates 52–61; T. A. Holland, "A Study of Palestinian Iron Age Baked Clay Figurines, with Special Reference to Jerusalem: Cave 1," Levant 9 (1977): 121–55.

[168] Or possibly pillars for a roof.

[169] See G. Heider, The Cult of Molek. A Reassessment (JSOTSS 43; Sheffield: JSOT Press, 1985); J. Day, Molech: A god of human sacrifice in the Old Testament (Cambridge: Cambridge University Press, 1989).

[170] 2 Kings 16:3; 17:17; 21:6; Jer 32:35. The verb śārap, "burn," is used in 2 Kings 17:31; Jer 7:31; 19:5.

[171] A. R. W. Green, The Role of Human Sacrifice in the Ancient Near East (ASORDS 1; Missoula: Scholars Press, 1975); L. E. Stager, S. R. Wolff, "Child Sacrifice at Carthage—Religious Rite or Population Control?" BAR 10 (1984): 30–51.

Punic world.[172] The first possibility, that the fire ritual is only divination, not sacrifice, is not easily reconciled with other references that use burn (śārap), unless one assumes a complete misrepresentation of the practice on the part of the biblical writers. The second possibility, that Molek is a type of sacrifice (as in Punic sacrificial texts), not a deity, has gained more supporters, but it too must assume that the biblical writers completely misrepresented the sacrificial term. Particularly difficult is the passage in Lev 20:1–5 which concerns the parent who "gives his seed to Molek" (ntn lmlk). One could render the phrase "who gives his offspring for a molk sacrifice," but 20:5 describes the practice with a phrase of opprobrium that is used only of other deities: "to whore after Molek" (znh 'ḥry lmlk).

The questions still remain, who is Molek and does Yahweh have a role in the sacrificial ritual? Evidence for a Canaanite deity known primarily as Melek remains sparse and uncertain. Thus, as noted above, the term is best understood as a corruption of the title "king." Like the titles Lord (Ba'al, 'Adon) or Lady (Ba'alah[t], Rabat), the titles of king or queen were not restricted to a single deity. Melek does occur as an element in several names/titles for deities. According to 2 Kings 17:31, the Sephardites in Samaria burned (śrp) their children to the deities 'Adramelek and 'Anamelek. The Phoenician deity Melqart, whose name means "king of the city," was also known as the Ba'al of Tyre.[173] A deity less well known named Milk'ashtart (mlk'ṯtrt) had a temple south of Tyre in the Hellenistic period where he is also referred to as the god of Ḥamon ('l ḥmn).[174] The god of the Ammonites, Milkom, is a name formed with melek. And of course, in Jerusalem Yahweh is known as the King, the great King (Isa 6:5; Psa 48:2).

Thus there are several candidates for the Molek of the biblical text when the various biblical and extrabiblical references are taken together. Both Melqart and Milkom (cf. 1 Kings 11:7 MT) are plausible suggestions. No clear, extrabiblical evidence exists for their involvement in human sacrifice, although others have seen hints of this for both deities.[175] If Molek is one of the lesser known deities whose name is formed with

---

[172] O. Eissfeldt, *Molk als Opferbegriff im Punischen und Hebräischen und das Ende des Gottes Moloch* (Halle: M. Niemeyer, 1935).

[173] C. Bonnet, *Melqart. Cultes et mythes de l'Héracles tyrien en Mediterranée* (Studia Phoenicia VIII; Leuven: Societé des études classiques, 1988).

[174] KAI 19. See also S. Ribichini, P. Xella, "Milk 'astart, mlk(m) e la tradizione siropalestinese sui Refaim," *Rivista di studi fenici* 7 (1979): 145–58. If this deity can be identified with the more widely known Ba'al Ḥammon (below), it would confirm a connection between the titles Ba'al and Molek.

[175] Cf. Heider, *The Cult of Molek*, 175–79, 278–79, 404. For possible connections with child sacrifice in Transjordan, cf. J. Hackett, "Religious Traditions in Israelite Transjordan," in Miller, et al., eds., *Ancient Israelite Religion*, 131–34. She does not consider Milkom in this discussion.

melek, then we lack enough information to say anything certain about the cult.[176] And there is still the possibility that Molek is the epithet of one or more deities whose "other name(s)" elude modern investigators.

The difficulty in drawing firm conclusions is illustrated by the references in the book of Jeremiah. In chapter 19 the prophet is commanded to buy an earthenware pot and to break it as a sign against the practices in the valley of Hinnom and the Tophet located there. Jeremiah 19:5 names Baʻal explicitly as the deity to whom children are burned in the fire. Many scholars, however, see this reference to Baʻal as nothing more than a polemical reference without specific historical value: Baʻal is simply a term for any foreign deity.

> [The people] have built "high places" for Baʻal to burn (*śrp*) their children in the fire as burnt offerings to Baʻal, something that I never commanded, never said, nor that ever came to my mind.

It must be admitted that Jeremiah's vocabulary varies in the description of the "valley practices." Whereas 19:4 says that the Tophet is defiled by abhorrent practices for other gods (*'elōhîm 'aḥērîm*) that the people, their fathers and their kings did not know, Jer 9:14(13H) describes the people as going after the Baʻals as their fathers had taught them. Both phrases are part of the "Deuteronomistic language" of Jeremiah with its stereotypical polemics against foreign deities. Jeremiah 7:31 polemicizes against the "valley practices" at the Tophet without naming a deity, although the context is a sermon delivered in the temple precincts to worshippers of Yahweh. Jeremiah 2:23 polemicizes against valley practices associated with the Baʻals without naming the location as Hinnom. Jeremiah 32:35 contains the most extended comment, including a link between Molek and Baʻal:

> [The people] built the "high places" of Baʻal that are in the valley of Hinnom to cause their sons and daughters to pass through the fire for Molek (*h'byr b'š lmlk*), something that I did not command nor did it come to my mind to do this abomination in order to cause Judah to sin.

In light of the variety of description one must be careful in making sweeping judgments, but one must also ask whether the references to Baʻal(s) have not preserved the identity of at least one recipient of child sacrifice. The possibility of an affirmative answer comes in the comparison with extrabiblical texts. The deity to whom the thousands of child sacrifices were made at the Tophet in Carthage was named Baʻal Hammon.[177] He is frequently mentioned in the plentiful dedicatory inscrip-

---

[176] See the unconvincing reconstruction by M. Weinfeld, "The Worship of Molech and of the Queen of Heaven and its Background," *UF* 4 (1972): 133–54.

[177] Since Carthage was a Tyrian colony, one would expect some continuity between the Tyrian and Carthaginian pantheons. Thus it is possible that in

tions with his consort Tannit.[178] Greek and Latin writers later identified him with Kronos and Saturn respectively. But Baʿal Ḥammon is originally from the eastern Mediterranean area. His earliest reference is in a ninth-century inscription, as one of the deities of Samal in northern Syria.[179] He is mentioned in an amulet discovered near Tyre,[180] and south of Tyre at *Umm el 'Amed*, there is a temple for Milk'ashtart, the god of Ḥammon.[181] His name also occurs on a grave urn from Cyprus, which appears to be late eighth century in date and suggests a possible connection with the cult of the dead,[182] and in a sixth-century inscription from Malta.[183] A likely epithet for Baʿal Ḥammon is Baʿal 'Addir, known from neo-Punic references as the recipient of sacrifices.[184] The term 'Addir, "strong" or "mighty," can be compared with the first element in the name of the Sephardite deity, 'Adramelek, mentioned in 2 Kings 17:31 as the recipient of child sacrifice, suggesting another possible connection between Molek and Baʿal.[185]

Not all the "connections" listed above for Baʿal Ḥammon are firm,[186] and any specific connection with Jerusalem and human sacrifice also depends on the polemical language of Jeremiah. Nevertheless, the identification of Molek with Baʿal Ḥammon is plausible. Recent studies have proposed that Baʿal Ḥammon is an epithet of 'El, the high deity of

---

Carthage Baʿal Ḥammon was an epithet of Melqart. See W. Culican, "Melqart Representations on Phoenician Seals," *Abr Nahrain* 2 (1961): 41–54, for the royal motifs associated with Melqart.

[178] See conveniently KAI 85, 86, 87, 88.

[179] KAI 24:16.

[180] P. Bordreuil, "Attestations inédites de Melqart, Baal Hamon et Baal Saphon à Tyr," *Studia Phoenicia IV* (ed. C. Bonnet; Lipinski; Marchetti; Namur: Societé des études classiques, 1986), 77–86.

[181] KAI 19:4; see K. Galling, "Baal Ḥammon in Kition und die Ḥammanîm," *Wort und Geschichte. Festschrift für Karl Elliger zum 70. Geburtstag* (ed. H. Gese & H. P. Rüger; AOAT 18; Neukirchen-Vluyn, 1973), 67.

[182] Galling, "Baal Ḥammon in Kition," in Gese and Rüger, ed., *Wort und Geschichte*, 65–67.

[183] KAI 61:3–4.

[184] KAI 9:B 5; 112:2; 138:1.

[185] Yet another possible connection between Molek and Baʿal comes in the Ammonite seal of an official named בליס. For the seal, see L. Herr, "The Servant of Baalis," *BA* 48 (1985): 169–72. The connection depends on the conclusion that the theophoric element Baʿal is a reference to Milcom, the god of Ammon. According to R. Younker, "Israel, Judah, and Ammon and the Motifs on the Baalis Seal from Tell el-ʿUmeiri," *BA* 48 (1985): 177–79, the caduceus and lunar crescent symbolism on the seal have close parallels with symbols for Baʿal Ḥammon at Carthage. Younker suggests that Milcom is the Ammonite version of Baʿal Ḥammon, and that both terms are epithets of Canaanite 'El.

[186] See Y. Yadin, "Symbols of Deities at Zinjirli, Carthage and Hazor," *Essays in Honor of Nelson Glueck. Near Eastern Archaeology in the Twentieth Century* (ed. J. Sanders; New York, 1970), 199–231, who proposes that Baʿal Ḥammon was worshipped at Hazor in the LBA.

Syria-Palestine.[187] If that proposal is correct, it would strengthen the connection of rites of human sacrifice with Jerusalem where 'El was worshipped as Yahweh. Furthermore, the identification would account for the confusion between Yahweh, Ba'al, and Molek, as well as provide a plausible reason why 'El (= Ba'al Ḥammon) was addressed as the king.

At the same time, it must be admitted that the identification of Ba'al Ḥammon with 'El is not certain; the epithet Ḥammon could refer to the heat or smoke associated with sacrifice.[188] Ba'al Ḥammon, then, would be the epithet "Lord of the altar smoke."[189] This understanding would be quite interesting in light of the frequent polemical references to sacrificing with incense in Dtr H and Jeremiah. Finally, therefore, the cumulative evidence for the identification of Ba'al Ḥammon as *a* recipient of child sacrifice in Jerusalem is suggestive, not conclusive. Probably we should take the plural reference to Ba'als in Jeremiah as an accurate indication that more than one deity was involved with child sacrifice.

It is interesting to observe in this context the great lengths to which a theory will go to exonerate Ba'al from claims in the Dtr H and Jeremiah that 'Asherah was his consort and that he received child sacrifice. Olyan makes a learned defense against both charges while arguing in great detail that Ba'al Ḥammon received such sacrifices in the Punic world and that his consort, Tannit, should be identified with 'Asherah![190] For some reason he never seriously considers the possibility that an analogous situation had developed in Judah and that some persons sacrificed their children to a Ba'al (Ḥammon) in an act of devotion. It is not convincing to counter that Ba'al Ḥammon is really an epithet for 'El, because even if this is a correct identification, there are scores of inscriptional references over the centuries that refer to him as *Ba'al* Ḥammon. That legitimately identifies him, just as Tannit can be called the "face of *Ba'al*" (*pn b'l*) in the Punic and neo-Punic inscriptions even if she is "really" 'Asherah.[191]

There is still the question of Yahweh's relationship to child sacrifice. The protests of Yahweh (!) in Jer 7:31, 19:5, and 32:35, that such

---

[187] Cross, *Canaanite Myth and Hebrew Epic*, 24–28; Olyan, *Asherah and the Cult of Yahweh*, 62–69. The identification depends on the equation of Ḥammon with Mt. Amanus, the mountain of 'El in the Ugaritic texts, and the equating of Ba'al Ḥammon with 'El in the various inscriptions from Samal; cf. KAI 24:15–16 and 214:2–3 and 215:22.

[188] Both Donner and Röllig, KAI (vol. 2), 77–78, and Galling, "Ba'al Ḥammon in Kition," in Gese and Rüger, ed., *Wort und Geschichte*, suggest this meaning and hesitate on a firm identification of the epithet Ba'al Ḥammon with another deity.

[189] It is possible that an original epithet "Lord of Amanus" developed a popular etymology "Lord of the Smoke" based on its frequent use in sacrificial rites.

[190] Olyan, *Asherah and the Cult of Yahweh*. One should note that a number of scholars hold that Tannit is 'Ashtarte or 'Anat.

[191] KAI 78:2; 79:1; 175:2; 176:2. Cf. 'Ashtarte as the name of Ba'al (*šm b'l*) in KAI 14:18.

activities were never commanded nor considered, probably means that some in Judah thought differently. In light of other texts such as Gen 22, Judg 11:30–40,[192] Mic 6:6–7, and Ezek 20:25–26,[193] no doubt exists that some Judeans participated in the rite of child sacrifice, making their offering in the belief that Yahweh accepted the sacrifice. Not only are there protests from Yahweh but also from the people who claim in Jer 2:23 that what they have done was neither defilement nor directed to Ba'al. They are addressed:

> How can you say "I am not defiled; I haven't gone after the Ba'als." Look at your way in the valley, know what you have done. . . !

Such protest in Jeremiah's poetry confirms essentially the expanded material concerning child sacrifice in the prose texts[194] and thereby raises the most fundamental question for the interpretation of religious polemic in the OT: to what degree is the criticism of Molek and Ba'al also a criticism of Yahwistic practices judged unsound by the biblical writers? And with specific regard to child sacrifice, is it a practice earlier condoned in Israel as Yahwistic but now opposed? There is no simple answer to either question. That Jerusalem was a cosmopolitan city is clear from the material culture of the period, and it follows naturally that the city had a wide variety of cultic practices. The sacrificial rites in the valley of Hinnom were practiced within sight of the temple complex in Jerusalem. Some who participated in the rites apparently offered the sacrifice to Yahweh, or perhaps to Ba'al(s) and also to Yahweh, or even to Yahweh as the Ba'al or the King of Jerusalem. Since such rites were practiced by non-Yahwistic peoples as well, to describe them as "foreign" was technically true, but the real intention of the biblical writers was to label them unacceptable.

The gods could lay claim to human life. That perspective was widely shared in antiquity, and it accounts for certain practices in both animal and human sacrifice. The perspective is also shared by the biblical writers; thus Yahweh could demand that Abraham sacrifice his son Isaac

---

[192] D. Marcus, *Jephthah and His Vow* (Lubbock: Texas Tech, 1986), gives a thorough review of the passage and suggests that Jephthah did not actually sacrifice his daughter.

[193] This difficult text associates child sacrifice with Yahweh and the commandment to redeem the first born from a womb; cf. Exod 13:2, 12; 22:29. It is unlikely that Ezek 20:25–26 refers to the cult of Molek; see Day, *Molech*, 65–71.

[194] J. A. Soggin, " 'Your Conduct in the Valley.' A Note on Jeremiah 2:23a," *Old Testament and Oriental Studies* (Rome: Biblical Institute Press, 1975), 78–83; in the same volume "Child Sacrifice and the Cult of the Dead," 84–87. Soggin makes the connection between the poetic comment and the later prose texts, and in light of the newer investigations at Carthage suggests that "the valley" has a child sacrifice cult as part of a cult of the dead. Heider, *Cult of Molek*, also believes the cult of the dead was related to the sacrifices offered to Molek.

just as Yahweh could claim whatever opens the womb. In both examples, an animal substitute is allowed so that the principle of divine claim remains, but the practice of human sacrifice is not condoned. The desire to honor a deity and to provide something worthy of adoration (and useful for manipulation?) would lead some in Israel to offer the ultimate sacrifice. But it goes beyond the evidence to conclude that child (or human) sacrifice was widely condoned in Israel until the polemics of the Deuteronomistic Historian.[195] The references in the Dtr H imply that it was a practice that came in "officially" with Ahaz and Manasseh, and our sources do not allow us a closer look at earlier practices. There is no evidence that these rites were ever conducted in the temple, but the vigorous protests in the Dtr H and Jeremiah leave one with the impression that child sacrifice was considered a Yahwistic practice by some Judeans.

Solar Worship[196]

The references to the vessels for the sun (and other heavenly bodies) in the temple, and the horses and chariots for the sun associated with special temple precincts, make components of a solar cult in Jerusalem undeniable. Place names in Palestine such as Beth Shemesh, 'Ain Shemesh, Mt. Heres, Timnath Heres, and Maale Heres, serve as witnesses to the popularity of the sun.[197] In the post-biblical period the Jewish synagogues at Beth Alpha and Hammat Tiberias, whose mosaics depicted the sun chariot and the signs of the Zodiac, bear witness to the staying power of such symbolism (syncretism?) among the descendants of Israel.[198] A list of four "abominations" (tô 'ēbôt) in Ezek 8 supplies an example of solar worship as the culminating act of idolatry (8:16). In a vision Ezekiel sees a group of men in the inner courtyard of the temple, between the altar and the door to the temple itself, with their backs to the door and prostrating themselves toward the east and the sun.

Some references in the OT probably reflect the association of Yahweh with the light and power of the sun. Yahweh could be symbolized by the sun or identified with its movements (Pss 84:11[12H]; 19:1–6), but the sun (or any other heavenly body) was not to be venerated. Those practices condemned in Ezekiel and the Dtr H would range from those considered unacceptably syncretistic to those understood as apostasy from Yahweh in favor of a solar deity.

---

[195] Cf. the comments of R. de Vaux, *Studies in Old Testament Sacrifice* (Cardiff: University of Wales Press, 1964), 63–90.

[196] For added details cf. Stähli, *Solare Elemente im Jahweglauben*; and Smith, *The Early History of God*, 115–24.

[197] Josh 15:7, 10; Judg 1:35; 2:9; 8:13.

[198] G. Foerster, "The Zodiac in Ancient Synagogues and its Place in Jewish Thought and Literature," *EI* 19 (1987): 225–34.

Astrology and Divination[199]

The issue of solar worship is but one aspect of the more complicated issue of discerning the will and activity of deities through the movement of planets and stars. Perhaps some of the symbolic vessels in the temple dedicated to Ba'al, 'Asherah, and the host of heaven (2 Kings 23:4) served the process of observing and charting the heavens and then making the proper cultic response to a deity. One is tempted to see the triad of deities in 23:4 as the King and Queen of Heaven with their court, but this cannot be established definitively.[200] The next verse pertains to kǝmārîm priests, and those who burn incense to Ba'al, sun, moon, constellations and all the host of heaven. Surprisingly 'Asherah is not mentioned, and Ba'al is the only deity named who lacks an astronomical reference. One should hesitate to remove Ba'al from consideration for those reasons as suggested by some scholars. In Aramaic inscriptions attesting to the strong influence of late Assyrian religion, there are references not only to kǝmārîm priests, but to Shamash and Shahar (šhr) as sun and moon deities respectively.[201] The chief Assyrian deity of the period, however, was not Shamash but Assur, the God of gods. Perhaps in analogous fashion the rise of Ba'al (Shamēm, Shamēn),[202] the "Lord of Heaven," was a Phoenician and Aramean response which had its impact in Judah as well.

The precise relationship between Yahweh and Ba'al (Shamēm) during this period is a complicated one, and it is made more difficult by the account of Josiah's reforming activity. The reform account offers no information on the way Ba'al or the other deities had been integrated into Yahwism, but we should assume some kind of integration occurred, since the cult symbols of these deities were located in the Solomonic temple complex. For some Judeans the identification between Yahweh and Ba'al was easy to make; Yahweh was, after all, the "Lord of Heaven."

---

[199] La divination en Mesopotamie ancienne et dans les regions voisines (14th Meeting of the International Assyrological Conference; Paris: Presses Universitaires de France, 1966); H. Spieckermann, Juda unter Assur in der Sargonidenzeit, 257–73; Zatelli, "Astrology and the Worship of the Stars." See the long list of divining practices and terms in M. S. Moore, The Balaam Traditions: Their Character and Development (SBLDS 113; Atlanta: Scholars Press, 1990), 20–65.

[200] Cf. KAI 4 which names "Ba'al Shamēm, Ba'al[at?] of Byblos, and the assembly of the holy gods of Byblos" (wmphrt 'l gbl qdšm). If the second name is feminine, and thus another reference to the well known lady of Byblos, then an analogous triad with 2 Kings 23:4 exists. Cf. also the typical phrase of Assurbanipal (Rassam Cylinder I, 56), "Assur, Ishtar and the great Gods, my Lords."

[201] KAI 202:B 24; 214:2–3; 215:22; 222:A 9; 225:1, 9; 226:1.

[202] Ba'al Shamēm = Phoenician (שמם בעל); Ba'al Shamēn = Aramaic (בעל שמין). See the classic article by O. Eissfeldt, "Ba'alšamēm und Jahwe," Kleine Schriften (vol. 2; Tübingen: Mohr, 1963), 171–98.

Perhaps for others the identification was a collapse of Yahweh into the form of the popular Ba'al. Perhaps for some Yahweh was considered the Ba'al of Jerusalem in analogous fashion with Melqart in Tyre, a city or national deity, but not the Lord of Heaven who remained a separate deity.[203] Part of the difficulty in assessing the relationship between Yahweh and Ba'al also comes with the question of cultural influence. Neo-Assyrian influence is likely behind the deity list in 23:5 and the solar cult in 23:11. But did it come from Assyrian imposition or was it something mediated to Judah through Aramean and Phoenician contacts as the result of Assyrian political hegemony over the eastern Mediterranean? Whatever Assyria may have imposed on Judah by way of sacrificial ritual or cultic observance, the terminology used in 2 Kings 23 is primarily that of the Aramean-Phoenician world. The success of Neo-Assyria in military and political matters obviously would translate into a large religio-cultural impact. If Assyrian propaganda attributed success to Assyrian diviners and astrologers, then so might Phoenicians and Judeans to their own diviners if they adopted similar methods and developed them in accord with traditional vocabulary.

The altars on the roof of the temple's upper chamber (23:12) likely had a divinatory role. These would be official means of mediating between the heavens and earth, discerning signs for political and cultic activity, as well as offering service to various deities. These altars find their popular and unofficial parallel in Jer 32:29, with the reference to altars on the roof of homes. The increase in the use of private altars was a natural result of the increasing availability of incense and the influence of divination and "scientific astrology" from Assyria. Incense could substitute for whole burnt offerings and the use of blood typical in west semitic ritual, and its employment gave the individual more control over his or her cultic practice. Perhaps a factor in the reform measures of Hezekiah and Josiah was an attempt to control not only the regional "high places," long in use in Judah, but the growth of additional cult practices and even new cult centers which had developed as a result of increasing interest in divination and astral phenomena.

An increasing interest in divination would bring with it renewed employment of traditional means of discerning revelation and mastering one's fate. In the Canaanite world, one means of divination came through the cult of the dead (cf. 1 Sam 28). The references to the ancestral cults or cults of the dead in 2 Kings 23:24 come in the context of a general statement that Josiah removed disgusting things from the land (see pp. 85–87). These cults had a long history in Canaan and

---

[203]Ba'al Shamēm leads the list of Tyrian deities in the treaty between Ba'lu of Tyre and Esarhaddon; cf. R. Borger, *Die Inschriften Asarhaddons, Königs von Assyrien*, para. 69, IV, 10–14. See p. 76.

apparently developed a new popularity in the late pre-exilic period. The 'ōbôt and yiddə'ōnîm in 23:24 are probably references to cultic symbols of the ancestors by means of which the dead could communicate with those who sought their help. The mediums (called prophets?) too, no doubt, were removed along with the cultic symbols.

Conclusion

There is much to be said for the view that Assyrian imperialism of the ninth-seventh centuries was the catalyst for several cultural developments in the eastern Mediterranean. For example, official and unofficial movements can be observed in Egypt as responses.[204] The rise of "writing prophets" in Israel and Judah and the archaizing tendencies of Deuteronomy, no less than the various developments in cultic practice, owe much to this cultural imperialism. If older Israelite and Canaanite views of the host of heaven, divination and prophecy, the solar cult, incense burning as opposed to blood sacrifice, etc. were redefined in light of Assyrian influence, then so were the Yahwistic ideas that Yahweh had elected Israel, instructed Moses in the exclusivity of the Yahweh-Israel relationship, given Israel an inheritance, chosen a particular place for an earthly abode, and raised up prophets to declare his will (see chapter 4). The patterns depicted in the Dtr H for Ahaz and Manasseh, no less than for Hezekiah and Josiah, reflect the kinds of reactions to broad socio-political developments. Those of Ahaz and Manasseh followed one pattern of integrating Yahwism with the broader socio-political forces they encountered, while Hezekiah and Josiah followed a reformist pattern of Yahwism which also had its socio-political consequences. Both patterns were specific developments of a long-standing conversation in Israel concerning the nature of Yahwism and the religious identity of the people.

---

[204]Brunner, H., "Zum Verständnis der archaisierenden Tendenzen in der ägyptischen Spätzeit," and "Zeichendeutung aus Sternen und Winden in Ägypten," *Das Hörende Herz. Kleine Schriften zur religions- und geistesgeschichte Ägyptens* (ed. W. Röllig; OBO 80; Fribourg: Vandenhoeck & Ruprecht, 1988), 110–20; 224–29.

ISRAEL AS A RELIGIOUS COMMUNITY IN THE EXILIC AND POST-EXILIC PERIODS

3

THERE ARE VERY FEW WRITTEN SOURCES concerning life in Judah and Samaria during the period of the Babylonian exile.[1] The accounts of the murder of Gedaliah, which come near the end of the historical accounts preserved in the Dtr H and Jeremiah, effectively drop a curtain on continued existence in Palestine. This is not a coincidence but reflects the circles who compiled the post-exilic sources. These writers wanted to show that continuity between the pre- and post-exilic periods is provided by the Judean exiles and their descendants who return to Palestine under Persian rule.[2] Jews of the post-exilic period preserved and edited earlier documents, and added writings of their own in a process that lasted into the Maccabean period when the writings of the Hebrew Bible were completed. They are essentially responsible for the consonantal text of the Hebrew Bible and perhaps for major elements of the Septuagint.

In cultural terms, changes of great magnitude took place with the Babylonian exile. Israel lacked a reigning king and an operative temple. While the bulk of the middle and upper classes of Judah lived in Babylon as a minority, rural inhabitants of Judah continued to live under the

---

[1] E. Janssen, *Juda in der Exilzeit. Ein Beitrag der Entstehung des Judentum* (Göttingen: Vandenhoeck & Ruprecht, 1956).

[2] R. J. Coggins, "The Origins of the Jewish Diaspora," in Clements, ed., *The World of Ancient Israel*, 163–81. On the numbers of people deported and whose descendants later returned, see W. Schottroff, "Zur Sozialgeschichte Israels in der Persezeit," *VF* 27 (1982): 48–51.

control of the Babylonian administration. Property owned by the deportees was left unattended, or was divided and used by the "people of the land" who remained, or was taken over by local officials appointed by the Babylonians. At this time there were sizable Jewish populations in Egypt as well as scattered communities in other parts of the empire. Theologically the exiles grappled with the loss of home and autonomy in light of the difficult claims that Yahweh had judged them. Indeed there were elements of pessimism among the exiles concerning Yahweh's will and ability to bless them. They struggled culturally to maintain their identity over against the influence of the Babylonian state.

The anonymous prophet of the exile known as Second Isaiah is often credited with crucial insights that play a decisive role in the development of a practical monotheism.[3] The point can be overemphasized, as if only the trauma of exile could bring about the affirmation of Jewish monotheism, and then only as a response to contact with Persian Zoroastrianism.[4] In spite of the real advances in the analyses of Persian traditions,[5] it is premature to claim substantial Zoroastrian influence on Second Isaiah. The prophet's criticism of idolatry, sayings concerning judgment in the historical arena, vocabulary of servanthood, and the affirmations of Yahweh's universal sovereignty and uniqueness depend on earlier Israelite tradition.[6] The role of Israel as mediator of divine revelation, justice (mišpāṭ), and salvation (ṣedāqāh) was one answer to the "why" of exile, an answer derived from the affirmation of Yahweh as universally sovereign in judgment and righteousness (see pp. 230–31).

THE PERSIAN PERIOD (539–332 B.C.E.)

Whatever motives lay behind Persian benevolence in allowing subject peoples a greater autonomy and the opportunity to rebuild temples,[7] the Jews returning to Palestine brought with them the deter-

---

[3] H. Wildberger, "Der Monotheismus Deuterojesajas," Beiträge zur Alttestamentlichen Theologie. Festschrift für Walter Zimmerli zum 70. Geburtstag (Göttingen: Vandenhoeck & Ruprecht, 1977), 506–30.

[4] As proposed by H. Vorländer, "Der Monotheismus Israels als Antwort auf die Krise des Exils," 108–11.

[5] M. Boyce, A History of Zoroastrianism (vol. 1; Leiden: Brill, 1975).

[6] Wellhausen, Israelitische und jüdische Geschichte, 152, characterized the universalism of Second Isaiah as a transformation from national religion to "missionary religion." Israel had already faced forms of "missionary religion" in the popular Phoenician cults, whose success at spreading their religion is everywhere apparent in their colonies, and from the pressure of the Assyrians in the eighth and seventh centuries.

[7] A. Kuhrt, "The Cyrus Cylinder and Achaemenid Imperial Policy," JSOT 25 (1983): 83–97.

mination to resettle the promised land as a type of second exodus. Second Isaiah had spoken of the exaltation of Zion and the power of Yahweh's word. That powerful rhetoric came in a context in which it was not clear how many exiles had the will or the faith to return and face the difficulties of resettlement. But they returned in more than one stage and succeeded in rebuilding a modest temple and a small community around the former capital city. The area preserved the name of the former state and was known in Hebrew and Aramaic as Yehud.[8] The settlers also claimed the identity of Israel for themselves as heirs of the covenant Yahweh made with their ancestors.

1–2 Chronicles

The post-exilic narrative traditions in the OT are preserved primarily in 1–2 Chronicles and the books of Ezra and Nehemiah. Many scholars have concluded that essentially one "school" or circle was responsible for the four books. The books do share much in terminology and perspective, even to the extent that the end of 2 Chronicles is repeated as the beginning of Ezra, but these traits are better accounted for as similarities and redactional activity than as a unity of expression due to common authorship.[9] Chronicles provides a retelling of the pre-exilic history of Israel which presupposes a form of the Dtr H.[10] Ezra and Nehemiah concentrate on events in and around Jerusalem during the period of Persian rule.

The Chronicler's assessment of the pre-exilic period is intended to instruct a post-exilic audience concerning its identity as Israel. Nine chapters of genealogies begin the work, placing the twelve tribes of Israel in the context of world history and concluding with lists that make explicit the connection between the post-exilic audience and its ancestors.[11] Great emphasis is placed on Yahweh as the God of Israel who chose a dynasty (David) and a place (Jerusalem) for the benefit of Israel. Saul's reign is almost completely ignored, except to be used as a negative example, but the reigns of both David and Solomon are developed in detail as models to define an Israel closer to Yahweh's intention. The

---

[8] See E. L. Sukenik, "Paraleipomena Palaestinensia: I. The Oldest Coins of Judaea," *JPOS* 14 (1934): 178–82; U. Rappaport, "The First Jewish Coinage," *JJS* 32 (1981): 1–18.

[9] H. G. M. Williamson, *Israel in the Book of Chronicles* (Cambridge: Cambridge University Press, 1977); idem, "The Composition of Ezra i–vi," *JTS* 34 (1983): 1–30, provides a good survey of the literary theories and concludes convincingly that Ezra and Nehemiah must be considered separately from Chronicles. See the recent survey of the issues by P. Ackroyd, "Chronicles-Ezra-Nehemiah: the Concept of Unity," *ZAW Sup* 100 (1988): 189–201.

[10] S. McKenzie, *The Chronicler's Use of the Deuteronomistic History* (HSM 33; Atlanta: Scholars Press, 1984).

[11] J. P. Weinberg, "Das Wesen und die functionelle Bestimmung der Listen in I Chr 1–9," *ZAW* 93 (1981): 91–113.

Chronicler omits accounts of unsavory activity from both reigns in order to concentrate on the positive characteristics of obedience to divine instruction. The failures of both rulers were already known from the accounts in the Dtr H. In the exalting of David and Solomon, and in the "overlooking" of their failures, we should probably see several factors at work: a weariness with negative examples to explain divine judgment, an attempt to show how an attentive ruler could institute Yahweh's will, and the employment of the past as a means to portray messianic and theocratic ideals for the future.

David plays a role corresponding to that of Moses in mediating Yahweh's will to Israel. Moses received the torah from Yahweh at Mt. Sinai and delivered it to Israel, but he did not live to see its implementation in Canaan. David would receive the pattern for the temple and inspiration for its administration, but he would not live to see its fulfillment in the temple itself.[12] Just as Moses had a successor in Joshua, who led Israel in the period of the occupation, so Solomon would succeed David and rule Israel at the time the temple was completed. Jerusalem's supreme importance came with its divine designation as the site for the temple, a city which the Davidic dynasty would make the capital of Israel and where it would preside at the temple's completion. There is little future in debating whether David or Solomon has the primary role in Chronicles;[13] the fact that plans for the temple occupied both reigns is the key to placing their respective reigns in perspective.

It would be difficult to overestimate the importance the Chronicler attaches to the worship life in the temple at Jerusalem. A faithful cult at the Jerusalem temple is the key to Chronicler's understanding of Israelite identity. The glory days of empire and autonomy were past, but Israel could maintain its identity as the people of Yahweh by its joyful adherence to a torah piety centered on the majestic temple service. Since the temple service was restored, and if it could be maintained obediently, then the reign of the God of heaven could be celebrated in anticipation of further restoration.[14] Temple worship was the key for maintaining a

---

[12] S. J. De Vries, "Moses and David as Cult Founders in Chronicles," *JBL* 106 (1987): 619–39.

[13] For example, R. Mosis, *Untersuchungen zur Theologie des chronistischen Geschichtswerkes* (FTS 92; Freiburg: Herder, 1973) argues for an emphasis on Solomon. The parallels he suggests between Moses and Solomon (pp. 116–22, 130–35, 144–47) are not enough to set him apart from David. T. S. Im, *Das Davidbild in den Chronikbüchern. David als Idealbild des theokratischen Messianismus* (Frankfurt: P. Lang, 1985) argues for David. But his proposal—that Solomon was but a "continuation" (p. 111) of what David modelled—underestimates the role of Solomon in the Chronicler. David had historical priority, but Solomon does illustrate what can be accomplished by an obedient member of the dynasty.

[14] M. Saebo, "Messianism in Chronicles?" *Horizons in Biblical Theology* 2 (1980): 85–109.

Yahwistic identity and piety; moreover, it was also the centerpiece of the Chronicler's attempt to define an Israelite culture amidst the cultural confusion of the post-exilic period. Williamson and others have underlined the importance of the identity of Israel for the Chronicler. Israel is not just the community huddled around Jerusalem but includes any among the exiles who recognize the legitimacy of the temple to represent the service of the God of Israel. That perspective is confirmed by the Chronicler's detailed presentation of all Israel in the period of the united monarchy and the attention given to the reforms of Hezekiah and Josiah in the north. After the fall of the northern kingdom, Jerusalem represents the legitimate sanctuary for all Israel (2 Chron. 29–32, 34:1–35:19).

Ezra and Nehemiah

As with Chronicles, Ezra-Nehemiah represent torah observance as a key to Israel's identity. But as the two books make clear, defining Israel over against the various neighbors who would dominate Jerusalem requires some extreme measures. Ezra the priest and Nehemiah the governor[15] are alike in their attempt to give an official shape to Israelite identity in Jerusalem; at least this is the description given by the books bearing their names. Ezra represents priestly specialty in interpreting and applying the torah.[16] He is commissioned by the Persian court to bring back to Judah any exiles who would like to return. He also brings funds to assist in the temple service and appoints magistrates and judges to make rulings according to the torah (Ezra 7:12–26). And he is commissioned "to make inquiry concerning (*lbqr' 'l*) Judah and Jerusalem according to the law of God in your hand" (7:14). The Aramaic phrase for inquiry does not itself make clear how Ezra is to proceed, but it suggests that his primary task was to apply torah in the religious and cultural life of Jewish inhabitants in Yehud. Perhaps his objective of organizing the inhabitants according to the law of God is analogous to the phrase describing Jehoshaphat's reforms in 2 Chron 19:11: according to "the matter of Yahweh and the matter of the king."[17] There should be no doubt that the Ezra and Nehemiah reforms presuppose loyalty to the Persian court in political affairs.

Jewish identity according to the torah was the hallmark of Nehemiah's administrative measures. He rebuilt a wall around Jerusalem in

---

[15] The two terms used are *peḥāh*, Neh 5:14, and *tiršātā'*, Neh 7:65, 70(H69); 8:9; 10:1(2H). The latter is a Persian term.

[16] C. Houtman, "Ezra and the Law," *OTS* 21 (1981): 91–115, doubts that the *torah* Ezra brought back to Jerusalem was the Pentateuch in essentially its final form. His doubts are themselves unconvincing.

[17] As proposed by J. Blenkinsopp, "The Mission of Udjahorresnet and Those of Ezra and Nehemiah," *JBL* 106 (1987): 419.

order to give the city a functional identity (Neh 2:17–6:15). Then he was able to enforce a trade-ban in the city on the sabbath (Neh 13:15–21) as well as to provide a measure of security for the city's inhabitants. He instituted a policy of divorce between Jewish men and non-Jewish wives (Neh 13:23–29; cf. Ezra 9–10). The ban enacted by Nehemiah (and Ezra) against mixed marriages was intended to maintain a particular Jewish identity over against a perceived syncretism and cultic heterodoxy among Jews in the region. It is clear that the efforts of Nehemiah (and Ezra) were primarily directed at instructing and educating Jews along orthodox lines rather than executing the prophetic activity of condemnation.

Nehemiah also expelled a prominent figure in Jerusalem (Neh 6:17–19) from a room he used in the temple precinct. The expulsion of Tobiah the "Ammonite" is described as a response to the prescription in the book of Moses that no Ammonite or Moabite should enter the assembly of Yahweh (Neh 13:1–9; cf. Deut 23:3–5). It is a significant act because the very name Tobiah indicates a form of Yahwism, and his family was well-known in Jewish circles for centuries.[18]

Ezra 4:1f. prepares the reader for the theme of the true Israel in a retrospective section that describes the reaction of the "enemies of Judah and Benjamin" to the report that the "people from the exile" (*banê haggōlāh*) were building a temple in Jerusalem for Yahweh, the God of Israel. Here the term *banê haggōlāh* refers to those who returned from Babylonian exile, and it distinguishes them from those around them who are hostile to their activities. In the description of the Passover celebration in 6:19–22, the same phrase is used in conjunction with "those who had separated from the uncleanness of the peoples around them" (Ezra 6:21).[19] Even in Jerusalem the term "exiles" remains a mark of identification. Those who returned from exile, and their companions who separated from the "uncleanness" around them, constitute the legitimate Israel. We should see in these efforts of separation the continuing influence of the exile even in Yehud. Whereas "separation" in the exilic communities in Babylon helped maintain a Yahwistic identity, the same practice was used in Yehud to define a legitimate Yahwism over against perceived heterodoxy.

The "enemies" mentioned in Ezra 4 are at least partially identified with the "people of the land" in 4:4, probably those in and around Jerusalem who were not part of the returned exiles and who resented their presence. Some "enemies" were Yahwists and others were not. They are further identified in Neh 2:10 through the reactions of Sanballat the

---

[18] For a reconstruction and assessment of the important Tobiad family see B. Mazar, "The Tobiads," *IEJ* 7 (1957): 137–45, 229–38, and pp. 108, 117 in this chapter.

[19] The verb "separate" (*bdl*) is used frequently in Ezra and Nehemiah for the separation of the torah observing returnees from their unorthodox neighbors (Jewish or gentile). See Ezra 6:21; 8:24; 10:8f.; Neh 9:2; 10:29; 13:3, 28.

Horonite and Tobiah the Ammonite. Tobiah is also referred to as "the servant" (*'ebed*) which may define him in relation to Sanballat or as an official of the Persian administration. A third "enemy" is Geshem the Arab (Neh 2:19).[20] Like Tobiah and Geshem, Sanballat is the head of a notable family. That is implied from the references to him in Nehemiah. The appellative "Horonite" probably indicates his home was in Beth Horon, ca. thirteen miles northwest of Jerusalem. And as with Tobiah, the family of Sanballat is linked with prominent circles in Jerusalem. Indeed, Nehemiah records that his daughter had married into the high priestly family (13:28), which implies that Sanballat too was a Yahwist.

Nowhere in Ezra or Nehemiah is Sanballat described as a Samaritan, a term later used for the Jewish community around Shechem.[21] This has major implications for the more exclusive and separatist definition of Israel promulgated in Ezra and Nehemiah as well as for the dating of the final break between Samaritans and Jews (see pp. 108–9, 115). Differences between the inhabitants of Samaria and Judah were already centuries old in the Persian period, but Sanballat is an "enemy" because of his actions, not because he was from the province of Samaria. In fact, he was the "governor" (*pḥh*) of Samaria, two of his sons had Yahwistic names (Delaiah, Shelemiah), and his family continued in the administrative leadership of the province for decades. That information derives from extrabiblical inscriptions[22] and confirms the status attributed to him in the book of Nehemiah. The earlier of the two references can be dated to the year 408 B.C.E. and comes in the context of letters written by Egyptian Jews to both Samaria and Yehud. Apparently there was no ultimate break between Samaria and Yehud by the end of the fifth century.

The differences between Nehemiah and Sanballat represent the struggles for control of Yehud between prominent and wealthy families,

---

[20] Cf. Neh 6:1–19. For extrabiblical references to Geshem and a proposal for the extent of his political hegemony cf. W. Dumbrell, "The Tell el Maskhuta Bowls and the 'Kingdom' of Qedar in the Persian Period," *BASOR* 203 (1971): 33–44.

[21] The term occurs only once in the OT (2 Kings 17:29) and in that context means little more than settlers in the province of Samaria. Cf. R. J. Coggins, *Samaritans and Jews: The Origin of Samaritanism Reconsidered* (Atlanta: John Knox, 1975).

[22] A. Cowley, *Aramaic Papyri of the Fifth Century B.C.* (Oxford: Clarendon Press, 1923), doc. 30:17–18. From the Samaria papyri, which date a century later than Nehemiah, there is a reference to a son of Sanballat who was "governor" of Samaria. For chronological reasons this is a second Sanballat, perhaps the grandson of Nehemiah's opponent. Cf. F. M. Cross, "The Papyri and their Historical Implications," *Discoveries in the Wâd ed-Dâliyeh* (AASOR 41; ed. P. and N. Lapp; Cambridge: ASOR, 1976), 17–29; "A Report on the Samaria Papyri," *VTSup* 40 (1986): 17–26. The account in Josephus, *Antiquities*, 11.302–25, suggests the possibility that there was yet another Sanballat as governor at the time when Alexander the Great incorporated Samaria and Yehud into his realm. See p. 115.

yet the two figures also personify the differences between rival forms of Yahwism. The latter theme seems apparent from the cultural context of Ezra and Nehemiah but is not depicted clearly in the books themselves. It is a judgment made from the wider cultural context and from what is known of the subsequent relationship between Yehud and Samaria. Apparently the writers would not dignify the religion of Sanballat (or Tobiah) by an explicit reference to his Yahwism. He is regarded no differently than a gentile.

Perhaps we can be more precise about some of the differences between Nehemiah and his "enemies." Some of the tensions resulted from the oversight of Yehud by Samaria for a period of time before Nehemiah's arrival. We lack enough information to say much about that territorial administration in the decades immediately after the return of Jews from the Babylonian exile,[23] but the work of Ezra and Nehemiah represents fundamental changes in the life of Yehud. Nehemiah (and Ezra) succeeded in developing a Yahwistic community in Yehud focused on torah observance and temple worship, one committed to maintaining Jewish identity over against gentile religions and "heterodox" forms of Judaism. But control of the walled city and the temple also had crucial socio-economic consequences in the defining of orthodoxy. It has been suggested that the community function of the second temple differed somewhat from that of its pre-exilic counterpart.[24] The first temple was primarily a royal chapel intended to represent the official religion of the Judean state. The second temple too was supported by the state, but in this case the state was the Persian government who extended to the local inhabitants some measure of administrative control to live according to their ancestral laws. Following other examples in the Persian realm, the second temple under the Ezra-Nehemiah reforms probably played a large socio-economic role in the community (e.g., to loan money, to collect

---

[23] A. Alt, "Die Rolle Samarias bei der Entstehung des Judentums," *Kleine Schriften zur Geschichte des Volkes Israel* (vol. 2; Munich: Beck'sche, 1953), 316–37, proposed that Judah or Yehud was never an independent province until the arrival of Nehemiah in 445. He is followed by S. McEvenue, "The Political Structure in Judah from Cyrus to Nehemiah," *CBQ* 43 (1981): 353–64. Such a sweeping judgment is unlikely; see N. Avigad, *Bullae and Seals from a Post-exilic Judaean Archive* (Qedem 4; Jerusalem: Hebrew University, 1976), 3–36; H. G. M. Williamson, "The governors of Judah under the Persians," *Tyndale Bulletin* 39 (1988): 59–82; E. M. Laperrousaz, "Jérusalem à l'époque perse (étendue et statut)," *Transeu* 1 (1989): 55–65. Neh 5:15 probably refers to previous "governors" or administrators of Yehud, not Samaria. It is probable, however, that Samaria and other nearby territories had substantial influence on tiny Yehud.

[24] J. P. Weinberg, "Das BĒIT 'ĀBŌT im 6–4 Jr. v. u. Z.," *VT* 23 (1973): 400–414; idem, "Die Agraverhältnisse in der Bürger-Tempel-Gemeinde der Achämenidenzeit," *Wirtschaft und Gesellschaft im Alten Vorderasien* (ed. J. Harmatta, G. Komóczy; Budapest: Akadémiai Kiadó, 1976), 473–86; idem, "Das Wesen und die functionelle Bestimmung der Listen in I Chr 1–9," *ZAW* 93 (1981): 91–113.

taxes, to oversee the use of property). Full rights of participation in the temple were limited to those properly enrolled by family identity and having claim to ancestral holdings. This model has been called the *Bürger-Tempel-Gemeinde* because of the close association of socio-economic and political identity, and it offers a plausible setting for the emphasis on genealogy and ancestral holdings in the Persian period.

The expulsions of Tobiah and the son-in-law of Sanballat from the temple, therefore, exemplified more than just the expulsion of forms of Yahwism deemed unacceptable. Their expulsion had substantial socio-economic consequences as well. The families of Tobiah and Sanballat represented a wealthy, property-owning class opposed to the political emergence of the returnees with their claim to ancestral property. And they would have opposed attempts by the returnees to form the officially recognized political community in Yehud through the Ezra-Nehemiah reforms. It is noteworthy in this context that Nehemiah enacted social legislation to cope with a crisis of debts among many Jews around Jerusalem as one aspect of his reform measures (Neh 5). Another sign of the obligation of many Jews to the nobility that opposed Nehemiah is the comment that many were under oath to Tobiah (Neh 6:18). Apparently Nehemiah himself was well-to-do, and his legislation, if described accurately, means he exercised considerable authority as the governor appointed by Artaxerxes.[25] Perhaps his concern for indebtedness ought to be seen in the light of the social legislation in the Pentateuch.[26]

Once Nehemiah succeeded in gaining control of the city and the administration of the temple, his proposed reforms defined Judaism for the sub-province of Yehud. Eventually the Jews of Samaria would build their own sanctuary on Mt. Gerazim, and it is also possible that the final forms of Ezra and Nehemiah are written as "counterpropaganda" to that construction.[27] According to Josephus, during the reign of Antiochus IV

---

[25] See the discussion by H. Kippenberg, *Religion und Klassenbildung im antiken Judäa. Eine religionssoziologische Studie zum Verhältnis von Tradition und gesellschaftlichen Entwicklung* (SUNT 14; Göttingen: Vandenhoeck & Ruprecht, 1978), 49–76. He proposes that a "money economy" developed among the inhabitants of the land which was partially responsible for the large indebtedness of the small farmers, and that Nehemiah needed the strong backing of the Persian government to ameliorate their conditions. He compares Nehemiah's activity to that of Solon in Athens.

[26] E.g., Lev 25:25–55. See also the study of H. Kreissig, *Die socialökonomische Situation in Juda zur Achämenidenzeit* (Berlin: Akademie Verlag, 1973) based on Marxist principles of class analysis.

[27] Williamson, "The Composition of Ezra i–vi." The archaeological evidence suggests an early Hellenistic date for the first sanctuary on Mt. Gerazim. Cf. R. Bull, G. E. Wright, "Newly Discovered Temples on Mt. Gerazim in Jordan," *HTR* 58 (1965): 234–7; R. Bull, "The Excavations of Tell er Ras on Mt. Gerazim," *BA* 31 (1968): 58–72; R. Bull and E. F. Campbell, "The Sixth Campaign at Balâtah (Shechem)," *BASOR* 190 (1968): 4–19. See also the comments of R. T. Anderson,

(175–164) the Samaritans even claimed they were not Jews but Sidonians.[28] The Tobiad family also may have built a sanctuary at their compound east of the Jordan river, but this is uncertain.[29] The family remained involved in Jewish life and the affairs of Jerusalem for centuries.

We might see added significance in the work of Ezra and Nehemiah if, for example, we knew that one or both of them also intended to ensure the loyalty of Judah in light of the stirrings of rebellion in Egypt,[30] or that Ezra's reform brought with it a number of new elements originally intended for all the Jews of the province and not just those in Yehud.[31] But it is difficult to know whether Jews in Samaria or Yehud participated in any of the rebellions that periodically rippled through the Persian Empire,[32] and if so, whether Persian administrative control of Samaria and Yehud was combined or separated as a result, or even if Ezra actually preceded Nehemiah in his trip to Jerusalem as presupposed in the canonical version of the books.[33] There can be not doubt, however, that

---

"The Elusive Samaritan Temple," *BA* 54 (1991): 104–7, who cautions against identifying the ruins uncovered at Gerazim in the 1960s with the ruins of the Samaritan temple.

[28] *Ant.* 13.257–61. Although the inhabitants of Shechem undoubtedly represented several cultures, the bias of Josephus against them is clear from his report.

[29] This is a frequent supposition among scholars; see M. Hengel, *Judaism and Hellenism: Studies in Their Encounter in Palestine during the Early Hellenistic Period* (Philadelphia: Fortress Press, 1974), 272–77. However, there is no archaeological evidence that the impressive Hellenistic *qasr* at 'Araq el-Emir west of Amman was itself a sanctuary or was associated with one. On the excavations see N. Lapp, ed., *The Excavations at Araq el Emir* (AASOR 47; Cambridge: ASOR, 1983).

[30] E. Meyers, "The Persian Period and the Judaean Restoration: From Zerubbabel to Nehemiah," in Miller, et al., eds., *Ancient Israelite Religion*, 509–22, would interpret the Persian commissioning of Ezra and Nehemiah along these lines. See M. Dunand, "La défense du front mediterranéen de l'empire achémenide," *The Role of the Phoenicians in the Interaction of Mediterranean Civilizations* (ed. W. A. Ward; Beirut: American University, 1968), 43–51; and O. Margalith, "The Political Role of Ezra as Persian Governor," *ZAW* 98 (1986): 110–12.

[31] So K. Koch, "Ezra and the Origins of Judaism," *JSS* 19 (1974): 173–97.

[32] Cf. J. Morgenstern, "Jerusalem-485 BC," *HUCA* 27 (1956): 101–79; 28 (1957): 15–47; 31 (1960): 1–29; D. Barag, "The Effects of the Tennes Rebellion on Palestine," *BASOR* 183 (1966): 6–12. J. Betlyon, "The Provincial Government of Persian Period Judea and the Yehud Coins," *JBL* 105 (1986): 633–42, proposes the chronology of Persian period coins in Yehud reflects rebellions against Persian rule in the fourth century. Josephus records that the murder of a priest in Jerusalem near the end of the Persian period provoked a reprisal by the Persian general Bagoas; see the analysis of the account by H. G. M. Williamson, "The Historical Value of Josephus' *Jewish Antiquities* XI. 297–301," *JTS* 28 (1977): 49–66.

[33] The chonological issues are succinctly summarized in G. Widengren, "The Persian Period," *Israelite and Judaean History* (ed. J. Hayes, J. M. Miller; Philadelphia: Fortress, 1977), 503–9.

this period played a decisive role in shaping subsequent forms of Judaism. The books of Ezra and Nehemiah represent the period as a struggle to define orthodoxy and the political future of Yahwism in Yehud. They are another example in the OT of an intra-Yahwistic debate over the attempt to define orthodoxy. The Judaism of their reforms is presented as the solution to a grave crisis which threatened the very existence of Yahwism.

In virtually all matters, the post-exilic community of Yehud was smaller and poorer than its pre-exilic counterpart, extending for just a few kilometers north and south of Jerusalem.[34] Jerusalem was considerably reduced in size from its former extent. Nehemiah's walls probably enclosed only the upper areas of the 'ophel, the eastern hill of Jerusalem.[35] And the second temple was also quite modest in comparison to the edifice of Solomon, a fact which underlines the comparative poverty of the exiles who must have faced difficulty in establishing claims to property as well as difficulty in producing a livelihood. Nehemiah even instituted a draft to move people into the city of Jerusalem (Neh 11:1–36).

The Material Culture of the Period

The material culture of the period shows that trade played a large role in Palestine of the Persian period and that luxury goods were highly prized.[36] Trade came through the Phoenician ports and overland from the east. The coastal area shows marked Phoenician influence with less. but varying degrees of influence in the hill country of Samaria and Yehud. Greek pottery and cultural objects are known from the late, pre-exilic period on the coast, a phenomenon that increases throughout the Persian period before the advent of Alexander and his successors. Achemaenid influence is best seen in the control of security and taxation; otherwise, the material culture reflects a wide assortment of contacts. The cultural record also shows a number of sites were fortified in the period and destroyed; most of these were located outside the borders of Yehud. These sites presuppose the consequences of both struggles between factions seeking freedom from Persia and internal struggles of local rivals.

Stern ascribes a dominant influence in material culture to the Phoenicians. Two common phenomena in Palestine are *favissae*,[37] i.e., pits or caves for discarding votive vessels, and small, cuboidal incense

---

[34] E. Stern, *Material Culture of the Land of the Bible in the Persian Period 538–332 B.C.* (Jerusalem: IEJ, 1982), 245–49, proposes a somewhat larger province. His evidence is to take the maximum range suggested by the biblical references to Jewish settlements and to add to them any location where a Yehud seal was found.

[35] H. G. M. Williamson, "Nehemiah's Walls Revisited," *PEQ* 116 (1984): 81–88.

[36] E. Stern, *Material Culture of the Land of the Bible in the Persian Period*; his "Achaemenid Clay Rhyta from Palestine," *IEJ* 32 (1982), 36–43; his "A Favissa of a Phoenician Sanctuary from T. Dor," *JJS* 33 (1982): 35–54.

[37] Stern, *Material Culture*, 158–95; "A Favissa of a Phoenician Sanctuary."

altars. The *favissae* imply worship centers or temples located near them, but examples of cultic sites in Yehud have proved elusive.[38] Stern concludes that in cultural matters there are essentially two Palestines; the coast is dominated by Phoenician culture while much of the hill country is a mixture of Phoenician influence and the continuation of the older IA culture of Judah and Israel.

Yahwism in Upper Egypt During the Persian Period

The most important extrabiblical references to Judaism in the period come from Aramaic documents belonging to diaspora Jews stationed in the Persian garrison at Elephantine in Upper Egypt.[39] Some have identified the religion witnessed in the Aramaic documents as a continuation of the official, pre-exilic polytheism of Israel. That is a difficult judgment to make. The Jewish community had a temple in Elephantine for the worship of Yahu (= Yahweh) before the invasion of the Persian Cambyses in 525. Egyptian priests conspired to have the structure destroyed, and a priest from the Jewish community wrote letters to the governors of Samaria and Yehud asking for their assistance in getting permission from the Egyptian governor to rebuild it. Two copies of the letter sent to the governor in Yehud are preserved.[40] The letter implies that there was no deep split between Yehud and Samaria at this time, and it demonstrates that there were established contacts between Elephantine and the Palestinian Jewish communities.[41]

The religious affiliations of the various inhabitants of the site are not easy to reconstruct, since Jewish soldiers comprised only a segment of the area inhabitants. In the documents there are references to Yahu the Lord of Heaven (*yhw mr' šmy'*), a variation of a term one meets with frequency in the post-exilic period as the God of heaven,[42] and to Yahu who dwells in Yeb (*yhw škn yb brt'*). Yeb is the name of the garrison at Elephantine.[43] The temple is also called the "altar house of the god of

---

[38] Y. Aharoni proposes a Persian-period Yahwistic temple at Lachish was overlooked by the earlier excavations by Starkey; cf. *Lachish V. The Sanctuary and the Residency*, 3–11. But even if this proposal is correct, Lachish was probably outside the jurisdiction of Jerusalem.

[39] Cowley, *Aramaic Papyri of the Fifth Century B.C.*; A. Vincent, *La religion des judéo-araméenes d'Elephantine* (Paris: Geuthner, 1937).

[40] Cowley, doc. 30, 31. The date is the seventeenth year of Darius, 408 B.C.E.

[41] Cowley, doc. 32. This document seems to be the recording of the oral reply from Samaria and Yehud brought back by a messenger.

[42] Cowley, 30:15. See D. K. Andrews, "Yahweh the God of the Heavens," *The Seed of Wisdom. Essays in Honour of T. J. Meek* (ed. W. S. McCullough; Toronto: University of Toronto Press, 1964), 45–57.

[43] E. Kraeling, *The Brooklyn Museum Aramaic Papyri. New Documents of the Fifth Century B.C.* from the Jewish Colony at Elephantine (New Haven: Yale University Press, 1953), 12:2.

heaven."[44] According to the letter sent to Yehud, the sacrificial cult included cereal offerings (*mnḥh*), incense offerings (*lbwnh*), and whole burnt offerings (*'lwh*).[45] There are also references in the papyri both to Jews who swear by 'Anatyahu[46] and Ḥerembetel,[47] which may be references to other deities worshipped among the Jews, and to contributions for 'Anatbetel and 'Ashembetel[48] as well as for Yahu.

It is possible, for example, that at least some of the contributions to deities other than Yahu were made by non-Jews. Also, in a letter for Elephantine/Syene found at Hermopolis, there is a reference to a house of Bethel and also to a house for the Queen of Heaven, which indicates the presence of other temples in the community.[49] The proverbs of Ahiqar found at Elephantine mention yet other deities, so that in addition to the question of the ethnic mix, there is the problem of distinguishing between what is part of an operating religious tradition at Elephantine and what is primarily rhetorical.[50] Moreover, some have suggested that the name 'Anatyahu does not refer to a goddess but to a personification of Yahu, and something analogous would be possible for the name Ḥerembetel as well. On these grounds the supposed polytheism of the Jews at Elephantine would be markedly reduced.

The crucial factor in assessing Judaism at Elephantine is the temple cult. From the references preserved, only Yahu is worshipped there. The apparent exclusiveness of the temple cult, however, does not mean that the veneration of other deities is rejected by (all) the Jews of Elephantine, that swearing by 'Anatyahu is only a reference to Yahweh's providence, or that Jewish cultic practices were in accord with the reform measures recently instituted by Ezra and Nehemiah. We should see in the phrase, "Yahu, the Lord of Heaven," an attempt to depict the worship of Yahweh as the worship of a universal high God (the God of heaven). That depiction is likely a common denominator between Elephantine and Jerusalem, apart from any other traditions employed by Jews in Upper Egypt. In the letter from the governors of Samaria and Yehud, the request is made to the Egyptian governor that the "altar house of the 'God' of Heaven" be restored. There is no reference in the letter to Yehohanan, the high priest in Jerusalem who had been addressed in the request from Elephantine; nor, in naming specific sacrifices, is there any

---

[44] Cowley, 32:3–4; *byt mdbḥ' zy 'lh šmy'*.

[45] Cowley, 30:21, 25.

[46] Cowley, 44:3. Cf. Vincent, *La religion*, 622–53. He suggests Anat is the consort of Yahweh at Elephantine.

[47] Cowley, 7:7–8. Cf. Vincent, *La religion*, 562–621.

[48] Cowley, 22:124, 125.

[49] E., Bresciani, M. Kamil, *Le lettre aramaiche di Hermopoli* (Rome: Accademia Nazionale des Lincei, 1966), 398.

[50] J. M. Lindenberger, "The Gods of Ahiqar," *UF* (1982): 105–17.

reference to whole burnt offerings. Perhaps the unmentioned priest would disapprove of the sacrificial cult outside of Jerusalem (based on the stipulations of Deuteronomy?), or perhaps the governor's reply reflects the knowledge that animal sacrifices were offensive to some Egyptians. A further communication from five elders of the Jewish community also lacks a reference to whole burnt offerings.[51]

The founding date of the community in Elephantine is unknown. The Jewish temple antedates the invasion of Cambyses, and it is probable, therefore, that some of the Jewish practices reach back to the Babylonian period if not to the latest pre-exilic period. The papyri come from the end of the fifth century and give only glimpses of the relationship between the practice of Yahwism in Egypt and that in Palestine, but there is enough contact to suggest that even in an isolated place like Upper Egypt, a small garrison of Jewish soldiers understood themselves to be part of the larger community of Judaism. They are called "Jews,"[52] and in a letter that is unfortunately damaged, they receive instructions about celebrating the Festival of Unleavened Bread and apparently the Passover.[53]

Judaism in the Persian Period

Contacts between Egypt and Palestine have implications for understanding the issues facing all Jews of the Persian period. The fact of the diaspora raised the issue of defining Yahwism for each community as well as its relationship to its "homeland" in Palestine. We should see, therefore, in the differing emphases of the Chronicler and Ezra-Nehemiah, attempts to formulate a Judaism centered in the Jerusalem temple which would be a standard for all Jews.[54] The Chronicler emphasized the roles of Hezekiah and Josiah in presiding over a restored cult of Israel that served both north and south. Ezra and Nehemiah apparently brought with them a number of the practices of the exiles regarding "separation from uncleanness" and incorporated them into the Jewish community they formed in Yehud, thus preserving a link between the "homeland" and the practice of Judaism in Babylon, the largest diaspora community.[55]

---

[51] Cowley, 33.

[52] Cf. *yhwdyn* (Jews) in Cowley 20:2, and *yhwdy'* (Jewish) in Cowley 21:2.

[53] Cowley, 21. See P. Grelot, "Etudes sur le 'Papyrus Pascal' d'Eléphantine," *VT* 4 (1954); idem, "Le Papyrus Pascal d'Eléphantine: Essai de Restauration," *VT* 17 (1967): 201–7. Cf. the discussion in B. Porten, *Archives from Elephantine. The Life of an Ancient Jewish Military Colony* (Berkeley: University of California Press, 1968), 122–33.

[54] At a later period, Jews in Jerusalem sent letters to Egyptian Jews concerning the Festival of Lights, Booths and the Feast of the Fire (2 Macc 1:1–2:18).

[55] There is limited evidence in the eastern diaspora for a renewal of Yahwism among Jews; see E. Bickerman, "The Generation of Ezra and Nehemiah," *Studies in Jewish and Christian History* (vol. 3; Leiden: E. J. Brill, 1986), 299–326. For a

By virtue of geography and heritage, only the Jerusalem temple could play the unifying role. Even an incidental reference in Ezra is a helpful illustration. According to the historical résumé of Ezra 5, the building of the second temple came at the instigation of the prophets Haggai and Zechariah (see pp. 232–33). The books of Haggai and Zechariah (and Joel and Malachi) have a different thrust to them than the narratives of Ezra and Nehemiah, yet they are one in their support for a purified cult at the temple in accordance with the torah.[56]

THE HELLENISTIC PERIOD IN PALESTINE AND THE END OF THE OLD TESTAMENT PERIOD (332–165 B.C.E.)

Alexander the Great's conquest of the Near East (333–323 B.C.E.) brought with it profound influences on the subsequent cultural development of the area. Greek pottery and luxury items were already well known in the coastal areas of Palestine during the Persian period and even to some degree in the hill country areas of Yehud and Samaria. But with the transfer of political hegemony from Persia to Greece, all of Palestine would reflect Alexander's greatest success, the transmission of Greek culture (Hellenism) to conquered peoples. Alexander himself did not live long enough to establish his vision of world order in any detail; however, two of his successors, the Ptolemies in Egypt and the Seleucids in Syria, established forms of political rule that directly influenced the Jewish communities under their rule.

Hengel's thorough study of the impact of Hellenism on Judaism makes a detailed investigation of the topic superfluous.[57] It is sufficient to say that elements of Greek culture thoroughly permeated Palestine in the decades that followed Alexander's conquest, and thus segments of Judaism had assimilated the Greek language and aspects of the Hellenistic world view. Other segments of Judaism remained less influenced and hostile, but they could not avoid its impact. It must be stressed that "Hellenizing does not mean simply making something Greek."[58] Hellenism in the ANE was the product of the encounter between Greek culture and the semitic east which changed both entities.

---

possible identification of a lay group of Jews with strict interpretations of the torah, see J. Blenkinsopp, "A Jewish Sect of the Persian Period," *CBQ* 52 (1990): 5–20.

[56] The use of the term torah in the post-exilic prophets supports the close identification of torah observance and temple cult. See A. Renker, *Die Torah bei Malachi* (FTS 112; Freiburg: Herder, 1979).

[57] M. Hengel, *Judaism and Hellenism*. See also E. Will, C. Orrieux, *Ioudaïsmos— Hellènismos* (Nancy: Presses Universitaires, 1986); E. Bickerman, *The Jews in the Greek Age* (Cambridge: Harvard University Press, 1988).

[58] O. Kaiser, "Judentum und Hellenismus," *VF* 27 (1982): 88.

The symbiosis between Hellenism and semitic-oriental cultures produced new opportunities for Jewish thought and new challenges to Jewish identity. Apart from the possibility of influence on the writer of Ecclesiastes, there is little evidence of direct Hellenistic influence on the writers of the OT. Daniel, of course, is an exception. It is a book that emerged during the early crisis period of the Maccabean revolt (ca. 167–65 B.C.E.) at what might be termed the end of the OT period (see pp. 118–22). The influence on Jewish intertestamental literature, however, is profound, with one of the greatest achievements coming in the form of Greek translations of the Hebrew Bible. In much of the diaspora, Jewish documents were compiled in Greek, and even in Palestine Greek was increasingly used (e.g., 1–2 Maccabees).

According to Josephus, major changes took place first in the province of Samaria.[59] Sanballat, the leader of the Jews of Samaria, received permission to build a temple on Mt. Gerazim. Morever, he installed his son-in-law Manasseh as priest, who was from the high priestly family in Jerusalem, making the sanctuary a rival to the temple in Jerusalem. Much of Josephus' report sounds like a garbled version of Neh 13:28, which it may be,[60] but the Samaria papyri make it indisputable that there was another Sanballat in the ruling family of Samaria on the eve of the Greek conquest of Palestine, and the building of the Samaritan sanctuary in the early Hellenistic period concurs with the date suggested by the excavator of *Tell er Ras* (Mt. Gerazim).[61] *Tell Balaṭah*, biblical Shechem, was again inhabited at this time period, which provides a plausible origin for the later Samaritan community in Shechem.

Not only did the Samaritan community in Shechem grow further estranged from the Jewish community in Jerusalem, but the community in Jerusalem itself suffered tensions. Some of these problems in Jerusalem were the result of life under the administrative control of the Ptolemies (301–198) and later the Seleucids (198–167). The two empires struggled repeatedly against each other with the Jewish communities caught in the middle. Some tensions were the result of the differing reactions to Hellenism in cultural matters. Other problems perhaps were inherited from the Persian period and never fully resolved.[62] The accumulation of these problems, the rising power of Rome which influenced the balance of political power, and the misguided policies of Antiochus IV Epiphanes in particular, led to a crisis in Jerusalem in the years 175 and following.

---

[59] *Antiquities*, 11.302–25.

[60] See L. L. Grabbe, "Josephus and the Reconstruction of the Judean Restoration," *JBL* 106 (1987): 236–44; and D. R., Schwartz, "On Some Papyri and Josephus' Sources and Chronology for the Persian Period," *JSJ* 21 (1990): 175–99.

[61] See note 27 above.

[62] See O. Margalith, "The Political Background of Zerubbabel's Mission and the Samaritan Schism," *VT* 41 (1991): 321–23.

The Maccabean Revolt

First and Second Maccabees and the writings of Josephus (*Ant.* 12.234–434) afford the best introduction to this last phase of OT history.[63] First Maccabees is concerned with the priestly Hasmonean family from the village of Modein which is credited with a major role in the uprising against Seleucid control and the policies of Antiochus IV (175–164 B.C.E.). Eventually the Hasmoneans supplant the Zadokite line and take up the office of the high priest as well as that of military and political leadership (1 Macc 10:15–21; 13:41; 15:1–2). Second Maccabees gives fewer dates and covers a shorter period of time, concentrating on the restoration of the temple cult after its defilement from the reforms imposed by Antiochus IV. Both books attribute a major part of the crisis to the involvement of the Seleucid rulers in Jewish affairs and to leading figures in Jerusalem who cooperated with them.[64]

Any reconstruction of the events leading up to the Maccabean revolt in 167 must take into account several factors.[65] The two key variables concern: (a) the internal cultural divisions among Jews in Jerusalem and the surrounding province, and (b) the purposes behind the oppressive policies of Antiochus IV, which were a catalyst for the revolt if not the principal provocation. It is certain, for example, that within Judaism there were movements which represented various positions concerning the influence of Hellenism and the orthodoxy of the temple cult, but we lack enough evidence to identify them clearly.[66] We might suppose that antecedents of those movements later known as Pharisees, Sadducees, and Essenes had already formed under Seleucid rule early in the second century. Indeed, were more source material available, these antecedents would likely reflect some of the tensions and

---

[63] See further J. Goldstein, *I Maccabees* (AB 41; Garden City: Doubleday, 1976); *II Maccabees* (AB 41A; Garden City: Doubleday, 1983).

[64] See 1 Macc 1:11–15 and the references to "lawless men from Israel" who make a covenant with the Gentiles and "abandoned the holy covenant;" 2 Macc 4:7–17 makes references to a "Greek way of life" and the "increase of Hellenization" under the priesthood of Jason.

[65] The classic study is that of E. Bickerman, *The God of the Maccabees: Studies on the Meaning and Origin of the Maccabean Revolt* (SJLA 32; Leiden: E. J. Brill, 1979); the German original was published in 1937. See also V. Tcherikover, *Hellenistic Civilization and the Jews* (Philadelphia: Jewish Publication Society, 1959), 152–203; Hengel, *Judaism and Hellenism*, 175–210; Goldstein, *I Maccabees*, 104–60; idem, *II Maccabees*; 84–112; K. Bringmann, *Hellenistische Reform und Religionsverfolgung in Judaa. Eine Untersuchung zur jüdisch-hellenistische Geschichte [175–163 v. Chr.]* (Göttingen: Vandenhoeck & Ruprecht, 1983); S. Derfler, *The Hasmonean Revolt. Reaction or Revolution* (ANETS 6; Lewiston: Edwin Mellen Press, 1990); J. Sievers, *The Hasmoneans and Their Supporters. From Mattathias to the Death of John Hyrcanus I* (SFSHJ 6; Atlanta: Scholars Press, 1990).

[66] See, for example, the allusive references in Dan 11:28f.

movements already formed in the Persian period.[67] One group known as the Ḥasidim (the pious ones) is named in 1–2 Maccabees, but the Ḥasidim are difficult to define and to relate to other movements.[68]

Cultural Divisions Among Jews

The Tobiad family is noted often enough in extrabiblical sources to illustrate the continuity with problems from the Persian period.[69] The family had a base of power in the Transjordanian region of Ammanitis. At various times the family had military influence and tax-farming rights in the region which allowed for the great accumulation of wealth. The Tobias known from Josephus and the Zeno papyri was even married to the sister of the Jerusalem high priest Onias II. For several reasons there are doubts about the strictness of Tobias' Judaism, but none concerning the influence of his family in Jewish affairs. The Tobiads have been used as an example of the Hellenizing tendencies of the upper classes in Jerusalem and the surrounding area which led to the crisis under Antiochus IV Epiphanes.[70] Although the importance of this class and cultural distinction can be overemphasized, one can see how concerns regarding religion and culture in the Persian period took similar forms in the later Hellenistic period. It is quite clear that 1 and 2 Maccabees represent the impact of Hellenism on Judaism as a major reason for the crisis under Antiochus IV.[71]

The narrative sources also reveal problems and intrigue within the high priestly line, and as a result, problems with the administration of the Jerusalem temple.[72] The struggle between Jason and Menelaus for

---

[67] See J. Blenkinsopp, "Interpretation and the Tendency to Sectarianism: An Aspect of Second Temple History," *Jewish and Christian Self-Definition* (vol. 2; ed. E. P. Sanders; Philadelphia: Fortress Press, 1981), 1–26, 299–309; and A. Rofé, "The Onset of Sects in Postexilic Judaism: Neglected Evidence from the Septuagint, Trito-Isaiah, Ben Sira, and Malachi," *The Social World of Formative Christianity and Judaism* (ed. J. Neusner et al.; Philadelphia: Fortress Press, 1988), 39–49.

[68] 1 Macc 2:42 (reverence for the Torah); 7:12–14 (support for the line of Aaron); 2 Macc 14:6 (associated with Judas Maccabeus). See P. R. Davies, "Ḥasidim in the Maccabean Period," *JJS* 28 (1977): 127–40; J. Kampen, *The Hasideans and the Origin of Pharisaism: A Study in 1–2 Maccabees* (SBLSCS 24; Atlanta: Scholars Press, 1988).

[69] Josephus, *Antiquities* 12.160–228, 239–241; V. A. Tcherikover, A. Fuks, *Corpus Papyrorum Judaicarum* (vol. 1; Cambridge: Harvard University Press, 1957) doc. 1, 2, 4, 5; J. A. Goldstein, "The Tales of the Tobiads," *Christianity, Judaism, and Other Greco-Roman Cults. Studies for Morton Smith at Sixty* (ed. J. Neusner; Leiden: E. J. Brill, 1975), 91–121.

[70] See Hengel, *Judaism and Hellenism*, 267–303.

[71] 2 Maccabees actually uses the Greek terms "Hellenism" (*Hellēnismos*) and "Judaism" (*Ioudaismos*) to describe the conflict during this period. See 2 Macc 4:13 and 2:21.

[72] 2 Macc 3:1–5:20; cf. 1 Macc 1:11–15 and Josephus, *Ant.* 12.237–240.

the high priesthood polarized segments of the Jewish community and provoked armed conflict. Onias III, a Zadokite and the high priest at the time of Antiochus' accession, was removed in favor of his brother Jason, who promised the Seleucid ruler additional revenue. In turn, Menelaus won the appointment as high priest by promising even more than Jason. Thus Antiochus began his reign (175 B.C.E.) with problems in Jerusalem. According to 2 Maccabees, Onias III represented the piety expected of the office, while Jason and Menelaus are branded as Hellenists and opportunists. Eventually Onias III is murdered (2 Macc 4:30–38).[73] Apparently Jason even sought to change Jerusalem into a Greek polis and to enroll its inhabitants as citizens of Antioch (2 Macc 4:9). This would have changed the legal status of the city and tied its leadership even closer to the Seleucid administration.

Antiochus IV Epiphanes

Antiochus himself played a key role in bringing tensions to the point of conflict. Polybius reported he was nicknamed *Epimenes* ("madman") as a pun on his title of *Epiphanes* (manifestation of Zeus), and that he was capable of erratic behavior.[74] Some have concluded from Polybius' description that Antiochus' erratic character, combined with his great love of Greek culture, accounts for his religious persecution of Jews. There is also evidence that he was greedy and in need of funds, and that his taking of temple funds led to rebellion.[75] If the legal status of the city had been changed with the reforms of Jason (2 Macc 4:10–17), and if Antiochus was recognized by the properly enrolled citizens as the founder of the cult for the new Hellenistic city, then perhaps he believed he had a legitimate right to use the Jerusalem temple funds.

On two occasions Antiochus campaigned against Ptolemaic Egypt (170–168), but he was frustrated by circumstances and Roman pressure from taking any advantage of his initial victory.[76] On both occasions

---

[73] The Jewish temple built at Leontopolis in the second century B.C.E. by Onias IV (son of the murdered high priest) was one response to religious policies in Jerusalem. See the contradictory information given by Josephus in *War*, 1.31–33; 7.423; *Ant.*, 12.387–388; 13.62. Cf. M. Delcor, "Le Temple d'Onias en Egypte," *RB* 75 (1968): 188–203; R. Haywood, "The Jewish Temple at Leontopolis: A Reconsideration," *JJS* 33 (1982): 429–44.

[74] Polybius, 26. Ia, 10; 26. I, 1–14. Polybius 31.10 and Livy 41. 20, 8, mention his devotion to Olympian Zeus in Athens.

[75] Josephus, *Ant.* 12.249; 1 Macc 1:29; 2 Macc 5:21, 24–26. According to Polybius, 31. 10, Antiochus robbed several temples. Bringmann, *Hellenistische Reform und Religionsverfolgung in Judaa*, concentrates on the socio-economic background to the revolt and persecution.

[76] Dan 11:30 and the reference to the *kittim* (=Romans); 1 Macc 1:20; 2 Macc 5:1f.; Josephus, *Ant.* 12.244–247.

either Antiochus or his army turned on Jerusalem. After the second campaign Jerusalem was in armed conflict because there was a rumor of Antiochus' death, and Jason had attacked his rival Menelaus in another round of struggle over the high priesthood and political control of Jerusalem. Antiochus attacked the city and garrisoned troops in the Akra, a fortified citadel in Jerusalem.[77] It is very difficult, however, to reconstruct in chronological order the series of events that led to the revolt, and none of the sources provide adequate reasons for the religious persecution that so occupied the Jewish writers.[78] Any reconstruction must bear in mind the concerns of the sources which provide the primary avenue of approach to the issue.

First Maccabees 1:41–64 and 2 Macc 6:1–11 describe idolatrous forms of worship forced on the temple cult in Jerusalem by Antiochus and his supporters. It is difficult to accept these statements as evidence of a forced shift to Greek religion; rather, they should be interpreted as efforts to establish a Jewish tradition in Jerusalem consonant with a Syro-Phoenician Hellenism and one which abolished Jewish particularism. Both passages suggest Antiochus wished to establish a form of unity in his realm which required certain common cultic practices.[79] The references to the worship of Olympian Zeus and the rites of Dionysus in the latter passage suggest Hellenistic forms of worship foreign to traditional Judaism; but this impression is misleading. Hellenic names had been adopted elsewhere in Syria-Palestine to represent semitic deities and local cults.[80] Furthermore, the sexual activity depicted in the temple precincts is not a common form of Greek religion[81] and likely reflects Syro-Phoenician fertility rites. Zeus Olympus, therefore, is almost certainly a reference which employs Greek terminology for the Syro-Phoe-

---

[77] 1 Macc 1:33–40; Josephus, *Ant.* 12.252; cf. the cryptic reference in Dan 11:38–39.

[78] Goldstein, *I Maccabees*, 106–23, proposes that the best source for Antiochus' policies comes from the period in which he was held a prisoner in Rome. His religious persecutions of Jews were the result of copying Roman strictures against certain philosophies. It is an intriguing and plausible thesis but one which must read much into the primary sources of 1–2 Maccabees.

[79] V. Tcherikover, *Hellenistic Civilization and the Jews*, 182, 398, emphasizes that there is no other evidence for the imposition of a common cult over his entire realm by Antiochus IV.

[80] See, for example, the references to Olympian Zeus (=Ba'al Shamem) at Tyre, Josephus, *Ant.* 8.145, 147, and to Heracles (=Melqart), 2 Macc 4:18–20. See also the inscription dedicated to Zeus discovered at Beisan, B. Lifshitz "Der Neues Akairos und des Zeus Bachkos in Beisan (Skythopolis)," *ZDPV* 76 (1961): 186–90, which identifies Zeus as the god of the height and possibly as Dionysus (=Bacchus). Scholars differ on the question whether the "reforms" of Antiochus in the temple cult were polytheistic (so, for example, Goldstein in his commentaries) or monotheistic (so Hengel, *Judaism and Hellenism*, 283–92).

[81] 2 Macc 6:4 does attribute these practices to the Gentiles.

nician Ba'al Shamem, the "Lord of Heaven."[82] Eusebius reports, for example, the equation of the Phoenician Lord of Heaven (βεελσαμην) with the Greek deity Zeus.[83] The circumstances "forced" on the Jerusalem cult represent a Hellenistic pattern of resignifying a semitic deity.

In light of these comments, it is very unlikely that the worship of Yahweh was replaced in the Jerusalem temple; instead the Seleucid reforms attempted to represent Yahwism in the form of Hellenistic and Syro-Phoenician cult practices. Even earlier in the diaspora, the habit of referring to Yahweh as the God of heaven had gained wide currency among Jews; but the attribution of the *name* Zeus or that of Ba'al Shamem for Yahweh was too syncretistic for many Jews. It is also probable that non-Jews or heterodox Jews introduced additional cults into the city of Jerusalem. One thinks immediately of the religious rites of the forces loyal to Antiochus who lived in the citadel (1 Macc 1:33–40; Dan 11:38–39).

Apparently the altar of sacrifice in the temple courtyard was also adapted for the new, syncretistic cult (cf. 1 Macc 1:54, 59 and 2 Macc 6:7). Bickerman plausibly suggested the adaption was a form of bomolatry where the altar becomes not just the place of sacrifice but an object of veneration itself.[84] Perhaps additional stones with an inscription or engraving representing Olympian Zeus were added to the altar platform. In any case, there is also the possibility that sacrifices made on behalf of the emperor were understood by some as sacrifices to the emperor, i.e., as part of an emperor cult unacceptable to conservative Jews. As noted above, both 1 and 2 Maccabees attribute a number of the religious-cultural problems to the cooperation between some Jewish priests and the Seleucid administration, and the temple cult is best explained as a result of this cooperation. The cult was an amalgam of Hellenistic and semitic practices designed to incorporate Judaism more fully into the commonalities of an eastern Hellenism and to overcome

---

[82] See the discussion of other possibilities for identifying Zeus Olympus in K. Koch, *Das Buch Daniel* (Darmstadt: Wissenschaftliche Buchgesellschaft, 1980), 136–40. The equation of Zeus Olympus with Ba'al Shamem depends on the references to the "abomination of desolation" (*šiqqûṣ məšōmēm*) in Dan 9:27, 11:31, 12:11, as a pun on the phrase "Lord of Heaven." Cf. Ba'al with *šiqqûṣ*, a term for an idol or horror, and Shamem (*šāmēm/šamayîm*) with the similar sounding term *məšōmēm* which means desolation. The Syriac version translates the reference to Olympian Zeus in 2 Macc 6:2 as *b'l šmyn*.

[83] *Preparation of the Gospel* 1, 10, 17. According to Josephus, *Ant.* 12.261, the Samaritans asked Antiochus that the deity worshipped on Mt. Gerazim be known by the Greek name Zeus Hellenios. There is no change of deities, only a change in terminology. Cf. 2 Macc 6:2 which refers to the name Zeus Xenios as called by the people of that region (Shechem). The discrepancy between the two names is unclear, but perhaps 2 Macc 6:2 preserves the new title and the reference of Josephus is a polemical one.

[84] Bickerman, *The God of the Maccabees*, 69–71.

Jewish particularism.[85] What the books of Maccabees brand as Hellenistic and idolatrous included a variety of Yahwistic practices opposed by the writers.

The End of the Old Testament Period

First Maccabees consciously adapts themes from the Hebrew Bible as means of describing the contributions of the Hasmonean family to the struggles over the control of Jerusalem. First, Mattathias and his five sons are like the Judges and heroes of old. The book draws a distinct line between Jews who support Judas (called Maccabeus, 2 Macc 8:1) and his brothers, and those who do not. The struggles of the Jews led by the Hasmoneans are depicted as if they represent a struggle of *Israel* against its foreign and idolatrous oppressors, although as noted previously, Jews in the former province of Yehud were divided into several factions.[86] Second, once power is consolidated in the hands of Simon, the last surviving of the five brothers, there is still much to be done in the way of incorporating Jews and territory into his realm. His son John Hyrcanus, for example, would destroy the Samaritan temple on Mt. Gerazim and force an interpretation of Judaism upon Idumeans.[87] It seems plain in retrospect that the Hasmonean family fought for more than the removal of Hellenistic rites in the temple and the lifting of oppressive policies regarding the practice of Judaism. Their rise to power is another aspect of the struggle among Jews for political and cultic control of Jerusalem as well as the result of struggles against Seleucid control.

Whatever triggered the Maccabean revolt, the crisis is described in 1–2 Maccabees as a struggle for the identity of Judaism and the right to claim continuity with the Israel of old. The crisis and its aftermath reveal considerable differences among Jews themselves over the proper response to Hellenism and the proper role of Palestinian Judaism as a community among other nations. Apparently there was no consensus on the best way to express the particularities of Judaism in a time when political and social forces urged accommodation toward the ideal of cultural unity.

Thus at the end of the OT period we see particular illustrations of a pattern widely followed in previous centuries. From the accounts of the Judges to the accounts of the Maccabees, factions within Israel described varieties of Yahwism they opposed as apostasy, lumping them together

---

[85] This conclusion accounts for the opposition to circumcision and the books of Torah, as well as the advocacy of eating pork and conducting sacrifices for the Seleucid king.

[86] 1 Macc 5:55–62; 16:2. In the latter reference Simon reminds his sons that their family had fought the "wars of Israel."

[87] Josephus, *Ant.* 13.254–258.

with practices attributed to non-Yahwists and gentiles. Their goal in every instance was the defining of an acceptable Yahwism and a faithful Israel over against those practices considered unacceptable. What becomes the scripture principle or normative tradition in the faith communities of Judaism and Christianity is one result of their efforts.

PART TWO

RELIGION AND CULTURE ACCORDING TO SOME
OLD TESTAMENT TRADITIONS

THE TRANSFORMATIONIST VISION OF DEUTERONOMY

4

INTRODUCTION

Deuteronomy is formulated as the final addresses of Moses delivered before his death to the assembled Israelite tribes in Transjordan.[1] As a "last will and testament," these speeches and poems are intended to instruct and persuade their hearers to maintain the covenant that Yahweh had made with them at Horeb (Sinai). Repeatedly the book appeals to the hearts and memories of its hearers, setting before them the blessings of obedience to the covenant and the curses for disobedience, and urging Israel to choose life and not death. It is the one book in the Pentateuch that contains provisions for its public reading at a national festival (31:9–13) as well as instructions for teaching Yahweh's stipulations in the family (6:6–25). These two institutional settings—a national festival and an Israelite family—indicate the comprehensive range of Deuteronomy's concern. All Israel is called to respond to divine instruction (*tôrāh*) for its institutional life in the promised land of Canaan.

Deuteronomy represents the land of Canaan as both the promised land for Israel and a snare to Israel in maintaining its obedience to Yahweh. Canaan is a symbol of blessing and curse, life and death; it is a gift of Yahweh to Israel where the covenant with Yahweh can be implemented, but it is also the home for several peoples whose practices

---

[1] The best collection of bibliography and evaluation is that of H. D. Preuss, *Deuteronomium* (Darmstadt: Wissenschaftliche Buchgesellschaft, 1982).

can seduce Israel from its calling. Thus the rhetoric of persuasion in the book underscores the transforming power of Yahweh's covenant for life in Canaan. Israel is called to eradicate all impediments to the covenant and to implement the covenantal stipulations in its institutional life.

A basic outline of Deuteronomy is as follows:

I. First address of Moses   1:6–4:40
II. Second address of Moses   5:1b–26:19
    A. Narration and Application   5:1b–11:32
    B. Ordinances and Application   12:1–26:19
III. Third Address of Moses   27:1–30:20
IV. Provisions for Moses' Successor and Preservation
    of this Torah   31:1–29
V. Moses' Song   32:1–43
VI. Moses' Tribal Blessings   33:2–29
VII. Death of Moses   34:1–12

Closer critical examination of Deuteronomy does nothing to contradict the sense of appeal to the hearers, but it does reveal more complicated literary arrangements in the book than is obvious from the outline above. Scholars have long observed that a core of statutes and ordinances (the Deuteronomic Code) is embedded in the second address (II,B above) and that those elements which follow it (III–VII above) are a heterogenous collection with complex literary and tradition-history backgrounds. Deuteronomy, therefore, must be compared on the one hand with other legal *corpora* in the Pentateuch (primarily the Book of the Covenant, Exod 21:1–23:19), and on the other hand with narrative materials from a variety of sources. The narrative sources cannot be limited to the Tetrateuch, but for obvious stylistic and thematic reasons they must include the Former Prophets and the prose sections of Jeremiah as well.

The setting of Moses' farewell oration to Israel is in Transjordan on the plains of Moab (Num 33:50, Deut 1:5). Most scholars, however, have concluded that as a public document Deuteronomy emerged historically in penultimate form during the reforms of Hezekiah or Josiah in pre-exilic Judah (see pp. 78–90). This Deuteronomy of the late eighth/seventh century was based on earlier literary models if it is not already a document itself. It reached essentially its current form during the Babylonian exile. According to 2 Kings 22, a book of the torah of Yahweh was discovered during Josiah's reign while the temple was under repair (622/21 B.C.E.). After hearing the book's contents, the king called Judah to renew its covenant (*bərît*) with Yahweh. Josiah then proceeded to enact a series of nationalistic and religious measures (2 Kings 23). The "discovered" book of the torah (called the Book of the Covenant in 2 Kings 23:2) should be identified with Deuteronomy or an earlier form of it. The narratives in 2 Kings 22–23 represent the book as primarily provoking reform. The Chronicler also records the discovery of the book in Josiah's reign but does not base all of the king's reforming efforts on it.[2]

To link Deuteronomy with Josiah's reform, while correct, is too slender a base upon which to analyze the book. The reform movements which gave birth to the book are older than the seventh century,[3] although the final form of Deuteronomy (and the Dtr H) is no earlier than the late exilic period. Fundamentally Deuteronomy is (1) the sum of Mosaic torah and (2) the last word of the Pentateuch. These two characteristics are interrelated and form the basis for any satisfactory interpretation. Deuteronomy is also a recapitulation of Israel's life that makes adherence to torah a life or death issue. And by casting Mosaic Yahwism in the form of covenant renewal, Deuteronomy shapes the whole Pentateuch. This is a literary judgment on the function of Deuteronomy as the final voice of the Pentateuch, but it is also a historical judgment. Those circles responsible for Deuteronomy are probably responsible for the essential shape of the Pentateuch.[4] Deuteronomy, therefore, is the most comprehensive statement in the Pentateuch of the application of torah to the life of all Israel.

The vocabulary and theological concerns of Deuteronomy also exhibit influence from classical prophecy[5] and the wisdom traditions.[6] Furthermore, close examination of Deuteronomic style has shown that much of this style is a type of scribal prose of the late pre-exilic period in Judah.[7] These three elements combine to suggest scribal circles for the compilation of Deuteronomy, the Dtr H, and Jeremiah as public documents. There are narratives in 2 Kings 22 and Jeremiah 36 where just such scribal circles are intimately bound with the preservation of the book of the torah and the scroll of the prophet Jeremiah. The scribe

---

[2] 2 Chron 34:1–35:19.

[3] E. W. Nicholson, *Deuteronomy and Tradition* (Philadelphia: Fortress Press, 1967), 1–17, 37–57; M. Weinfeld, "The Emergence of the Deuteronomic Movement: The Historical Antecedents," *Das Deuteronomium. Entstehung, Gestalt und Botschaft* (BETL 68; ed. N. Lohfink; Leuven: University Press, 1985), 76–98.

[4] As proposed by R. Rendtorff, *The Old Testament: An Introduction* (Philadelphia: Fortress Press, 1986), 157–63.

[5] Particularly Hosea, Micah, and Zephaniah; J. Blenkinsopp, *A History of Prophecy in Israel* (Philadelphia: Westminster Press, 1982), 105–6, 118–25, 138–46. See also J. Scharbert, "Zefanja und die Reform des Joschija," *Künder der Wortes: Beiträge zur Theologie der Propheten; Josef Schreiner zum 60. Geburtstag* (ed. L. Ruppert; Würzburg: Echter, 1982), 237–54.

[6] M. Weinfeld, *Deuteronomy and the Deuteronomic School* (Oxford: Clarendon Press, 1972), 244–319. See the evaluation of this proposal by C. Brekelmans, "Wisdom Influence in Deuteronomy," in Gilbert, ed., *La Sagesse de l'Ancien Testament*, 28–38.

[7] J. Muilenburg, "Baruch the Scribe," *Proclamation and Presence. Old Testament Essays in Honour of Gwynne Henton Davies* (ed. J. I. Durham, J. R. Porter; Richmond: John Knox, 1970), 232–34.

Shaphan and his son Ahikam are named in 2 Kings 22. Both are employed in government service. Shaphan figures principally in the reading and authenticating of the newly discovered book. Ahikam later spoke for Jeremiah after his disastrous temple sermon (Jer 26). Two other sons of Shaphan assisted Jeremiah in his prophetic efforts: one named Gemariah allowed his office overlooking the temple courtyard to be used by Baruch to read from the prophetic scroll (Jer 36), and another named Elasah took a letter of Jeremiah to Babylon (Jer 29). Two grandsons are also mentioned. Micaiah, the son of Gemariah, is briefly noted in the account of the prophetic scroll in Jer 36, and the other, Gedaliah, the son of Ahikam, was appointed governor of Judah by the Babylonians after the destruction of Jerusalem. And of course there are Baruch, Jeremiah's scribal companion, and his brother Seraiah, a diplomat who also assisted Jeremiah (Jer 51:59). The family of Neriah was apparently well integrated into Judean political circles.[8]

It is precisely in these scribal families (and in others), whose job it was to compile and interpret documents and to carry out political assignments, that one would meet the combination of abilities to "represent" Moses, to engage in an interpretation of a law code, to shape previous documents and traditions of earlier political history into the Dtr H, and to preserve the biographical narratives of Jeremiah, one of the prophets like Moses whom Yahweh had raised up. Such scribal circles would have been educated in the wisdom traditions, privy to the decision-making apparatus of state, and possessed of the largeness of vision necessary to speak of a transformation of all Israel. They had seen firsthand the ominous signs of national failure and partook of the spirit of Moses in calling all Israel to renew their commitment to the majestic Horeb covenant.

Perhaps the most adequate source theory for the Dtr H is that which sees the composition in two major strands, one which is pre-exilic and linked with the reign of Josiah, and a second which is exilic.[9] The first strand would contain some materials from the former northern kingdom as well as from Judah preserved by supporters of the reform movements in the period of Hezekiah. The second strand would have the impact of exile and the destruction of the Judean state in the foreground in addition to passing along the materials of the reform movements from the earlier period. Deuteronomy, therefore, would have two primary editions, one written during the period of Josiah's reign, and the second during the exile.

---

[8] For further details, J. A. Dearman, "My Servants the Scribes: Composition and Context in Jer 36," *JBL* 109 (1990): 403–21.

[9] So A. D. H. Mayes, *The Story of Israel between Settlement and Exile. A Redactional Study of the Deuteronomistic History* (London: SCM Press, 1983). He provides a good discussion of the compositional issues.

ISRAEL AS THE PEOPLE OF GOD

"There is no God but Yahweh and Israel is his (servant, i.e., prophet)." In this brief statement Wellhausen[10] captures much of the essence of Deuteronomy. The God who speaks at Horeb is Yahweh, and the people addressed are collectively called Israel. Deuteronomy represents both deity and people as unique. Yahweh liberated a community from slavery in Egypt, chose them freely as a special possession among all the peoples of the earth, and set them apart to live obediently in a land promised to their ancestors. The covenant ethos of Horeb, therefore, is fundamentally a community ethos. Modern English translations often obscure an essential indication of this community identity in Deuteronomy by failing to note the mixing of the second person singular and plural in the addresses to Israel. The community is the object of Moses' words whether addressed with singular or plural pronouns. Indeed, the community is referred to repeatedly as "all Israel."[11]

Deuteronomy understands Israel to be bound together by social obligations as a result of its historical experience. In one sense Israel is a community of brothers,[12] like a large family where kinship and shared experience give every member of the community a certain status. This is reflected in the term brother ('āḥ), used in the sense of *fellow-Israelite*. Even those of the community who have lost property and social autonomy are known as brothers.[13]

Israel, therefore, is addressed as the people of Yahweh, an ideal community, whose great privileges have great responsibilities as their consequence.[14] Everything about Israel's life that Moses mentions de-

---

[10] J. Wellhausen, *Israelitische und jüdische Geschichte* (8th edition; Berlin: G. Reimar, 1921), 152. The quote comes from his discussion of the Babylonian exile.

[11] Deut 1:1; 11:16; 13:12; 18:6; 21:21; 29:1; 31:1, 7, 11; 34:12. In 31:30 the people are called "the whole congregation (kol-qahal) of Israel." See further, J. Schreiner, "Volk Gottes als Gemeinde des Herrn in deuteronomischer Theologie," *Segen für die Völker. Gesammelte Schriften zur Entstehung und Theologie des Alten Testaments* (ed. E. Zenger; Würzburg: Echter, 1987), 253–55; and G. Braulik, "Das Deuteronomium und die Geburt des Monotheismus," in H. Haag, ed., *Gott. der einzige*, 115, who both ascribe a major influence in Deuteronomistic theology to the concern for "ecclesiology."

[12] L. Perlitt, " 'Ein einzig Volk von Brüdern.' Zur deuteronomischen Herkunft der biblischen Bezeichnung 'Bruder.' " *Kirche. Festschrift für Günther Bornkamm zum 75. Geburtstag* (ed. D. Lührmann, G. Strecker; Tübingen: J. Mohr, 1980), 30–52. Deuteronomy uses the term "brother" or "brothers" forty eight times in a variety of contexts as a means of identifying Israel or an individual member of the community.

[13] See Deut 15:2–3, 7, 9, 11–12. According to 15:12, "brother" is not necessarily gender related but includes male and female "Hebrews," i.e., Israelites.

[14] G. von Rad, *Das Gottesvolk im Deuteronomium* (BWANT 47; Stuttgart: W. Kolhammer, 1929); A. Causse, "L'idéal politique et social du Deutéronome. La fraternité d' Israël," *RHPR* 13 (1933): 289–323.

pends on seeing this connection between privilege and responsibility. Moses speaks of the "today"[15] of continuing transforming power like that the previous generation saw and experienced at Horeb. Yet this same Moses warns his generation that the only Israel to have a future is an Israel wholeheartedly obedient and responsive to Yahweh's instruction. It is essential, however, to stress that privilege comes first. The community of Israel is Yahweh's by virtue of promises made to the ancestors and by virtue of Israel's deliverance from slavery in Egypt (4:37–40).

Israel's privilege is described with distinctive vocabulary. Three times in the book Israel is referred to as Yahweh's *səgullāh*, a "peculiar treasure" or "prized possession" (Deut 7:6; 14:2; 26:18). The term is known from cognate sources as a reference to special relations between a vassal and sovereign or between a human ruler and deity.[16] In Deuteronomy the term is descriptive of Israel as a community, expanding on the use of *səgullāh* in Exod 19:5 (discussed below). Israel became Yahweh's *səgullāh* through divine choice. This is clearly seen from the use of *səgullāh* in 7:6 with its related vocabulary of privilege:

> For you are a "holy people" (*'am qādôš*) belonging to Yahweh your God; Yahweh your God "chose" (*bḥr*) you for himself as a "prized people" (*'am səgullāh*).

Moses' declaration that Israel is a "holy people" is paralleled by the phrase "prized people." Both phrases are a result of Israel's election by Yahweh.[17] Israel's privilege of holiness does not begin with an assumption of moral standing, i.e., something inherently superior about the people; it signifies Israel's status as a people set apart for a particular purpose.[18] That this election is a privileged position is indicated by the parallel term *səgullāh*. Israel's status results from the deep mystery of Yahweh's discretionary choice. No motive on Yahweh's part is given except that of an active love (Deut 7:7, *ḥšq*, *'hb*) consistent with promises Yahweh made to Israel's ancestors.

The reference to Israel's ancestors is another indication of the community's identity. The Israel whom Moses repeatedly challenges with the decisive "today" is a generation which has a prior history with Yahweh through its ancestors. It seems strange to modern sensibilities to put it that way, but Moses' appeal is to a generation that does not have to repeat the mistakes of its ancestors—i.e., its parents who perished in the wilderness. Yahweh's saving presence previously revealed through

---

[15] E.g., Deut 5:3; 8:18; 11:26, 32; 26:17–18.

[16] Weinfeld, *Deuteronomy*, 226.

[17] See Deut 4:37; 7:7; 10:15; 14:2, for additional references to Yahweh's choice of Israel.

[18] See 28:9 in context of 28:1–14.

exodus and covenant can be this people's experience as well. Thus Moses instructs the parents to teach their children:

> We were slaves of Pharaoh in Egypt, but Yahweh brought us out from Egypt with a mighty hand. . . . He brought us out from there in order that He might bring us to give us the land which he promised to our fathers (Deut 6:21, 23).

In this instruction the experiences of one generation become that of another. In a similar manner, the fruit of promises to a past generation, "the land promised to the fathers," becomes the inheritance of later generations. In the confession associated with the first fruits offering, an Israelite worshipper who will live in the land of Canaan shall confess that a "wandering (or perishing) Aramean was my father" (Deut 26:1–10). And the confession goes on to affirm (vv. 8–10) that Yahweh has given Israel the land. The land flowing with milk and honey is a central symbol of Yahweh's faithfulness in Deuteronomy,[19] but Deuteronomy is equally emphatic that Israel must not misuse the gift or see the possession of the land as a result of its prowess. Canaan and its non-Israelite inhabitants can be a snare as well (7:12–9:6).

Another theme in this intergenerational dynamic comes in the requirement of the current generation to declare its loyalty through acceptance of the Horeb torah. This theme comes through in the awkwardly worded introduction to the Decalogue in 5:2–3:

> Yahweh our God made a covenant with us at Horeb; not with our fathers did Yahweh make this covenant but with us, we, these here today, all of us (who are) alive.

The emphasis in v. 3 on "today"(*hayyôm*) is vital for understanding Deuteronomy's insistence that Israel must commit itself anew to Yahweh. "Today," says Moses, you should know that the Horeb covenant is for us. We are those who heard the commanding voice of Yahweh at Horeb. To maintain the emphasis on "today" and the current generation of hearers, Moses seemingly denies that Yahweh made a covenant with the previous generation, a denial which is inconsistent with the canonical tradition. Yahweh did indeed make such a covenant with the previous generation (Deut 2:19–3:15)! That generation perished because of its disobedience. Moses' denial, therefore, is a literary device for undergirding the "today" of decision for the hearers.

The long address in 9:1–29 should be interpreted similarly, but with one unexpected shift of vocabulary. Moses' plea to Yahweh on behalf of his audience is more than just a reminder to Yahweh of past dealings with Israel's ancestors. As expected, Moses' audience is identified with

---

[19] P. D. Miller, Jr., "The Gift of God. The Deuteronomic Theology of the Land," *Int* 23 (1969): 451–65.

its ancestors in Yahweh's previous promissory and redemptive activity; for Yahweh to destroy the current generation for its failures would be to undo a work already set in motion through the treatment of the ancestors. The unexpected turn comes in the designation of the people as Yahweh's inheritance *(naḥalāh, vv. 26, 29)*.[20] The shift is a subtle but strategic one. Canaan is Israel's *naḥalāh*, promised to the ancestors for their descendants. Israel is to give thanks to Yahweh for this inheritance (Deut 26:5–11). But Israel itself (not the land!) is Yahweh's inheritance. The expected relationship—that Israel is the result of the promises made to their ancestors for land, progeny, and blessing (Gen 12:1–3)—is both acknowledged and transformed in the confession that they are uniquely Yahweh's own inheritance.

This intergenerational dynamic reflects a deeply rooted pattern in Deuteronomy. Moses' audience is the people of God, loved by Yahweh through the ancestors, one with another generation in the suffering of Egyptian bondage and the experience of redeeming activity. Yet this same audience is at a crossroads in Moab, facing the choices of whole-hearted obedience to Yahweh's revealed torah (and the entry into their inheritance) or disobedience and accompanying disaster. The generation finds itself between promise and fulfillment. Yahweh's saving act in Egypt is behind it and the full possession of its inheritance is ahead of it. Israel at the crossroads is faced with the question of the continuing transforming power of Horeb. Can the torah define its life as a covenant people, and will such a torah be *life-giving* once Israel enters its inheritance?

Moses, the servant of Yahweh,[21] addresses Israel at the crossroads. He is a divinely appointed teacher and prophet whose farewell address assumes the paramount importance of torah for Israel's future. It is assumed that Israel could not safeguard its identity without torah; nothing else could insulate Israel from the corruption of Canaan's other inhabitants. It is also assumed that Israel can be instructed to keep the torah. These assumptions about Israel's teachableness and the applica-bility of torah to all of life are part of what some scholars describe as Deuteronomy's "humanism."[22] Although anachronistic, the term is a reminder that Deuteronomy inculcates obedience to Yahweh's revealed will not in a narrow, sectarian sense, but in a full-orbed, confident embrace of a world Yahweh created and rules over. "To Yahweh belong the heavens, even the heavens' heavens, and the earth, and all that is in it" (10:14).

---

[20] Cf. 32:9.

[21] P. D. Miller, Jr., " 'Moses My Servant.' The Deuteronomistic Portrait of Moses," *Int* 41 (1987): 245–55.

[22] Weinfeld, *Deuteronomy*, 282–97; S. D. McBride, "Polity of the Covenant People," *Int* 41 (1987): 244.

The assumption of Israel's teachableness balances other elements in Deuteronomy where a more pessimistic spirit is evident, notably in the long list of curses for covenant disobedience (Deut 28:15–68). Israel's teachableness has several aspects to it. For example, Moses reminds (zkr) Israel of its past. At one level this is simply a homiletical device; Moses can recall either positive or negative illustrations for instructional purposes. Instructive reminders, however, must persuade hearers of their relevance and then impel these hearers into action. The goal of such Mosaic instruction is a wiser Israel, fully cognizant of the threats to its existence, yet committed to the transforming power of the Horeb covenant.

Israel's assumed fitness for instruction also has its corollary in Israel's ability to commit itself to the claims of covenant. More than once Moses will speak, indeed command, that Israel respond to Yahweh with all its "heart" and "soul" (Deut 6:5; 10:12), two terms in Hebrew whose meanings are not adequately represented when their equivalents are used in modern, Western societies. "Heart"(lēb/lēbāb) refers primarily to the will and understanding, and only secondarily to the emotions. "Soul"(nepeš) has several related senses, but in Hebrew it primarily means the life or personality of an individual. A human being does not (just) possess a soul, but in a primary sense is a soul. Thus the call to love Yahweh "with all the heart and soul" could be rendered colorlessly in English as "with all the will and intentionality that a person can muster."

Strangely enough to moderns, Moses seems never to doubt the possibility of this command's implementation. Israel can be seduced or diverted from its high calling, but it is a calling both fit and worthy of its allegiance. There is no speculation that Israel is inherently incapable of adhering to divine instruction (cf. Deut 30:11–14). That Israel is capable of loving Yahweh and implementing torah, however, is not based on a general view of human capability. Everything crucial in Deuteronomy depends on Yahweh's unique acts of self-revelation and providence to which a properly prepared and instructed Israel can respond suitably.

> The Lord your God will circumcise your heart and the heart of your offspring, to love the Lord your God with all your heart and with all your soul, in order that you will live.[23]

The ideological nature of Deuteronomy comes through clearly in its emphasis on the uniqueness of Yahweh and "all Israel." Behind these claims are faded memories of loose tribal associations which rarely acted in concert, a divisive period of the dual monarchy where "Israel" existed in two different states dominated by monarchical rule, and other forms of regionalism which would undermine a cohesive form for the people of

---

[23] Deut 30:6. The larger context of 30:1–11 presupposes the fact of exile and the priority of divine initiative in restoring the people.

Yahweh. The authors ignore all forms of political divisiveness and propose an ideal form of community based on Yahweh's election and promise as the only adequate basis for defining Israel. Only an Israel so defined and instructed in the ways of torah can "live."

The chief obstacle to Israel in the book of Deuteronomy is the Canaanites, the indigenous inhabitants of the promised land. Even the goodness of the land of Canaan offers temptations to Israel to forget its identity and the source of its blessing, but the emphasis of Deuteronomy falls on the land's inhabitants and their seductive practices which can lead Israel to destruction.[24] In many ways the Canaanites define the polar opposite of the ideal Israel. They are a symbol of what Israel should not be but is in danger of becoming. They are to be avoided or destroyed, for the snare of their religion imperils the continuing existence of Israel.[25]

Given the fact that the material culture of Israel was Canaanite, the portrayal of the Canaanites as a snare to Israel is a remarkable *tour de force* on the part of Deuteronomy. It is, in fact, likely that the various practices opposed by Deuteronomy are lumped together and all attributed conveniently to non-Israelite origin (see pp. 30–35). One can observe this in the discussion over the nature of prophecy in Deut 13. The source of defection from Yahwism (as defined by Deuteronomy) can come from within Israel. So the passage begins, "if a prophet should arise among you," and goes on a few verses later to note what happens if a family member suggests the worship of gods other than Yahweh (13:1, 6–7). And it is clear from a close reading that the "other gods" are not just Canaanite but from far away as well.[26]

THE NATURE OF THE COVENANT

At Horeb Israel heard the voice of Yahweh delivering the ten commandments (Deut 4:33; 5:4). Together these commandments are called Yahweh's covenant (4:13),[27] and they are a summary of Israel's responsibility. The various commandments (*miṣwôt*), statutes (*ḥuqqîm*) and ordinances (*mišpāṭîm*) in the code of chapters 12–26, therefore, are commentary and elaboration on this covenant Yahweh gives to the

---

[24] Deut 8:7–20. According to this text, the Canaanites are not of one nation and have more than one deity. In 7:1 the inhabitants are attributed to seven different nations.

[25] See Deut 7:1–5; 12:2–3; 13:6–18. See further the discussion of the anti–Canaanite theme in G. Schmitt, *Du sollst keinen Frieden schliessen mit den Bewohnern des Landes* (BWANT 11; Stuttgart: W. Kohlhammer, 1970).

[26] See the discussion below. The reference to the gods from far away (Deut 13:7) probably reflects the cults made popular by the Assyrians, Arameans and Babylonians.

[27] "His covenant" (*bərîtô*).

generation entering Canaan.[28] Many of them are also closely related to the *mišpāṭîm* of the Covenant Code in Exod 21:1–23:19 and serve as supplements and elaborations on them. Collectively they are called Yahweh's torah,[29] mediated through Moses, for life in the promised land. The maintenance of torah by Israel is faithfulness to the covenant instituted by Yahweh.

The relationship Yahweh established with Israel at Horeb has been variously described, but the traditional term "covenant" is still the most widely used designation in English. "Covenant," moreover, is the typical rendering of the Hebrew term *bərît*. Scholars have long debated the etymology of the Hebrew term, its precise connotation in a variety of literary sources, and the historical development of the idea of a relationship between Yahweh and the people in Israelite religion.[30] For Deuteronomy the concept of covenant is wrapped up in the reciprocal statement that Israel is Yahweh's people and Yahweh is its God. It is a concept broader (and older) than can be grasped by the use of the term *bərît* in Deuteronomy or in any other biblical text.

Perhaps the particular emphasis of Deuteronomy would reformulate the reciprocal statement in the following manner: "it is the relationship of an indivisible Yahweh with his complete and undivided Israel."[31] The concepts of both Yahweh and Israel had suffered fragmentation, and the Deuteronomistic formulation of the covenant sought to reinstate a coherent identity for the covenant giver (Yahweh) and the recipient.

However the precise term *bərît* is translated, the concept of reciprocal relationship as defined above is essential in Deuteronomy. At times in Deuteronomy the word *bərît*, or more precisely Yahweh's *bərît*,[32] does refer to this relationship. The possessive qualification "his" is important since Yahweh established the people as his inheritance. There is no reference to "Israel's" covenant anywhere in Deuteronomy. Elsewhere, the relationship between God and people is linked to the promises Yahweh previously swore to Israel's ancestors. This oath is also a *bərît*.[33] Thus

---

[28] The vocabulary for the prescriptive elements in torah varies; cf. 5:1, 31; 6:1, 20; 7:11; 11:1; 12:1; 27:10.

[29] Cf. Deut 4:8; "What great nation is there that has such righteous statutes and ordinances (*ḥuqqîm ûmišpāṭîm ṣaddîqîm*) as this whole torah (*kol hattôrāh*)?"

[30] E. W. Nicholson, *God and His People. Covenant and Theology in the Old Testament* (Oxford: Clarendon Press, 1986). See the extended review by K. Kitchen, "The Fall and Rise of Covenant, Law and Treaty," *Tyndale Bulletin* 40 (1989): 118–35.

[31] S. Herrmann, "Die konstruktive Restauration. Das Deuteronomium als Mitte biblischer Theologie," *Probleme Biblischer Theologie. Gerhard von Rad zum 70. Geburtstag* (ed. H. W. Wolff; Munich: Kaiser, 1971), 162.

[32] Deut 4:13, 23; 8:18; 17:2; 31:16, 20; 33:9.

[33] Deut 4:31. This chapter is a focal point for recent literary analysis of Deuteronomy and should be assigned to the exilic strand. D. Knapp, *Deuteronomium 4. Literarische Analyse und theologische Interpretation* (Göttingen: Vandenhoeck

the "covenant" with Israel is established at Yahweh's initiative, and although a disobedient generation can disqualify itself, the relationship between Israel and Yahweh is based ultimately on Yahweh's self-binding oath.

The reciprocal relationship between any particular generation of Israel and Yahweh is conditional. The call to decision and covenant renewal is central to Moses' farewell address, and the long list of curses for covenant disobedience in Deut 27 and 28 serves to underline this theme of conditionality. In the introduction to the Sinai pericope (Exod 19:4–6a)[34] Yahweh makes a conditional statement of the covenant with Israel. It is so closely related in theme and vocabulary with Deuteronomy that some scholars would label the passage (19:3b–6) "proto-deuteronomic" or as the creation of a Deuteronomic editor:

> You have seen what I did to the Egyptians, that I bore you on eagles' wings and brought you to myself. Now, if you will listen to my voice and keep my covenant, then you shall be my treasured possession *(səgullāh)* from all the peoples, for all the land *(hā'āreṣ)* is mine. And you shall be to me a priestly kingdom *(mamleket kōhanîm)* and a holy people *(gôy qādôš)*.

The goal of the Deuteronomic address is to point forward to the establishment of this kind of community in Canaan. Not only is Israel a people, Israel is a nation *(gôy)*.[35] And as a state it must have an ethos or even a culture that reflects its identity as the covenant people of Yahweh.

The language of covenant in Deuteronomy, therefore, is derived in part from the political context of the eighth/seventh centuries. Deuteronomy combines elements of two well-known ANE literary models that were frequently employed by the Neo-Assyrians: vassal treaties and law codes.[36] Both models had long histories in the ANE and were concerned with recognized standards of fidelity in the public realm. More specifically, the treaties were concerned with the loyalty of a vassal and the law codes with the defining of an acceptable social order by a monarch. The result of this influence in the compilation of Deuteronomy is no crude imitation of either but the adaptation of aspects from both to the concept of covenant renewal between Yahweh and Israel.

& Ruprecht, 1987) denies the chapter was composed essentially as a unit. With his atomistic analysis, one doubts any composition could pass the test successfully.

[34] H. Wildberger, *Jahwes Eigentumvolk. Eine Studie zur Traditionsgeschichte und Theologie des Erwählungsgedankens* (AThANT 37; Zürich: Zwingli Verlag, 1960) remains a useful study.

[35] Deuteronomy refers to Israel as a nation *(gôy)* in 4:6–8; 26:5. In 7:6 and 14:2 the phrase is "holy people" *('am qādôš)* not "holy nation" *(gôy qādôš)*. The terms *'am* and *gôy*, when used for Israel, are probably synonymous in Deuteronomy.

[36] See R. Frankena, "The Vassal Treaties of Esarhaddon and the Dating of Deuteronomy," *OTS* 14 (1965): 122–54; Weinfeld, *Deuteronomy*, 146–57; Kitchen, "The Fall and Rise of Covenant."

One should note specifically that the code in Deut 12–26 differs considerably in two respects from its counterparts in the ANE: (1) it is promulgated by God through Moses rather than by a monarch; (2) it is thoroughly integrated into a narrative context without which the code itself would make little sense. These two literary characteristics are shared with the other legal corpora of the Pentateuch. Where the code of Deuteronomy differs with the other two major collections (Exod 21:1–23:19 = the Book of the Covenant; Lev 17–26 = the Holiness Code) is in setting and audience. The setting is the plains of Moab just prior to the occupation of the promised land, and the audience is the second generation after the exodus from Egypt. In Deuteronomy the setting and audience are literary devices to emphasize that what Moses promulgates is a renewal of a covenant which had already been established before Israel ever has a human king or complete possession of its own land.

As with the extrabiblical law codes, there is considerable doubt whether the Deuteronomic code in 12–26 has the force of state law.[37] It is more likely that the code of stipulations functions similarly to the narrative testimonies in Deut 1–11, calling readers/hearers to consider their responsibility in maintaining a correct relationship with Yahweh, the God of Israel, but illustrating that responsibility by way of precepts. M. Noth proposed in a classic essay that the stipulations reflect the continuing ideal of an older, pre-monarchical tribal confederation (an amphictyony) of Israel as it was remembered during the monarchy.[38] His theory of an Israelite amphictyony has been criticized for good reason, but his explanation still points in the right direction. Deuteronomy's constitution attempts to instruct an Israel which is defined ideally and not always with up-to-date political terms. Behind the particulars of the code stand the philosophy and goals of reform-minded circles under the monarchy, but even so Deuteronomy remains homiletic instruction. It represents covenant renewal for all Israel, not primarily a new covenant or the charter for state policy.

THE RESPONSIBILITIES OF ISRAEL IN THE COVENANT

All elements of the Deuteronomic address assume Israel's responsibilities to the covenant established by Yahweh. As noted above, these

---

[37] B. Jackson, "Ideas of Law and Legal Administration: A Semiotics Approach," in Clements, ed., *The World of Ancient Israel*, 205–22. This common view of the codes is disputed by R. Westbrook, "Biblical and Cuneiform Law Codes," *RB* 92 (1985): 247–64.

[38] "The Laws in the Pentateuch: Their Assumptions and Meaning," in *The Laws in the Pentateuch and Other Studies* (Philadelphia: Fortress Press, 1967), 2–60.

are the responsibilities resulting from Israel's election. They are to be enacted in Israel's institutional life in Canaan, i.e., in the public realm of community life.[39] A central facet of Israel's duties is indicated by the attention given the appointment of judges in Deut 1:9–18; justice should be a hallmark of Israel. The passage develops retrospectively the account of Moses' appointment of judges described in Exod 18:1–27. First Moses asks the people to select some wise and experienced men whom he might appoint as heads of Israelite tribes:

> Discern between your brothers and judge rightly *(ṣedeq)* between a man and his brother (or with) his alien. Do not show partiality in judgment *(mišpāṭ)*; listen to small and great cases alike. Don't be diverted by anyone, for justice *(mišpāṭ)* belongs to God. Difficult matters you shall bring to me (1:16b–17).

The Deuteronomic edition (1:9–18) passes over the surprising element in the Exodus account whereby Jethro, Moses' father-in-law, advises Moses on the need for judges to help the people (Exod 18:17–23). Second, while in the Exodus account Moses chooses *(bḥr)* the judges and appoints them as heads of the people, in Deuteronomy the process has more input from the people who are themselves to make the initial selection of wise and experienced men. Third, in keeping with the emphases of the Deuteronomists, the characteristics of the judges receive more attention than in Exodus 18. These heads *(rō'šîm)* are to be strict adherents to impartiality; no perverting of justice is allowed due to favoritism or to the social standing of those under their jurisdiction.[40] Fourth, although there is a difference between a brother *('āḥ)* and a resident-alien *(gēr)*, both deserve the same standard of justice.

These last three characteristics underline the theme of justice and right administration in Deuteronomy. Yahweh's people must be characterized by social rectitude and integrity at the center of their institutional life, an emphasis that Deuteronomy shares with the pre-exilic prophets (see chapter 5). But with this shared emphasis comes a critical difference as well. Deuteronomy seeks to give institutional expression to the concept of justice through sermon and stipulation, and to create an Israelite ethos in the culture of Canaan to maintain the covenant. The pre-exilic prophets cite few stipulations from the torah and announce Yahweh's judgment on Israel and Judah for institutional failure. In all likelihood, one reason for the zeal with which Deuteronomy calls for the

---

[39] H. Cazelles, "Droit public dans le Deutéronome," *Das Deuteronomium. Entstehung, Gestalt und Botschaft* (BETL 68; ed. N. Lohfink; Leuven: University Press, 1985), 99–106; L. Stulman, "Encroachment in Deuteronomy: An Analysis of the Social World of the D Code," *JBL* 109 (1990): 613–32.

[40] There are references to judges and their responsibilities in 1:16; 16:18; 17:9, 12; 19:17–18; 21:2; 25:2. All but the first reference come in the legal core (Deut 12–26) of the book. See below.

transformation of all Israel comes from the prophetic announcements of Israel's failures.

Deuteronomy's transformationist vision begins with the acknowledgment that wisdom and justice among Israel's leadership are indispensable and must remain a hallmark of Israel in the promised land. Thus the Deuteronomic law code adds details to the Mosaic institution of appointed judges (Deut 16:18–20; 17:8–13). On the one hand, cities (literally "gates") must have judges who will deliver a right judgment (*mišpāṭ ṣedeq*)[41] and who show no partiality. For certain difficult cases, a central court with a priest and a judge will also be established at a site Yahweh will choose from among the tribes. On the other hand, anyone in Israel who shows contempt for the rulings of justice at this high court is to be executed. As Moses charged all of Israel concerning the local court system: "What is right *(ṣedeq)*, and that only, you shall pursue so that you might live and possess the land Yahweh your God is giving you" (16:20).[42]

The Responsibilities of Israel's Leaders[43]

The Deuteronomic teaching on the responsibility of Israel for justice in its institutional life forms part of a more general emphasis on the importance of institutional leadership in Israel. Deuteronomy has more about the various leaders in Israelite society than either the Book of the Covenant or the Holiness Code have in their respective contexts. In its present form Exodus—Numbers has more about specifically priestly duties, but less (or even nothing) concerning the criteria for evaluating judges, prophets, kings, leadership in war, etc. than Deuteronomy. With its reformist zeal, Deuteronomy exhibits wide interests in and concerns for institutional life in Israel. Israel's institutional life must reflect the nation's character as Yahweh's people in a land promised to them, in contrast to the Canaanites living in the land whose influence in every area must be overcome or eradicated.

Judicial Courts

The high judicial court, which replaces Moses as the last court of appeal, has both priestly and lay judges (Deut 17:9–13; cf. 19:17). Perhaps

---

[41] As noted above, Deuteronomy has the theme of righteousness (*ṣdq/ṣdqh*) and justice (*špṭ/mišpāṭ*) in common with the legal tradition in Israel, though Deuteronomy gives it special emphasis. Cf. Deut. 1:16; 6:25; 9:4–6 (which denies any merit to Israel's righteousness); Deut. 19:17–18; 25:1, 15; Deut. 32:4 and Deut. 33:21 (Yahweh's justice and righteousness).

[42] J. Milgrom, "The Ideological Importance of the Office of the Judge in Deuteronomy," *Isac Leo Seeligmann Volume. Essays on the Bible and the Ancient World* (ed. A. Rofe and Y. Zakovitch; Jerusalem: Rubinstein's, 1983), 129–39.

[43] U. Rüterswörden, *Von der politischen Gemeinschaft zur Gemeinde. Studien zu Dt 16,18–18,22* (BBB 65; Frankfurt: Athenäum, 1987).

the division of labor on the high court was between cultic and secular matters, but if so, that is not made clear in the description of the court's duties. What is of more interest to Deuteronomy are the standards to be represented by the judges (above). All Israel is to support these standards. Not only are judges *(šōpəṭîm)* presupposed for the cities (16:18; 25:1–3), so also is a judicial role for elders *(zəqēnîm)* in Israelite settlements. At times the elders serve as witnesses (21:18–21), at other times they serve a judicial function (22:13–19). To define the court system more closely one might resort to source analysis to separate older and younger traditions, but in doing so one might miss what was of chief concern to Deuteronomy: the attempt to claim all of Israel's institutional life for the implementation of Mosaic torah. Who precisely was responsible as a judge in specific institutional settings is of less interest than that all Israel know the implementation was essential for its survival.

The King

Deuteronomy is the only book of the Torah to address directly the role of the Israelite king (17:14–20). As is typical of Deuteronomy, the passage is concerned with defining and protecting the legitimate role of the royal office in Israel, while underscoring the king's responsibility to rule under the authority of Mosaic torah. This latter fact, and not questions about the tradition-history of the passage or its pre-Deuteronomic existence, is crucial for understanding the significance of the passage. The king is like a judge. He must demonstrate integrity and piety in public life. He must resist accumulating wealth or becoming entangled in business or political alliances. He must be Israelite, a "brother" *('āḥ)* who has a leadership role among family. He should have access to Mosaic torah and should read it faithfully so that his actions demonstrate proper reverence toward Yahweh. There is no mention of a separate covenant between Yahweh and king. It is assumed that Israel will have a king like the other nations, but the king must be one of Yahweh's own choosing (17:14–15). In fact, the method of Yahweh's choosing is not even cited; what is at issue is first of all divine initiative and concomitant royal responsibility to torah.

Prophets

Yahweh's word is mediated through prophets, Moses himself being the paradigm (18:22; 34:10–12). Special care must be taken in listening to prophets, for they speak with the authority of Yahweh (18:19). Once more Deuteronomy takes up a topic of concern held in common with the pre-exilic prophets. The role of prophetic assessment requires critical discernment on the part of Israel. One method of discernment is the pragmatic test of accuracy; if the word of the prophet does not come true in historical experience, then Israel should not heed the prophet's word.

Moses describes his successor(s) as a mediator of Yahweh's word. Yahweh will see to it that Israel has the authoritative interpretation it needs to interpret the Horeb revelation for coming generations. Deuteronomy, therefore, emphasizes the prophetic office because of: its continuity with the Mosaic tradition ("Moses" could continue to speak), prophecy's ability to predict and interpret the future, and prophecy's peculiar ability to call for reform and repentance. What remains at issue is whether the written copies of the torah which Moses is leaving with Israel will be interpreted faithfully by the prophets, and whether Israel will adhere to the torah.

Prophets who lead Israel astray should be dealt with harshly. Judgment must be the consequence for the perversion or misuse of prophecy. Death, even the destruction of Israelite cities, may be required to eradicate the lure of polytheism or reliance on deities other than Yahweh (13:1–18, [2–19H]). This harsh approach presupposes that at least some of the prophets who rely on a deity other than Yahweh were Israelite. Although such prophetic acts are by no means implausible, the stipulations of chapter 13 blur the distinction between the failures of Israel and the seductions of various Canaanite practices.

The Levitical Priesthood

The degree to which Deuteronomy distinguishes between the responsibilities of priests and levites is unclear.[44] Yet as with prophets, Deuteronomy upholds a prominent place in public affairs for priests and levites. Special concern is expressed for the levites who have no inheritance in Canaan, who live in various towns in Israel, and thus who do not regularly officiate at the central sanctuary (12:12, 19; 14:27–29). Priests serve before Yahweh's presence at the central sanctuary (10:8–9; 18:1–8). They rule on matters pertaining to clean and unclean (24:8). They have a place on the central court as a judge (17:9–12). Priests also teach, a duty Deuteronomy underscores as especially significant. Those instructed include the king (17:18), litigants (17:9–11), and the worshipping congregation (31:9–13). And like the prophets, they represent Mosaic torah in their spheres of influence. The emphasis on teaching is consistent with the transformationist vision of Deuteronomy: Israel can be and must be instructed, otherwise Israel's "secret sins" can bring ruin upon it (27:14–16).

The Organization for War

The care that Deuteronomy takes toward the regulation of institutional life in Israel extends even to the exercise of war (20:5–20). Two

---

[44] R. Duke, "The Portion of the Levite: Another Reading of Deuteronomy 18:6–8," *JBL* 106 (1987): 193–201.

different types of officials are named as responsible for martial organization. One group (*šōṭərîm*) is associated with the muster of soldiers from
the general population. The other group (*śārîm*) is responsible for commanding segments of the troops. The regulations presented in chapter
20 have a mixture of kerygmatic, idealistic, and judicial intentions.
Concern for those mustered into service is one priority. That warfare is
Yahweh's prerogative is another. It is assumed that those engaged are
not just Israel's enemies but also Yahweh's. No narrative in the Hebrew
Bible portrays Israel at war in precisely this manner, which indicates the
kerygmatic and idealistic features behind the martial stipulations. Perhaps the inclusion of these regulations for warfare is the best indication
of the breadth of the transformationist vision of Deuteronomy. Even the
description of warfare, with its unique combination of kindness and
severity, is an instrument by which Yahweh challenges Israel to be
obedient to divine instruction.

THE REJECTION OF SYNCRETISM AND POLYTHEISM

The covenant Yahweh establishes with Israel excludes the worship
of other deities in Israel. Such a bland statement is quite inadequate to
convey the seriousness with which Deuteronomy takes this viewpoint
and promulgates it. The most common phrase of opprobrium used in
Deuteronomy is that of "other gods" (*'elōhîm 'aḥērîm*) which occurs
eighteen times.[45] It is a general term spread throughout the book and
represents all the practices of all the non-Israelite inhabitants of the land.
They are a snare, and their acceptance in Israel is a matter of the gravest
consequences. As a result, the Deuteronomists are not concerned to be
fair or particularly informative about the practices they oppose. The
references to cultic paraphernalia and practices are little more than
summary references (7:1–6; 12:2–3).

> This is what you should do to them: their altars (*mizbəḥôt*) you should tear
> down and their standing stones (*maṣṣēbôt*) you should shatter; their *'ašērîm*
> you should cut down and their divine images (*pəsîlîm*) you should burn
> with fire (7:5).

A closer look at the language, however, does reveal that these are
references to the cultic paraphernalia of a typical Canaanite worship site.
Altars for sacrificial service and images to represent the deities are the

---

[45] 5:7; 6:4; 7:4; 8:9; 11:16, 28; 13:3, 7, 14; 17:3; 18:20; 28:14, 36, 64; 29:25;
30:17; 31:18, 20. The phrase is characteristic Deuteronomistic language and is also
found in the Dtr H. In the covenant renewal language of Exod 34:14 one finds a
similar prohibition of the worship of another deity (*'ēl 'aḥēr*). Cf. the affirmation
in the song of Moses that "Yahweh alone (*bādād*) led us and there was no foreign
god (*'ēl nēkār*) with him" (Deut 32:12).

easiest terms to identify. The other two are more difficult. The *'ašērîm* are feminine fertility symbols of carved wood and/or cultivated plants (see pp. 79–84). It is not clear whether the plural reference is to multiple symbols per site or whether it is a collective term for the type of symbol commonly used at a site. Behind the plural term is the name of the well-known goddess, 'Asherah.[46] She or they (the symbolic representations of fertility) could be worshipped in her/their own right and as a consort for a male deity.

The general use of standing stones in public ritual was typical of Israelites and the other Canaanite peoples alike (see p. 15). Deuteronomic opposition is based first of all on the possessive pronoun "their." Since these stones are supposedly used for other deities, they should be eradicated. But the opposition to using them may go further than that, since even their employment in Yahwistic circles is open to abuse and misunderstanding. For example, they can be understood as "representations" of Yahweh in a manner foreign to the iconoclasm of Deuteronomy, or they can be used as more universal symbols which syncretistically assimilate Yahweh into a Canaanite pantheon, or they can represent the male aspect of Yahweh (phallus).

Surprisingly there are no polemical references to Ba'al in Deuteronomy other than a reminder of the entanglement with Ba'al [of] Peor in 4:3. According to a longer version of the entanglement (Num 25:1–9), those involved in the transgression were executed. The lack of references in Deut is surprising for two reasons. First of all, one would expect the struggles with the Ba'al cults in Israel, which are narrated in the longer Dtr H,[47] to have a detailed anchor point in the farewell address of "Moses." Secondly, even the reference of 4:3 is brief considering the fact that the tribes are represented as encamped near Beth Peor (3:29; 4:46). Moses is even buried opposite Beth Peor (34:6). One would expect a more extended use of the incident at Beth Peor from Moses, since it fits the theme of grave consequences for idolatry and apostasy, and it is so close at hand.

These observations are best accounted for by the assumption that the terminology in Deuteronomy for entanglement with foreign deities is general and polemical, and that Ba'al is an appellative for more than one deity (see pp. 39–45). The reference to Ba'al [of] Peor indicates but one form of that entanglement, the only account of involvement with Ba'al in the Pentateuch. Such apostasy was still a possibility for the audience of "Moses," yet the Ba'al [of] Peor did not necessarily represent the dominant form of apostasy opposed by the Deuteronomists. Apostasy at Beth Peor is cited primarily as a reminder of the consequences of idolatry. This conclusion is indirectly supported by non-polemical uses of the term

---

[46] W. Maier, *Ašerah: Extra biblical Evidence.*
[47] Above all in the Elijah/Elisha cycle in 1–2 Kings.

baʻal in both noun and verb forms in the legal "core" of Deuteronomy.[48] The Baʻalism of the eighth/seventh centuries had taken on several forms and developed as part of newly emerging sacrificial and divinatory cults. Its various practices could be subsumed under the common phrase "other gods" (ʼelōhîm ʼaḥērîm).

Idolatry in the form of graven images (see pp. 30–39) receives more attention in Deuteronomy than Baʻal. There are, for example, the first and second commandments of the Decalogue which literally deny a place for any other deity before Yahweh,[49] and which prohibit the manufacture of an image to be worshipped.[50] The term pesel (image) is the same one used in the summary statements of 7:5 and 12:3 and refers to something handmade that represents a deity.[51] And even though Deuteronomy shares the prohibition against images with Exodus and Leviticus,[52] the concern is more pronounced in it than in the other two. In his first address (4:15–19), "Moses" reminded the audience that when Yahweh spoke the Decalogue to them from the fire at Horeb, they saw no form at all (kol təmûnāh), but heard only a voice. For this reason they should be careful not to provoke Yahweh by making an image (pesel) of any form (semel), male or female, of any type of living creature, or even of the heavenly bodies.[53] This last reference is noteworthy, for it names the sun, moon and stars, and all the host of heaven (kol ṣābāʼ haš-šamayim), and likely refers to types of astrological cults which identified various deities with astronomical phenomena. Certain forms of these cults are quite old in Canaan, but they received new impetus and development from the Assyrian domination of Syria-Palestine in the eighth and seventh centuries B.C.E. (see pp. 84–99). Even so, the Deuteronomic terminology is general and polemical; in a summary statement elsewhere, worship of the host of heaven is simply one form of the forbidden veneration of "other deities" (17:3).

---

[48] 15:2 = an "owner" or "creditor;" 22:22 = "husband" (Baʻal) and "wife" (Baʻalat instead of MT bəʻulat); 21:13; 24:1, 4 = as the verb "to marry."

[49] 5:7 [Exod 20:4] = "You shall have no other deities besides me" (literally, before or beside my face).

[50] 5:8–9 [Exod 20:5–6]. The singular form for image is probably a stylistic element designed to reinforce a comprehensive ban on divine images, i.e., not one at all of any likeness (kol təmûnāh). There are plural references to "them" (=images) in v. 9.

[51] The verb psl is used in both Exod 34:1 and Deut 10:1, 3, to refer to Moses' carving of the stone tablets for the Decalogue. In Deut 27:15 a curse is pronounced on anyone who makes a carved image (pesel) or a molten image (massēkāh). They are made by a craftsman (ḥārāš) and are an abomination (tôʻabat) to Yahweh.

[52] Exod 34:11–17; Lev 19:4; 26:1.

[53] According to P. D. Miller, Jr., "The Most Important Word: The Yoke of the Kingdom," Iliff Review 41 (1984): 24, Deut 4 is "a commentary on the Prologue and First and Second Commandments" and 4:16–18 "is the most elaborated form of it [the second commandment of the Decalogue] in the Scriptures."

WORSHIP AND RITUAL

All that Deuteronomy holds dear about worship is related to the significance of the confession of Yahweh's "oneness."[54] As formulated in the *Shema*, "Yahweh our God is *one* Yahweh." Israel should respond to the affirmation by loving Yahweh unreservedly and wholeheartedly. According to 6:1, 25, this is "the commandment."[55] Even in a document that so emphasizes the corporate identity of Israel, the commandment comes in the context of family life. One should not overlook the premium that Deuteronomy attaches to the family and individual religious practices, recording a number of non-priestly, individual practices not mentioned elsewhere in the Pentateuch.[56] No doubt this results from the perception of Deuteronomy's author(s) that Yahwistic practices generally in vogue lacked the comprehensiveness and vitality to maintain Israel's identity in a period of crisis.

Grammatically and thematically the affirmation of Yahweh's oneness in 6:4 is linked with the verses that follow. Both 6:4 and 5 are formulated as a critique of a popular conception of Yahweh and its consequences.[57] Behind the brief affirmation is the critique of the perception that Yahweh took on many forms, depending on the place of revelation. Without Yahweh's oneness and integrity Israel could not be whole. If Yahweh had many forms, then so could the covenant. Polyyahwism would lead inevitably to a fragmented Israel, unable to resist the seductions of Canaan and easily tempted to supplement Yahweh's shifting identity with "specialist deities" whose strengths lay in particular areas. The affirmation of Yahweh's oneness is actually a positive formulation of the prohibition: "You shall have no other gods before me."[58] On the one hand, it is a comprehensive oneness that needs no supplemen-

---

[54] Deut 6:4–9. On the translation of 6:4 see R. W. L. Moberly, " 'Yahweh is one': the translation of the Shema," *VT Sup* 41 (1990): 209–15. Preuss, *Deuteronomium*, 19, 100, lists those who propose 6:4f. was the beginning of the first edition of Deuteronomy under Josiah.

[55] *hammiṣwāh hazzō't*; N. Lohfink, *Das Hauptgebot. Eine Untersuchung literarischer Einleitungsfragen zu Dtn. 5–11* (ABib 20; Rome: Pontifical Biblical Institute, 1963).

[56] R. Albertz, *Persönliche Frömmigkeit und offizielle Religion. Religionsinterner Pluralismus in Israel und Babylon*, 169–78.

[57] M. Rose, *Der Ausschliesslichkeitsanspruch Jahwes. Deuteronomische Schultheologie und die Volksfrömmigkeit in der späten Königszeit* (BWANT 106; Stuttgart: Kolhammer, 1975), 134–42.

[58] P. D. Miller, Jr., "The Most Important Word: The Yoke of the Kingdom," 19, describes 6:4–5 as the "mirror image of the first part of the Decalogue. One can virtually write the history of Israel as a history of this primary commandment and its effects. It is often a negative history, but the negative judgment is made on the basis of this canon, this measuring rod."

tation or assistance from other deities. On the other hand, it is not quite a monotheistic affirmation in the modern sense, for there is a recognition that many gods compete for human allegiance.

The command to love Yahweh follows in a straightforward manner from this interpretation of Yahweh's oneness. There is no sphere of human life from which Yahweh's comprehensive oneness is excluded. One should love Yahweh unreservedly because there is no need for a divided allegiance. A comprehensive torah with its application at home and in the daily patterns of life requires no less. The family's importance as the locus of education and piety is assumed in the Deuteronomic comments, but they are not primarily a call to develop only a family piety. The family in Israel must take its identity from the larger family Yahweh redeemed (6:20–25):

> When your son asks you, "What is the purpose[59] of the testimonies, the statutes and the judgments which Yahweh our God commanded you?" And you shall say: "we were slaves in Egypt . . . and it will be righteousness for us if we take care to observe all of this commandment before Yahweh our God as he commanded us."

Deuteronomy's understanding of the one place of sacrificial worship also follows consistently from the affirmation of Yahweh's "oneness." Just as Yahweh chose (*bḥr*) Israel from among the peoples as a special possession, so Yahweh will choose (*bḥr*) a place (*māqôm*) from among the tribal lands to cause his name to dwell there (12:5).[60] The choice of one particular place is first of all to distinguish Israel from Canaan's other inhabitants who have many corrupting sanctuaries and practices. The one place concerns Israel's identity. As a place of pilgrimage for all of Israel, the place will be a visible sign of Israel's unity and Yahweh's oneness.[61] Second, it will mean less of certain kinds of worship—notably ritual slaughter with the manipulation of blood (see pp. 80–88)—since these activities should only be carried out at the central sanctuary. Behind this paradoxical "reduction" of worship is the historical experience that Israel had worshipped at numerous sanctuaries and had not maintained the strict Yahwistic confessionalism and practices enjoined by Deuteronomy. Neither pilgrimage sites[62] nor pilgrimage

---

[59] Literally the question is "What are the . . . ," but the context makes it clear that the meaning and purpose is the point.

[60] For discussions of the centralization formula in Deuteronomy, cf. Preuss, *Deuteronomium*, 12–19; N. Lohfink, "Zur deuteronomistischen Zentralisationsformel," *Bib* 65 (1984): 297–329; J. McConville, *Law and Theology in Deuteronomy* (JSOTSS 33; Sheffield: JSOT Press, 1984), 21–38.

[61] See especially von Rad, *Das Gottesvolk*, 51: "The institution of cultic unity made impossible every individualistic or particularistic splintering. The one people (*Volk*) worship the one God at one sanctuary."

[62] Judg 21:19 and 1 Sam 1:3.

festivals are an innovation,[63] but limiting certain ritual activities to one place is a Deuteronomic innovation designed to impose reform from the top down. Such innovation is preferable to the widely varying practices where "each one does what is right in his own eyes" (Deut 12:8).

Sacrificial practices limited to the central sanctuary include whole burnt offerings ('ōlōt), ritual slaughter (zabāḥîm), tithes (ma'śarôt), and a variety of voluntary offerings.[64] On the one hand, the central sanctuary will have enormous influence. Cultic personnel formerly employed in local sanctuaries will be transferred to the central sanctuary. It will require a large administrative staff to oversee the storage and distribution of the accumulated goods such as the tithes. Though it is not stated specifically, there is an assumption of a larger role for the royal government in sanctuary affairs, and thus a closer relationship between royal administration and the official expression of Israelite religion at the central sanctuary.

On the other hand, non-sacrificial practices could be carried on in local sanctuaries and within extended families. As always, Deuteronomy keeps the family in mind.[65] The profane slaughter of animals for food was not forbidden, just regulated to preserve a Yahwistic identity (Deut 12:15–16). Clearly, however, these prescriptions faced an uphill battle with segments of the populace. Their prerogative in carrying out local cultic activities would be severely curtailed in the Deuteronomic attempt to define more adequately the identity of Yahwism for all of Israel. As a balance to this curtailment, Deuteronomy repeatedly uses the verb rejoice (śmḥ) as the descriptive term for ritual activity of the household at the central place.[66] There is even an extraordinary provision for those who could not make a pilgrimage with their tithe to the central place at the appointed time. They are to exchange their tithe for money, come later to the central place and buy whatever they would like, cattle, wine, etc. in order to eat before Yahweh and to rejoice (Deut 14:22–26).

Surprisingly Jerusalem is never named in Deuteronomy.[67] Shechem is the only place explicitly named where the people are commanded to offer sacrifice when they settle in the land. They are to build an altar of unhewn stones on Mt. Ebal and to offer sacrifice, rejoicing before the Lord.[68] Of course, there is little doubt that the Deuteronomy of Josiah's reform intended the place of pilgrimage to be Jerusalem. The description of the place where Yahweh chooses for his name to dwell is used of

---

[63] Exod 23:14–19a. Deut 16:1–16 assumes these festivals, while elaborating on their ritual and mandating their observance in the central place.

[64] The lists in 12:6, 11, differ in the enumeration of this last category. On the sacrifices, see McConville, *Law and Theology*, 39–67.

[65] Typically the reference is to your "house" or "houses."

[66] E.g., Deut 12:7, 12, 18; 14:26; 16:11.

[67] Jerusalem is not named specifically in the Pentateuch either.

[68] Deut 27:2–8; cf. Josh 8:30–32; 24:1–27.

Jerusalem in the Dtr H.[69] But the reference to Shechem is quite remarkable for the claim to represent all Israel if not also a clue to the
antecedents of the book of Deuteronomy. It had been the site of revelation to the ancestors and a center of tribal Israel. In the early IA, the
city had a temple dedicated to "God of the Covenant" (Judg 9:46).[70]
Nothing less than a symbol for all Israel, a place long associated with
Yahwistic ceremony and covenant renewal, would suffice as a forerun-
ner of the place that Yahweh would choose.

The one sanctuary where Yahweh and Israel meet reflects the
comprehensive oneness of both deity and people. Deuteronomy lays
stress on the one place as it does on the prohibition of divine images, but
with little explanation in either case. In both cases we would be amiss if
we sought only a political explanation. Deuteronomy opposes those
forces which would fragment the people of God and dilute its identity or
that of its deity. The multiplicity of sanctuaries (and divine images) could
lead to such fragmentation, and so they are opposed.

BLESSING AND CURSE AND THE NEED FOR ISRAEL'S OBEDIENCE

The terminology of blessing (*brk*, *'šr*) and curse ('*rr*, *qll*) emerges
prominently in the heterogenous collection of materials following the
torah code of 12–26. It is particularly prevalent in chapters 27–28 and
crucial for the understanding of the last of Moses' "last words" in chapter
33. The blessing of Moses in chapter 33 is integral in the scheme of
Deuteronomy, like that of the patriarchal blessing of Jacob in Gen 49.
Jacob's blessing foreshadowed the future of Israel's tribes in general and
the transition from an extended family in Egypt to a nation located there.
Moses' blessing also foreshadows the future of Israel in general and the
transition from the last wilderness generation to the first generation
since Jacob's sons to live in the promised land.

For Deuteronomy, blessing is that sphere of existence which is the
result of the implementation of torah in the land of Canaan. Curse is
semantically and theologically the opposite of blessing and is the result
of rejecting the efficacy of torah for Israel's life in Canaan. This is made
clear in the list of blessings and curses in chapter 28. But blessing is also
something Deuteronomy claims Israel has already experienced in its
history with Yahweh. In his historical summary Moses reminds the
people that:

---

[69] See the references in Weinfeld, *Deuteronomy*, 324–26.
[70] A Hurrian text discovered at Ugarit preserves the same phrase; see P. C.
Craigie, "El brt. El dn (RS 24.278,14–15)," *UF* 5 (1973): 278–79.

Yahweh your God has blessed you in all the works of your hands.[71] He knew your walking in this great wilderness. These forty years Yahweh your God was with you; you did not lack a thing (Deut 2:7).[72]

Blessing is linked with Yahweh's presence and active providence, something Israel had already experienced and would continue to experience if it would respond to Yahweh's commandments. Indeed, Israel's proper response would be a blessing to Yahweh.[73] The curses which Moses declares in 11:26–29 and 28:15–68 would come upon Israel if it refused to obey the voice of Yahweh. The vast majority of references to both blessings and curses in Deuteronomy are mentioned in the context of Israel's (future) life in Canaan,[74] but it should be noted that blessing preceded curse just as Yahweh's election of Israel preceded the requirement of their obedience to Yahweh's revealed torah. Israel could perceive something of the horror of curse since it had experienced Yahweh's providential blessing in bringing it to the promised land.

Deuteronomy also uses synonyms for blessing and curse in making the claim that Israel must choose the direction of its future which Yahweh has opened up for it:

> See I set before you this day life and good, death and evil . . . life and death, blessing and curse (Deut 30:15, 19).

But in pointing to the open way before Israel with the consequences of blessing or curse, Deuteronomy could not help but enjoin the choice of life, or better, cleaving (*dbq*) to Yahweh the source of Israel's life.[75]

If Israel needed motivations for keeping torah,[76] then Deuteronomy supplied them. The most frequent motive comes in the reminder that Israel was a slave in Egypt. Just as Yahweh had been compassionate and redeemed Israel, so individual Israelites should obey the stipulations of torah in a compassionate and good-hearted manner.[77]

---

[71] Reading the plural form with the versions.

[72] According to 23:6 (5H), Israel had also experienced Yahweh's power to transform Balaam's curse into a blessing.

[73] Deut 8:10.

[74] Frequently Deuteronomy links material prosperity and length of days in Canaan to Israel's obedience. See 4:25, 40; 5:16, 29 (30H), 30; 6:3, 18; 11:9, 21; 12:25, 28; 22:7; 30:18.

[75] Deut 30:20.

[76] On this aspect of torah in Deuteronomy and elsewhere see R. Sonsino, *Motive Clauses in Hebrew Law: Biblical Forms and Near Eastern Parallels* (SBLDS 45; Chico: Scholars Press, 1980).

[77] Deut 5:15; 15:15; 24:18. Cf. 9:26; 13:5 (6H); 16:17; 21:8.

POLITICS AND RELIGIOUS IDEOLOGY IN DEUTERONOMY

Deuteronomy defines a state in theological terms and is, therefore, a political document. In the history of its investigation some scholars have proposed that Deuteronomy is more specifically a plan for national reform or a type of theocratic restoration, whether originally based in Israel (i.e., the northern kingdom) before its fall to Assyria, or whether first drawn up and then published in Judah.[78] In any case, the interpreter must also take into account the marked ideological and utopian character[79] of the book which takes its particular form during the political crises of the eighth/seventh centuries, and which seeks nothing less than a complete transformation of Israel's identity in light of certain fundamental theological principles.

Although it is correct to link Deuteronomy with Josiah's reforming efforts, Deuteronomic theology did not emerge *de novo* in the seventh century B.C.E. Herrmann underlines this point and several others in his discussion of Deuteronomy as a constructive restoration. In his view Deuteronomy attempted to make concrete an understanding of the state that had existed previously in theoretical and ideological thought, an understanding also rooted in various national traditions.[80] In Herrmann's assessment, it is wrong to identify Deuteronomy too closely with a treaty form from the ANE or even a covenant renewal document based on a formula such as Yahweh is the God of Israel and Israel is the people of Yahweh. Deuteronomy is a compendium of thoughts put together in a systematic and ideological form, centered around the concepts of cultic

---

[78] For references and views see A. Welch, "The Problem of Deuteronomy," *JBL* 43 (1929): 291–306; A. Alt, "Die Heimat des Deuteronomiums," *Kleine Schriften zur Geschichte des Volkes Israel* (vol. 2; Munich: Beck'sche, 1953), 250–75; S. Herrmann, "Die konstruktive Restauration," in Wolff, ed., *Probleme Biblischer Theologie*, 155–71; McBride, "Polity of the Covenant People," 229–44.

[79] On these terms see the work of K. Mannheim, *Ideology and Utopia* (London: Routledge and Kegan Paul, 1936). He understands that ideology and utopia are similar (both use ideas as instruments to advance social interests), but that utopian thinking also has a transforming dynamism for its adherents that allows them to project a new image of social reality. See also B. R. Wilson, *Magic and the Millennium. A Sociological Study of Religious Movements of Protest Among Tribal and Third-World Peoples* (London: Heinemann, 1973), 25–26, who describes utopian views as more radical than reformist since the utopian world view requires the complete replacement of the existing social organization. In these senses Deuteronomy is not only an ideological work but also a utopian one.

[80] "S. Herrmann, "Die konstruktive Restauration," in Wolff, ed., *Probleme Biblischer Theologie*: "The admonitions and models for a future Israelite common essence" (p. 156); "a pre-conceived work of ideas," in one sense a "theoretical document" (p. 157).

unity and cultic purity, and bound together with the idea of a definable "all Israel."[81]

Deuteronomy is as much the end product of a long, complicated process of theological reflection as it is a distinctive voice emerging in the eighth/seventh centuries. Its presuppositions have obviously influenced the OT presentation of Israel's life in Canaan; as Herrmann states, "the whole history of the occupation of the land and the formation of the states comes in a Deuteronomistic redaction." He also claims that "the theology of the Old Testament is finally a theology oriented to the standards of Deuteronomy."[82] This latter claim about OT theology is an overstatement. It would be more adequate to say (as he does elsewhere) that Deuteronomy contains "the basic questions of OT theology *in nuce.*"[83] But without careful qualification even that is an overstatement. The relevant OT documents develop their response to these questions independently, and the affirmations in Deuteronomy do not dictate their conclusions.

The interpretation of McBride has features in common with that of Herrmann, also emphasizing the political and ideological aspects of Deuteronomy. For him torah is too easily equated with "instruction" in the sense of moralizing or homiletical application. In Deuteronomy torah is nothing less than "covenant law, the divinely authorized social order that Israel must implement to secure its collective political existence as the people of God."[84] Deuteronomy offers a "charter for a constitutional theocracy," a "comprehensive social charter, perhaps uniquely appropriate to the peculiar covenantal identity that Israel claimed for itself and which was the product of mature reflection on this identity."[85] It would be inadequate, therefore, to stress the spirit of inculcation to the exclusion of the spirit of political implementation in "Deuteronomic constitutionalism."

The comments of both Herrmann and McBride demonstrate how important Deuteronomy is for its distinct approach to the question of religion and culture. Life in Canaan, the inheritance of all Israel, must be transformed by the application of *tôrāh* to Israel's public life. From the king on down to individual families, *tôrāh* must inform and transform the people of God, or Israel perverts its election and becomes perverted

---

[81] Ibid., 158–64. Herrmann proposes the OT does not preserve treaty or covenant documents, but only various accounts concerning the conclusion of such public ceremonies.

[82] Ibid., 167.

[83] Herrmann does say this (p. 156), but goes on to claim that OT theology has its center (*Zentrum*) in Deuteronomy.

[84] McBride, "Polity of the Covenant People," 233.

[85] Ibid., 236–38. Like Herrmann, McBride cautions against identifying Deuteronomy too closely with treaty forms and law codes from the ANE.

through the influence of Canaanite religion. The Canaanites, then, must be destroyed or avoided, or Israel will fail its calling from Yahweh. Election, promised land, and life-giving torah are interwined in the covenant relationship between Yahweh and Israel; they are the building blocks of the constitutional transformation of Israel proposed by Deuteronomy.[86]

Conclusion

It is precisely Deuteronomy's passionate insistence that Israel faces life-and-death decisions in the land of Canaan that gives the book its particular approach to the question of religion and culture. Indeed it would be unfair to Deuteronomy to say that its approach insists only on life-or-death decisions without noting that such decisions lead to life-and-death struggles. Political ideology and utopian hope infuse Deuteronomy's zeal for an Israel transformed by the Horeb covenant; it is a zeal for a covenant community dedicated exclusively to the service of Yahweh in the land of Canaan. One would expect no less in the last words of Moses to all Israel.

> I call heaven and earth to bear witness today that I have placed before you life and death, blessing and curse. Choose life so that you may live, you and your descendants, loving Yahweh your God, listening to his voice, and clinging to him. That is your life and the extension of your days, that you may live in the land which the Yahweh promised to give to your fathers, to Abraham, Isaac, and Jacob (Deut 30:19–20).

---

[86] According to Deut 30:1–10, a future transformation of Israel comes after Israel's exile among the nations. Yahweh will circumcise Israel's heart and bring the exiles back to the promised land. Then Israel will be able to love Yahweh wholeheartedly and live obediently in the promised land. This passage almost certainly belongs to the exilic circles responsible for the final form of the book.

THE PRE-EXILIC PROPHETS AND THE PARADOX OF ISRAELITE CULTURE

5

ISRAELITE PROPHECY HAS BEEN REGARDED frequently by interpreters as the most distinctive element in the OT. This view was common among many earlier critical scholars who attributed to the pre-exilic writing prophets a decisive role in Israel's theological development. Current trends suggest a return to this view among many scholars, since the later dating of the narrative traditions in the OT places the pre-exilic prophets—and particularly the eighth-century prophets—as the earliest representatives of several key ideas.[1] This current trend typically assumes too much innovation for the prophets, but it does reflect accurately that they represent forms of Yahwism at critical moments in Israel's history.[2]

Recent sociological and anthropological approaches to Israelite religion have given attention to the place of prophets in their society.[3]

---

[1] This trend is clear from the helpful survey of E. Nicholson, "Israelite Religion in the Pre-exilic Period. A Debate Renewed," *A Word in Season. Essays in Honour of William McKane* (JSOTSS 42; ed. J. D. Martin and P. R. Davies; Sheffield: JSOT Press, 1986), 3–34.

[2] See R. Rendtorff, "Reflections on the Early History of Prophecy in Israel," *JTC* 4 (1967): 14–34; and J. Blenkinsopp, *A History of Prophecy in Israel*, 53–79, for a discussion of the lines of continuity between the earlier prophets and the writing of classical prophets of the eighth century and later.

[3] R. Wilson, *Prophecy and Society in Ancient Israel* (Philadelphia: Fortress Press, 1980); D. Petersen, *The Roles of Israel's Prophets* (JSOTSS 27; Sheffield: JSOT Press, 1981); R. P. Carroll, "Prophecy and Society," in Clements, ed., *The World of Ancient Israel*, 203–25. From a cross-cultural perspective, see T. W. Overholt, *Channels of Prophecy: The Social Dynamics of Prophetic Activity* (Minneapolis: Fortress, 1989).

One firm result is the recognition that the prophets were not the kind of individualists they were often assumed to be. Whether they participated in the central social institutions of their society or whether they existed on the periphery, prophets had supportive communities which valued their efforts and preserved their words. Behind every prophetic book, therefore, stand not only the prophet but also those who agreed with the prophet's (often negative) assessment of contemporary society. From the stage of oral delivery to the stage of final preservation, the prophetic words are interpreted within the context of a religious community.

Prophecy and monarchy were intimately related. The theocentric emphasis of the prophets was influential during the period when Yahweh's anointed ruled in Israel or Judah, though historically prophecy outlasted the monarchy. The pre-exilic prophets of the eighth and seventh centuries B.C.E. especially had a common element among their various emphases which allows them to be treated together. The common element is derived from a paradoxical assessment of Israelite society by the prophets. On the one hand, these prophets addressed an Israelite culture with its own developed institutions and national character and found them all utterly lacking in a Yahwistic ethos necessary for national survival. Their assessment of corporate failure was one part of the paradox. On the other hand, Israel's and Judah's continuing historical existence depended on the character of their central institutions;[4] not only because they represented symbolically the people's identity but also because they represented Yahweh's gifts to sustain public life. The prophets' assumption of the symbolic role of the central institutions was the other part to the paradox. What was assumed as central to the identity of society (its central institutions) was judged by these prophets as central to society's failure.[5]

The "paradoxical element" in the prophetic critique is not a key to explain everything that is significant about the pre-exilic prophets; it is, however, a description of a common ingredient in their approach to religion and culture. The Yahwism they represented stood in a paradoxical relationship to the Yahwism they perceived represented in Israelite society. This paradoxical approach can be developed by considering the prophetic books of the period under five categories: the role of the

---

[4] H. Utzschneider, *Prophet vor dem Ende. Zum Verhältnis von Geschichte und Institution in der alttestamentlichen Prophetie* (OBO 18; Fribourg: Universitätsverlag, 1980) has analyzed the prophet Hosea from the perspective of the interrelatedness (*die Bindung*) of national history and the character of the national institutions. He understands that prophecy too is a recognized institution in Israel. Utzschneider depends on the work of P. Berger and T. Luckmann, *The Social Construction of Reality*, for his emphasis on what public institutions represent about a society's self-perception.

[5] See further, W. McKane, "Prophet and Institution," *ZAW* 94 (1982): 251–66.

prophets, their understanding of their audience as the people of Yahweh, their criticism of worship, their assessment of the monarchy, and the relationship between prophecy and society.

THE ROLE OF PROPHETS ACCORDING TO THE PROPHETIC BOOKS

The pre-exilic prophetic books provide some evidence for the roles of the prophets in Israelite society. As with many of the prophecies, those concerned with prophetic roles have a polemical aspect associated with them. Nevertheless they are valuable indicators not only for the prophets themselves but also for the communities which preserved the prophecies as ongoing witnesses to Yahweh's word for Israel. Prophecy is represented as an institution in Israel and Judah, bound in an integral way with other institutions such as temple and monarchy, but it is an institution that offers a critique of Israel and Judah's identity. This role is common to all of the earliest "writing" prophets regardless of differences of social setting. Amos, for example, may be an outsider in Israel; Isaiah perhaps is a patrician in Jerusalem. The activities of both assume that prophetic activity has an institutional nature recognized by their society.

Much of the prophetic assessment of the prophets' contemporaries was negative, and the books which preserve this assessment instructed their readers concerning the defeat of Israel and Judah at the hands of Assyria and Babylonia respectively. Several communities of faith who sought answers to the verdict of history, and who expressed hope for the future, did so on the basis of the words of the prophets. The books, therefore, address the people of God across the generations, even though most of the individual prophecies originally addressed more specific contexts. But both the prophets themselves and the later, edited books share one common feature: They originated in circles or communities who carried out a ministry to the larger society of which they were a part. Answer, criticism, and hope are all given confessionally, that is, the prophets and their editors perceived God's activity in the historical process and spoke definitively from that perspective. This conclusion does not mean that the books (Amos, Micah, etc.) are essentially an invention of later circles to explain the trauma of Israel and Judah's demise. On the contrary, an Amos or a Micah had exercised a prophetic calling to an Israel or a Judah before the states collapsed, and from their prophetic perspective, they believed Yahweh enabled them to see the consequences of state activity. The compilers of the books did make editorial changes and adaptations, but they did so in order that the prophets' words might continue to instruct subsequent generations. From a time considerably before the collapse of Israel, there were prophets who spoke to their contemporaries about righteousness and judgment, deliverance and hope.[6] The prophets of the eighth century and later were heirs of this activity and contributors to it.

The Eighth-Century Prophets

Amos has a brief recital of Yahweh's saving activity on behalf of Israel in 2:9–12. The theme is the gift of the land to those Yahweh delivered from Egypt and preserved in the wilderness. Such brief recitals are not uncommon in the prophets, but Amos carries the theme of Yahweh's saving activity past the exodus and occupation generations and links it with prophetic activity itself (vv. 11–12).

> And I raised up prophets from your sons and Nazirites from your children. Is this not so Israel (says Yahweh)? But you made the Nazirites drink wine, and you commanded the prophets not to prophesy.

Little is known about the Nazirites, but apparently they lived in communities or circles in the midst of the larger community of Israel where they maintained traditions which they dedicated to the service of God. As a result, they played a distinctive role in their society. Abstinence from wine was one tradition; others included forgoing the cutting of hair and touching corpses.[7] The reasons for their special practices are not given, but perhaps abstinence from wine was their witness to Yahweh's sustaining power outside the cultivated land (cf. 2:10b). Just as the wilderness generations had no wine to drink—and had to depend on Yahweh even for water—so the Nazirites passed up the privilege of wine as a symbolic act of witness to Yahweh's saving activity.

Some prophets had a similar profile and can be categorized as a group who stand as interpreters of God's continuing activity in the midst of Israelite society. Their prophetic activity also set them apart from the society as a whole. The effect of their public speaking must have been such that on occasion the larger community sought to silence them. Part of the reason for this is surely that the prophets spoke with conviction about the future.[8] A second reason is that some prophets were outside the control of priests or other officials, offering a critical assessment of Israelite society. And since they spoke in the name of Yahweh, there was

---

[6] K. van der Toorn, "From Patriarchs to Prophets. A Reappraisal of Charismatic Leadership in Ancient Israel," *JNWSL* 13 (1987): 191–218, proposes early prophets had central roles among the tribes even before the monarchy. As the monarchy took over more and more functions of state administration, the political power of the prophets was reduced, but not their role mediating Yahweh's word to their society.

[7] Num 6:1–21.

[8] Amos 3:7 represents the view that Yahweh doesn't act without revealing his counsel to his servants, the prophets. This comment is most likely editorial and represents the view of the community which preserved Amos' words, but even so, it is a valuable indicator of how certain groups perceived the prophets.

no higher authority to which those offended might appeal. That is a crucial point in the exchange between Amos and the priest Amaziah in 7:10–17. Amos claims he was not a member of a prophetic group that made its living predicting the future for clients, but that he uttered his prophecies at the direct command of Yahweh.[9] Amaziah could forcibly evict Amos from Israel or perhaps have him arrested for treason against the state (cf. 7:9), but he was unable to countermand Amos' sense of call.

Hosea associates prophecy with the work of Moses in leading Israel up from Egypt.[10] Moses represented Yahweh's judging word to Pharaoh and liberating word to Israel in ways that could not be controlled through official channels. Something of this same assumption of freedom to prophesy (and to state harsh and unpopular things) is behind the statement in 6:5–6 that Yahweh had struck Israel through the prophets and had slain with the words of his mouth. The difficult saying in 12:10 (11H)—about Yahweh speaking to the prophets and about their parabolic prophecies—follows a brief recital of saving history and thus links Israel's past with the prophetic preaching. In some respects this passage is similar to Amos 2:9–12, linking past and present together. Hosea even understands Israel's place in Yahweh's economy to be analogous to a watchman/prophet (9:8).

In the book of Isaiah the prophet's response to Yahweh's self-revelation is consistent with the sketch of prophetic activity drawn from Amos and Hosea. Yahweh speaks to Isaiah in the temple in a way that the priest, who has regular cultic and pastoral duties, is usually unable to portray (6:1–13). The word which Isaiah hears is definitely a judgmental one and not something that easily becomes a part of regular cultic practice! Another indication of prophetic roles in society is the brief statement that Isaiah had disciples with whom he shared his prophecies when rebuffed by the leading elements of Judean society (8:16).[11]

In line with these previous statements is Micah's brief claim (3:8) that he was "full of strength,[12] justice and power, to declare to Jacob his

---

[9] Amos' answer to Amaziah in 7:14 lacks a verb. Literally the Hebrew text reads: "no prophet I and no prophet's son I," and one must supply either the present or past tense of the verb *to be*. I *am* no prophet . . . or I *was* no prophet. Another important definition of a prophet comes in 7:15 with the claim that Yahweh took (*lqḥ*) Amos and told him to go (*hlk*) and prophesy (*nb'*). This vocabulary should be compared to the phrase in Isa 6:8, where Yahweh speaks in the heavenly assembly: "Whom shall I send (*šlk*) and who will go (*hlk*) for us?"

[10] E. Zenger, " 'Durch Menschen zog ich sie . . . ' (Hos 11,4). Beobachtungen zum Verständnis des prophetischen Amtes im Hoseabuch," in L. Ruppert, ed., *Künder der Wortes: Beiträge zur Theologie der Propheten; Josef Schreiner zum 60. Geburtstag*, 183–201.

[11] C. Hardmeier, "Verkündigung und Schrift bei Jesaja. Zur Entstehung der Schriftprophetie als Oppositionsliteratur im alten Israel," *Th Gl* 73 (1983): 119–34.

[12] The Hebrew text of the first line in 3:8 has "spirit (*rûaḥ*) of Yahweh" after

transgression and to Israel his sin." Perhaps Mic 7:7–8 is to be understood in the light of the prophet's expectancy that Yahweh would vindicate him in spite of his detractors, but the context of the saying is too difficult to make the connection clear.

The Prophets of the Seventh Century and Later

Similar lines of development characterize the remaining pre-exilic prophets, though the details vary in the books that result from their activity. Zephaniah, for example, who depicts the judgment to fall on Judah at the coming day of Yahweh, is possibly the great-grandson of Hezekiah.[13] If the attribution is correct, it would place the prophet among reforming circles opposed to the policies of Manasseh. The large books of Jeremiah and Ezekiel both stem from the exile and early post-exilic periods. Jeremiah is a prophet in the mold of Moses according to "his book,"[14] while Ezekiel is portrayed as a watchman[15] to whom Yahweh has revealed his unalterable judgment. In both cases, the books depict a prophet with an unpopular message who is virtually unable to resist Yahweh's claim upon him.

Prophetic opposition to the canonical prophets is a theme which develops throughout the pre-exilic period. Hosea offers some evidence of prophetic opposition, and this comes in language difficult to interpret (9:7b–8). Micah similarly has a couple of references (Mic 2:6–11; 3:5–7). Zephaniah mentions prophetic opposition in Jerusalem, and this comes to light in a general list of Jerusalemite inhabitants opposed to his judgmental and reformist prophecy (Zeph 3:3–4). With Jeremiah, however, comes opposition in virtually all forms. He faces persecution from the king and the priests, and even opposition from his family. Prophetic opposition comes from several places (Jer 23:9–40; 28:1–17). One source comes from those who apparently oppose Jeremiah's exclusive reliance on Yahweh, or from their perspective, Jeremiah's denial of the validity of Ba'al's word. Others obviously are appalled at his preaching of judgment and his condemnation of Judean society. Certainly others are most offended at the political implications of his prophecies, one of which is

the term strength (kōaḥ). The phrase sits awkwardly in the verse, and many scholars believe it is an editorial insertion noting the source of the prophet's strength and convictions.

[13] Zeph 1:1. The verse is editorial, and Hezekiah is not identified as a (former) king.

[14] C. Seitz, "The Prophet Moses and the Canonical Shape of Jeremiah," ZAW 101 (1989): 3–27.

[15] Ezek 3:17. See, R. Clements, "The Ezekiel Tradition: prophecy in a time of crisis," Israel's Prophetic Tradition. Essays in Honour of Peter R. Ackroyd (Cambridge: Cambridge University Press, 1982), 119–36. Habakkuk, who was appalled at the failures of Judah (1:2–4), is also depicted as a watchman in 2:1–2.

submission to Babylon. Most intriguing is the account of the confrontation between Jeremiah and Hananiah of Gibeon (Jer 28). Both speak in the name of Yahweh and both believe that Yahweh will bring back the exilic community from Babylon. Hananiah, however, is unable to fathom the depth of Judean failure, the nature of divine judgment as Jeremiah represents it, or the extent of the changes which the future will bring upon the people of God. Jeremiah represents the view that the prophets before him were known for their prophecies of war, disaster and pestilence; the prophecy of peace is the one particularly in need of divine confirmation (28:8). Here we may have a summary statement about prophecy that owes as much to the editors of the book as to Jeremiah himself, but it characterizes in a compressed and one-sided way a dominant theme of Jeremiah's canonical predecessors.

Ezekiel likewise faced explicit opposition of a similar kind (Ezek 13). He too would have been opposed by many because of the harshness of his language and the bizarre nature of his symbolic acts.[16] In many ways the language of judgment reaches its harshest and most uncompromising level in the book of Ezekiel. The prophet even interprets the previous history of Israel and Judah as a series of failures to respond adequately to divine revelation. Here the paradoxical dimension in the prophetic assessment comes sharply to the foreground. Ezekiel sought to portray Israelite and Judean failure as longstanding facts, as if the people of God had persistently resisted making a faithful response to Yahweh's electing activity in their previous history. Of course, there are elements of a theodicy in Ezekiel's argument as the fact of Israelite and Judean exile looms in the background. Ezekiel represents judgment as Yahweh's reaction to persistent disobedience.

Beginning with the exilic prophet Second Isaiah, prophecy changes its approach. No longer is the preaching of judgment the dominent theme, especially in the absolute form of future announcements of judgment. Second Isaiah, for example, is every bit the evangelist for Yahweh's new acts of salvation for Israel as Jeremiah and Ezekiel had been in announcing Yahweh's judgment. For the anonymous prophet the paradox is not that of failure against Yahweh's grace but the paradox of Yahweh's saving intentions for the heirs of the disobedient in exile, indeed, even for the ends of the earth, with these heirs of the disobedient playing a key role in the divine plan.[17]

---

[16] B. Lang, "Street Theater, Raising the Dead, and the Zoroastrian Connection in Ezekiel's Prophecy," *Ezekiel and His Book. Textual and Literary Criticism and Their Interrelation* (BETL 74; ed. J. Lust; Leuven: University Press, 1986), 297–316, discusses the sources for Ezekiel's bizarre activity.

[17] D. Van Winkle, "The Relationship of the Nations to Yahweh and to Israel in Isaiah xl-lv," *VT* 35 (1985): 446–58.

Post-exilic prophecy would take its lead from the prophets of the previous era (see pp. 230–35). For example, the largest prophetic book of the post-exilic period, Zechariah, begins with the acknowledgment that prophecy is now heir to a long tradition. Moreover, the previous prophets whom Yahweh designates as "my servants the prophets" can be understood by the post-exilic generations as preachers of repentance so that they will understand where their ancestors went wrong.

> Return (*šûb*) to me says Yahweh of Hosts, and I will return (*šûb*) to you. . . . Do not be like your ancestors to whom the former prophets proclaimed. . . . Return (*šûb*) from your evil ways and deeds (Zech 1:3–4).

This vocabulary is not unique to Zechariah but can be found in Jeremiah and 1–2 Kings, both of which are exilic compositions in their final form. But with Zechariah the language is joined with prophecies to build the temple and to reform life around Jerusalem. And post-exilic prophecy becomes increasingly intent on depicting Yahweh's future acts of restoration, as if to say that the difficulties of the present era are but a prelude to Yahweh's decisive transformation of the world.

Symbolic acts are common to the role of the prophets in the public eye. Hosea and Isaiah gave symbolic names to children as a public witness to their words (Hos 1:2–9; Isa 8:1–4); Jeremiah wore a yoke to illustrate servitude to Babylon (Jer 27–28); Ezekiel portrayed several short enactments of exile and destruction (Ezek 4–5). But there is more symbolism to their public activity than these generally recognized acts. They collected disciples or companions who helped with the preservation of their prophetic words. And together, prophet and disciple formed a community to represent the prophetic word symbolically for their generation. Both scroll and (small) community became prophetic symbols of Yahweh's word to the people.

In summary, the pre-exilic prophetic books depict the prophets as representatives of Yahweh's word to Israel and Judah in times of crisis. Their public posture meets with opposition and persecution from representatives of the state government and temples. Their words and communities stand over against the failures of the state as the prophets perceived them. And undoubtedly the facts of defeat and exile at the hands of the Assyrians and Babylonians influence the shape and the predominantly negative tone of the prophetic books. In their final form, however, the books preserve a triple role for the prophets and their critique: (1) their words confirm the necessity of divine judgment on Israel and Judah; (2) their words instruct generations after the fact of judgment concerning activities to avoid; and (3) their words point to Yahweh's future acts of compassion and restoration.

THE PROPHETS' AUDIENCE: ISRAEL AND JUDAH AS THE PEOPLE OF GOD

Everything essential about the prophetic preaching presupposes that Israel and Judah have been designated as the people of God. The prophets' primary audience is a corporate one; Israel (and Judah) is addressed as a community called into existence by Yahweh.[18] Both the prophets and their later "books" speak of this divine-human relationship with varied terminology and emphasis, but they are one in their assumption of its importance. This is best demonstrated by an examination of the theme in the four earliest writing prophets, Amos, Hosea, Isaiah of Jerusalem, and Micah, and by a briefer look at succeeding prophetic books.

Amos

Although Amos vigorously represented certain oppressed classes, his message is primarily directed against Israel in a corporate sense. He assumes that Israel is not just the designation of a state but also of a community whose character and ethos should be determined by the revelation of God.[19] The book of Amos has three major sections which are due to the prophet's editors (1:1–2:16; 3:1–9:10; 9:11–15). The first section is comprised mainly of oracles against various nations, with the last and longest against Israel. Many scholars question whether all of the oracles are original to Amos, especially the one directed against Judah in 2:4–5.[20] Even if there are editorial additions, the first two chapters still reflect a theme of Amos' oral preaching: Yahweh exercises historical sovereignty over the nations and holds them morally accountable for their actions. Moab, for example, is criticized for an atrocity against Edom and has a future judgment pronounced against it (2:1–3); the relationship between Moab and Israel is not the reason for judgment. An atrocity of one people against another occasions the judgment. Moab's atrocity transgresses the moral order Yahweh has instituted to which

---

[18] On the importance of the name Israel in the prophets, see L. Rost, *Israel bei den Propheten* (BWANT 19; Stuttgart: W. Kohlhammer, 1937); G. A. Danell, *Studies in the Name Israel in the Old Testament* (Uppsala: Appelbergs, 1946), 110–269. The approach of Danell is to take the prophetic books in their received form, while Rost attempts to separate editorial layers from the original words of a prophet and then to seek a precise historical background for a prophetic saying when possible.

[19] On the varied uses of "Israel" in Amos, cf. H. W. Wolff, *Joel and Amos* (Philadelphia: Fortress, 1977), 164.

[20] The language of the oracle against Judah has some vocabulary in common with Deuteronomy (e.g., Torah, statutes) and the crimes are unlike those cited in 1:3f. Even if editorial, the prophecy against Judah presupposes the state had been shown Yahweh's special favor, and this favor is presupposed also in the (editorial?) announcement of the reconstitution of Davidic rule in 9:11–12.

any community can be held accountable. Israel too is subject to judgment like any other morally responsible agent, but that is not the primary point of the long oracle against it in 2:6–16. Israel's perceived crimes are decidedly reprehensible when contrasted with Yahweh's providential care for its ancestors (2:9–11). The very land Israel inhabits is a gift from Yahweh its God, who has also provided prophets and Nazirites for Israel's ongoing instruction. In short, Israel's enumerated crimes are crimes against divine grace.

The fulcrum of the book is 3:1–2, a passage which introduces the second and major section of Amos' prophecy (3:1–9:10) and which underlines the theme of Israel's election by Yahweh. Verse 2 states the theme succinctly:

> You only have I known (*yd'*) of all the families of the earth,
> Therefore, I will bring upon (*pqd 'l*) you all your iniquities.

"To know" in this context means more than knowledge about Israel; it includes knowledge of the most intimate and personal kind. The second verse surprisingly links the coming judgment with this special relationship. Since Israel is the beneficiary of special knowledge of Yahweh, the nation stands under the judgment of its own behavior which Yahweh will bring upon it.

The book of Amos contains two other terms which presuppose the claim of 3:2a. In the dirge of 5:1–2 Israel is depicted as a fallen virgin (*bǝtûlāh*) who had not remained pure for her spouse. Similarly, in the visions of judgment in 7:1–8; 8:1–2 the term "my people Israel" is used by Yahweh to designate the community under impending doom.[21]

Amos, always the disputant, states in a surprising passage that Yahweh had acted decisively in the previous histories of other nations besides Israel (9:7). Though sharply worded, the point is *not* to deny the election of Israel by God as affirmed in 3:1–2 but to demonstrate Yahweh's freedom to act in the historical process and to confirm Israel's culpability for its fate. In its own way, 9:7 underlines the importance of divine activity in the historical process and sets the stage for the claim that Yahweh can call any community to account for its actions.

Hosea

Hosea is the only northern prophet whose prophecies resulted in a book attached to his name. Although Amos' primary audience also was Israel, he was a Judean from Tekoa. Hosea's public career apparently lasted longer than that of Amos, stretching close to the time when the

---

[21] 7:8, 8:2. Cf. Yahweh's call to Amos to go and prophesy to "*my people* Israel" in 7:15; the announcement that the "sinners of *my people*" shall perish in 9:10; and the announcement of the better days for "the remnant of *my people*" in 9:14.

capital city of Samaria fell to the Assyrians.[22] In several ways, however, the books of Amos and Hosea are different. Hosea preserves even more references to the canonical story line of the past and to public institutions than does Amos. And much of the book's language is typical of the agricultural terminology of Canaan (see pp. 177–82).

Hosea does recognize and employ the designation of Israel as "my (i.e., Yahweh's) people"[23] and Yahweh as Israel's God.[24] His frequent depiction of Israel's failures makes extended use of the imagery of prostitution (harlotry) and adultery. Two of his primary models for depicting the relationship between Yahweh and Israel come from the sphere of family relationships. Yahweh is the husband or parent, Israel is the wife or child.[25] Both models go to the heart of Israel's identity before Yahweh and serve to underscore the paradoxical element in the prophetic critique: how can a child or spouse act like this? Moreover, the book has three references to the Hebrew word bərît, normally translated as "covenant,"[26] a word that developed into a common term for the Israelite-Yahweh bond. The term serves to identify Israel as a community obligated to Yahweh and to establish a basis for criticism (Hos 8:1–2).

Previous generations of scholars often contrasted the "natural bond" assumed in early Israel with the theme of election and subsequent responsibility introduced by the writing prophets.[27] No such distinction can be made in Hosea's vocabulary; he uses the language of "natural bond" (children, spouse) and that of election and covenant. Indeed, the language in 11:1–9 mixes the various concepts. His vocabulary for Israel combines concepts from the Canaanite agricultural sphere with the creative adoption of the national traditions of exodus, covenant binding, and Yahweh's gift of the land. The stress falls on the assumption that

---

[22] J. J. M. Roberts, "Amos 6:1–7," *Understanding the Word. Essays in Honor of Bernhard W. Anderson* (JSOTSS 52; ed. J. T. Butler et al.; Sheffield: JSOT Press, 1985), 155–66, proposes Amos' prophetic career also continued until at least 738. This is several years later than normally assumed, and it would make him Hosea's prophetic contemporary even if Amos' later years were spent in Judah.

[23] 1:9 [literally "not my people"]; 2:25[E]; 4:6, 8, 12; 7:1; 11:7. On Israel as the people of Yahweh see 5:9; 9:10; 11:1; 12:13. It is probable that the "house of Yahweh" in 8:1 is a reference to the land and people as a single entity.

[24] 2:25[E]; 4:6; 12:10; 13:4; 14:2. Cf. Amos 4:12a.

[25] Chs. 1–3, 11.

[26] 2:20; 6:7; 8:1. See A. S. Kapelrud, "The Prophets and the Covenant," *In The Shelter of Elyon. Essays on Ancient Palestinian Life and Literature in Honor of G. W. Ahlström* (JSOTSS 31; ed. W. B. Barrick, J. R. Spencer; Sheffield: JSOT Press, 1984), 175–83. Kapelrud states that the covenant relationship between Yahweh and Israel-Judah was central to the prophets, but that this relationship could be expressed in more ways than the term bərît. Furthermore, he thinks the prophets did not use the term bərît very much because many in their audience understood it as Yahweh's obligation to protect the nation.

[27] For bibliography and details, cf. E. Nicholson, *God and His People*, 3–27.

Yahweh's prior activity in forming the nation is the only adequate means to define Israel's identity,[28] and that any activity on Israel's part which fails to reflect this identity is reprehensible.

Isaiah

The book of Isaiah is a collection of prophecies and naratives that represents more than the work of a single individual from the eighth century. That is clear from the variety of historical backgrounds presupposed by segments of the book, which is typically divided into three major sections (1–39; 40–55; 56–66). When taken as a whole, the book is structured in such a way as to transcend any one particular historical context. We should begin, however, with those prophecies that likely originated with the Isaiah of eighth-century Jerusalem and were collected among an initial group of disciples. The first chapter introduces several themes that are taken up and used throughout the book. In each case, there is no reason to doubt that the concepts are as old as the eighth century, even though their employment throughout the book presupposes their continued use.

Isaiah begins with Israel depicted as less intelligent than domesticated animals when it comes to knowing their proper place (1:2–3).

> Listen O heavens and be attentive O land,
> I have raised children to maturity, yet they rebel against me!
> An ox knows its owner, and the donkey its master's crib;
> (How can it be that) *Israel* does not understand, that *my people* have no discernment?

The parallelism of 3b makes clear that Yahweh's people are called Israel. Even a Judean prophet can use the name Israel since it represents Yahweh's people as a community and not just a political entity. Moreover, a frequent designation of Yahweh as the "Holy One of Israel" serves to underline the theme of Israel's election. The term is first encountered in 1:4 and is spread through various sections of the book.[29] Yahweh's holiness is a key theme to Isaiah of Jerusalem (6:1–13), and the designation

---

[28] See further, H. D. Neef, *Die Heilstraditionen Israel in der Verkündigung des Propheten Hosea* (BZAW 169; Berlin: de Gruyter, 1987) for a treatment of the passages concerning Yahweh's activity in the past upon which the prophet bases his critique of the present.

[29] 5:19, 24; 10:20; 12:6; 17:7; 29:19, 23 [the holy one of Jacob]; 30:11, 12, 15; 31:1; 37:23; 40:25; 41:14, 16, 20; 43:3, 14, 15; 45:11; 47:14; 48:17; 49:7; 54:5; 55:5; 60:9, 14. Cf. 5:16; 57:15. See A. Van Selms, "The Expression 'the Holy One of Israel,' " *Von Kanaan bis Kerala. Festschrift für Prof. Mag. Dr. Dr. J. M. P. van der Ploeg O. P.* (AOAT 211; ed. Delsman et al.; Neukirchen-Vluyn: Neukirchener Verlag, 1982), 257–69.

of Yahweh as the "Holy One" or the "Holy One of Israel" was a phrase used by the prophet and taken up later by those responsible for the book.

Two other phrases for the elected community come from the spheres of family relations and landed property. In 1:8 comes the first reference to the forlorn "daughter (of) Zion."[30] Zion *herself* is addressed and not someone or something that belongs to her, regardless of the fact that translations habitually render the phrase as "daughter *of* Zion." The name Zion refers to the temple mount in Jerusalem or to the city of Jerusalem as a whole (see pp. 56–60). The cultural presumption is that a daughter is legally and morally under the care of her father, and so, likewise, Jerusalem is specially Yahweh's "daughter." She is the seat of the Davidic dynasty and the royal temple, two major institutions (symbols) Yahweh gave to Israel. Indeed, the concept of Zion as Yahweh's daughter can be augmented with the term "virgin,"[31] since both daughter and virgin can be used of the elect community as a whole.[32]

The "song of the vineyard" in 5:1–7 concerns the frustration of an owner whose careful tending of the vineyard did not result in the production of decent grapes. The analogy of the frustrated owner with Yahweh's perplexity over the behavior of Israel and Judah is made apparent with the prophetic conclusion in verse 7.

> For the vineyard of the Lord of Hosts is the house of Israel,
>   and the people of Judah [are] his delightful plant.
> He waited for justice, and (look!) bloodshed,
>   For righteousness, and (look!) a distressful cry.

The concept of ownership and investment for return comes through distinctly in the song. And though the language is from a different social setting than that used in chapter 1, the various terms share a common presupposition. Israel and Judah belong to Yahweh.[33]

According to Isa 7:17, the prophet regarded the division of the kingdom after Solomon's death as a great horror. He tells Ahaz of judgment to come (Assyria), which is comparable to the division of the kingdom. Significantly, the prophet refers to the time when Ephraim "turned away" (*sûr*) from Judah. The name Israel is not used for the northern kingdom in this passage since it also has the positive sense of the people of God that transcended the political boundaries of the day.

---

[30] 10:32; 16:1; 37:22 ["virgin daughter Zion]; 52:2; 62:11. Cf. Psa 9:15[E]. The phrase is used a number of times in Jeremiah and Lamentations.

[31] 37:22; cf. Lam 1:15.

[32] 22:4 ["daughter (of) my people"= "my daughter people"]; cf. Jer 4:11; Lam 4:10.

[33] J. Høgenhaven, *Gott und Volk bei Jesaja. Eine Untersuchung zur biblischen Theologie* (Leiden: E. J. Brill, 1988) proposes that Isaiah only uses Israel as a designation for Judah after the fall of Samaria in 721. While his argument is plausible, he assumes the ability to date prophetic oracles rather precisely.

Micah

Micah, the last of the eighth-century prophets, was from the Judean countryside. The vocabulary used in his book for the people of God is much like that of Isaiah.[34] Both Israel and Judah and their respective capitals of Samaria and Jerusalem are addressed.[35] In certain instances *Israel* may also mean the people of God.[36] Judeans are addressed as "my people,"[37] as are certain classes of people oppressed by the leaders of Jacob and rulers of the house of Israel.[38] In their present context, the references to these oppressive leaders are best understood as polemical references to Judean leaders. According to 3:12 their corrupt leadership will lead to the destruction of Jerusalem. It is possible, however, that originally Micah directed these and other prophecies against the kingdom of Israel and their application to Judah is due to editorial arrangement. On the other hand, the accepted use of Israel/Jacob as terms for the people of God makes possible the application to Judah as well. The term *Israel* is certainly addressed to the people of God in 6:2 as is the reference to Jacob in 4:2. Unfortunately, neither 4:1–5 nor 6:1–8 can be assumed to be creations of the prophet Micah.[39] They are either adaptations of traditional forms of speech by Micah or later, editorial contributions.

Jeremiah and Ezekiel

The prophetic books of Jeremiah and Ezekiel are the result of intensive theological reflection stemming from the Babylonian exile. Jeremiah conducted his prophetic ministry in Jerusalem during the last years of the Judean monarchy through the capitulation of the city for

---

[34] Perhaps the best study of the traditions of Israel upon which the prophet depended is that of W. Beyerlin, *Die Kulttraditionen Israels in der Verkündigung des Propheten Micha* (FRLANT 54; Göttingen: Vandenhoeck & Ruprecht, 1959). His dependence on the theory of an early Israelite amphictyony does not invalidate his traditio-historical analysis.

[35] E.g., 1:1 [editorial], 5–6.

[36] E.g., 1:13, 15 [?]; 2:12 [later addition?]; 3:8?; 4:14 [later addition?]; 5:1 [later addition?]. See the interpretation of 1:10–16 by C. Shaw, "Micah 1:10–16 Reconsidered," *JBL* 106 (1987): 223–29, where the author proposes a date for the passage at the time of the Syro-Ephraimite war or even slightly earlier. If correct, a phrase such as the "glory of Israel" in 1:15 would refer to the region of Judah.

[37] 1:9; 2:4; 6:3, 16.

[38] 3:3, 5. Additionally, there are references to "daughter (of) Zion" in 4:8, 10, 13; "daughter Jerusalem" in 4:8 for Judah. Some, if not all, of these references may be later additions.

[39] The case of 4:1–5 is complicated by its appearance (with minor changes) in Isa 2:2–5 and the adaptation of 4:3 in Joel 4:10. The use of the term Jacob in the book of Isaiah is relatively common, but if the references in 2:3, 5 are not considered, there are no clear examples of Judah addressed as Jacob in the eighth-century material.

the second time to the Babylonians in 587 B.C.E. His book comes from circles associated with reformist movements in Judah and bears a strong Deuteronomistic stamp (see pp. 125–29). Ezekiel carried out his prophetic ministry among the exiles in Babylon, and his book comes from circles committed to renewal through priestly application of Torah. In both cases we should think of the prophets as members of renewal communities whose words were preserved and edited over the course of a generation or two.

The book of Jeremiah addresses the people of God with a number of the terms already employed in other prophetic books. They come from the spheres of family life, social relationships, and agriculture. The familiar name *Israel* refers to the people of God as an elect community,[40] to the northern kingdom in distinction to Judah,[41] and to exiled remnants of the northern kingdom.[42] "Jacob" and "Ephraim" refer to the northern kingom or its exiled remnants.[43] The southern kingdom is called Judah or "daughter (of) Zion." "My people" is a corporate address to Israel as the people of God or to either kingdom. And, of course, there is the language of covenant (*bərît*) as the term to define the relationship between Yahweh and the elect community.[44]

The analogies of the daughter or spouse are developed in a variety of ways. A youthful Israel was set apart (*qdš*) for Yahweh in the time of wilderness wandering (2:2–3).[45] At the exodus event Yahweh took Israel by the hand to lead it out from slavery as its Lord (31:32).[46] Unfaithfulness to Yahweh is described in the familiar terms of sexual infidelity and promiscuity (2:20–3:10). The analogy of divorce depicts the estrangement between Yahweh and Israel (3:1–5). The latter passage is based on the divorce regulation in Deut 24:1–4 which holds that once a woman is legally divorced from one husband and marries another, she can no longer remarry the former husband after a subsequent divorce or the death of the second husband. Such a second marriage pollutes both land and community and is an affront to Yahweh. The analogy developed in Jer 3:1–5 assumes the sinfulness of the wife *Israel* to her first husband *Yahweh*, and that her promiscuity has, in effect, married her to other lovers.

---

[40] E.g., 2:3–4; "my people Israel" in 7:12.

[41] E.g., 3:6.

[42] E.g., 30:3; "the remnant of Israel" in 31:7 [likely a gloss or scribal addition].

[43] E.g., 30:10; 31:9.

[44] A socio-political model of covenant is found in Jer 34. A Deuteronomistic formulation of covenant comes in 11:1–10.

[45] M. DeRoche, "Jeremiah 2:2–3 and Israel's Love for God during the Wilderness Wanderings," *CBQ* 45 (1983): 364–76.

[46] The verb used is *baʿal* and describes the activity of Yahweh as husband or owner. Cf. Deut 24:1 where it is used for the taking of a wife. In noun form the word means master, owner, or husband.

Another analogy depicts Israel and Judah as faithless sisters, with Judah unable to learn from the tragic demise of her sister (3:6–10). The analogy makes sense only in the context of family relations where the conduct of the sisters shames the parents. As with the case of divorce and remarriage in 3:1–5, the sphere of family relationships defines the proper relationship between the people and Yahweh as well as the consequences of breaking the family's integrity.

The use of "covenant language" in the book is not due solely to the influence of Deuteronomy; however, as noted earlier, there is a marked increase in the use of covenant terminology in comparison with the earlier prophets. Of the prophets of the Assyrian period, only Hosea used the actual term bǝrît to define the Yahweh-Israel relationship, and then only sparingly. The book of Jeremiah has points of contact with the Hosea material[47] and Deuteronomy,[48] and in one sense it is a combination and development of these two similar traditions. Jeremiah 11:1–10, for example, is deeply influenced by the Deuteronomistic account of the Sinai covenant.

> Hear the words of this covenant (bǝrît). . . . Cursed ('rr) is the one who does not obey the words of this covenant (bǝrît) which I commanded your fathers in the day I brought them out from the land of Egypt . . . saying: listen to my voice and do them . . . and you will be my people and I will be your God . . . in order to establish the oath which I swore to your fathers to give to them the land . . . (2–5).
>
> . . . [The Judeans] have turned to the iniquities of their fathers who refused to listen to my words and they followed after other gods to serve them . . . (9–10).

While this vocabulary is at home in the formulations of Deuteronomy, it is not typical of prior prophetic preaching. This is especially true of the references to the fathers and Yahweh's oath to them to grant them the land of Canaan. Aspects of this thinking are quite old and traditional, but the formulation comes from the Deuteronomistic circles. Jeremiah the prophet was likely influenced by Deuteronomy and the Deuteronomistic reforms, and perhaps he employed their rhetoric on occasion. The perspective of the passage, however, clearly betrays not only the influence of Deuteronomy but also the historical experience of Judah's demise, and it owes its final form to the circles who preserved and shaped the prophet's words during the exile.

---

[47] A. Deissler, "Das 'Echo' der Hosea-Verkündigung im Jeremiabuch," in L. Ruppert, ed., Künder der Wortes: Beiträge zur Theologie der Propheten; Josef Schreiner zum 60. Geburtstag, 61–77.

[48] W. Thiel, Die deuteronomistische Redaktion von Jeremia 1–25 (WMANT 41; Neukirchen-Vluyn: Neu-kirchener Verlag, 1973); Die deuteronomistische Redaktion von Jeremia 26–45 (WMANT 52; Neukirchen-Vluyn: Neukirchener Verlag, 1981).

The well-known prophecy of the new covenant in Jer 31:31–34 is probably a development of Jeremiah's that is influenced by Hosea and Deuteronomy. It is introduced by a prophetic announcement that Yahweh will make a new covenant (bərît ḥadāšāh) with Israel in the future. The old covenant, i.e., that relationship initiated by Yahweh with Israel's ancestors, is no longer valid because of Israel's failure. Yahweh took Israel's ancestors by the hand and led them out of Egypt as their "owner" or "husband," yet that generation and the generation addressed by Jeremiah failed in their fidelity to the covenant. The analogy with marriage is assumed for the old covenant; Israel's role as obedient spouse or partner is defined by Yahweh's "torah." Yahweh's "new" covenant also has its normative expression in tôrāh, but this involves a tôrāh made almost instinctive for the covenant partner through Yahweh's act of engrafting it upon the heart. Most amazing of all, as with the question of divorce and remarriage in 3:1–5, Yahweh freely declares pardon for the guilty in a sovereign decision not mandated by either the marriage laws or the political models of covenant.

Elsewhere in Jeremiah, the future covenant between Yahweh and the people is depicted as an "eternal" ('ôlām) covenant, like that established between Yahweh and night and day. Since kingship and priesthood are Yahweh's gifts for maintaining corporate life, the future covenant can be defined through these two institutions as well.[49] One must always keep in mind the institutional focus of such future prophecy. With the demise of Judah at the hands of the Babylonians, the various remnants of people faced the fundamental questions of the future shape of their cultural and institutional life.

Israel is by far the most frequent designation for the audience in Ezekiel.[50] Apparently the prophetic preference for the old, transnational designation for the people of God is a conservative element in his preaching. From the perspective of the exile, it was as if the very repetition of the term *Israel* reminded the audience that the Judean state no longer existed as Judah, and that any who would survive the calamity of exile would do so as members of Israel.

Under the influence of his priestly background, Ezekiel joined cultic language of clean and unclean to the traditional prophetic analogy of sexual infidelity. The people of God are (porno)graphically depicted as a faithless wife who had been nurtured by her spouse from infancy, or as two faithless sisters, both of whom shamelessly flaunted their infidelity.[51] Ezekiel was heir to centuries-long employment of this analogy between

---

[49] 31:35–37; 32:40; 33:14–26.

[50] The term Israel occurs ca. 186 times in the book, while Judah occurs 15 times. Cf. W. Zimmerli, "Israel im Buche Ezechiel," *VT* 8 (1958): 75–90.

[51] Chapters 16, 23.

Israel's failure and sexual infidelity, and his harsh depiction of Israel's failures left nothing to the imagination.

As with Jeremiah, the book of Ezekiel presupposes that Israel is heir to a covenant relationship with Yahweh. Indeed, it is the normative stipulations of this covenant as understood by the prophet that confirmed the worst about his audience.[52] Similarly, the restoration of Israel comes through an everlasting (*'ôlām*) covenant, a covenant of peace (*šālôm*), where Yahweh grants those things which Israel's failures have indicated she is powerless to do for herself.[53]

The temple comes in for special consideration in Ezekiel. Yahweh, invisibly enthroned in the temple, departs from his place in the midst of the people because of their idolatrous pollution and moral transgressions.[54] One should not overlook in this departure scene what it presupposes for the defining of Ezekiel's audience. *Israel*, by definition, had the presence of Yahweh at its very center. Such an understanding of the people of God gathered around their divine Lord went back to the accounts of the exodus from Egypt. And since *Israel*, by definition, had Yahweh at the center of its existence, the future restoration of Israel is depicted with a new temple in its midst.[55]

By way of summary, the prophets employ a variety of images and diverse vocabulary to define Israel and Judah in their relationship to Yahweh. The symbolic language includes references to Israel and Judah as Yahweh's spouse, son, daughter, vineyard, and house; Yahweh has given them land, fertility, kings, temples, priests, prophets, Nazirites, and instruction (*tôrāh*), and has claimed them through a covenant (*bərît*). The prophetic critique asserts that all of these gifts and institutions have been abused and become rotten. To borrow the symbolism of a cultivated plot of land (Isa 5:1–7), one expects a tended vineyard to produce grapes for its owner. Instead it produced rotten grapes. That expectation and the pain over its failure succinctly illustrate the prophetic critique: the paradox of what Israel and Judah were called to be in comparison with what they had become.

PROPHETIC CRITICISM OF PUBLIC WORSHIP AND THE PEOPLE OF GOD

Perhaps there is no subject about which the prophets are more critical than public worship and related, ritual activities among the people of God.[56] And their pointed critique of the public cult is basic to

---

[52] 16:1–8; 17:1–8; 20:1–39.

[53] 16:59–62; 34:23–25 [cf. Jer 33:14–26); 36:26–30; 37:15–28.

[54] Chapters 1–2, 8–11.

[55] Chapters 40–48.

[56] An older, comprehensive treatment of the issues is in R. Hentschke, *Die Stellung der vorexilischen Schriftpropheten zum Kultus* (BZAW 75; Berlin: A. Töpel-

the paradoxical nature of pre-exilic prophecy. It is directed at the primary religious institutions of Israel and Judah, many of which were supported by the state, and it is based on alternative conceptions of how these institutions should perform. There are two major elements in their criticism. One concerns misconceptions of worship offered to Yahweh. The other element—which is often related to the first—concerns the influence of syncretism or apostasy in worship. Their critique of popular piety can play a role in both cases. A common theme among the prophets is a contrast between the Yahwism they represent and other forms of Yahwism practiced by their contemporaries.

A well-known passage in Amos 5:21f. is typical of the prophetic representation of Yahweh's attitude.

> I really despise your feasts, and I have no pleasure in your assemblies;
> even if you make whole-burnt offerings, [they will make no difference].[57]
> Your gifts I reject, and I will take no notice of your peace-offerings.
> Remove from before me your noisy songs, to the sound of your lute I will not listen.
> Let justice (*mišpāṭ*) roll down like waters, and righteousness (*ṣədāqāh*) like a perennial stream.

Interpreters have long debated whether Amos (and other of the prophets) rejected public worship itself as vain, ritualistic attempts to appease God or whether the language of categorical rejection serves the purpose of pointing out the incongruity between public worship and the public ethos. Granting a degree of variability, the latter position better reflects the prophetic critique. The best clue for understanding Amos is careful consideration of his vocabulary. His audience would naturally associate the vocabulary of ritual sacrifice and offerings with public worship. But where would Amos and the other prophets get their vocabulary of justice and righteousness? That vocabulary too has its place in the language of worship, as the book of Psalms demonstrates.[58]

---

mann, 1957). For a recent survey of the issues, cf. H. J. Boecker, "Überlegungen zur Kultpolemik der vorexilischen Propheten," *Die Botschaft und die Boten. Festschrift für Hans Walter Wolff zum 70. Geburtstag* (ed. J. Jeremias, L. Perlitt; Neukirchen-Vluyn: Neukirchener Verlag, 1981), 169–180.

[57] The meaning of the first clause of v. 22 is disputed. The Hebrew particles (*kî-'im*) that begin the verse can be translated as "Even if. . . . " or as "But if (you make whole burnt offerings). . . . " The latter translation assumes that an editor, horrified that Amos so categorically rejects the efficacy of worship, inserted the phrase so that readers would know that a serious effort at worship such as whole burnt offerings would be efficacious. Another problem concerns the second phrase of v. 22. My rendering assumes that a phrase has inadevertently fallen out or been overlooked.

[58] "There is not one concept from the social message of the prophets which did not also play a large role in these [Lament and Thanksgiving] psalms;" so S. Holm-Nielsen, "Die Sozialkritik der Propheten," *Dekender Glaube. Festschrift für C. Heinz Ratschow* (ed. O. Kaiser; Berlin: de Gruyter, 1976), 14.

The prophets, then, derived much of their vocabulary from the language used in worship because public ritual was the richest and most widely used source of religious vocabulary for Israel.

It is widely recognized that many of the psalms have their origin in public worship, whether that took place at local shrines or at the chief centers of pilgrimage during the festival seasons.[59] For the multitudes who could not read, the psalms would be a chief source of instruction and a primary means by which they "absorbed" the ethos of Yahwism. Those psalms which have survived in the OT are but a portion of those used in cultic ceremony and personal piety, and like the hymns and prayers used in any place and time, they can be much older than the generation that continues to use them. Even when the language is "updated," much of the traditional character of a psalm often remains. The psalms and related public ritual, therefore, are an excellent source for the vocabulary held in common by the prophets and their audiences.

The Example of Amos

To continue with the example of Amos, 5:21–23 has a number of parallels in the psalms. God has established his throne or rule with justice and righteousness.[60] God loves ('hb) justice and righteousness.[61] God acts with justice and righteousness on behalf of the poor and oppressed.[62] Judgment (mišpāṭ) is something God brings or appoints; or God "enters into judgment" on behalf of someone.[63] The concern in several of the psalms of lament is for the integrity or righteousness of an afflicted one who prays that God would vindicate his or her case (mišpāṭ).[64]

Both Amos and the psalms use the same language in the context of human activity in the social process. To affirm that God loves justice and righteousness implies already that such activity is expected among the people of God. "Blessed are those who practice justice (mišpāṭ) and who do righteousness (ṣədāqāh)."[65] Indeed, there are a few psalms known as the temple-entrance liturgies which focus on the character of those who would present themselves before Yahweh in worship (Pss 15; 24:1–6).[66]

---

[59] For a discussion of prophecies in cultic settings which are now embedded in certain psalms, see A. Johnson, The Cultic Prophet and Israel's Psalmody (Cardiff: University of Wales Press, 1979).

[60] Pss. 9:8; 36:7; 89:14; 97:2.

[61] Pss 33:5; 37:28.

[62] Pss 25:9; 37:35–40; 76:9–11; 94; 140:13; 146:7.

[63] Pss 1:5; 7:7; 37:5–6; 109:6–7 = judgment in the judicial process; 143:2.

[64] Psa 17:2 = "my just case;" see also 35:23.

[65] Psa 106:3. The psalm is likely post-exilic, but this affirmation is not new to the post-exilic period.

[66] See M. Weinfeld, "Instructions for Temple Visitors in the Bible and in Ancient Egypt," Studies in History and Literature of Ancient Egypt (Scripta Hierosolymitana 28; ed. S. Groll; Jerusalem: Magnes Press, 1982), 224–50, for a compara-

Who may reside in your tent O Yahweh; who may dwell in your holy mountain?

One who walks in integrity (tāmîm), who acts righteously (ṣedeq), and who speaks the truth ('emet) from his heart (15:1–2).

A number of the lament psalms are prayers to Yahweh for vindication in the social process, usually through aspects of the judicial system or in the political arena. The vocabulary of righteousness and justice takes on the hue of innocence/rectitude and fairness/acquittal respectively as Yahweh is implored to oversee the affair to a satisfactory conclusion. Therefore, neither justice nor righteousness is understood as an abstract term. They refer to the integrity of relationships and the maintenance of the health of the community. This is especially true with the term *righteousness*, since it also means innocence in charges of wrongdoing. To pronounce someone innocent (i.e., righteous) is to make a judgment about a specific relationship or case and not a blanket statement about moral standing. In similar fashion, to do *justice* is first of all to do what is proper in a given case or in a specific relationship.[67] Since priests and other cultic personnel could figure prominently in the discernment of guilt or innocence, it is only natural that public worship employ a vocabulary also used in public institutions. The judicial system, for example, would be another source of this "public language" used by the prophets.[68]

The general criticism of worship in Amos 5:21f. has a significant corollary in the prophet's criticism of particular pilgrimage sanctuaries.[69] Bethel is well known both from the ancestral traditions and as a royal sanctuary established by Jeroboam I. Dan, too, was established as a state sanctuary by Jeroboam (1 Kings 12:29–33). Gilgal was primarily a cultic site, which was located near the Jordan river and associated with early Israel's settlement of the land (Josh 4–5; cf. Judg 3:19). Beersheba

---

tive discussion of temple entrance requirements; and S. Steingrimsson, *Tor der Gerechtigkeit. Eine literaturwissenschaftliche Untersuchung der sogenannten Einzugsliturgien im AT: Ps 15; 24, 3–5 und Jes 33, 14–16* (St. Ottilien: EOS Verlag, 1984).

[67] The verb špṭ has the connotation of rule, administrate as well as to judge or to do justly.

[68] Cf. Exod 23:1–8 as an example. On the use of the public language of justice and righteousness in the ANE see M. Weinfeld, " 'Justice and Righteousness' in Ancient Israel Against the Background of 'Social Reforms' in the Ancient Near East," *Mesopotamien und seine Nachbarn. Politische und kulturelle Wechsel-beziehungen im Alten Vorderasien vom 4. bis 1. Jahrtausend v. Chr.* (vol. 2; ed. H. J. Nissen, J. Renger; Berlin: D. Reimer Verlag, 1980), 491–519.

[69] Amos 4:4–5; 5:4–6; 8:14; cf. H. Barstad, *The Religious Polemics of Amos* (VT Sup 34; Leiden: E. J. Brill, 1984), 47–58. Barstad argues against the consensus of biblical scholars that Amos was quite concerned about syncretism in Israel's faith. Not all of his analysis is convincing, especially his interpretation of 2:6–8, but his work is a valuable corrective to previous assumptions about Amos' work.

was located in the Judean Negev, considerably south of the other sites, under the administration of Judah. It was associated with the ancestors Abraham, Isaac, and Jacob.[70] Finally, the capital city of Samaria is named, since it must have had some form of shrine under royal patronage (1 Kings 16:32; Hos 8:5).

It is difficult to reconstruct precise details from the polemical comments, but these pilgrimage sites apparently fall under the double condemnation of worship noted above. First of all, the sacrificial rites ignore the connection intended between worship and ethics, so that the prophet's ironic word reverses the result expected in performing the rites (4:4a): "Go to Bethel and transgress, to Gilgal and increase transgression!" This is not an overt reference to apostasy but a judgment on the inadequacy of Yahwism practiced at the sites. In this context the prophet employs the terminology associated with worship to present an "insider's critique." Similarly he speaks for Yahweh to worshippers of Yahweh (5:4–5a): "Seek (drš) me and live; do not seek Bethel, do not go to Gilgal, and do not cross over to Beersheba." There is also the likelihood that a regional temple played a role in the economy. Though the explicit OT evidence is scanty, temples in the ANE often served as banking centers. Their association with the state links the government with the collection of tithes and offerings. Thus Amos' criticism of land accumulation, taxation, and debt-slavery practices may be directly related to his criticism of the cult.[71]

A goal of the pilgrimage was to seek Yahweh so that the worshippers might live, i.e., to offer acceptable worship and to apprehend Yahweh's will for their lives. The phrase "to seek Yahweh" in the context of a pilgrimage site would include the mediation of Yahweh's will to the worshippers by priests and prophets. The verb "seek" (drš) can be used also for what Yahweh "seeks out" or "requires" from worshippers.[72] Apparently Amos finds fault with both the motives of the worshippers and the Yahwism represented at the pilgrimage sites.[73]

---

[70] Gen 21:31–33; 26:23–33; 28:10; 46:1–5.

[71] For references see J. A. Dearman, "Prophecy, Property and Politics," *Society of Biblical Literature 1984 Seminar Papers* (ed. K. H. Richards; Chico: Scholars Press, 1984), 387.

[72] Mic 6:8. Cf. the comments below on the text.

[73] It is possible that much of Amos' criticism of the northern sanctuaries comes because he is a Judean and affirms the legitimacy of only the Jerusalem cult; so M. E. Polley, *Amos and the Davidic Empire. A Socio-Historical Approach* (Oxford: Oxford University Press, 1989), 83–111. It seems, however, that the same argument could be made for the book of Hosea if all the positive statements about David and Jerusalem are authentic to the prophet. Cf. G. I. Emmerson, *Hosea. An Israelite Prophet in Judean Perspective* (JSOTSS 28; Sheffield: JSOT Press, 1984), 56–116, who accepts much of the Judean material as authentic to Hosea, but still reckons with further changes made by Judean editors. Apart from an overempha-

Amos 8:14 criticizes the oaths taken at pilgrimage sites. There are hints of unacceptable syncretism in the phrases "guilt of Samaria," "your god, O Dan," and perhaps in the "way of Beersheba." A number of commentators see in the term "guilt" (*'ašmāh*) a reference to either the goddess 'Ashima or 'Asherah.[74] A divine name fits the nature of the oath, whereas "guilt" is clearly a polemical reference. Likewise, to speak of Dan's god rather than of Yahweh is a backhand criticism of the state sanctuary. The problem of the Beersheba reference comes in the different possibilities to interpret the term "way."[75]

These criticisms hover between charges of unacceptable syncretism on the one hand and outright apostasy on the other (see pp. 78–99). The latter charge is explicit in Amos 5:25–27, but this difficult text, which has Neo-Assyrian terminology and references to astral deities, is probably the work of a later redactor.[76] Amos represents a Yahwism that is equally valid in Dan or Beersheba, a Yahwism that addresses Israel as a whole and that is an exclusive cult based on the confession that Yahweh delivered Israel from Egypt and gave them the land of Canaan. The pilgrimage sites had fragmented Yahwism into a number of different forms and diluted the normative tradition represented by the prophet with a variety of syncretistic additions.

Isaiah

Isaiah 1:10–17 is similar in some respects to Amos 5:21–24, coming in the initial chapter of the book as a general critique of worship. In 1:10–12, the precincts of the Jerusalem temple and ritual activities are mentioned.

> Hear Yahweh's word O leaders of Sodom,
> Listen to the teaching (*tôrāh*) of our God O people of Gomorrah.
> What do the multitude of your sacrifices mean to me, says Yahweh;
> I am satiated with your whole burnt offerings . . .
> I have no pleasure in your blood sacrifices . . .
> When you present yourselves before me,
> Who required you to trample my courts?

Though the language of the passage is extreme, it is clear that Yahweh does not categorically reject ritual activity. Prayer, for example, is not rejected as a means to approach Yahweh, but the particular prayers of worshippers in the temple precincts are rejected.[77] And as with the

---

sis on Amos' nationalism, Polley's intriguing thesis offers fresh insight into prophetic polemics in the eighth century.

[74] Barstad, *The Religious Polemics of Amos*, 143–80.

[75] Ibid., 191–201.

[76] Ibid., 118–26.

[77] V. 15. The spreading out of the hands is a common posture for public prayer.

passage in Amos, the conclusion appeals to the worshippers to wash (i.e., purify) themselves and to perform those tasks associated with the care for the less fortunate in society. The two passages share the term justice (mišpāṭ),[78] with the passage in Isaiah making additional reference to the widows and orphans (literally the "fatherless"), those categories of inhabitants most at risk in Judean society.

Isaiah's "song of the vineyard" in 5:1–7 is also directed at the gathered community in which the prophet employs the normative terms of justice (mišpāṭ) and righteousness (ṣədāqāh) found in Amos 5:24. There is no reason to see a direct link between the two prophets other than a common concern for the character of the people addressed. Both presuppose that the normative ethos expressed in worship by the people of God is not made effective in the community's social institutions. The prophets have a synthetic, or perhaps better stated, a wholistic understanding of community character. What is celebrated and proclaimed in public worship is not the language of idealism but the substance of community identity: the people of God are who God has called them to be. This is the fundamental presupposition of the prophetic critique of Israelite and Judean society.

One should interpret the "call" of Isaiah (6:1–13) in the context of worship and community ethos. Isaiah apprehends Yahweh's revealed holiness (qādôš) in the temple, and as a result, recognizes his and the people's uncleanness (ṭm'). He has seen *the* King, Yahweh of Hosts, whose glory (kābôd) fills the earth and is especially revealed in the Jerusalem temple. This account demonstrates at once the inner connection between temple and land, worship, and community ethos. The temple is the symbolic point of intersection between the land, those who inhabit the land, and Yahweh. The temple and its precincts symbolically represent each of these parties in their interrelationship. Yahweh's revelation does not stop with this demonstration of holiness, but continues with a request for an obedient messenger to the people.[79] The prophet's confession of uncleanness and his voiced "here am I, send me," leads to the ritual removal (kpr) of his uncleanness and his commissioning as a messenger.

The paradoxical element in the prophetic critique of worship is seen in the opening verse of the caustic oracle in 1:10–17. Those addressed are the people of God; but Isaiah's language, which presupposes this identity, actually reverses the terminology as a means to portray the utter incongruity of the people's identity with their activity. Sodom and Gomorrah are the antitype of the people of God! The well-cared for

---

[78] V. 17 contains the noun justice as the object of an imperative ("seek justice"), and the verbal form (špṭ) in the imperative ("do justly for the widow").

[79] The repeated "this people" in vv. 9–10 is probably a conscious avoidance of the traditional "my people."

vineyard in 5:1–7 produced rotten grapes; Yahweh's revealed holiness in 6:1–5 demonstrates the people's uncleanness. Isaiah of Jerusalem depends on the traditions of Yahweh's choice of Jerusalem and David to demonstrate perceived inadequacies of Yahwistic worship.[80] There are also hints of unacceptable syncretism in the Yahwistic cult, but these references are difficult to interpret.[81]

Hosea

Hosea's depiction of worship in Israel is complicated by the many references to activity that is both political and cultic in nature, and by the editorial process of the book's preservation which makes relationships between various oracles difficult to establish. Moreover, it is difficult to strike a proper balance between the prophet's acceptance of the widely employed fertility symbols of his day and his specific criticism of Israel's unreflective dependence on them. It is obvious, for example, that Hosea perceived a widespread, syncretistic influence among his contemporaries that blurred the distinction between Yahweh and the other gods of Canaan (see pp. 35–45, 73–78). This is clear from the prophecy that in the future Israel will no longer call Yahweh "my Ba'al."[82] There are also references to cults of other deities which served as rivals to the various Yahwistic practices.[83]

All of Hosea's language presupposes the close interrelationship between Yahweh, Israel, and the land. The land Israel inhabits came to it through the providential activity of Yahweh. As noted above, Hosea knows the accounts of exodus from Egypt and the wilderness sojourn of Israel. These accounts define who Israel is. Yahweh has been their God since Egypt and entered into a covenant relationship with Israel in the wilderness, a relationship comparable to a marriage. The land of Canaan is granted to Israel as a means by which Israel can be fruitful and multiply. Hosea also associates prophetic leadership with Israel's early history. "By a prophet Yahweh brought Israel up from Egypt, and by a prophet [was Israel] preserved" (12:14).[84] In this context Hosea also cites

---

[80] C. Evans, "On Isaiah's Use of Israel's Sacred Tradition," *BZ* 30 (1986): 91–96. Cf. H. Niehr, "Bedeutung und Funktion kanaanäischer Traditionselemente in der Sozialkritik Jesajas," *BZ* 28 (1984): 69–81. Niehr identifies a number of Canaanite elements he believes Isaiah incorporates in his criticism of Jerusalem. While he is correct to emphasize that these are urban elements, he overemphasizes the difference between Israel's semi–nomadic heritage and the socalled Canaanite vocabulary used by the prophet.

[81] E.g., Isa 2:20; 8:19; 28:18; 29:15–16.

[82] Hos 2:16 (18H).

[83] E.g., 2:8 (10H), 13 (15), 17 (19); 11:2; 13:1.

[84] The prophet associated with the exodus is a reference to Moses. It is not clear whether the second reference also is to Moses or is to another figure raised up by Yahweh, such as Samuel. Hosea 12:10(11H) associates prophetic

the examples of Jacob, the ancestor of Israel, whose unethical behavior typifies Israel, and whose serving (*šmr*) in Aram for a wife is like the prophetic activity in preserving (*šmr*) Israel.

Hosea 4:1–3 is a hinge passage that makes the transition from the accounts of Hosea's family life to the prophetic speeches directed toward Israel. Again the connection between Yahweh, Israel, and land is clear from the outset.

> Hear the word of Yahweh O Israelites, Yahweh has a suit with the inhabitants of the *land*;
> There is no truth (*'emet*), no loyalty (*ḥesed*), and no knowledge of God in the *land*.
> [Instead there is] swearing, lying, murder, theft and adultery.
> They [the inhabitants of the land] burst forth, one act of bloodshed after another.
> Therefore the *land* mourns, all its inhabitants languish;
> the animals of the field, the birds of the air, even the fish of the sea disappear.

The connection between Yahweh, land, and people is a symbiotic one to the extent that both Yahweh and the land are repulsed by the activity of Israel. Each of the three plays a role in the sustaining of the triangular connection. What Israel does as a community affects its symbiotic relationship with Yahweh and its larger environmental context (i.e., the land). According to Yahweh's charge (*rîb*) against Israel, they lack the normative elements that sustain community and they do those things which pollute their relationships with Yahweh and their environmental/cultural context.[85]

Harlotry (*zənûnîm*) is a term of opprobrium used by Hosea to describe Israel's activity (e.g., 1:2). Even his marriage and children become vehicles for the charge of faithless activity against Israel. Scholars have long debated whether the events described biographically in chapters 1–2, and autobiographically in chapter 3, are literary constructs or actual reflections of the prophet's family life. Did Hosea really marry a prostitute and give the judgmental names to the children? Or did he

---

activity with the interpreting of Israel's national history in figures of speech. Apparently the references to Jacob in chapter 12 are an example of this prophetic activity.

[85] Several charges in 4:2a employ the same vocabulary as the Decalogue: murder (*rṣḥ*), theft (*gnb*), adultery (*n'p*). Since Hosea employs the traditions of exodus and wilderness sojourn, and uses the term covenant (*bərît*) to describe the Yahweh-Israel relationship, his terminology in 4:2 is probably derived from the Sinai–Horeb tradition. He also uses the term *tôrāh* in the sense of instruction or teaching (8:1, 12), but not as a summary term for Yahweh's revealed will (*hattôrāh*, the torah) as in Deuteronomy. The references are not citations of the Decalogue as the epitome of torah, but on the other hand, one should not regard Hosea as an innovator in his use of the Decalogue material.

enter into marriage with the best of intentions only to learn through subsequent experience about his wife's promiscuity (and then use his painful experience as a device for prophecy)? Or are the accounts parabolical in nature, designed to instruct an audience but not to report historical fact? The events in question are best understood as actual events from his personal history which are not reported simply as biography or autobiography. They are symbolic acts intended from the beginning as instruction for Israel, and they are written confessionally as such.[86] Gomer is an adulterous wife and mother, and she *is* Israel. Her children too *are* Israel: the generation of Israel which will reap the consequences of corporate failure. Hosea, whose anger and pain are depicted in the divorce proceedings of chapter 2, represents Yahweh, the aggrieved husband of Israel and parent of a wayward generation. Even in its editorial form Hos 1–3 embodies the word of Yahweh through the medium of symbolic description. The three chapters are not a private report but are intended as public prophecy.

Just what kind of activity underlies the description of Gomer's harlotry is also debated. It is possible but unlikely that she represents prostitution in the modern sense of sexual acts for financial gain. Gomer is charged with what Israel does, which is to seek the favor of the *ba'alîm*, literally "lords" or "masters,"[87] who are fertility deities that bless or withhold favor in the procreative process. Chapter 4 uses the same terminology of harlotry to describe Israelite activity that is used to describe Gomer's activity. In a fertility religion public worship thoroughly integrates the rhythm of the agricultural cycle with the particular circumstances of a given culture. It is probable, therefore, that ritual acts of sex, sacred marriage ceremonies enacted by priestly classes and royalty, and other sacramental efforts were made to ensure the vitality of the agricultural cycle and thus the maintainance of community wholeness. And it is more likely that this is the activity with which Gomer (=Israel) is charged. After all, the fertility of family, flocks, and crops is a powerful inducement for religious activity on the part of cult officials and worshippers alike. When joined with polytheism, the belief that there are multiple divine powers at work in the cosmos who should be served, fertility religion finds its models for divinity in the male-female sexual polarity. A deity's sexual identity is closely associated with his or her sphere of activity in the cosmos. And even the cosmos itself is

---

[86] S. Amsler, "Les prophètes et la communication par les actes," *Werden und Wirken des Alten Testaments. Festschrift für Claus Westermann zum 70. Geburtstag* (Göttingen: Vandenhoeck & Ruprecht, 1980), 194–201, has moved beyond the form-critical analysis of prophetic acts to emphasize their role in the communication process.

[87] The use of the plural term in 2:15 (17E) makes it clear that more than one deity is in mind.

dependent on the successful integration of different, divine powers to ensure its continuing viability.[88]

Hosea's criticism of Israelite culture and public worship is primarily directed at syncretism, polytheism, and the related divinization of sex, not at the concept of fertility religion as such. The prophet does not assume that fertility religion per se is wrong or that it is primarily a Canaanite phenomenon which "seduced" Israel. In certain senses Yahweh is a fertility deity, although there is no place for a consort or partner for Yahweh.[89] Moreover, the prophet opposes the use of the title Ba'al for Yahweh because of the confusion the term created for Israel. Yahweh gives the gifts associated with the agricultural cycle such as wine and oil. And Yahweh is depicted in the roles commonly parceled out to different deities in the various forms of fertility religion. Thus Yahweh has both male and female roles in zoomorphic imagery, is compared to the sustaining dew of the summer season, and is even described in biological symbolism as a cypress tree.[90] Some elements from this analogical theology are intended as a contrast to Israelite behavior, but the substance of the language is compatible with basic elements of fertility religion. Yahweh is not just the Lord of history and revealed paradigmatically in certain events, Yahweh is also the sustainer of the agricultural cycle and intimately related to the cosmos in all its life-supporting variety.

It would be wrong, therefore, to portray Hosea and the fertility religion of Canaan simply as opposing forces. The relationship is more complicated than that. Given that Israel is Yahweh's chosen community in Canaan, and given that Yahweh's sovereignty includes those activities necessary for a fruitful community, the natural rhythm associated with the agricultural cycle is compatible with the affirmation of Yahweh's unique acts in the historical process. Or so Hosea assumes. The criticism of fertility religion in Hosea is a criticism of its excesses, which reflect polytheism, magic, superstition, and eroticism.

Hosea is particularly harsh in assessing the priesthood, since it bears special responsibility for the conducting of public worship and the instruction of Israel in the ways of Yahweh (Hos 4:6–11). What is not as clear is the extent to which priests played a role in the Israelite political

---

[88] D. Kinet, *Ba'al und Jahwe. Ein Beitrag zur Theologie des Hoseasbuches* (Frankfurt: Lang, 1977) has a helpful discussion of ba'alism and the fertility cult, but he depends too much on the Ugaritic texts for his material.

[89] Some scholars have proposed slightly emending Hos 14:9a to read: "Ephraim, what have I to do with idols, I am his 'Anat (*'ntw* for *'nyty*) and his 'Asherah (*w'šrtw* for *w'šwrnw*)." Even if this emendation is correct, which is far from certain, it represents Yahweh as fulfilling the functions of a consort or feminine deity, not as the divine husband of a female deity. Cf. M. Weinfeld, "Kuntillet 'Ajrud Inscriptions and Their Significance," *SEL* 1 (1984): 122–23.

[90] 5:12, 14; 6:3; 11:10; 13:7–8; 14:5–7E.

process, which also comes under severe criticism by Hosea. The initial verse of 4:6–11, which perhaps reflects the introductory Sinai pericope (Exod 19:3–6), has Yahweh rejecting his people in language associated with priestly activity.

> My people are destroyed for the lack of knowledge;
> Since you have rejected knowledge, I reject you from priestly service[91]
> before me.
> Since you have forgotten the instruction (*tôrāh*) of your God, I will forget your children.

This passage includes the term "knowledge" (*da'at*), which is quite important to Hosea. As noted earlier, "to know" implies more than cognizance of facts, but includes intimacy and other relational aspects between persons. Features of Yahweh's relationship with Israel are founded on past historical experience; this must be transmitted comprehensively enough so that subsequent generations also "know" or have "knowledge" of Yahweh.

Another saying with a similar context pairs the knowledge of God with loyalty (*ḥesed*) over against sacrifice and whole burnt offerings (6:6). Such a categorical statement is a corporate address intended for Israel as a whole, but it is an Israel that still has appropriate priestly duties to perform. This seems clear in light of a related saying associated with the prophet Samuel:

> Has Yahweh as much pleasure in whole burnt offerings and sacrifices as with obedience to Yahweh's voice?
> Behold, to obey is better than sacrifice, to follow [Yahweh's word is better] than the fat of rams (1 Sam 15:22).

The context of the saying in 1 Samuel discloses that sacrifice and ritual are acceptable activities. The two issues of dispute concern Saul's obedience to the prophetic word (the command to slay Agag), and his failure to wait for Samuel in order to begin sacrificial ceremonies.

As does Amos, Hosea criticizes of the pilgrimage sanctuaries.[92] His criticisms of priests, sacrificial rites, and syncretism, lead directly to his criticism of these state-supported institutions. He mentions Gilgal and Bethel,[93] but says more about the activities of Samaria than Amos.[94] A complicating factor comes with the references to Samaria and Ephraim. These are synonyms for the state, since Ephraim was the central tribe. Samaria too can stand for the ruling house and thus can represent the state as well. Hosea also criticizes the multiplication of altars, which can

---

[91] The piel infinitive of *khn*.

[92] E.g., 4:15. See Emmerson, *Hosea*, 117–45.

[93] In 4:15 Bethel (= house of God) is polemically called Beth 'Aven (= house of iniquity). cf. 5:8; 10:5.

[94] 8:5–6.

refer to the activities at the state-sponsored sanctuaries as well as to private and non-Yahwistic cults in Israel.[95] It is difficult to make a distinction in Hosea between an acceptance of Bethel or Gilgal as legitimate sanctuaries and an opposition to the particulars of the cults practiced there. The categorical rejection of their cultic activities has a good parallel in the rejection of monarchy. Hosea does not reject Israel's monarchy because he supported the exclusive right of the Davidic dynasty, but because the monarchy had failed totally in its responsibilities.[96]

One element of syncretistic excess opposed by Hosea is the making of divine images.[97] Hosea's scorn for such activity presupposes an understanding of Yahwism that forbids the making of images, probably derived from the first and second commandments of the Decalogue (see pp. 36–39). Hosea is better understood as a representative of this viewpoint in Israel rather than as its first promulgator. Apparently he opposed image-making on various grounds depending on the particular practice in view. In 8:4f., for example, the making of images ('aṣabbîm) from silver and gold is linked with the making of kings and officials. Perhaps these idols represent various ba'als in the form of royal symbols closely identified with the ruling house. Some of them may even represent Yahweh. The calf named in 8:5–6 is probably a Yahwistic symbol of virility. The references in 4:12 imply divination rites which can be associated with images. Images, therefore, are considered too syncretistic or as polytheistic, and are associated with magical and manipulative practices.[98]

Micah

The well-known passage in Mic 6:1–8 is, in reality, a summary statement of the prophetic theme that worship and ethics are intimately related. As a summary statement it is difficult to know what part, if any, Micah played in its composition. In form it is an indictment of the

---

[95] 8:11, cf. 14; 10:1–2, 8; 12:2.

[96] Emmerson, *Hosea*, 117–45, would first distinguish between Hosea's criticism of the cult and the prophet's own acceptance of the legitimacy of the sanctuaries. She then attributes any categorical rejection of the sanctuaries to Judean redactors who supported the centralization of worship in Jerusalem. It is better to see the categorical rejection of the sanctuaries as reflecting Hosea's own assessment of their failure.

[97] 8:4–7; 10:5; 11:2, 9.

[98] Similar elements are found in the critique of syncretism and polytheism in Zephaniah 1:4–6 and 3:2. That seventh-century Judean prophet names the "remnant of Ba'al," the "host of Heaven," heterodox priests (kəmārîm), and either the Ammonite deity Milcom or Molek, a deity associated with human sacrifice. Cf. J. Scharbert, "Zefanja und die Reform des Joschija," *Künder der Wortes: Beiträge zur Theologie der Propheten; Josef Schreiner zum 60. Geburtstag* (ed. L. Ruppert; Würzburg: Echter, 1982), 237–54.

audience named three times as the people of God.[99] Through the prophet, Yahweh reminds the indicted of the deliverance from Egypt and of the leadership of Moses, Aaron, and Miriam. The reference to Moses is understandable, but why reference to Aaron and Miriam? The latter two represent the institutions of priesthood and prophecy that grow out of the Mosaic office (and family) and their corresponding ritual activity. Yahweh sent[100] Aaron and Miriam too. Their leadership comes in the context of Yahweh's righteous deeds (ṣidqôt)[101] and can be contrasted with the activity of Balaam, who sought to curse Israel by cultic and prophetic means. Worship must have the righteousness of Yahweh as its focal point, and the historical experiences of Israel's deliverance in exodus and wilderness are the normative examples of that righteousness. Worship is properly a response to Yahweh, who through redemption and nurture has called a people into existence. Worship is manipulation unless it provides Israel with a corresponding ethos for social institutions. The "answer" or better conclusion to the indictment of 6:1–5 is the affirmation in 6:6–8 that Yahweh has declared what is good: not a vast number of sacrifices or offerings, not even the supreme sacrifice of children (see pp. 90–96), but to do justice (mišpāṭ), to love loyalty (ḥesed), and to walk circumspectly with God.

Jeremiah

In a number of ways, Jeremiah was an heir of earlier prophecy. Within the large book of Jeremiah are withering criticisms of public worship, particularly in the so-called temple sermon.[102] Both the relationship between worship and ethics and the problem of syncretism are clearly spelled out. Jeremiah delivers a word to those who enter the temple precincts to worship Yahweh.

> Do not put your trust in the false litany, "this is Yahweh's temple, Yahweh's temple, Yahweh's temple." If you reform[103] your ways and deeds, if you do justice (mišpāṭ) . . . if you don't oppress . . . and shed innocent blood in this place, and follow other deities to your own harm, then I will dwell with you[104] in this place, in the land I gave to your ancestors (7:4–7).

The longer version of the sermon in chapter 7 leaves no doubt that a doctrine of the temple is a primary theme. Not only are there the

---

[99] 6:2, 3, 5.

[100] 6:4. The verb is šlḥ, the same verb used in the Deuteronomistic and later literature to describe Yahweh's activity in sending "his servants, the prophets."

[101] 6:5. Literally the term is "righteousnesses," but this rendering is far too abstract for the acts of deliverance presupposed in the term.

[102] Accounts of the "sermon" and its aftermath are in chapters 7 and 26.

[103] Literally "make good."

[104] The Hebrew text can be read as "then I will allow you to dwell in this place, in the land."

repeated references to this place (*māqôm*), but there is also a reference to Yahweh's place (*māqôm*) at Shiloh[105] as an example of a previous temple (symbol) that in and of itself could not sustain Israel. At issue is whether the temple in Jerusalem, which is called by Yahweh's name,[106] is a good luck charm which protects Judah from harm regardless of national character and activity, or whether the temple is the place where worship brings participants into Yahweh's righteous presence and confirms them in the responsibility to uphold Yahwistic practices.

Yahweh's exclusive claim upon Israel is reflected in the name theology of the Jerusalem temple. That is an important concept in Deuteronomy and also an indication of the editorial slant of the sermon. Those scholars who see a considerable difference between the prophet Jeremiah and his Deuteronomistic editors often claim that the prophet himself did not hold such a high view of the temple. If that is the case, the question of the source of Jeremiah's opposition to the worship of other deities in Judah still remains. For him it is a question of the identity and character of Yahwism. Yahweh was Israel's God before its settlement in Canaan, and he is the one who brought Israel to the land. As noted above, this relationship is an exclusive one on the analogy of a marriage covenant. The indictment which begins the prophecies of Jeremiah makes just that case (Jer 2:2–13). The paradox of Judean faithlessness is depicted in the frustrated cry to visit other lands to see if they too have "exchanged"[107] deities, though in Israel's case, what they get in the exchange is neither divine nor of any value (2:10–13).

The book of Jeremiah contains references to more than one "foreign" deity, so it is a mistake to assume that the official Judean cult had simply exchanged a Yahwistic cult for another, official cult. The variety of names and practices presupposes a range of syncretistic and polytheistic practices; some of these would be a form of Yahwism, others assume a different cult altogether (see pp. 84–99). Chapter 7 contains references to the worship of Ba'al and "other deities,"[108] "abominations,"[109] the Queen of Heaven,[110] "detestable things" placed in the temple,[111] and the

---

[105] 7:12 describes the temple at Shiloh as the place where Yahweh formerly caused his name to dwell.

[106] 7:11, 14. This statement is a parallel to the statement that Yahweh's name dwells at a site.

[107] The verb is *ymr/mûr* in the hiphil which has the connotation of a formal exchange such as that of property.

[108] 7:9. The book has both singular (e.g., 2:8; 23:13, 27) and plural references (2:23; 9:14) to Ba'al. The phrase "other deities" is common in Deuteronomy and 1–2 Kings as a summary term for syncretistic polytheism and idolatry.

[109] 7:10. The Hebrew term is *tô'ēbôt*. It is frequently used in priestly language and by Ezekiel.

[110] 7:18. She is also named in 44:17–19, 25.

[111] 7:30. The Hebrew term is *šiqqûṣîm*. Cf. 4:1; 13:27; 16:18; 32:34. It is a

"high places of Topheth" in the valley of Hinnom where children are burned in a fire.[112] In his poetry Jeremiah prefers the analogies of harlotry and sexual desire to describe these practices, where he also makes fun of divine images.[113]

Ezekiel

Ezekiel's criticism of syncreticism and idolatry is more strident than that in Jeremiah, but at the same time it is more general. His is a defense against any encroachment of the exclusive relationship between Yahweh and Israel which focuses upon the temple cult. In typically priestly language he describes the "abominations" (tô'ēbôt) in the temple complex which profane Yahweh's name and ultimately force the departure of Yahweh's presence[114] from the temple. There are references to divine images in the temple complex, carvings in the temple itself, ritual weeping for Tammuz, and solar worship. Elsewhere Ezekiel employs the familiar analogy of harlotry to describe the defection of Israel and Judah from Yahweh.[115]

The book of Ezekiel presents the temple as the focal point of the people's identity as well as the place of worship. This is clear in the vision report of temple-land restoration in chapters 40–48. With the restored temple, all of Jerusalem will be transformed and even renamed.[116] The elaborate detail provided for the temple complex is derived from priestly circles, and it projects a future so glorious as to prevent any misunderstanding concerning Yahweh's exclusive claim on Israel (see pp. 193–94).

In summary, the preoccupation of the prophets with Israel's cultic failures was a recognition that the worship of Yahweh provided Israel with its necessary identity and ethos. In their assessment, for Israel to pervert its worship was for Israel to pervert its identity and the integrity of its institutional life. Cultic failure was not attributed to a single cause, but is described variously as idolatry, syncretism, and outright defection from Yahweh.

THE PROPHETIC ASSESSMENT OF THE MONARCHY AND STATE ADMINISTRATION

The treatment of kingship in the pre-exilic prophets clearly raises the question of editorial work in the production of their books. Many

---

frequent term in Ezekiel as well.

[112] 7:31. Cf. 32:35 and the reference to the "high places" (bāmôt) of Ba'al.

[113] 2:14–37; 5:7–9. Jer 17:1–4 makes disparaging references to the multitude of altars and female fertility symbols ('šrym).

[114] Ezek 8–11. Literally Yahweh's "glory," visibly manifested to the prophet, departs from the Holy of Holies (11:22–23).

[115] Ezek 16; 22–23.

[116] 48:35; The name will be "The Lord is There."

scholars have reconstructed a twofold editorial process in the texts concerning kingship whereby the prophetic sayings are supplemented with a pronounced Davidic (Judean) and eschatological orientation. This practice denied to the prophets any detailed shape or much content to their future hope, which had to be supplied by later editors. It is obvious that extensive editorial work has taken place in the prophetic books, but one cannot generalize on the extent to which that has obscured or changed earlier sayings regarding the role of the monarch. In every instance one must ask about the coherence of prophecies concerning the future of monarchy, or of any element of future hope, in light of the prophet's other sayings.

Generally speaking, criticism of the monarchy is assumed when royal representatives or appointees holding public office are criticized. This can be true also of criticism directed at Jerusalem or Samaria, since these are royal cities as well as state capitals. Finally, one should distinguish between criticism of a particular monarch or public leader and the assumption (sometimes implicit) on the part of the prophet that the office itself is in need of radical transformation.

Amos

Amos is an excellent example of the problems involved in assessing the prophetic attitude toward monarchy and resulting forms of state administration. As already noted, Amos understands that the identity of Israel was formed before the rise of kingship (2:9–11; 3:1–2; 9:7). We might say, therefore, that monarchy itself was not an issue for the prophet, but the type of rule he encountered was of utmost importance for the content of his message. The core of his message was "the end has come on my (i.e., Yahweh's) people Israel" (8:2).[117] His sayings concerning monarchy and state administration should be interpreted in light of this fundamental point.

The sequence of Amos' visions underscores the point that judgment upon Israel is unalterable.[118] Israel's sanctuaries will be laid waste and Yahweh will rise against the house of Jeroboam with the sword. In political terms one might understand this saying in 7:9 as treason. At the very least it places the ruling dynasty in the same failed category as Israel's religious practices. In fact, it is unlikely that Amos would have made much distinction between the failures of the monarchy and the failures of Israel's practice of religion at the chief sanctuaries. Both fall under the prophet's corporate critique of Israel since they are insep-

---

[117] See J. Hayes, *Amos. The Eighth-Century Prophet* (Nashville: Abingdon Press, 1988), 207–8, for a different reading of this saying. He underestimates the force of this last vision to project the irrevocability of corporate judgment.

[118] Amos 7:1–9; 8:1–3.

arable.[119] For example, the criticisms which name Samaria demonstrate that Amos speaks of the capital city in all its official capacities.[120]

In those sayings where the social criticism is more broadly based, Amos often intends to indict those with official roles or connections to the state. His criticisms of the administrative-judicial system are a case in point.[121] The judgment upon Israel takes into account the various official structures which give legitimacy to public activities. This is the principle by which to understand Amos' critique. Israel has failed; its societal institutions are rotten, and like the wall in need of reconstruction (7:7–8), it must first be torn down.

According to the conclusion of the prophet's book, there is still a future for "my (i.e., Yahweh's) people Israel" (9:11–15). After announcing the end of Israel, how can this be? In the view of many scholars the conclusion is an example of editorial work by the prophet's disciples. Almost certainly this is correct for 9:13–15, which clearly presupposes the exile of Israel from its land. But it is not as clear that 9:11–12 also fits in this category.[122] The verses in question read:

> In that day I will raise up the booth of David which has fallen, and I will close its breeches. Its ruins I will repair and I will rebuild it as in the days of old, so that they may possess the remnant of Edom and all the nations that are called by my name—says Yahweh of Hosts who is doing this.

Possibly this hopeful prophecy presupposes the exile of Israel and Judah from their land. But it is also possible that Amos himself was rooted in the tradition that Yahweh had made an eternal promise to David's line and that any legitimate form of government for Israel must have a Davidic monarch.[123] Such a view is supported by the claim in 1:2 that "Yahweh roars from Zion and offers his voice from Jerusalem," but this verse also may be editorial.[124] Thus we are left with major decisions about the prophet's approach which are dependent on precise but difficult judgments about the authenticity of certain sayings.

---

[119] G. W. Ahlström, *Royal Administration and National Religion in Ancient Palestine.*

[120] 3:9–11, 3:12, 4:1–3, 6:1–6, 8:14. On the importance of Samaria as the national administrative center, see J. A. Dearman, *Property Rights in the Eighth-Century Prophets,* 25–27. According to Hayes, *Amos,* 154–55, the term "virgin of Israel" in 5:2 refers to Samaria and not to the nation as a whole. If so, Samaria is singled out as particularly responsible for the failures listed in 5:1–17.

[121] E.g., 5:7–15.

[122] Wolff, *Joel and Amos,* 350–55, presents the case for 9:11–12 as an editorial addition.

[123] See the discussion in M. E. Polley, *Amos and the Davidic Empire* (New York: Oxford, 1989). Polley does attribute this view to Amos and calls it "nationalism."

[124] So Wolff, *Joel and Amos,* p. 121.

One can say that the book of Amos does not condemn Israel simply because it had rebelled from the political control of the Davidic dynasty in Jerusalem. The premonarchic traditions of election, exodus, and conquest are considered legitimate indications of Israel's identity as well as the basis for its judgment. The house of Jeroboam and its administrative-cultic institutions had failed. That conclusion sufficiently accounts for the announcement that the end had come upon Israel, even if it is not a complete explanation. Even if the future shape of government is Davidic, it is Yahweh's people "Israel" who are replanted in the land.

Hosea

Even more complex editorial issues face the interpreter of Hosea and the prophet's view of kingship.[125] As with the book of Amos, one should interpret Hosea's rejection of Israel's monarchy in light of his rejection of the viability of all the nation's public institutions. This proposal does not depend on a judgment for or against the authenticity of the hopeful sayings in 1:11 (2:2H) and 3:5, though these two texts are important for an interpretation of the prophet's understanding of kingship.

Hosea 3:5 states that in the future Israel will "seek Yahweh their God and David their king." If the prophecy reflects Hosea's own hope for the future and not just that of a later Judean editor, it possibly shows the power of the prophet's pro-Judean sympathies.[126] This view is supported by the contrast between the judgment on Israel and the deliverance promised for Judah in 1:6–7,[127] but the prophecy concerning Judah is likely an editorial comment. So probably is the reference to David their king in 3:5. However, the prophecy concerning the future of Judah and Israel together in 1:11 (2:2H) is likely that of Hosea himself:

> The Judeans and the Israelites will gather themselves together and make for themselves a common head (rō'š 'eḥād), and they will spring up from the land, for great is the day of Jezreel.

Hosea avoids the pretentious and potentially divisive word king (melek) in favor of a more neutral term. Even if the reference to David their king

---

[125] A. Gelston, "Kingship in the Book of Hosea," OTS 19 (1974): 71–85; G. Emmerson, Hosea: An Israelite Prophet in Judean Perspective (JSOTSup 28; Sheffield: JSOT, 1984), 56–116. On redaction-critical issues and the book of Hosea, see G. Yee, Composition and Tradition in the Book of Hosea. A Redaction Critical Investigation (SBLDS 102; Atlanta: Scholars Press, 1987).

[126] G. Swaim, "Hosea the Statesman," Biblical and Near Eastern Studies. Essays in Honor of William Sanford LaSor (ed. G. Tuttle; Grand Rapids: Eerdmans, 1978), 177–83. Most scholars view either the whole verse or at least the reference to "David their king" as editorial.

[127] The attempt by F. Andersen and D. N. Freedman, Hosea (AB 24; Garden City: Doubleday, 1980), 188–96, to read 1:7 as the continuation of a prophecy of judgment seems improbable.

in 3:5 is authentic, which is not likely, one should be cautious in branding Hosea a Judean nationalist. He more clearly represents a religio-political tradition of Israel's indivisibility before Yahweh which includes an acceptance of monarchy. As Amos, Hosea understands that Israel's identity was established before the advent of the monarchy and that this identity has important consequences for Israel's institutional life.

Closely related to the work of the king is that of the princes (śārîm).[128] They too are included in the prophetic critique, for they represent the military and administrative-judicial arms of government. It would be unwise, therefore, to distinguish between the political and cultic failures of Israel's rulers. The policies of the ruling house have failed, and Israel will suffer the consequences.[129]

The precise political background to Hosea's rejection of the Israelite monarchy is not well known, but we should attribute his negative assessment to the political intrigue (2 Kings 15:8–31) and failed policies of Israel's last years rather than some pre-monarchical ideal of rule that could dispense with kingship.[130] When the prophet proclaims in Yahweh's name (8:4) that Israel "made kings but not from me (i.e., Yahweh) and made princes but I did not know (them)," this has to do with the coronation and appointment of rulers chosen by means other than Yahweh's approval. Nevertheless, we should not miss the categorical rejection of Israel's government by Hosea. While it possibly presupposes a pro-Judean bias, it most certainly reflects one aspect of the prophet's larger, institutional critique of Israel. Monarchical rule, like the Yahwistic cult, had failed.

Isaiah

Isaiah of Jerusalem also offers a severe critique of Judah's monarchy and administrative-judicial system. Unlike Amos and Hosea, he depends almost totally on the identity given Judah with Yahweh's choice of David's house and the city of Jerusalem as the location of the national temple. The theme of the righteous-city-gone-bad comes in the first chapter (1:21–26). According to the prophetic critique, Jerusalem formerly was the city of faithfulness (qiryāh ne'emānāh), with the attributes of justice (mišpāṭ) and righteousness (ṣədāqāh), but had disqualified herself from such an epithet by the actions of her leaders.[131] These leaders are her princes (śārîm) who had the roles of judges (šōpəṭîm) and

---

[128] 3:4; 7:3, 5; 8:10; 13:10. There is some overlap with the term judges (šōpəṭîm) in 7:7 and 13:10.

[129] See especially 8:1, 3.

[130] See literature in note 125 above.

[131] Isaiah uses feminine imagery here. Jerusalem is portrayed as a whore. See E. W. Davies, Prophecy and Ethics. Isaiah and the Ethical Tradition of Israel (JSOTSS 16; Sheffield: JSOT Press, 1981), 90–112.

counselors (yô'aṣîm) as well. What is true of Jerusalem and her leaders also holds for the leadership of the nation as a whole.[132]

Unfortunately we do not know precisely what it is meant by Yahweh's restoration (šûb) of judges and counselors in Jerusalem as in a former time (ri'šōnāh). Perhaps it refers to the Jebusite past,[133] but more likely it refers to the initial rule of David in the city and its seat as the administrative center for the nation. The reference in 1:26 is important because it demonstrates that Isaiah's critique of the Judean capital depends on an understanding of how the city should function as the locus of Yahweh's righteous rule.

A similar dynamic exists for the critique of the ruling Davidic monarch. In the famous prophecy directed to Ahaz in Isa 7:4–9, the rulers of Damascus and Samaria are rejected in their attempt to take Jerusalem and to depose the Davidic monarch. Isaiah's counsel presupposes that Ahaz, a descendant of David, is an heir to the promise of Yahweh toward the Davidic line and that Ahaz should have confidence in Yahweh's faithfulness to his promise. Ahaz's rejection of Isaiah's counsel has certain negative consequences (7:10–25), but the very promise of the child Immanuel's birth in 7:14 should be understood as a reflection of the promises associated with the Davidic line.

Another famous prophecy should be associated with this period of Ahaz's rule (Isa 9:1–7).[134] After the successful invasion of Tiglath Pileser III and his subsequent annexing of much of Israel in 733/32 B.C.E., Isaiah offers a prophecy of hope for the northern territories now under Assyrian rule. This prophecy also reminds its hearers of the kind of rule expected from the Davidic line. Those people who walk in darkness shall see a great light . . . rejoicing shall take place:

> For a child is born to us; a child is given to us, and the government shall be upon his shoulder. And his name shall be called Wonderful Counselor, Mighty God, Everlasting Father, Prince of Peace. Of the increase of his government and of peace there will be no end, upon the throne of David and his kingdom, to establish it and to found it in justice (mišpāṭ) and righteousness (ṣədāqāh), from now until forever—the zeal of the Lord of Hosts shall do this.

---

[132] See Isa 3:13–15 which names the elders (zəqēnîm) and the princes (śārîm) of Yahweh's people as culprits. In Isa 10:1 the prophet indicts those who make unjust statutes (ḥōqəqîm ḥiqqê-'āwen).

[133] Niehr, "Bedeutung und Funktion kanaanäischer Traditionselemente in der Sozialkritik Jesajas," BZ 28 (1984): 70–71, proposes Isaiah depends on mythological and specifically Jebusite elements for his depiction.

[134] 8:23–9:6 in Hebrew. A recent treatment of royal ideology in Isaiah concentrating on chapters 6:1–9:6; 11:1–9, is A. Laato, Who Is Immanuel? The Rise and Fall of Isaiah's Messianic Expectation (Abo: Abo Academy Press, 1988).

Traditional Christian readings of this passage should not obscure the intended criticisms of policies during Isaiah's day. The language of the prophecy is probably taken from a coronation ritual that gave official expression to a messianic hope in Judah.[135] Messianic in this instance refers to the hopes associated with the rule of the Davidic line. The prophecy is actually full of political language with its references to government (misrāh), throne (kissē'), and kingdom (mamlākāh) founded in justice and righteousness. Neither the failures of the northern kingdom nor those of Judah could thwart Yahweh's zeal to bring this rule of peace to reality.[136] But it is obvious from Isaiah's criticism of Judean society that the rule of Ahaz does not embody the characteristics associated with messianic rule even in provisional form. Nevertheless, the expectations associated with the Davidic rule provided a standard by which administrative rule could be assessed.

Micah

The book of Micah also contains prophecies harshly critical of Israel and Judah along with those which depict the future rule of the Davidic dynasty and the international significance of Jerusalem. Literary criticism and historical analysis have had a field day carving up the book into different authors representing different periods of biblical history,[137] which often meant that the sayings about a new David or the exalted role of Zion were considered post-exilic additions to the original words of the prophet.[138] As noted previously, such decisions of date and authorship are quite difficult to make, especially in a book of only seven chapters. Nonetheless, even if virtually the whole book is assigned to the prophet of the eighth century,[139] we are still left with the difficulty of interpreting the contradictory words of destruction and deliverance.

Like Isaiah, Micah criticizes the administration associated with Jerusalem and its officials. This is quite clear from the prophecies in 3:1–12 which name the leaders by various titles and conclude with an announcement that Jerusalem itself will be destroyed. The announcement of Jerusalem's destruction assumes the same fate for the temple

---

[135] See J. Beker, *Messianic Expectation in the Old Testament* (Philadelphia: Fortress Press, 1980), 37–47; W. Harrelson, "Prophetic Eschatological Visions and the Kingdom of God," *The Quest for the Kingdom of God: Studies in Honor of George E. Mendenhall* (Winona Lake: Eisenbrauns, 1983), 117–26.

[136] One should compare Psalms 2, 72 and Isa 11:1–9. The importance of Jerusalem in this righteous rule is more apparent in these texts than in Isa 9:1–7. Cf. also Isa 2:1–5 = Mic 4:1–4.

[137] See K. Jeppesen, "New Aspects of Micah Research," *JSOT* 8 (1978): 3–32, for a history of discussion.

[138] 5:1–6 (4:14–5:5H)—new David; 4:1–13—future Zion.

[139] So D. Hillers, *Micah* (Hermeneia; Philadelphia: Fortress Press, 1984).

and the monarch.[140] One might conclude that Micah, too, took his critique of Judean society from the expectations of a just rule associated with the Davidic house, but this will only partially explain the source of his criticism. Unlike his contemporary Isaiah, Micah also quotes certain traditions associated with tribal Israel in 6:4–5. Even the reference to Davidic rule in 5:2, if authentic, names Bethlehem and not Jerusalem as the origin of the Davidic hope. It is as if to say that the pretensions of royalty in Jerusalem are rejected in favor of a type of pan-tribal rule from the old family of Jesse.

Jeremiah and Ezekiel

The books of Jeremiah and Ezekiel have extensive material directed at the ruling monarch as well as material projecting a prominent role for the community's political leader in a future reconfiguration of Israel.[141] Behind the preservation of every passage in the books stands the fact of the Babylonian exile and the important role the two books play in interpreting the tragedy of Judean (and Israelite) failure. One can still discern elements of political views in the criticisms of a Jeremiah or Ezekiel, particularly against Zedekiah. For example, in both cases their criticisms of the kings and their foreign policies reflect a measure of support for what is sometimes termed the "pro-Babylonian party,"[142] those who counseled political submission to Babylon, but it must be stressed that this identification is but one facet of the prophetic critique and is by no means the key to a comprehensive interpretation of their political views.[143]

One can observe in the heading of Jer 21:12 evidence for the collection of prophecies about the monarch. The king is evaluated in terms of the attributes associated with the house of David.

---

[140] This identification of the monarch with the fate of the capital city is important to keep in mind when assessing the claim that the eighth-century prophets did not include the king in most of the prophecies of judgment.

[141] E.g., Jer 21:1–23:8; Ezek 17:1–24; 34:1–24.

[142] J. Wilcoxen, "The Political Background of Jeremiah's Temple Sermon," *Scripture in History and Theology. Essays in Honor of J. Coert Rylaarsdam* (ed. A. Merrill, T. Overholt; Pittsburgh: The Pickwick Press, 1977), 151–66; K. F. Pohlmann, *Studien zum Jeremiabuch. Ein Beitrag zur Frage der Entstehung des Jeremiabuches* (FRLANT 118; Göttingen: Vandenhoeck & Ruprecht, 1978), 183–207. See the discussion in B. Lang, *Kein Aufstand in Jerusalem. Die Politik des Propheten Ezechiel* (Stuttgart: Katholisches Bibelwerk, 1980). While he concentrates on Ezekiel, Lang also discusses briefly the general issue of the prophets and their political loyalties (p. 5–8, 11–14).

[143] In the same manner, the fact that Hosea rejected alliances with Egypt and Assyria (Hos 5:13; 7:11; 9:6?; 10:4), or that Isaiah rejected reliance upon Assyria, are but the outworking of their conviction that such alliances are a rejection of Yahweh's sovereignty.

O House of David, thus says Yahweh: judge justly (*mišpāṭ*) in the morning[144] and deliver the robbed (*gāzûl*) from the hand of the oppressor ('*ôšēq*) . . . (Jer 21:12).

The verbs "judge" (*dîn*) and "deliver" (*nṣl*) are in the plural, which implies that the instruction to the ruling house applies to both the king and his officials in charge of judicial administration. The vocabulary of the injunction is rooted in the duties of the monarch to uphold the attributes of justice and righteousness. These attributes are defined by Yahweh and should be embodied in the activities of the Davidic dynasty.

The various prophecies in Jer 22 give both negative and positive references to the role played by the king in safeguarding these fundamental values. Josiah, for example, could eat and drink as a king, but he also "did justice and righteousness," and "judged [fairly the case of] the poor and needy." Such activity illustrates what it meant for a king "to know" Yahweh.[145] Jehoiachim, however, is described in criminal terms as an agent of oppression ('*ôšēq*) and violence (*mərûṣāh*).[146]

Zedekiah does not receive a favorable verdict from Jeremiah either. As previously noted, Zedekiah is involved in activities against the Babylonian overlords to whom he has sworn a loyalty oath before Yahweh. On the one hand, Jeremiah has nothing good to say about him or his officials (21:1–11, 12–14; 24:1–10). On the other hand, the very name of the king ("Yahweh is righteous" or "My righteousness is Yahweh") is used quite polemically as the basis for a new ruler from David's line who will embody the righteousness reflected in the king's name, a righteousness so lacking with Zedekiah and among his officials.[147]

The book of Ezekiel preserves far more about kingship than the opposition of the prophet to the rebellious policies of Zedekiah, but it is correct to see in the prophet's criticisms of the king a rejection of the king's foreign policies.[148] Included in the criticism of the ruling house are princes (*nəśî'îm*)[149] and shepherds (*rō'îm*)[150] who have perverted their place of responsibility in society in several ways. It is difficult to know who bore the title of prince or shepherd, and to know what were their roles, but it is likely that both terms are related to the workings of the

---

[144]The morning is likely a reference to the traditional time when the king or his representatives held court for administrative-judicial affairs.

[145]Jer 22:15–16.

[146]Jer 22:13–19.

[147]Jer 23:1–6. A number of scholars hold that this passage comes from Jeremiah's editors not from the prophet himself; cf. 34:14–26. Part of the problem is the lack of integration on the part of Jeremiah himself or his editors between the future era where a new David will reign and the era of the "new covenant" (Jer 31:31–34).

[148]Discussed thoroughly in Lang, *Kein Aufstand in Jerusalem*.

[149]Ezek 22:6–12.

[150]Ezek 34:1–10.

royal house and its institutional duties. In a future time a restored Israel will be united under one from David's line who can be called a shepherd (rô'eh) and a prince (nāśî') as well as king (melek).[151]

The book of Ezekiel ends with nine chapters depicting the restoration of the twelve tribes of Israel gathered around a transformed Jerusalem and a rebuilt temple. This section combines detailed observations concerning the structure of the new community with visionary and symbolic language. One goal of the concluding section is the depiction of a new Israel gathered around the new temple in the new city[152] with a new leader. The terrain of Palestine will be altered to fit the construction of the new city and temple, and several descriptions of the cultic life reflect both reformist and visionary ideals. This combination of reform and vision is behind the depiction of the community's leader ("the prince").[153] References to former kings of Israel are made in passing (43:6–9); otherwise, there is no mention of a king. Any "royal" duties are performed by the prince. The choice of the term nāśî' instead of melek implicitly criticizes royal activity as experienced in the pre-exilic period. This is most distinctly indicated in the injunction that the "princes" shall no longer "oppress" (yônû) Yahweh's people and that they must "do justice and righteousness" (ûmišpāṭ ûṣədāqāh 'aśû).[154] In the ideal community of the future, the ruler will not continue any patterns of abuse from previous practices.

The polity of the restored community in Ezekiel, therefore, is not antimonarchical. The book shares a critical assessment of royal practices with other pre-exilic books, but the office itself is not done away with. In light of the reference to the Davidic ruler in Ezek 37:24–25—who is called both melek and nāśî'—there is no convincing reason to see the political structure of Ezek 40–48 as anti–Davidic simply because the terms melek and David are lacking. For example, we should not assume the temple polity is opposed to a high priest simply because no such person is named in these chapters. More plausibly, we should see the duties of a high priest included in the duties of the nāśî' and in the collective work of the Zadokites.[155]

---

[151] Ezek 37:24–25. On the nature of the nāśî' in Ezekiel see J. D. Levenson, *Theology of the Program of the Restoration of Ezekiel 40–48* (HSM 10; Missoula: Scholars Press, 1976), 55–107. He proposes convincingly that the melek/rô'eh/nāśî' in Ezek 37:24f. should be identified with the nāśî' in the visionary section in chapters 40–48. See discussion below.

[152] The city of Jerusalem is renamed as "Yahweh is there" (48:35).

[153] Hebrew nāśî'. See Ezek 44:3; 45:7, 16–17, 22; 46:2, 4, 8, 10, 12, 16–18; 48:21–22.

[154] Ezek 45:8–9.

[155] Levenson, *Theology of the Program of Restoration*, 75–107, describes the nāśî' as an "a-political messiah." Apparently he uses this term to describe an office curbed of the royal excesses known from the pre-exilic period. One doubts,

PROPHECY AND SOCIETY

The sharp-edged words of the pre-exilic prophets raise the question of the prophetic intention in delivering them. The history of interpretation reveals a number of interesting answers that vary considerably.[156] Scholars have concluded that the prophets were demagogues, utopian thinkers, fifth column agents for the eastern powers, ardent patriots, or idealistic reformers, among other things. There are dimensions of truth in each of these proposals with the exception of the notion that the prophets actively worked for the Assyrians or Babylonians. In no case, however, does a label such as demagogue, utopian, or reformer adequately identify a pre-exilic prophet. In every case this inadequacy has to do with the theological character of prophecy which drives the interpreter to grapple with the prophet's conception of God and human responsibility rather than only with sociological and political categories.[157]

Most discussions of the pre-exilic prophets begin with their severe critiques of Israel and Judah. This has led to discussion over the function of announcing judgment. Is the announcement of judgment the primary intention of the prophet, or should these prophecies be interpreted as drastic calls for reform?[158] The explicit call to repentance is less frequent than the announcement of judgment, so that the question at one level is whether the more frequent form of public speech (the announcement of judgment and related statements) is the best indication of prophetic intention. Stated differently, was the prophets' intention essentially a doxology of judgment in which the audience is called to acknowledge the correctness of divine judgment, or was their intention to change their audiences behavior by their harsh language?[159] There is no final answer

---

however, if an office that combines administrative and priestly duties can be described as "apolitical."

[156] See the survey in B. Albrektson, "Prophecy and Politics in the Old Testament," *The Myth of the State* (ed. H. Biezais; Stockholm: Almqvist and Wiksell, 1972), 45–56; and the idiosyncratic study of M. Silver, *Prophets and Markets. The Political Economy of Ancient Israel* (Boston: Kluwer-Nijhoff, 1983).

[157] The importance of the prophets as "thinkers" whose writings are interpreted adequately only by careful attention to their world view is underscored in the two-volume work by K. Koch, *The Prophets* (Philadelphia: Fortress Press, 1983–84). Even if his own proposals are not equally convincing, he has shown the inadequacy of purely sociological or political categories of interpretation. Moreover, his work shows that attempts to place individual prophets in a certain theological tradition (e.g., wisdom, David/Zion, Sinai covenant) can be helpful, but they too are ultimately inadequate.

[158] See the discussions in O. Keel, "Rechttun oder Annahme des drohenden Gerichts?" *BZ* 21 (1977): 200–218; J. Barton, "Begründungsversuche der prophetischen Unheilsankündigung im Alten Testament," *EvT* (47 (1987): 427–35.

[159] Put this way, the question is applicable not only to the pre-exilic prophets but to the Dtr H as well.

to the question, since the only access to the prophets' intention is through the books edited and shaped around the theme that Yahweh's primary word to the prophets' audiences was one of imminent judgment. Subsequent generations of readers might well find motives for repentance in the prophets' books, and in doing so, they would confirm a significant reason for preserving the prophets' words: that they might avoid the sins of their ancestors, and that they might open themselves to the possibility of Yahweh's new creation to come.

If one asks the question of prophetic intention from another angle—namely, where are the instructions for a properly functioning Israel—one finds little or nothing for detailed programs. This is most easily seen when comparing the social legislation of Deuteronomy with the scattered prophetic texts. Scholars have long observed that the contents of Deuteronomy were influenced by the activities of the pre-exilic prophets, but even though Deuteronomy gives far more legislative detail concerning the shape of an ideal Israel than any prophetic book, a number of scholars question if even Deuteronomy was intended as a state policy (pp. 150–52).[160] In any case, the search for detailed proposals for reform in the pre-exilic prophets is essentially a dead end.[161]

If it is true, then, that the prophets announced disaster as the consequence of institutional failure, it is also true that the prophets used the same vocabulary for the depiction of a future community that they used for present critique.[162] The institutions they criticized are the same ones that characterize a transformed Israel: monarchy, temple, promised land, Jerusalem, Sinai covenant, etc. It should be stressed that the future community is understood as a gift of Yahweh, a transformation of corrupt circumstances, not as the result of human reformation. The particular angle of prophetic critique perceived a close connection between public activity and its future consequences: thus the paradoxical view that the people of Yahweh would end in disaster because Yahweh would bring upon them the consequences of their activity. But having emphasized that aspect of divine activity for their day, the prophets also announced the paradox of grace: Yahweh would transform their society

---

[160] As an example, Koch, *The Prophets* (vol. 2), 1–11, describes the legislation of Deuteronomy as "law in the shadow of prophecy" and a "practical utopia."

[161] Silver, *Prophets and Markets*, interprets the prophets as idealistic but misguided reformers whose legitimate concern for the poor caused them to make overdrawn judgments about the economies of the day. Silver underestimates not only the role of the king and state administration in controlling the institutions criticized by the prophets but also the devastation of the economy brought on by military defeat and tribute in the ninth–seventh centuries, and he fails to see the prophetic critique of socio-economic policies as an integral part of the prophets' overall criticism of the nation.

[162] This is succinctly illustrated in Hos 2:19–23 (21–25H).

and its institutions beyond judgment and thus fulfil the promise of Israel's identity as his people.

Conclusion

The observations of this chapter derive from perceiving a deep-seated, paradoxical element in the prophetic relationship to Israelite society. On the one hand, the prophets assumed that an Israel or a Judah could be defined adequately only as the people of Yahweh, and in their critique they applied the definition rigorously. In this activity the prophets were not innovative but radical in their principles of application. To a certain degree they were idealists and utopian thinkers as well, and they would have been dissatisfied with most cultural expressions of Yahwism. This posture is their strength and their weakness.

> In their uncompromising assertion of the principles on which the Israelite cult was ultimately founded the great prophets were indeed utopians. If they had been reasonable and pragmatic we should probably never have heard from them.[163]

On the other hand, the prophets' negative assessment of the fundamental institutions of pre-exilic Israel and Judah proved to be indispensable to the communities of faith which sought to maintain a Yahwistic identity in the aftermath of exile. Their words may not have been reasonable, but they proved to be community-sustaining in the long run. Their assessment presupposed an understanding of corporate identity which operated at more than one level, challenging their audiences to rethink the definition of an Israel, a people of Yahweh, or even the nature of Yahweh.

Some responsibility for the paradoxical nature of the prophetic critique surely goes back to the communities which compiled the prophetic books, since they took seriously the prophets' challenge to the national identity. On occasion, the prophets themselves will have favored a given policy (e.g., non-alliance in political affairs) or even a particular king (e.g., Josiah). The disciples who preserved the prophecies, however, were concerned to account for the facts of defeat and exile as Yahweh's announced and just judgment but not as Yahweh's last word. It is likely, therefore, that these disciples have arranged the prophecies and underscored the tone of judgment they carried. But it is highly unlikely that editorial effort created the paradoxical nature of the prophetic critique. Such an approach to religion and its cultural expression is inherent in the prophetic insistence on a theological definition of Israelite society. Their radical critique sought to understand failure in theological terms

---

[163] Albrektson, "Prophecy and Politics," in Biezais, ed., *Myth of the State*, 56.

and to bear witness to Yahweh's new creative acts in the future.[164] Their efforts become a legacy which the canon of scripture preserves for Jews and Christians in any culture.

---

[164]The term "radical theocentricity" used by P. Joyce to describe the theological position of Ezekiel could be extended profitably to the other, pre-exilic prophets, once allowances are made for variation in terminology and emphasis. See his *Divine Initiative and Human Response in Ezekiel* (JSOTSS 51; Sheffield: JSOT Press, 1989), 89–105.

WISDOM AND RELIGION AS A CULTURAL SYNTHESIS   **6**

INTRODUCTION: WISDOM IN ISRAELITE CULTURE AND RELIGION

For the purposes of the following discussion, "wisdom" is defined first as a broad cultural movement in Israel and second as a set of documents in the OT (Proverbs, Ecclesiastes and Job). Both forms of the definition are rather arbitrary, but they are adequate for the discussion at hand. A dominant concern of wisdom in Israel or any of the nations of the ANE is the relationship between human community and the world, particularly as that relationship concerns the activity and limits of an individual. Wisdom concerns the human "art of steering" through the vicissitudes of life and attempts to understand the consequences of human activity for good and evil. These concerns presuppose an openness to the instruction of human experience and the values enjoined upon an individual by the culture in which he or she lives.

One of the clearest connections between the broad wisdom movements in the ANE and the particular traditions of the OT comes in the book of Proverbs. An individual proverb is a sentence or brief saying comparing or contrasting observable phenomena;[1] the book of Proverbs, therefore, is a collection of collections of such sayings along with brief poetic addresses. Because the books of Ecclesiastes and Job share the concerns of wisdom and elements of the proverbial approach, they are also included in the discussion. A case can be made as well for other

---

[1] J. M. Thompson, *The Form and Function of Proverbs in Ancient Israel* (The Hague: Mouton, 1974).

literary traditions in the OT. For example, a few psalms (e.g., Psa 34) and probably features of the apocalyptic writings (see pp. 236–40) deserve some consideration in a full treatment, as do the books of Ecclesiasticus (Ben Sira) and the Wisdom of Solomon from the Apocrypha.[2]

The wisdom movement in Israel is a subset of a broad, international phenomenon in the ANE.[3] Some interpreters in the past have found this close link of the Israelite wisdom movement to neighboring cultures to be a theological difficulty so that the wisdom traditions, however defined, were relegated to a subsidiary place in the evaluation of the OT. Only after the wisdom traditions of the ANE were integrated into the Israelite sphere and were "nationalized" and "integrated with Yahwism" did they have much relevance for theological interpretation.[4] And even then problems remained; the wisdom books preserved little or nothing about the designated "central affirmations" of the OT concerning the promises to the ancestors, the revelation at Sinai, covenants with Moses and David, etc. For other interpreters, this commonality with a widely recognized, international phenomenon became a positive component, and the lack of references to Yahweh's acts in the history of Israel was taken to be an affirmation of pluralism in theological matters. Within the canon of scripture these latter interpreters found a non-authoritarian tradition which allowed for a more interdisciplinary and interconfessional approach to the theological enterprise.[5]

Part of the problem for interpreting the wisdom traditions in the OT came with the assumption that originally "wisdom" was a secular concept in early Israel and only in the process of its integration into Yahwistic circles did the wisdom movement take on theological characteristics. This assumption is different from the perception that the wisdom movement in Israel shared much in common with other ANE cultures, but in the history of interpretation these two issues are interwoven. With all the difficulties and differences that remain in the

---

[2] R. N. Whybray, *The Intellectual Tradition in the Old Testament* (BZAW 135; Berlin: de Gruyter, 1974); see his "The Social World of the Wisdom Writers," in Clements, ed., *The World of Ancient Israel*, 227–50; R. Murphy, *The Tree of Life. Exploration of Biblical Wisdom* (New York: Doubleday, 1990).

[3] See the relevant essays in *The Sage in Israel and the Ancient Near East* (ed. J. Gammie, L. Perdue; Winona Lake: Eisenbrauns, 1990).

[4] J. Fichtner, *Die altorientalische Weisheit in ihrer israelitisch-jüdischen Ausprägung. Eine Studie zur Nationalisierung der Weisheit in Israel* (BZAW 62; Giessen: A. Töpelmann, 1933), 124.

[5] Details in W. Brueggemann, *In Man We Trust* (Richmond: John Knox, 1972); D. Morgan, *Wisdom in the Old Testament Traditions* (Atlanta: John Knox, 1981). On the question of the distinctiveness of the wisdom literature in the OT in light of its ANE context and other OT traditions, see F. J. Steiert, *Die Weisheit Israels—ein Fremdkörper im Alten Testament? Eine Untersuchung zum Buch der Sprüche auf dem Hintergrund der ägyptischen Weisheitslehren* (FTS 143; Freiburg: Herder, 1990).

interpretation of wisdom, the assumption is no longer valid that wisdom was originally a secular concept in the older cultures of the ANE or in early Israel. Two interpreters have demonstrated this point in detail, both by recourse to Egypt and Mesopotamian literature as well as the earliest elements in the biblical book of Proverbs.[6] Wisdom in the ANE has a central place in the attempt to comprehend a moral order in the cosmos and in human affairs. This order is not a closed system but is a creation of the gods or a process in which they are active. Even the so-called secular proverbs which do not overtly mention a deity still presuppose that human activity stands under a larger scheme of "world order" established by the gods in which human activity engenders a positive or negative reaction. The approach initially taken by Gese and Schmid, and now widely shared by scholars, is a vital contribution to the place of wisdom in Israel and is presupposed in what follows.[7]

To understand the place of the wisdom movement in Israelite culture, it should be remembered that the function of the wisdom traditions within the OT itself is more relevant than the question of the wisdom movement's origins. Nevertheless, the questions of wisdom in Israel and wisdom's origins are interrelated. No doubt one source of wisdom in Israel was the family, since it was the primary societal institution for nurture and education. Closely related to the family were the clan and village.[8] Tekoa, for example, is the home of a wise woman who is able to elicit an emotional response from the king to a fictitious

---

[6] H. Gese, *Lehre und Wirklichkeit in den alten Weisheit. Studien zu den Spruchen Salomos und zu den Buche Hiob* (Tübingen: J. C. B. Mohr [Siebeck], 1958), 1–50 and H. H. Schmid, *Wesen und Geschichte der Weisheit. Eine Untersuchung zur altorientalischen und israelitischen Weisheitsliteratur* (BZAW 101; Berlin: A. Töpelmann, 1966); *Gerechtigkeit als Weltordnung* (BHT 40; Tübingen: J. C. B. Mohr [Siebeck], 1968); "Altorientalisch-alttestamentliche Weisheit und ihr Verhältnis zur Geschichte," *Altorientalische Welt in der alttestamentlichen Theologie* (Zürich; Theologischer Verlag, 1974), 64–90. Gese still used the term "nationalizing" (p. 3) to describe the process by which Israel assimilated wisdom traditions. Both he and Schmid reckon with a considerable development within the wisdom movement in Israel.

[7] Regarding Israelite wisdom, see the perceptive discussion of Yahwism and the sapiential search for order in J. Crenshaw, "Murphy's Axiom: Every Gnomic Saying Needs a Balancing Corrective," in *The Listening Heart. Essays in Wisdom and the Psalms in honor of Roland E. Murphy, O. Carm.* (ed. K. Hoglund et al.; JSOTSS 58; Sheffield, 1987), 1–17; and L. Perdue, "Cosmology and the Social Order in the Wisdom Tradition," in Gammie and Perdue, eds., *The Sage in Israel*, 457–78.

[8] E. Gerstenberger, *Wesen und Herkunft des 'apodiktischen Rechts'* (WMANT 20; Neukirchen-Vluyn: Neukirchener Verlag, 1965); W. Richter, *Recht und Ethos. Versuch einer Ortung des weisheitlichen Mahnspruches* (SANT 15; Munich: Kaiser, 1966); H. J. Hermission, *Studien zur israelitischen Spruchweisheit* (WMANT 28; Neukirchen-Vluyn; Neukirchener Verlag, 1968), 81–92; C. Westermann, *Wurzeln der Weisheit: die ältesten Sprüche Israels und andere Völker* (Göttingen: Vandenhoeck & Ruprecht, 1990); C. Fontaine, "The Sage in Family and Tribe," in Gammie and Perdue, eds., *The Sage in Israel*, 155–64.

story and then use his response as a means to persuade him to a course of action (2 Sam 14:1–22). In this same account, the wise woman from Tekoa says that David "has wisdom like the wisdom of an angel of God" (14:20),[9] which alludes to other key sources of wisdom, namely, the monarch and the royal court. The knowledge of the monarch is a prominent theme in the ANE, since rulers cultivate or are granted a special relationship with the gods and are thus the recipients of divine revelation.[10] Court bureaucracies also developed the duties of scribes who specialized in forms of science and divination (see pp. 237–39).

It is with David's son Solomon, however, that the OT particularly associates wisdom. Solomon seeks wisdom from Yahweh for the governing of the people and then employs it juridically 'and administratively (1 Kings 3:3–28). According to his request, Solomon asks Yahweh for a "listening heart to judge your people and to discern between good and evil."[11] In addition to these accounts, Solomon is described as the recipient of divinely given wisdom, a wisdom that surpassed two widely recognized repositories of wisdom, namely, the "sons of the East" and Egypt.[12] Moreover, Solomon collects proverbs and songs which are part of his larger interest in the material world, and he is able to answer the questions of the Queen of Sheba (1 Kings 10:1–10).

Schmid, among others, states that with the rise of the state in Israel came the expected sociological and theological development of wisdom traditions. Yahweh would play the same role of author and guardian of the world order that the Egyptian and Mesopotamian deities played for their respective states. In Israel the administrative apparatus of the state had reached a point by Solomon's reign that schools and scribal guilds had an institutional setting. In turn, this institutional setting would foster the growth of a variety of wisdom movements and sapiential skills, although one should not assume that the didactic emphasis in proverbial wisdom has its "life setting" in schools. Moreover, we should not assume the reference to Solomon's collecting of proverbs (1:1; 25:1) confirms that he collected all the material in the book of Proverbs, even though there is no reason for skepticism concerning his part in the process. The biblical traditions concerning royal and court wisdom suggest a parallel

---

[9] Literally, "my Lord is wise (ḥākām) like the wisdom (ḥokmāh) of the angel of God to know everything that is in the land."

[10] L. Kalugila, The Wise King. Studies in Royal Wisdom as Divine Revelation in the Old Testament and Its Environment (CB/OT 15; Lund: Gleerup, 1980); R. N. Whybray, "The Sage in the Israelite Royal Court," in Gammie and Perdue, eds., The Sage in Israel, 133–140.

[11] 1 Kings 3:9: "listening heart" (lēb šōmēʻa), "judging" (špṭ), "discerning" (byn, hiphil).

[12] 1 Kings 4:29–34 (5:9–14 H). The sons of the East are likely early Arab tribes. Cf. Job 1:3. G. Bryce, A Legacy of Wisdom (Lewisburg: Bucknell University Press, 1979) treats the relationship between Egyptian and Israelite wisdom.

with Egypt, where the collection and study of wisdom was institutional-ized.[13] This institutional setting would be important for the preservation of written materials and their study. Even so, we should hesitate to put too much weight on schools in Israel in the early pre-exilic period. Above all we should be skeptical of an earlier theory that described this period in Israel as the "Solomonic enlightenment."[14]

The book of Proverbs mentions Solomon three times, once in the prologue to the book (1:1), once in the heading to a collection of sayings (10:1), and once by reference to the work of Hezekiah's men in collecting Solomonic proverbs (25:1). The Solomonic references explicitly unite Israel's history and proverbial wisdom. At a minimum, the last reference presupposes interpretational activity at the royal court at the end of the eighth century. Two other collections have headings in the book. Chapter 30 begins with a reference to the words of Agur, and chapter 31 begins with a reference to the words King Lemuel's mother taught him. No king named Lemuel ruled in Israel, and the reference to him demonstrates the international character of the wisdom movement as well as its associa-tion with royal courts.

Like most OT books, Proverbs is probably post-exilic in its final form, and as a collection of sayings and brief addresses, its contents are derived from several centuries of transmission and study. Concerning the book itself, a number of interpreters have proposed that chapters 1–9 are later than 10–29, providing something of an introduction to the seemingly random collection of sayings which follow. Indeed, chapters 1–9 do function as instructions which introduce the following chapters, but the attempt to divide the book into datable layers presupposes an evolution-ary scheme for the wisdom movement that is difficult to confirm.[15] One could conceivably argue, for example, that chapters 1–9 are actually

---

[13] K. Kitchen, "Egypt and Israel During the First Millennium B.C.," *VTSup* 40 (1986): 109–23. For a study of Egyptian wisdom from the first millennium see M. Lichtheim, *Late Egyptian Wisdom Literature in the International Context* (OBO 52; Fribourg: Universitätsverlag, 1983); D. Römheld, *Wege der Weisheit. Die Lehren Amenemopes und Proverbien 22,17–24,22* (BZAW 184; Berlin: de Gruyter, 1989).

[14] For references and discussion, cf. R. N. Whybray, "Wisdom Literature in the Reigns of David and Solomon," in Ishida, ed., *Studies in the Period of David and Solomon and Other Essays*, 13–26.

[15] Parallels with Egyptian instructions make a clear-cut distinction between chapters 1–9 and 10–29 rather difficult; cf. C. Bauer-Kayatz, *Studien zur Proverbien 1–9. Eine form- und motivgeschichtliche Untersuchung unter Einbeziehung ägyptischen Vergleichsmaterials* (WMANT 22; Neukirchen-Vluyn: Neukirchener Verlag, 1966), 15–75. A different type of evolutionary scheme is proposed by W. McKane, *Proverbs. A New Approach* (Philadelphia: Westminster, 1970). For a convincing critique of this developmental model cf. F. M. Wilson, "The Yahwistic Redaction of Proverbs Reconsidered," in Hoglund, et al., eds., *The Listening Heart*, 318–27.

earlier than the material in 10–29,[16] but the criteria for assessing this view are not clear.[17]

Ecclesiastes, a post-exilic book in origin, uses the literary device of a Solomonic autobiography as a means to convey the limits of wisdom. Solomon, therefore, serves as the collector par excellence of wisdom in the OT and into the intertestamental period.[18] There is a parallel here with David and his association with psalmody and the temple cult in Jerusalem. In the case of Solomon, however, the Dtr H affirms his reception of wisdom from Yahweh and his discerning employment of it, but the Dtr H also records that wisdom itself was no guarantee of Solomon's infallibility.[19]

The wisdom movement in Israel was not homogenous; it drew upon various sources for its contents: family, clan, gifted individuals, monarch, and royal courts. The wisdom movement sought insight through observation and experience, and guidance from those with knowledge of the world and human interaction. In one sense wisdom was characterized by the information and advice accumulated in the central social institutions of Israelite culture. It was an accumulation of knowledge that had much in common with institutional life throughout the ANE.

THE WISDOM MOVEMENT AND THE BOOK OF PROVERBS

Two characteristics of wisdom cannot be overlooked for an interpretation of the book of Proverbs and what it presupposes about the relationship between religion and culture. Both have already been mentioned in the introduction. The first is the presupposition of an order to the cosmos and in human experience which wise persons may observe and by which they seek to pattern their lives. The second concerns the lack of explicitly Yahwistic concerns such as the election of Israel, the covenant made with Abraham, Israel, David, the torah given at Sinai, etc. Taken together, these two characteristics point to an approach to the question of religion and culture which is distinctive of wisdom. The wisdom movement seeks insight into the orders of creation and human community, and guidance for piety before God through its cultural setting. As a part of the created order, a culture mediates insight and

---

[16] So B. Lang, *Wisdom and the Book of Proverbs. An Israelite Goddess Redefined* (New York: Pilgrim Press, 1986).

[17] In the reconstruction of Lang, *Wisdom and the Book of Proverbs*, personified wisdom in Proverbs 1–9 is modelled after an Israelite goddess who was a divine patronness of the Israelite schools. Neither the location of "wisdom instruction" in Israelite schools nor (especially) the existence of an Israelite goddess particularly devoted to such instruction can be adequately demonstrated from the proverbial texts themselves.

[18] E.g., the deuterocanonical Wisdom of Solomon.

[19] 1 Kings 11:1–6. The description of Solomon's failures is cast in typical Deuteronomistic style. See further discussion below.

guidance to wise observers who compare their experience with the observations handed down by their ancestors.[20]

As befits these characteristics of wisdom, the social settings for proverbial wisdom are quite broad. While the emphasis is on the individual, the institutional settings are primarily those encountered in public life. Home, family, marriage, children, city, agriculture, gossip, and reputation, are all subjects taken up in wisdom literature, while references to a particular state or formative historical events are not mentioned. One might generalize that if Deuteronomy and the pre-exilic prophets emphasized certain views of Israel before Yahweh, proverbial wisdom emphasized certain views of the place of the individual in the created order. For example, there is only one reference to Israel in the book of Proverbs, and it occurs in the superscription to the book. The circumstance is similar for Judah; the nation is mentioned once in a heading in 25:1. Jerusalem is not mentioned at all. Kings and rulers are mentioned (e.g., Prov 14:28), since their influence is often felt in daily life, but it is monarchy and politics in generic form that one meets in the proverbial wisdom. If one removed the references to Solomon and Hezekiah, there is nothing in the book of Proverbs that indicates it is Israelite except the references to Yahweh (below).

Admittedly the references to Yahweh in the book make no sense apart from Israel, and this fact is quite relevant for an overall evaluation of proverbial wisdom, but if a generic term for deity replaced all references to Yahweh, the point about proverbial wisdom's cultural anonymity would hold. The approach of proverbial wisdom begins in whatever culture potential sages find themselves. One may search for and find valid guidance for activity in the culture in which one lives. Even the knowledge of divine activity is mediated to individuals through the culture in which they live. The Yahwism of the book of Proverbs will accept this cultural approach but will insist finally that behind the general term "divine activity" stands a specific deity. The approach is both universal and particular; it is universal because of the view that a created order stands behind any culture and all human experience, and it is particular because the Lord of the created order is Yahweh.[21]

Social Settings of Proverbial Wisdom

Proverbial wisdom influenced education and the socialization process, though it is doubtful if a precise institutional setting for it can be recovered from the book of Proverbs. For example, the frequent address

---

[20] See the discussion of "common sense" as a cultural form by C. Geertz, "Common Sense as a Cultural System," *Antioch Review* 35 (1975): 5–26.

[21] See further, L. Boström, *The God of the Sages: The Portrayal of God in the Book of Proverbs* (CBOT 29; Stockholm: Almqvist & Wiksell, 1990).

"my son" could well refer to instruction in schools, but it could refer equally well to the instruction received at home.[22] Proverbs 1:8–19 exemplifies this emphasis on instruction and shows the universal aspect in the proverbial approach. A son is advised to avoid the company of sinners (*ḥaṭṭā'îm*), who are defined as thieves. Of course, the Decalogue contains explicit prohibitions against stealing and coveting, and Israel transmitted this as the speech of God.[23] But neither the Decalogue prohibitions nor even God are mentioned by the parents. Instead they remind their son that theft has its own consequences which will bring ruin on its perpetrators.

One is tempted to see a class ethic in proverbial wisdom with its emphasis on discipline, prudence, work, and its sometimes negative view of poverty, but this will not hold for the book of Proverbs as a whole.[24] One also finds sympathy for the poor and the view that poverty can result from oppression.[25] Matters such as foresight, keen observation, and openness to instruction are not the properties of any particular class, nor is there convincing evidence that such matters were taught or discussed only in specific classes.[26]

The many, so-called secular proverbs conveniently introduce the distinctive wisdom approach that emerges from such broad social settings. For example: "Better is a serving of vegetables with love there, than the fattened ox and hatred with it" (15:17, cf. 17:1). Formally this saying is a "better proverb" where two situations are juxtaposed and one judged better (*ṭôb*) than the other. A small but potentially vital clue to the setting of such a saying comes from the Hebrew particle *šām*, translated as "there." A serving of vegetables represents the food of the average person eaten within the family setting, a setting which is described as "better" than the food of a festival or a king if the latter setting also includes disharmony. It is presupposed that the bonds of family and the simple food eaten in that setting are good; whereas so-called good food

---

[22] The address to the son(s) is primarily in Prov 1–9, but not exclusively. Cf. Prov 23:15, 19; 24:21.

[23] Exod 20:15, 17; Deut 5:19, 21.

[24] See the discussion in R. Gordis, "The Social Background of Wisdom Literature," *HUCA* 18 (1944): 77–118, who proposes that the wisdom writers of the OT were from the upper class. A more adequate analysis is made by R. N. Whybray, *Wealth and Poverty in the Book of Proverbs* (JSOTSS 99; Sheffield: JSOT Press, 1990), who concludes that the variety of views on wealth and poverty in the book of Proverbs results from the fact that Proverbs is comprised of collections of material which originated from different segments of Israelite society.

[25] Prov 13:23, cf. the LXX which has righteous for poor (!). See also 14:20–21; 19:17; 21:13; 22:22–23.

[26] Cf. the discussion in B. W. Kovacs, "Is There a Class-Ethic in Proverbs?" *Essays in Old Testament Ethics* (ed. J. L. Crenshaw, J. T. Willis; New York: KTAV, 1972), 171–89.

is bad if the setting in which it is eaten is ruined. The accent falls on the terms love (*'ahabāh*) and hatred or disfavor (*śin'āh*) in the social setting of eating together. There is an experienced "good" in the sharing of a meal where there is love that outweighs the reputed "good" of a feast where the community is destroyed by hatred.

One might be tempted to read such a statement through Marxist eyes and see in it the advice to the poor to be satisfied with what they have. That would be a mistake; the proverb is a specific judgment about what fosters human community and what ruins it. By definition a proverb makes such a judgment concretely and not abstractly. A number of elements go into the making of community or its ruin, so that either a proverb illumines by analogy or another one must be sought as appropriate. No authority is stated for the proverb; the point of the proverb is not to reflect upon itself but to interpret a facet of human experience.

Another proverb of different form has a similar function. "Rarely set foot in your neighbor's house, lest he have his fill of you and hate you" (25:17). On the surface this proverb illustrates the definition of wisdom as "the art of steering." The problem of disharmony or hatred (*śin'āh*) between neighbors is an age-old one, but the stress of this saying falls on the discernment of the one who might offend. It is beyond the formal nature of a saying to give qualifications or exceptions to its interpretation; these things require a different saying with its own uniqueness. Thus there is no attempt to define how many visits to the neighbor is enough or when a neighbor is cross with you. The proverb leaves completely undiscussed whether the offended neighbor is rational, secretive, or paranoid, but it invites the hearer to observe carefully the consequences of his or her activity.

The focus on the consequences of activity for the hearer (i.e., the visitor to the neighbor) is more overt than the emphasis on the activity of the hearer of the first example (i.e., eating in an atmosphere of love or hatred), but the difference of effect is more apparent than real. In both cases, the hearers are invited to examine the consequences of their (common) activity for the good or ill it brings. A third saying shows the value proverbial wisdom attaches to the receptivity of a hearer by way of a common contrast between folly and wisdom. "A rebuke to one with discernment [impresses] more than a hundred blows [impress] a fool" (Prov 17:10). Left unstated in the compressed proverb is the appropriateness of the rebuke to the discerning one; perhaps the rebuke's justification is assumed, but the emphasis again falls upon the discernment of the one who changes his or her activity as a consequence of the rebuke.

Examples such as these sayings can be multiplied dozens of times in proverbial wisdom. The sheer brevity of the proverb leaves many elements assumed, but the general approach is consistent. A person in a wide variety of cultural circumstances can learn from experience and observation or not. Both experience and observation are reliable teachers for many facets of life. Wisdom, therefore, which relies heavily on experience and observation, can be described in explicit and specific terms, can be learned through observation, and can be imparted to those willing to learn. The difference between those who learn and those who do not portrays the basic distinction in proverbial wisdom between the wise and the foolish—or in vocabulary more overtly "moral" and "religious" to the Western mind—the distinction between the righteous and the wicked.[27] Because the subject matter varies considerably so does the vocabulary used, but the distinction between the wise/righteous and foolish/wicked is basic to proverbial wisdom.

The "Two-Way Doctrine" of Wisdom

The "two-way doctrine" expressed in proverbial form describes succinctly what experience and observation have learned about the consequences of human activity.[28] For example, the last named proverb (17:10) contrasts the reaction of the discerning one (*mēbîn*) with the fool (*kəsîl*).[29] Other contrasting categories include the righteous (*ṣaddîqîm*) over against the wicked (*rəšā'îm*),[30] the diligent (*ḥārûṣ*) over against the slack (*rəmiyyāh*),[31] the prudent (*'ārûm, 'arûmîm*) over against the naive (*petî, pətā'îm*),[32] the rich (*'āšîr*) over against the poor (*rāš, dal*).[33] The categories can overlap as seen in the equation of poverty/slackness and diligent/rich.[34] The "two-way doctrine" which employs these kinds of distinctions is concerned to point out the forces which the respective activities have set in motion. A fool, for example, acts foolishly and incurs folly. Action and consequence are joined like the activity of sowing and reaping. In the examples of diligence and wealth, or slackness and poverty, the connections between the acts and consequences are plausible (and observable), but they should not be considered inevitable; proverbial wisdom also knows about the connection between greed and riches and between poverty and oppression.[35]

---

[27] R. B. Y. Scott, "Wise and Foolish, Righteous and Wicked," *VT Sup* 23 (1972): 146–65. Scott notes that the two pairs of terms are analogous but not interchangeable. This is correct, but he also concludes (wrongly I believe) that the contrast between righteous and wicked is more religious and a later development than the contrast between wise and foolish.

[28] J. Crenshaw, *Old Testament Wisdom. An Introduction* (Atlanta: John Knox, 1981), 79–99.

[29] Prov 12:15, 23; 15:7, 21; 17:12; 29:11.

[30] Prov 10:11; 11:8, 23; 12:26.

[31] Prov 12:24, 27.

[32] Prov 14:15, 18.

[33] Prov 14:20; 19:4.

[34] Prov 10:4.

[35] See Prov 11:4, which contrasts righteousness with riches; 11:24–26, which criticizes the greed that motivates some wealthy persons; and 13:23, which

Much effort has been expended on the analysis of the "act-consequence" relationship in proverbial wisdom.[36] A saying such as "the one
who digs a pit will fall in it; and whoever rolls a stone, it will return to
him,"[37] apparently understands the connection between act and consequence as the parade example of the cosmic order. Such a proverb does
not describe digging pits and rolling stones as meaningful activities in
and of themselves, but uses them by analogy to describe human activity
in general. But does this saying reflect the perception by the sages of a
mechanistic system in the cosmos that is also operative in any culture?
And if so, what role does divine activity play in this system? Taken as a
whole, neither the proverbial wisdom in Proverbs, nor the wisdom of
Ecclesiastes and Job, understands the act-consequence relationship to be
a mechanistic system. In every case it is the doctrine of the mysterious
nature of divine activity that undermines a rigid predictability in the
act-consequence relationship. This rejection of a predictable act-consequence relationship is observed most clearly in the Yahweh proverbs.
For example:

> There is no wisdom (ḥokmāh), no insight (təbûnāh), no counsel ('ēṣāh) over
> against Yahweh; the horse is prepared for battle, but to Yahweh [belongs]
> the victory (Prov 21:30–31).

Such a statement concentrates on the mysterious nature of divine
activity. According to pragmatic wisdom, one must prepare carefully for
war and make strategic plans (Prov 20:18, 24:6). No one will deny the
value of strategy and preparation, but such precautions cannot prevail
against Yahweh. As is typical with the compressed saying, no reason is
given that Yahweh might favor one side over another; it is simply
acknowledged that Yahweh's own purposes transcend even the best
preparations for human achievement. "Many are the plans (maḥašābôt)
in a person's heart, but the counsel ('ēṣāh) of Yahweh will stand."[38]

In theological terms, the Yahweh proverbs become more a confession about divine activity and less an explanation about circumstances
easily predicted by an observant sage. These sayings affirm the mystery

---

acknowledges that injustice also causes poverty.

[36] On the theme in Israelite religion, see K. Koch, *Um das Prinzip der
Vergeltung in Religion und Recht des Alten Testaments* (Darmstadt: Wissenschaftliche
Buchgesellschaft, 1972). An essay by Koch in the volume has been translated into
English; "Is There a Doctrine of Retribution in the Old Testament?" *Theodicy in the
Old Testament* (ed. J. L. Crenshaw; Philadelphia: Fortress, 1983), 57–87. For a
discussion of the issues in Proverbs, cf. C. A. Keller, "Zum sogenannten Ver-
geltungsglauben im Proverbienbuch," *Beiträge zur Alttestamentlichen Theologie.
Festschrift für Walter Zimmerli zum 70. Geburtstag* (Göttingen: Vandenhoeck &
Ruprecht, 1977), 223–38.

[37] Prov 26:27.

[38] Prov 19:21. Cf. 20:24.

of divine activity as well as divine participation in the act-consequence relationship. For example:

> To a man belong the deliberations of the heart, but from Yahweh comes the answer of the tongue. A person judges his ways to be respectable, but Yahweh judges the motives (*rûḥôt*). Set before Yahweh your works, and your plans will be established. Yahweh has made everything for his own purpose, even the wicked (*rāšāʿ*) for the day of evil (Prov 16:1–4).

Set side by side in these four verses are confessional statements that link Yahweh with activity over and above human planning (16:1–2, 4) and those which understand divine activity in conjunction with the act-consequence relationship (16:3).

Even without the contribution of explicitly confessional material, proverbial wisdom reached the insight that the "two-way doctrine" could not be hardened into a dogma that ignored the particularity of a saying. As one response the editor (?) of Proverbs placed two seemingly contradictory sayings beside each other (26:4–5). This juxtaposition is not a coincidence but a way to stress that a proverb's application is limited to the particular and concrete.[39] There are appropriate times and inappropriate times to answer a fool, but the proverb itself cannot define the correct response. Wisdom is needed for the application of proverbs and not just in the apprehension of order in human experience. Thus 26:7 points out that a proverb (*māšāl*) in the mouth of fools [is like] the legs of the lame which do not work.[40] A proverb does not interpret human experience correctly because someone has claimed it so. Proverbial authority depends finally on the power of a saying to persuade its hearers of its particular relevancy.

Wisdom and Creation

On the basis of the two speeches of personified wisdom in Prov 1:20–33 and 8:22–31, it is fair to characterize proverbial wisdom in the book of Proverbs as a response to the "self-witness of creation."[41] Creation itself conveys a sense of order and meaning which *is* wisdom, and when perceived by human beings, this wisdom can instruct them in responsible patterns of behavior. However, the term "creation" and the

---

[39] K. Hoglund, "The Fool and the Wise in Dialogue," in Hoglund, et al., eds., *Essays in Wisdom and the Psalms in honor of Roland E. Murphy, O. Carm.,* 161–80, would explain the editorial activity differently but agrees with the function that contradictory sayings keep the proverbs from being extended into general dogma.

[40] Prov 25:11 is a positive statement of the principle. Cf. 15:23.

[41] G. von Rad, *Wisdom in Israel* (Nashville: Abingdon, 1972), 144–76. See further, H. J. Hermisson, "Observations on the Creation Theology in Wisdom," *Israelite Wisdom: Theological and Literary Essays in Honor of Samuel Terrien* (Missoula: Scholars Press, 1978), 43–57.

pronoun "itself" reveal at least two difficulties for the modern Western mind. Creation is typically associated with a doctrine of beginnings and is apprehended impersonally. Neither point is consistent with proverbial wisdom. Creation refers less to an absolute beginning and more to the sensory realm of human experience in the cosmos, to an environment upheld by God over against the forces of chaos which threaten to undo it. Nor does proverbial wisdom understand Yahweh's relationship to creation as impersonal, but almost as a "thou," since Yahweh has established relationships with the varied elements of creation. These differences account for the number of so-called creation texts in the OT which occur in a variety of genres and which associate creation as much with continuing divine activity as with past events.[42]

A succinct statement of von Rad reflects an understanding among the wise in Israel regarding the scope of divine activity and creation:

> [Israel] did not keep faith and knowledge apart. The experiences of the world were for her always divine experiences as well, and the experiences of God were for her experiences of the world.[43]

It is an overstatement on von Rad's part to put the matter so generally for Israel, but his claim does capture a vital aspect in the approach of wisdom. Precisely in the world of daily experience and trial, proverbial wisdom claims a person encounters God. This is a confession of faith which adds new perspective to the value of cultural analysis and Israel's understanding of cosmology.

Proverbs 8:22–31 furnishes the most intricate treatment of the relationship between Yahweh and creation in the wisdom literature.[44] What gives creation its "self-witness" is the mediation of wisdom between Yahweh and the human species, a wisdom personified as present from the beginning of Yahweh's creative activity and thus privy to the means by which the creative order is upheld. Wisdom speaks:

> Yahweh created (*qnh*) me at the beginning of his way, before his works of old. From eternity I was made (*nsk*), from the beginning, earlier than the land. When no great depths existed I came forth (*ḥll*) . . . Before the mountains were set in place, before the hills, I came forth (*ḥll*) . . . When He established the heavens I was there . . . I was beside him as a workman;[45]

---

[42] See the collected essays in *Creation in the Old Testament* (ed. B. W. Anderson; Philadelphia: Fortress Press, 1984).

[43] Von Rad, *Wisdom in Israel*, 62.

[44] G. Landes, "Creation Tradition in Proverbs 8:22–31 and Genesis 1," *A Light Unto My Path: Old Testament Studies in Honor of Jacob M. Myers* (ed. H. N. Bream et al.; Philadelphia: Temple University Press, 1974), 279–93; R. Murphy, "Wisdom and Creation," *JBL* 104 (1985): 3–11.

[45] Since wisdom (*ḥokmāh*) is feminine, some scholars who translate the term *'āmôn* as "workman," conclude the attribution is to Yahweh who is referred to in the previous word "*his* side." See, for example, P. Bonnard, "De la Sagesse

daily I was his delight, playing before Him at all times, playing in his land, and my delight is with the human species.

The best parallels to this passage come in Egyptian texts which have the Egyptian goddess *Ma'at* playing before other Egyptian deities. Since *Ma'at* represents the concepts of justice and order, the correspondence is close. In such a case there is always the danger of assuming dependence between the biblical text and the Egyptian model, and ignoring the differences that still exist between the two.[46] Wisdom (*ḥokmāh*), a feminine noun, is personified as a female in wisdom literature but not on the basis of a single metaphor.[47] It is probable that key components in Wisdom's personification are developed from Israelite models of the female rather than from extrabiblical parallels.[48]

Much of the precise relationship between Wisdom and Yahweh depends on the translation of the difficult verbs in 8:22–25 and the even more difficult noun ('*āmôn*) in 8:30a. The verbs *qnh, nsk,* and *ḥll* can all refer to the process of begetting and child bearing, which, if read in conjunction with the translation of '*amōn* as "darling child,"[49] makes wisdom essentially the child of Yahweh.[50] The Egyptian parallels noted above support this interpretation, but it is not a satisfactory explanation overall. In the first place, Wisdom's significance comes in the fact that she delights in the human species and mediates to them her knowledge of creation's orders. In functional terms she must be more than a delightful child. There is also the conceptual difficulty in the language of begetting and giving birth which is only partially alleviated because the terminology is metaphorical. A relevant parallel is the metaphorical "begetting" of the king by Yahweh as proclaimed in the royal theology, where similar terminology is used.[51] Overall, the translation offered above includes something of the intimacy proposed in the model of begotten child,

---

personnifiée dans l'Ancien Testament à la Sagesse en personne dans le Nouveau," in Gilbert, ed., *La Sagesse de l'Ancien Testament,* 119–23.

[46] In addition to Bauer-Kayatz, *Studien zur Proverbien 1–9,* 93–97, cf. O. Keel, *Die Weisheit spielt vor Gott: Ein ikonographischer Beitrag zur Deutung des məsaḥāqät in Spr 8, 30f.* (Göttingen: Vandenhoeck & Ruprecht, 1974).

[47] As noted above, she can be characterized even as a workman.

[48] C. Camp, *Wisdom and the Feminine* (Sheffield: Almond Press, 1985).

[49] Repointed as '*amūn.*

[50] For an interpretation emphasizing the vocabulary of procreation, see G. Yee, "An Analysis of Prov 8:22–31 According to Style and Structure," *ZAW* 94 (1982): 58–66. Cf. the similar reconstruction of Lang, *Wisdom and the Book of Proverbs,* 60–70.

[51] See Psa 2:6–7, which uses the verb *nsk* (cf. Prov 8:23); *yld,* a parallel term with *ḥll* as demonstrated in Deut 32:18 (cf. Prov 8:24–25); and the address to the king as "my son" which can be compared with the child (*yeled*) who bears the government on his shoulders in Isa 9:6 (5H).

but it also preserves something of Wisdom's insightful role in the creative process and authority to instruct based on what she knows.

The most critical clue to the significance of wisdom and the created order comes in the report that "*in* wisdom (*bəhokmāh*) Yahweh founded the earth, *in* understanding (*bitbûnāh*) He established the heavens" (3:19). That wisdom is here understood as a characteristic of Yahweh is confirmed by the following verse which reports that "with His knowledge (*bəda'tô*) the great depths were broken up." For the personification of wisdom in 8:22f., this means she is functionally Yahweh's self-communication through the witness of creation. This is the primary theological development made in proverbial wisdom from the standpoint of Yahwism. Even the model of religion and culture which most affirms the contributions of culture for theological understanding does so from the confessional standpoint that creation is a form of divine communication. "Wisdom, which appears to be a singularly human endeavor, is in reality the human response to a transcendental overture."[52] From this perspective, the universal element in the wisdom approach is validated because wisdom is subsumed under the creative lordship of Yahweh.

Because, in essence, she knows what Yahweh knows, Wisdom speaks like a prophetess (Prov 1:20–33).[53] She shouts in the street and offers reproof to those who deserve it. Like Yahweh she can pour out her spirit; in the day of calamity she can be called upon. Those who would reject knowledge, therefore, will not choose the fear of Yahweh (1:29).

The Fear of Yahweh

This last phrase in 1:29, the "fear of Yahweh" permeates the book of Proverbs, running like a thread through the longer instructions in chs. 1–9 as well as in the sayings collections of chs. 10–29.[54] The term "fear" (*yr'*) occurs in both noun and verb forms. According to 1:7 the "fear of Yahweh is the beginning of wisdom." Fear of Yahweh is an appropriate summary for proverbial wisdom and apparently was intended as such by the book's editors. Fear is primarily the response of awe that leads to reverence and then obedience. And when combined with the term

---

[52] F. M. Wilson, "The Yahwistic Redaction of Proverbs," in Hoglund, ed., *The Listening Heart*, 317.

[53] Bauer-Kayatz, *Studien zur Proverbien 1–9*, 119–34, points out that this passage is much more dependent on Israelite forms of speech, particularly prophetic, than the first person speech of wisdom in 8:22–31. Cf. P. Trible, "Wisdom Builds a Poem. The Architecture of Proverbs 1:20–33," *JBL* 94 (1975): 509–18.

[54] Prov 2:5; 3:7; 8:13; 9:10; 10:27; 14:2, 26–27; 15:16, 33; 16:6; 19:23; 22:4; 23:17; 24:21; 31:30. See P. J. Nels, *The Structure and Ethos of the Wisdom Admonitions in Proverbs* (BZAW 158; Berlin: de Gruyter, 1982), 97–101: "The *yir'at Jahweh* [fear of Yahweh] . . . is the scope or sphere in which wisdom is possible and conceivable . . . Wisdom as the cognitive ability to recognise the created order and the ethos which it demands, is only possible within the *yir'at Jahweh*" (p. 100).

"beginning" (rē'šît), fear of God underlines the confession that wisdom ultimately points away from itself to the mystery of Yahweh. Proverbial wisdom generally speaking worked from observations in specific contexts toward the goal of an ever-greater comprehension of the created order. In such an approach lies the basis for the scientific enterprise and at least the possibility of apprehending truth wherever encountered. But the very success in observing human experience led inevitably to the realization that wisdom is not so easily mastered. Thus the motif that the fear of Yahweh is the beginning of wisdom meant paradoxically that wisdom can be defined only *theologically* not anthropologically and that its proper role is a circumscribed one. The way is then prepared for wisdom's eventual identification with Torah and its integration with prophetic and cultic traditions.

THE WISDOM MOVEMENT AND THE BOOKS OF JOB AND ECCLESIASTES

It is tempting to read the books of Job and Ecclesiastes as dialogue partners with the proverbial wisdom contained in the book of Proverbs. According to several interpreters, Job and Ecclesiastes are the result of a crisis in the wisdom movement,[55] where the optimism of the two-way doctrine gave way to a radical rethinking of the act-consequence relationship.[56] The distinctive treatments in Job and Ecclesiastes of themes held in common with the international wisdom movement lend support for such a reading, but one should be wary of attributing the place of either book in the OT primarily to their function as dialogue partners for Proverbs. On the one hand, it is more likely that the book of Job is preserved because of the universal appeal of the story[57] and the fact that the memory of a righteous Job was widely known in antiquity (Ezek 14:14, 20). Ecclesiastes, on the other hand, is associated with Solomon and earns a place in the conversation on that basis.[58] Each book shares

---

[55] See discussion in F. Crüsemann, "Hiob und Koheleth. Ein Beitrag zum Verständnis des Hiobbuches," in Albertz, ed., *Werden und Wirken des Alten Testaments*, 373–93.

[56] J. Crenshaw, "The Birth of Skepticism in Ancient Israel," *The Divine Helmsman. Studies on God's Control of Human Events, presented to Lou H. Silberman* (ed. J. Crenshaw and S. Sandmel; New York: KTAV, 1980), 1–21.

[57] J. Gray, "The Book of Job in the Context of Near Eastern Literature," *ZAW* 82 (1970): 251–69; G. L. Mattingly, "The Pious Sufferer: Mesopotamia's Traditional Theodicy and Job's Counselors," *The Bible in Light of Cuneiform Literature* (ANETS 8; ed. W. W. Hallo et al.; Lewiston: Edwin Mellen, 1990), 305–348.

[58] It is also likely that Ecclesiastes and Proverbs were intended to be read together since both books are associated with the work of Solomon. See discussion below.

certain concerns which reflect a similar approach to the relationship between religion and culture, though they diverge considerably on other points.

The Wisdom Movement and Job

The bulk of the book of Job is taken up with dialogue between various parties—the satan and God, Job with his different companions, Job and God. This observation is a clue to the nature of the wisdom tradition where forms of dialogue as well as the preservation of proverbs have a long history. In spite of intense discussion over the form of the book and the stages by which it reached its present shape,[59] the dialogical nature of the book demonstrates the centrality of the sapiential approach in its formation. Job the individual cannot represent the unanswered problems of human suffering for everyone; however, his experience of suffering and his reactions to it are intended to instruct readers about the mysteries of human nature and the incomprehensible dimensions of divine activity. This general representation is more essential to the book's interpretation than a possible location of the book's author(s) in the Jewish aristocracy of the post-exilic period.[60]

In the initial verse of the prologue, Job is described as an inhabitant of Uz, a blameless (tām) and upright (yāšār) man, who feared God (yərē' 'elōhîm) and rejected evil. According to this same prologue, the writer's evaluation of Job and God's evaluation of Job are identical (1:8).[61] The land of Uz is not part of Israel but is likely east of the Jordan river,

---

[59] H. P. Müller, *Das Hiobproblem: seine Stellung und Entstehung im alten Orient und im Alten Testament* (Darmstadt: Wissenschaftliche Buchgesellschaft, 1978) provides a thorough introduction to the history of discussion concerning the book's interpretation. See also R. J. Williams, "Current Trends in the Study of the Book of Job," *Studies in the Book of Job* (ed. W. Aufrecht; Waterloo, Canada: Wilfred Laurier University Press, 1985), 1–27. For a deconstructionist approach to the internal tensions in the book—which have been investigated typically by literary critical and redactional schemes—see the essay by D. Clines, "Deconstructing the Book of Job," *The Bible and Rhetoric. Studies in Biblical Persuasion and Credibility* (ed. M. Warner; London: Routledge, 1990), 65–80.

[60] See the socio-historical reconstructions of Crüsemann, "Hiob und Koheleth," in Albertz, ed., *Werden und Wirken des Alten Testaments*, 386–93; and R. Albertz, "Der sozialgeschichtliche Hintergrund des Hiobbuches und der 'Babylonischen Theodizee,' " *Die Botschaft und die Boten. Festschrift für Hans Walter Wolff zum 70. Geburtstag* (ed. J. Jeremias, L. Perlitt; Neukirchen-Vluyn: Neukirchener Verlag, 1981), 357–72. In spite of a number of important observations about the possible location of the author(s) in the Jewish aristocracy of the post-exilic period, one senses the danger of controlling assumptions about the nature of the Judean upper classes in the period.

[61] See the stimulating but unconvincing attempt to question the traditional reading of Job's character by A. Brenner, "Job the Pious? The Characterization of Job in the Narrative Framework of the Book," *JSOT* 43 (1989): 37–52.

suggesting that Job himself is not an Israelite. This is consistent with the comparison of Job with the sons of the east (1:3) and the origin of one of Job's friends from Teman (2:11).[62] In the book there are no references to Israelite history or socio-political institutions (e.g., temple, monarchy). The vocabulary for deity is predominately generic; i.e., apart from the prologue and the speeches of Yahweh near the conclusion of the book, most references are to 'elōhîm, 'elôah, and šadday. Furthermore, the vocabulary of the book as a whole is full of rare words which lend to the work a pronounced individuality among the OT writings.

On balance of the evidence, Job is probably not an Israelite, but this does not deny the book a legitimate place in the Yahwistic tradition.[63] The book presupposes the cultural starting point of the wisdom movement as a whole—that God and moral purpose can be encountered in the human affairs of any culture—and proceeds to discuss these matters in light of Job's particular circumstances. In the book the God of creation and moral order is identified with Yahweh. Job's accusations and pleas are similar to the lament psalms of the OT,[64] and his defense of his activity assumes a definition of righteousness as faithfulness to the community (Job 29:7–17; 31:1–40). Job does not define himself explicitly by reference to Israel's torah or prophetic norms, but his moral criteria are consistent with a Yahwistic ethos. The assumption of a Yahwistic piety is also evident in the prologue where Job's "fear of God" applies to Yahweh (1:6–2:10).

Perhaps most importantly for the Yahwistic connection, the poem on the hiddenness and mystery of wisdom in chapter 28 shares this theme with proverbial wisdom.[65] Interpreters often contrast the affirmation of wisdom's hiddenness in Job 28 with the prophetic call of Wisdom to her audience in the book of Proverbs and then claim that this contrast is evidence for the development of wisdom thinking and for the critique of the proverbial two-way doctrine in the book of Job. The interpretation

---

[62] E. A. Knauf, "Supplementa Ismaelitica 4. Ijobs Heimat," *BN* 22 (1983): 25–29, locates Uz in northwest Arabia and would date the book to the sixth century B.C.E. Both are reasonable conjectures. Because of certain Aramaic influences in the Hebrew text of Job, post-biblical traditions, and the reference to Uz the son of Aram in Gen 10:23, some scholars would locate the land of Uz in the Hauran, south of Damascus.

[63] See J. J. M. Roberts, "Job and the Israelite Religious Tradition," *ZAW* 89 (1977): 107–14.

[64] See M. Bič, "Le juste et l'impie dans le livre de Job," *VT Sup* 15 (1966): 33–43; C. Westermann, *The Structure of the Book of Job* (Philadelphia: Fortress Press, 1978). The comparison with the laments is important to understand the dialogues in the book but it is not the decisive clue to the form of the book as Westermann concludes.

[65] S. Geller, " 'Where is Wisdom?': A Literary Study of Job 28 in Its Settings," *Judaic Perspectives on Ancient Israel* (ed. J. Neusner et al., Philadelphia: Fortress Press, 1987), 155–88.

has much to commend it as long as it is recognized that seeds of these developments are also found within proverbial wisdom in the book of Proverbs.[66] It is with the explicitly Yahwistic proverbs that a sense of mystery and inscrutableness in apprehending divine activity is also part of proverbial wisdom's approach (pp. 209–10, 213–14). Thus the approach of the book of Job originates in the broad wisdom movement of the ANE, while the particular "Joban" emphases come from the intersection between the traditional story of innocent suffering and the ethos of Yahwistic wisdom.

One is tempted to read the story of Job in light of the Babylonian exile of Judah and its effect on Yahwistic piety,[67] but very little in the account of Job itself is made clearer because of this reconstructed historical background. In fact, two central features of the story mitigate against the exile as the origin of the story of Job, even though it is quite possible that the book reached its final form in the post-exilic period. The first feature concerns the "wager" between the satan and Yahweh.[68] Nowhere else in the OT is (the) Satan made responsible for the fact of the exile, and the point at issue in the wager is not the guilt of Job but the motive for his righteousness. The second feature concerns the emphasis on the mysteries of creation in Yahweh's speeches to Job.[69] Here Yahweh's rehearsal of the intricacies of creation is a reminder to Job that his own questioning of the moral order and human fate takes place in a context he only dimly perceives. Admittedly, both features are relevant to the question of exile, but neither seems occasioned by it.[70] The book holds Yahweh's just government of the created order and the essential validity of Job's complaint in an uneasy and unresolved tension. It is inconceivable to the author(s) that Yahweh's method of moral rule can

---

[66] The poem on the hiddenness of wisdom concludes: "the fear of Yahweh, that is wisdom; and to turn from evil [that is] insight" (28:28). Even if this comment is an editorial addition to the theme of wisdom's hiddenness, it still reflects the application of Yahwism to the proverbial wisdom of Job.

[67] Perusal of commentaries and secondary literature demonstrates that a number of interpreters have followed this option. See J. Lévêque, "La datation du livre de Job," *VT Sup* 32 (1981): 206–19.

[68] The term does not describe the interchange between Yahweh and Satan very accurately, though it is commonly used. It is true that the other OT references to Satan are post-exilic (Zech 3:1; 1 Chron 21:1).

[69] See V. Kubina, *Die Gottesreden im Buche Hiob. Ein Beitrag zur Diskussion um die Einheit von Hiob 38,1–42,6* (FTS 115; Freiburg: Herder, 1979). She provides a full discussion of the double speech of Yahweh to Job and the frequent supposition that originally the story had only one reply of Yahweh to Job's pleas.

[70] J. van Oorschot, *Gott als Grenze. Eine literar- und redaktionsgeschichtliche Studie zu den Gottesreden des Hiobsbuches* (BZAW 170; Berlin: de Gruyter, 1987) proposes that the final form of the Yahweh speeches (and thus the book of Job as a whole) opposes an understanding of the exile in wisdom circles as a proportional punishment for sin.

be accounted for by the canons of human reason any more than the suffering of the righteous can always be assessed adequately from the human perspective. Over and over again Yahweh reminds Job either that he was not there to observe divine activity or that he does not know the reasons why other creatures do what they do. Yet surprisingly, Yahweh accepts Job's questions[71] and rejects the defense of divine justice offered by Job's companions. They, like the satan, thought all relationships between Yahweh and his creation are capable of rational explanation.

The exile of Israel and Judah raises the questions of divine justice and the place of Israel among the nations. The suffering of Job raises the questions of divine justice and the place of an individual in the created order. Job and (for example) Amos or Deuteronomy raise parallel issues that need not be collapsed one into the other. For all they have in common, the story of Job takes on the dialogical form of the "what if" scenario. His impressive righteousness contrasted with his tremendous suffering comprises the extreme "test case" for belief in Yahweh's moral providence. If the relationship between Yahweh and Job remains intact, then so does the case for human piety and divine integrity. The answers to the dilemma of Job (if they can be classified as answers) are founded in three affirmations: (1) True wisdom leads to the confession of human limitation. Wisdom does not yield all of her secrets to the assertive or persistent. (2) The created order watched over by Yahweh supplies a context for the divine-human encounter. While the righteousness of individuals cannot be predicted safely by their station in life, Yahweh affirms the importance of human integrity in the face of pain and suffering. (3) Yahweh's own integrity is affirmed in spite of claims to the contrary. This integrity is not subject to a rational explanation but is a confession derived from the divine-human encounter.

Job, therefore, stands within the cultural approach of the wisdom movement. Deep questions about Yahweh's moral rule (integrity) and the ubiquitous search for the meaning of piety are addressed without overt reference to torah, prophets, or the history of Israel. It is an example of faith seeking understanding in the interchange between wise tradition and human experience. Finally, however, the theological claims of Yahwism stamp the approach to the international setting and the universal quest for understanding. Whatever Job has heard takes second place to what he apprehends in the divine-human encounter (42:1–6).

---

[71] Job's "repentance" in his final reply (42:6) and Yahweh's restoration of Job (42:7–17) in the prose epilogue are both tangible expressions of acceptance. Job's repentance demonstrates his acceptance that he cannot gain an adequate perspective on Yahweh's moral rule, and in effect, ceases to consider Yahweh his enemy. Yahweh accepts Job's claim that he did not incur his suffering because of his sin and demonstrates this acceptance by restoring Job's circumstances.

While remaining mysterious, Yahweh is no generic deity, and Job's fate is no predictable outworking of the cosmic order.

The Wisdom Movement and Ecclesiastes

The sage(s) responsible for the book of Ecclesiastes shows more of the personal reflective style than any other writer(s) in the OT. Koheleth, the Hebrew term translated in English as Ecclesiastes or "the preacher,"[72] is clearly rooted in the international wisdom movement and is a vigorous participant in the dialogue over meaning and purpose in human affairs. The book's vocabulary strongly implies a post-exilic date for the work, and it is probably one of the youngest works in the OT.[73]

In any satisfactory interpretation of Ecclesiastes there are two closely related issues in assessing the book's composition. These concern (1) the different voices represented in the work, and (2) the contradictory nature of a number of sayings. One editorial voice is evident in the heading to the work and in the introductory statement of the book's dominant theme (1:1–2): "The words of Koheleth, the son of David, king in Jerusalem; vanity of vanities, says Koheleth . . . everything is vain."[74] Likewise, the concluding verses in 12:8–14 represent comments about Koheleth and are editorial. The contradictory nature of individual sayings is represented by seemingly "orthodox wisdom" sayings such as 3:17 and 7:12,[75] in light of the skeptical spirit so obvious in most of the book.

Current trends in interpretation are much less inclined than previous analyses to attribute all "positive" statements in Ecclesiastes to an orthodox editor.[76] These trends are to be welcomed, because the criteria for assessing genuine sayings as opposed to editorial additions in a work

---

[72] For the history of interpretation and discussions of current approaches: see R. Murphy, " Qohelet Interpreted: The Bearing of the Past on the Present," *VT* 32 (1982): 331–37; the (two) books by D. Michel, *Qohelet* (Darmstadt: Wissenschaftliche Buchgesellschaft, 1988), *Untersuchungen zur Eigenart des Buches Qohelet* (BZAW 183; Berlin: de Gruyter, 1989); and the work by M. Fox, *Qoheleth and His Contradictions* (BLS 18; Sheffield: Almond Press, 1989).

[73] The recent efforts by D. Fredericks to question the post-exilic dating are not conclusive; see his *Qoheleth's Language: Re-evaluating its Nature and Date* (ANETS 3; Lewiston: E. Mellen Press, 1988).

[74] The meaning of the word *hebel*, often translated "vain," is discussed at some length by both Michel, *Untersuchungen*, 40–51; and Fox, *Qoheleth*, 29–48, who independently of each other suggest "absurd" as the best rendering. Both cite the French existentialist A. Camus as a stimulus for their conclusion.

[75] One should add the conclusion of the epilogue in 12:13–14 to the orthodox sayings, although many interpreters distinguish between the writer(s) of the epilogue and the composer of the sayings in the book.

[76] Among the works cited by Michel and Fox, the study by J. A. Loader, *Polar Structures in the Book of Qohelet* (BZAW 152; Berlin: de Gruyter, 1979), is a good example of an attempt to wrestle with the compositional and theological complexities of Ecclesiastes as a whole document.

of the small size and great complexity of Ecclesiastes are quite subjective. Indeed, Koheleth might find the attempt to distinguish between what he recorded and what the "editors" added as a parade example of vanity and striving after wind. At the same time, the book manifestly exhibits at least two different figures, the voice(s) that introduce(s) Koheleth and provide(s) the epilogue, and the voice of Koheleth himself. The most satisfactory approach to the book is that which attributes the whole work to one individual (or "school") who contributes everything: both voices, the introduction, the autobiographical account of Solomon, the sayings collections, and the epilogue.[77] This author may have used an earlier pseudonymous form of a Solomonic autobiography which showed the consequences of Solomon's loss of Yahwistic wisdom, but he developed it for his own purposes rather than waiting until the epilogue to correct the world view that he opposed.

The literary depiction of Solomon, therefore, is the key to interpreting the book as it stands,[78] especially in the book's internal dialogue, which reflects the Israelite wisdom movement's grappling with meaning and purpose in human existence before God.[79] Solomon is depicted not just as a king but as a disillusioned and pensive older man, a sage faced with the inequities of life and a recognition of the limits of human knowledge. Two traditions in the OT are crucial to understand this depiction: (1) the portrait of Solomon in 1 Kings 3–12 as the apogee of human wisdom who failed to be guided by that wisdom late in his life; (2) the tradition of Solomon as the great collector of wisdom sayings as preserved in Prov 1:1–7; 10:1; 25:1.[80] Solomon represents in his own

---

[77] This is essentially the conclusion of Fox, *Qohelet*. For literary comparisons to the use of autobiography and first-person observations in Ecclesiastes, see O. Loretz, *Qohelet und der alte Orient. Untersuchungen zu Stil und theologischer Thematik des Bucher Qohelet* (Freiburg: Herder, 1964), 145–66, 212–17.

[78] This claim depends on the conclusions that (1) the "Solomonic memoir" begun in 1:12 carries all the way through the book, including the sayings collections in 3:15–12:7, and (2) that the editorial voice and the voice of Solomon go back to the same author. The majority view in modern critical studies is represented in the following statement which minimizes the Solomonic fiction: "As is well known, the literary fiction of royal authorship [of Ecclesiastes] fades away after the second chapter, to return again in the epilogue;" J. L. Crenshaw, "Wisdom and Authority: Sapiential Rhetoric and its Warrants," VT Sup 32 (1980): 29.

[79] See the study of G. Wilson, " 'The words of the wise:' the intent and significance of Qoheleth 12:9–14," *JBL* 103 (1984): 175–92, who proposes that "the epilogue serves to bind Qohelet together with Proverbs and provides a canonical key to the interpretation of both" (p. 179).

[80] The reference to a work entitled the "acts of Solomon" in 1 Kings 11:41 also may have preserved information available to the compiler of Ecclesiastes. It is more likely, however, that the verse provided the compiler with a convenient phrase for the book's heading. 1 Kings 11:41 twice mentions the *dibrê šəlōmōh* which can be translated as "deeds" or "words" of Solomon.

complex and contradictory character the problems inherent in the wisdom movement. The compiler of the book uses Solomon to give voice to the contradictory nature of human existence, concentrating on the failure of the two-way doctrine to explain meaning in human affairs and the lack of comprehension on the part of the wise concerning divine activity. The absurd represented by Solomon is part of the author's own confession about human existence, but it leads finally to the conclusion stated in the epilogue (Eccl 12:13–14): a final reckoning is reserved for the future. As in the prologue to Proverbs, the epilogue to Ecclesiastes claims that the fear of God (in spite of absurdity) is the central teaching that true wisdom has to offer. It adds the important corollary that one should keep God's commandments (miṣwôt),[81] which probably reflects an assessment of Solomon's failure along the lines of the Deuteronomistic interpretation in 1 Kings 11–12. Therefore, one should read Proverbs and Ecclesiastes together as reflections on the significance of the wisdom movement in Israel and the failures inherent in the movement without safeguards.

In terms of a cultural approach, Ecclesiastes shares some characteristics with Job. For example, both compositions likely owe something to the frustration and resignation of the educated, upper classes in the post-exilic period.[82] Ecclesiastes, in the guise of Solomon, explicitly names wisdom and riches as pursuits which in themselves do not satisfy the human quest for meaning (1:12–2:11). But as with the portrait of Job, one must not ignore the use of Solomon as a paradigm whose life is meant to be instructive on a much wider scale than class or even nationality would suggest. This wider audience becomes clear in the poignant treatment of old age and in the injunction that to fear God and to keep his commandments are the duty of everyone (12:1–7, 13–14).

Ecclesiastes does for the empirical attempt to discern meaning in the course of events what Job did for the attempt to understand the reasons for suffering. Koheleth is a skeptic, but the source and direction of his skepticism deserve careful consideration. Michel explains his type of skepticism in the following manner: "His particularity originates in his skeptical questioning of traditional wisdom theories, especially that of the relationship between act and consequence and the possibility that

---

[81] There is no explicit reference to God's commandments in Proverbs, although several references assume that sapiential instruction is derived from divine authority on analogy with the commandments of Torah. See the discussion in Wilson, "Words of the Wise," 183–90. The epilogue of 12:13–14 seems to presuppose an identification of wisdom with God's commandments in a fashion similar to Sir 1:1–30; 2:16–17; 19:20; 24:1–34; and Wisd 6:17–20.

[82] See the references in note 60 above and also F. Crüsemann, "Die unveränderbare Welt. Überlegungen zur 'Krisis der Weisheit' beim Prediger (Kohelet)," *Der Gott der kleinen Leute. Sozialgeschichtliche Bibelauslegungen* (ed. W. Schottroff, W. Stegemann; Munich: Kaiser, 1979), 80–104.

insight into this relationship could guarantee a *yitrôn* [profit]."[83] This is essentially correct, but not quite the way to formulate Koheleth's skepticism, since what is at stake is not a question about divine activity as such[84] but the possibility of ascertaining knowledge about divine activity and purpose through events which transpire under the sun.

The most promising places to ascertain Ecclesiastes' brand of epistomological skepticism come in the poem on appropriate times (3:1–8) and in the reflections offered on it in 3:9–15. Unfortunately, the translation of the crucial verse 11 remains disputed.[85] The section begins with the affirmation that "for everything there is a season, and [also] a time for every purpose under heaven" (3:1). Such an affirmation is typical of the wisdom movement with its emphasis on the proper time for things[86] and its desire to assist the wise in recognizing a propitious opportunity. Thus, as the catalogue of opposites in 3:2–8 affirms, there is a time to give birth and a time to die, etc. But what profit (*yitrôn*) does one have through human labor in light of this affirmation of proper timing (3:9)?[87] The reply to this received wisdom begins not with the quotation of an alternative tradition but with a personal observation that God has given humans an activity or business (*'inyān*) to be occupied with:

> Everything (*hakkōl*)[88] God has made suitable (*yāpeh*)[89] in its time, also God has placed eternity (*hā'ōlām*)[90] in the human heart, except that humankind cannot find out what God has done from beginning to end (3:11).

---

[83] Michel, *Untersuchungen*, 27.

[84] Ecclesiastes contains quite a number of references to things God has done, even if the author represents them as bewildering; see references and discussion in H. P. Müller, "Wie Sprach Qohälät von Gott?," *VT* 18 (1968): 238–64; L. Gorssen, "La cohérence de la conception de Dieu dans l'Ecclésiaste," *ETL* 46 (1970): 282–324; W. Zimmerli, " 'Unveränderbare Welt' oder 'Gott ist Gott'?" *"Wenn nicht jetzt, wann dann?" Aufsätze für Hans Joachim Kraus zum 65. Geburtstag* (ed. H. Geyer; Neukirchen Vluyn: Neukirchener Verlag, 1983), 103–114.

[85] See J. L. Crenshaw, "The Eternal Gospel (Eccl. 3:11)," *Essays in Old Testament Ethics* (ed. J. L. Crenshaw, J. T. Willis; New York: KTAV, 1972), 23–55.

[86] See, for example, the discussion by von Rad, *Wisdom in Israel*, 138–43, on the doctrine of the proper time.

[87] This question is essentially a reiteration of 1:3, which with the initial statement in 1:2 ("vanity of vanities . . . everything is vanity"), provides the theme of the disillusioned Solomon in the book.

[88] The same term is used in 3:1 in the affirmation that "to everything there is a season" and in the pessimistic claim in 1:2 and elsewhere that "everything is vanity."

[89] The term typically means "attractive," but in the context of discussing the proper time, "suitable" or "appropriate" seems better; see Michel, *Untersuchungen*, 60; Fox, *Qoheleth*, 191.

[90] The term has received considerable attention. See the collection of possibilities by C. F. Whitley, *Koheleth. His Language and Thought* (BZAW; Berlin: de Gruyter, 1979), 31–32. H. P. Müller, "Theonome Skepsis und Lebensfreude—Zu Koh 1,12—3,15," *BZ* 30 (1986): 14–15, argues compellingly that the context requires a term related to the passing of time.

The verse outlines the fundamental problem for Ecclesiastes.[91] On the one hand, there is an affirmation of God's role in bringing the world into existence and in providing a suitable setting for the human species. Probably the author is creatively reinterpreting elements in the Genesis creation accounts,[92] though we should not see them as the only reference behind 3:11a. "Everything that God has made" refers not just to the world created in the past but to the "appropriate place" of particular events as set forth in the previous poem. Yet on the other hand, even if one affirms the reality of divine activity, one is unable to fathom the "why" of God's work or its place in any causal relationship between act and result. This crux is stated clearly in the first-person observation of 8:17: "I saw all the work of God,[93] [and] that no one is able to find out the work which is done under the sun . . . even if a sage says he knows, he cannot find [it] out."

The skeptic Ecclesiastes does not say how he knows that God's rule[94] contains the key to appropriate times, since the point of his protests is that much of what he observes does not occur at appropriate times or end with the results expected from the tradition of proverbial wisdom. Apparently, however, even the skeptic takes certain things on faith. Like Job, Ecclesiastes considers the God of creation and providence to be a given, but unlike Job, there is no theophany to underscore the importance of the divine-human relationship. Whereas Job finally gains his audience with God (Yahweh) only to be overwhelmed, Koheleth cautions circumspection in prayer because God is in heaven and the one who prays is on earth (Eccl 5:2). The gulf between heaven and earth is absolute and cannot be bridged satisfactorily from the human side. And

---

[91] So argued by M. Schubert, *Schöpfungtheologie bei Kohelet* (BEATAJ 15; Frankfurt: P. Lang, 1989), 125–62. He describes it as the conflict or dialectic between knowledge derived from observation and experience (*Erkenntnis*) and the affirmation of the God of creation based on confession (*Bekenntnis*).

[92] See C. Forman, "Koheleth's Use of Genesis," *JSS* 3 (1958): 336–43; H. W. Hertzberg, *Der Prediger* (KAT 17/4; Gütersloh: Gerd Mohn, 1963), 227–31.

[93] Gorssen, "La cohérence de la conception de Dieu," proposes that the work of God is the central theme of the book. The theme is also the key to the crisis faced in the book: "This [work of God] is precisely the work that the human cannot comprehend" (p. 314). Gorssen's fine study is hampered by his rendering of *hā'ōlām* in 3:11, which he translates as "ignorance," based on the meaning of "darkness/hidden" for the root *'lm*. See Eccl 12:14; Job 28:21; 42:3, and the similar rendering of *hā'ōlām* in 3:11 by J. Crenshaw, *Ecclesiastes* (OTL; Philadephia: Westminster Press, 1987), 97–98. Crenshaw translates the term as "the unknown." It is not a God-given ignorance which causes a problem in recognizing divine activity, but the God-given sense (expectation?) of the purposeful intent behind the course of time which seems contradicted by the inappropriateness or senselessness of many events.

[94] It is perhaps important to note that the book never uses the divine name Yahweh, but alway the generic term *'elōhîm* for deity.

with the failure of the best of proverbial wisdom to interpret the world adequately, Koheleth is adrift without a satisfactory revelatory source. Thus the inequities of providence give rise to a searching skepticism that assumes divine activity but also affirms the essential opaqueness of the world.

Just as Job exemplified the extreme case of virtue and undeserved suffering, Solomon reflected the extreme case of great wisdom and precious few assured results. Human observation, even if informed by the best of the wisdom movement, and even if given an exalted place in the life of a wealthy monarch, is unable to make coherent sense of the human condition. The scriptural traditions in the employ of the writer—the various creation accounts[95] and the accounts of the great wisdom (and failure) of Solomon—support this conclusion. For example, in line with the Gen 1–3 accounts, Koheleth affirms the "rightness" of the human species as well as its failures (7:29): "one thing I have found; God made the human species (hā'ādām) upright (yāšār), but they have pursued many 'alternatives'[96] (ḥiššəbōnôt)." The theme of human culpability is also found in the claim of 7:20 that "there is no righteous (ṣaddîq) man in the land who does good and does not sin (ḥṭ')." This statement probably reflects more than a creative reading of Gen 1–3; it also approximates a saying of Solomon in his prayer of dedication for the temple in 1 Kings 8:46: "there is no man who does not sin (ḥṭ')." Solomon, therefore, in his guise as Koheleth, is an illustration of his own claim of a universal human failing.

While it is clear enough that the book opposes the claims of an over-optimistic use of wisdom, obtaining a better understanding of the polemical nature of the book requires additional knowledge of those whom the writer opposed. Unfortunately Koheleth does not have "friends" like Job who represent a position argued against. One line of approach to the book attempts to isolate quotations or sayings to which Koheleth responds, but there is no consensus concerning the number of quotations or whether the author responds to them in a consistent manner.[97] Perhaps the best single reference comes in the claim of 8:17 that even a sage (ḥākām) cannot find out the work of God. If the wise man in 8:17 represents Koheleth's opponents, they are to be identified with sages who

---

[95] In addition to note 92 above, see the study by M. Schubert, *Schöpfungstheologie bei Kohelet*, who deals with more than just the Genesis accounts. His work has many important observations, but he downplays the creative reinterpretation of OT accounts in Ecclesiastes in preference for a more philosophical approach to the writer's work.

[96] The term has to do with the formulation of plans and methods of activity. In context the term means that while God made the human species to be upright, they have formulated other modes of activity and pursued them.

[97] See, for example, the discussion by R. Whybray, "The identification and use of quotations in Ecclesiastes," *VT Sup* 32 (1980): 435–51.

claim to know the work of God[98] in a manner which the author denies is possible given his own extended observations about the limitations of human knowledge.

The dispute over divinely given or determined times in Ecclesiastes suggests more than just an inter-sapiential debate. Koheleth also speaks about the search for the knowledge of divine activity from beginning to end (3:11), which may locate some of his opponents in circles representing forms of apocalyptic eschatology. If correct, this does not require full acceptance of von Rad's proposal that apocalyptic speculations arose from within the wisdom movement,[99] but indicates only that sapiential speculation and eschatological theories may be linked in the circles against whom Koheleth polemicized.[100] We know far too little about the make-up of specific parties or socio-cultural movements in the post-exilic period to be dogmatic concerning the broader dimensions of apocalyptically oriented groups (pp. 228–40).

Solomon, i.e., Koheleth, may have been adrift without an adequate revelatory source, but the author of the book was not without such sources. In his old age, the pensive and morally suspect Solomon could point out the problems with human existence before God; however, the author proposed two antidotes for the truly wise who had more to do than debunk the optimism and speculations of other sages or sink into despair over the opaqueness of the world. They are the concluding verses of the book:

> one should fear God and keep his commandments, for this applies to everyone (12:13). The future belongs to God who will bring into judgment every human work, even "everything hidden"[101] (12:14).

In the context of the book as a whole, these concluding comments do more than "correct" the skepticism of Solomon. Indeed, it is doubtful whether that is even an adequate description of their purpose, since the author shared some of the skepticism or disorientation Solomon repre-

---

[98] As noted previously, for several reasons it is very likely that Koheleth's opponents represent developments within the wisdom movement.

[99] Von Rad, *Wisdom in Israel*, 263–83.

[100] See the brief but illuminating comments in Michel, *Untersuchungen*, 126–37, who suggests that Eccl 7:1–10 may oppose the spirit of an apocalyptic pessimism. At least this much can be said: Koheleth knows and essentially accepts the view of the divine determination of times which was important to the conceptual schemes of apocalyptic. He denies, however, that even the sage can know definitively about the intention of God's work. Furthermore, his emphasis on the sameness of human experience in the world (1:4–11) effectively denies any "signs of the times" to the expectant apocalyptic sage.

[101] The Hebrew phrase '*al kol ne'lām*, which modifies human work, also reflects an understanding of the secret nature of divine work. What human observation may not see or comprehend is still known and assessed by God.

sents. The author used Solomon precisely because the failure of the great sage afforded him the literary medium to affirm the limitations of human wisdom in the face of life's inequities. Given the limitations of human wisdom and the seeming inscrutability of divine purpose, one must respond with a posture that moves beyond a strictly rational comprehension. One should hold fast to traditional claims of piety (fear) and ethics (commandments) even when the results of such activity do not make sense. Thus the author opts to place the final assessment of human activity in a future divine judgment.[102] In the meantime, however, he uses Solomon to voice his own perception of disorientation, while urging piety and obedience in the place of understanding.

Conclusions

Although the influence of the wisdom movement on the OT is greater than contents of the three books of Proverbs, Job, and Ecclesiastes, these three furnish the basis for an examination of the distinctive emphases of the movement's approach to culture. The three works reflect in varying degrees the international character of the wisdom movement and its empirical approach to human existence. Furthermore, in varying degrees they demonstrate profound wrestling with the place of wisdom in the development of Yahwistic theology and Israelite culture.

Each of the three works presupposes the importance of human observation and experience in the wisdom movement. Even in the book of Job, where the empirical element in human experience comes under critique, it is still presupposed as integral to the search for wisdom. Observation and experience, in turn, indicate two key elements in the wisdom movement's approach to culture. One is the emphasis on the observant individual who seeks to understand discrete data, a particular experience, or a set of events. The other concerns the collected observations of previous generations (e.g., the "two-way doctrine") which grant insights and warrants for discerning sages. Thus proverbial wisdom addresses the child or student in the book of Proverbs, Job's friends cite the wisdom they inherited, and Koheleth offers his individual reflections in light of certain expectations of what should be or will be profitable for an individual. In each case there is a tension between the variety of experience and the more stable norms of tradition, a tension which becomes acute in Job and Ecclesiastes.

---

[102]If it is correct that the author is in dialogue with sages who speculate about the future and claim insight into divine activity, the concluding verses presuppose an agreement that God's judgment lies ahead but perhaps a disagreement over the proper model of piety in the interim. One must hold to the commandments, whether or not God rewards such a response, or perhaps whether or not the purpose (value?) of the commandments is even understood.

Because of the accent on observation and experience, the wisdom movement was potentially the most open of all the literary traditions in the OT to a variety of influences. And this trait made the wisdom movement most open to insight from its cultural settings—wherever the movement took root. More specifically, two theological characteristics of the OT wisdom traditions shape their approach to culture. One is an affirmation of a theology of creation broadly understood. Human community in its larger environment is a manifestation of a creator, so that insight into the workings of any human community or natural environment provides instruction for the life of the wise. Secondly, the "fear of Yahweh/God" also anchors the wisdom movement in a particular theology. For both Proverbs and Job, Yahweh is the creator whose works deserve the response of awe and piety on the part of the wise. The value of wisdom lies in its ability to guide a sage in responding appropriately. Even if Yahweh's activity as creator or moral agent seems hidden to the sage, there is no suggestion that Yahweh is ultimately remote from either the human community or the world. Paradoxically, Yahweh is never mentioned in Ecclesiastes, though the the fear of God (*'elōhîm*) is noted several times. Since Ecclesiastes is post-exilic, the more generic term *'elōhîm* probably reflects nothing more than an attempt to maintain the universal implications of the author's reflections.[103] The affirmation of the fear of Yahweh/God sets the approach of wisdom in dialogue with other Yahwistic traditions and offers limits on the anthropological emphasis of wisdom. Nevertheless, observation and experience remained integral facets of the wisdom movement and primary reasons for an accommodating relationship between the wisdom movement and Israelite culture.

---

[103] The same attempt accounts for the general term "commandments" (*miṣwôt*) in 12:13 rather than the more specific term *tôrāh*.

RELIGION AGAINST CULTURAL IMPERIALISM: THE RISE OF APOCALYPTICISM AND THE BOOK OF DANIEL   **7**

INTRODUCTION

What is termed apocalypticism or apocalyptic thinking did not reach a mature stage in the Mediterranean world until the Hellenistic age and later,[1] although it has antecedents which reached back considerably earlier in the ancient world. Apocalypticism can be characterized in general terms as a world view (a "symbolic universe" to use a phrase proposed by P. Hanson)[2] with emphases on the cosmic scope of evil, the radical distinction between good and evil in the present age, the revelation of divine mysteries to the elect, and the hope for the imminent end to evil and the dawn of a new age of salvation. In defining apocalypticism more specifically, one must take care to distinguish between the literary analysis of documents which preserve such characteristics and the historical investigation of diverse communities with apocalyptic and eschatological world views.[3]

---

[1] See the important collection of papers in *Apocalypticism in the Mediterranean World and the Near East* (ed. D. Hellholm; Tübingen: J. C. B. Mohr [Siebeck], 1983).

[2] P. Hanson, "Apocalyptic Literature," in Knight and Tucker, eds., *The Hebrew Bible and its Modern Interpreters*, 465–88.

[3] For surveys of the discussion see J. M. Schmidt, *Die jüdische Apokalyptik. Die Geschichte ihrer Erforschung von den Anfängen bis zu den Textfunden von Qumran* (2d edition; Neukirchen-Vluyn; Neukirchener Verlag, 1972); J. J. Collins, "The Place of Apocalypticism in the Religion of Israel," in Miller, et al., eds., *Ancient Israelite Religion*, 539–58; P. R. Davies, "The Social World of the Apocalyptic Writings," in Clements, ed., *The World of Ancient Israel*, 251–71.

Literary analysis, in particular, has concentrated on defining the genre apocalypse (below), a prominent form of literature which gives expression to apocalypticism. The only apocalypse in the OT is the book of Daniel,[4] although there are literary antecedents related to apocalypticism in the OT beginning with the period of the Babylonian exile. Ezekiel, major sections of the Isaiah scroll (Isa 24–27, 40–66), and Zechariah, along with certain priestly and wisdom traditions, preserve these "proto-apocalyptic" elements. The book of Daniel itself quite likely incorporates a number of traditions from earlier centuries, but it reaches its final form no earlier than the crisis in Judah under Antiochus IV (ca. 168–64 B.C.E.), which included the persecution of Jews who maintained a strict adherence to the Torah in the face of pressures to do otherwise (see pp. 114–22). Daniel is more specifically described as a historical apocalypse because of its prominent use of historiography and because it does not preserve a journey into another world to receive revelation for its major character.

An apocalypse can be defined essentially as follows:[5]

> a genre of revelatory literature with a narrative framework, in which a revelation is mediated by an otherworldly being to a human recipient, disclosing a transcendent reality which is both temporal, insofar as it envisages eschatological salvation, and spatial insofar as it involves another, supernatural world.

The definition combines the essentials of form and content necessary for literary analysis. Furthermore, it leaves open the issues of setting and intention for the interpretation of a particular apocalypse, and it allows for the incorporation of other literary forms (e.g., vision reports, midrash) within the broader genre. The book of Daniel, for example, contains a narrative framework, accounts of revelation through dream reports and angelic mediation, a midrash on earlier prophecy, and references to the (eschatological) hope of the advent of God's kingdom and the resurrection from the dead. It should be noted, however, that the employment of the terms "eschatological salvation" and "another, su-

---

[4] A survey of the history of research on the book of Daniel is given in K. Koch et al., *Das Buch Daniel*. See also J. J. Collins, *Daniel, With an Introduction to Apocalyptic Literature* (FOTL 20; Grand Rapids: Eerdmans, 1984); A. LaCocque, *Daniel in His Time* (Columbia: Univ. of South Carolina Press, 1988).

[5] The definition is the result of a scholarly work group on defining an apocalypse. See the papers collected in *Apocalypse: The Morphology of a Genre* (Semeia 14; ed. J. Collins; Missoula: Scholars Press, 1979). The quotation is on p. 9. There is further discussion of the issues in defining an apocalypse in Collins, *Daniel, With an Introduction to Apocalyptic Literature*, 2–24. A similar and somewhat shorter definition is given by Davies, "Social World," in Clements, ed., *The World of Ancient Israel*, 254.

pernatural world" do more than give shape to form and content; they also indicate some of the concerns which motivated communities to preserve and study apocalypses.

As a relatively late development in Israel's history, apocalypticism is heir to a number of rich literary and theological traditions. One should not take this fact alone as an adequate definition of what apocalypticism is or as an explanation of why it is noteworthy. Apocalypticism is more than an amalgam of earlier literary and cultural traditions. The earlier traditions upon which apocalypticism depends, however, do provide avenues of approach in the search to comprehend its general function, and they especially inform the understanding of what Daniel represents about the practice of religion in the context of oppression.

THE DEVELOPMENT OF APOCALYPTICISM IN ISRAEL[6]

The Contribution of Prophecy

As a result of Judah's defeat and the subsequent Babylonian exile, prophetic voices among the people took on new tones and perspectives. The major prophetic books of Isaiah, Jeremiah, and Ezekiel were all edited in the exilic and early post-exilic periods, and each book offered a theological rationale for the failure of Judah (and also of Israel at an earlier date). The very fact that these books were edited, studied, and distributed is the best evidence that they intended to do more than account for failure and tragedy; they also intended to instruct readers about Yahweh's continuing activity in the aftermath of defeat and exile. Thus each book pointed to Yahweh's restorative activity and future blessing for the dispersed people (see pp. 195–98). Furthermore, each book shares the expectation that Yahweh would decisively judge and deliver Israel in the future. This common expectation was already a type of eschatology which would receive amplification and cosmic overtones

---

[6] P. von der Osten-Sacken, *Die Apokalyptik in ihrem Verhältnis zu Prophetie und Weisheit* (Munich: Chr. Kaiser, 1969); J. Z. Smith, "Wisdom and Apocalyptic," *Religious Syncretism in Late Antiquity* (ed. B. Pearson; Missoula: Scholars Press, 1975), 131–56; W. G. Lambert, *The Background of Jewish Apocalyptic* (London: Athlone Press, 1978); P. Hanson, *The Dawn of Apocalyptic* (Philadelphia: Fortress Press, 1979); O. H. Steck, "Weltgeschehen und Gottesvolk im Buche Daniel," *Kirche* (ed. D. Lührmann, G. Strecker; Tübingen: J. C. B. Mohr, 1980), 53–78; R. R. Wilson, "From Prophecy to Apocalyptic: Reflections on the Shape of Israelite Religion," *Anthropological Perspectives on Old Testament Prophecy* (Semeia 21; ed. R. Culley, T. Overholt; Chico: Scholars Press, 1982), 79–95; J. VanderKam, "The Prophetic-Sapiential Origins of Apocalyptic Thought," *A Word in Season. Essays in Honour of William McKane* (ed. J. D. Martin and P. R. Davies; JSOTSS 42; Sheffield, 1986), 163–76.

in the post-exilic period.[7] Post-exilic prophets such as Haggai, Zechariah, Joel, and Malachi would add their voices to the rising expectation that Yahweh would act decisively in the historical process on behalf of Israel and the nations. Pre-exilic prophecy had been tied closely to the monarchy, so that the loss of kingship and the profound effects of the exile led to radical shifts in the role and message of prophecy.[8]

A major addition to the Isaiah scroll made one form of this changed perspective clear with a stirring call to comfort the exiles in Babylon and with a proclamation of Yahweh's saving activity in returning the exiles to the promised land (Isa 40–55).[9] "Second" Isaiah was a prophet of the exilic community in Babylon who functioned as an outsider in two different ways. First, as an observer of the dominant Babylonian culture, he had sharp and sarcastic comments about the superstition and burden of the native cults (Isa 44:1–20; 46:1–7). Second, among the exilic community itself, he proposed that Yahweh was on the verge of new saving activity that would surprise and humble them (Isa 43:18–28; 45:20–25). The prophet's disputation speech and other forms of public address presuppose a keen observer at work.

When the prophet called his audience to "forget the former things" (Isa 43:18), he did not have in mind the long-held belief that Israel was the people of God. On the contrary, the prophet believed that Yahweh's promises toward Israel were sure and that the manifestation of his saving purpose in the historical arena would henceforth include a more positive role for Israel among the nations.[10] Their election and the future promise of their elevation in world standing were still valid. Indeed, belief in these things undergirded the prophet's call to the exilic community to prepare for Yahweh's new acts of salvation. The prophetic word to Israel was nothing less than the call to move from being a minority community in the dominant Babylonian culture to being Yahweh's servant in bringing salvation to the ends of the earth (see pp. 100–103, 159–60).

---

[7] See B. Vawter, "Apocalyptic: Its Relation to Prophecy," *CBQ* 22 (1960): 33–46; K. D. Schunck, "Die Eschatologie der Propheten des Alten Testaments und ihre Wandlung in exilisch-nachexilischer Zeit," *VT Sup* 26 (1974): 116–32. For a succinct and helpful discussion of future expectation in the OT see D. Gowan, *Eschatology in the Old Testament* (Philadelphia: Fortress Press, 1986).

[8] It is misleading to conclude as some scholars have done that prophecy comes to end with the demise of monarchy. See the helpful discussion in D. Petersen, "Rethinking the End of Prophecy," *Wünschet Jerusalem Frieden* (ed. M. Augustin, K. D. Schunck; Frankfurt: P. Lang, 1988), 37–64.

[9] B. W. Anderson, "Exodus Typology in Second Isaiah," *Israel's Prophetic Heritage: Essays in Honor of James Muilenburg* (ed. B. W. Anderson, W. Harrelson; New York: Harper and Row, 1962), 177–95.

[10] D. Van Winkle, "The Relationship of the Nations to Yahweh and to Israel in Isaiah xl-lv," *VT* 35 (1985): 446–58.

The prophets of the early Persian period, Haggai and Zechariah, concerned themselves primarily with the rebuilding of the temple in a community without a king and with the rekindling of expectation that Yahweh's decisive activity in the future was not far off (see p. 160). The first chapter of Zechariah (1:3–6) explicitly refers to the former prophets in the conviction that their preaching of judgment had reached its goal in the historical judgment of the exile. The prophetic words of the pre-exilic era were a prelude to a new era about to dawn. Both Haggai and Zechariah, therefore, represented a new emphasis on the future for the community that began to rebuild Jerusalem and the temple at the end of the sixth century. They wanted to encourage the faithful to build more than homes, a city, and a temple. In rebuilding the city and temple, the community must build in anticipation of Yahweh's coming acts of salvation and prepare themselves accordingly. Haggai placed great emphasis on the rebuilding of the temple in Jerusalem as preliminary activity to the day when Yahweh would shake the heavens and the earth and the glory of the second temple would exceed that of the first (Hag 2:6–9). Zechariah too represented the temple as a key to the community's identity.[11] The temple represented Yahweh's presence among the people, and its rebuilding symbolized the new age to come, a tangible sign to the faithful that even greater things would follow.

Both Haggai and Zechariah portrayed Zerubbabel, a descendant of Jehoiachin and heir to the throne of David, as evidence that Yahweh had the restored fortunes of the people in mind (Hag 2:20–23; Zech 4:1–14). Zerubbabel was the governor (*pahat*; Hag 2:21) appointed by the Persians in early post-exilic Jerusalem who also represented the Davidic hope for many in the community. Of course, there were also members of the Jewish community of the period who placed no political confidence in Zerubbabel,[12] but the combination of temple rebuilding and the presence of a Davidic heir fueled the fires of rising expectations among some Jewish circles. The abrupt disappearance of Zerubbabel doubtlessly dashed the hopes of some in the community, but his presence during the early post-exilic period helped both re-establish lines of continuity with the pre-exilic past and provide a symbol of restoration.

Visionary reports figure prominently in Zechariah, the largest book among the post-exilic prophets and a strategic link between classical prophecy and apocalypticism.[13] The book begins with a series of vision

---

[11] H. G. Schöttler, *Gott inmitten seines Volkes. Die Neuordnung des Gottesvolkes nach Sacharja 1–6* (TTS 43; Trier: Paulinus Verlag, 1987).

[12] On the different views of Zerubbabel see S. Japhet, "Sheshbazzar and Zerubbabel, Against the Background of the Historical and Religious Tendencies of Ezra-Nehemiah," *ZAW* 95 (1983): 218–29.

[13] R. North, "Prophecy to Apocalyptic via Zechariah," *VT Sup* 22 (1972): 47–71; S. Amsler, "Zacharie et l'origine de l'apocalyptique," *VT Sup* 22 (1972):

reports mediated to the prophet by an angel (1:7–6:15).[14] Vision reports themselves are not new to the prophetic movement (cf. Amos 7:1–9; 8:1–2), but their complex symbolism and frequency in Zechariah demonstrate their import for prophetic activity in the post-exilic period.[15] The concluding chapters of Ezekiel (40–48), for example, describe a future temple in the form of vision reports (Ezek 40:2)[16] containing complex and extended symbolism (see pp. 185, 193–94). Zechariah also emphasizes the future role of the temple in Jerusalem (cf. 8:20–23); the book concludes with the prophecy that Jerusalem will be the religious center of a new world order (Zech 14:16–21).[17]

Another motif taken over in post-exilic prophecy is the announcement of the decisive day of Yahweh.[18] As he had with the vision reports, Amos already used the expectation of a decisive day of the Lord on the part of his audience as an opportunity to announce that such a day would be a day of judgment for Israel (Amos 5:18–20).[19] However, the post-exilic prophecies in Haggai, Zechariah, Isaiah (Isa 56–66; 24–27),[20]

227–31; H. Gese, "Anfang und Ende der Apokalyptik dargestellt am Sacharjabuch," *ZTK* (1973): 20–49.

[14] C. Jeremias, *Die Nachtgesichte des Sacharja. Untersuchungen zu ihrer Stellung im Zusammenhang der Visionsberichte im Alten Testament und zu ihrem Bildmaterial* (FRLANT 117; Göttingen: Vandenhoeck & Ruprecht, 1977); D. Petersen, "Zechariah's Visions: A Theological Perspective," *VT* 34 (1984): 195–206.

[15] S. Niditch, *The Symbolic Vision in Biblical Tradition* (HSM 30; Chico: Scholars Press, 1983).

[16] Isa 1:1; Hab 1:1; Obad 1:1 and Nah 1:1 describe the prophetic contents of their respective books as a vision (ḥazôn). In the case of Isaiah, the description covers the editorial work of centuries. On the development from prophetic vision reports to vision reports in apocalypses, see K. Koch, "Vom profetischen zum apokalyptischen Visionbericht," in Hellholm, ed., *Apocalypticism in the Mediterranean World and the Near East*, 413–46.

[17] Chapters 9–14 of Zechariah are likely from the later period of Persian rule (or possibly from the early Hellenistic period). See R. A. Mason, "The Relation of Zachariah 9–14 to Proto-Zachariah," *ZAW* 88 (1976): 227–39.

[18] Y. Hoffmann, "The Day of the Lord as a Concept and a Term in the Prophetic Literature," *ZAW* 93 (1981): 37–50.

[19] The future hope expressed at the end of Amos refers to a decisive "in that day" (9:11) and to "days that are coming" (9:13f.). The latter reference concludes the book and is probably a post-exilic addition. Perhaps the reference in 9:11f is post-exilic as well. The short prophecy of Zephaniah is formulated on the expectation of the "day of Yahweh," a day that brings both judgment on and future deliverance of Judah. The book originates in the late pre-exilic period and already reflects elements of the increasing eschatological sense and more cosmic orientation given to the concept of the "day" of Yahweh in the post-exilic period.

[20] Some scholars have called Isa 24–27 the Isaianic apocalypse and date it to the Hellenistic period. It is more likely that 24–27 is late sixth or fifth century and should be called proto-apocalyptic. See the full discussion of date and intention in D. Johnson, *From Chaos to Restoration. An Integrative Reading of Isaiah 24–27* (JSOTSS 61; Sheffield: JSOT Press, 1988).

Joel, Obadiah, and Malachi are replete with examples of prophecies that refer to a decisive "day" of Yahweh's future activity.[21] In the cases of Joel, Obadiah, and Malachi, the expectation of a decisive "day" of Yahweh—when the fortunes of Israel will be dramatically and qualitatively reversed—dominates their respective depictions of the future.

Developing eschatological expectations in the post-exilic period became fertile ground for the use of visionary reports and announcements concerning Yahweh's future intentions. These expectations were one product of the culture shock of the diaspora and the minority status of Jews in the Persian Empire. There was no uniformity in the eschatological expectations; instead, dominant symbols from the pre-exilic period such as the Davidic monarch, Jerusalem, the temple, the Mosaic covenant, Elijah the prophet, even the heavens and earth of the old cosmic order, were transformed by the prophetic word into future symbols which would manifest the coming salvation of Yahweh. The eventual production of apocalypses owed much to the combination of eschatological expectation and visionary symbolism found in post-exilic prophecy.

Several scholars have drawn suggestive conclusions about the social setting of proto-apocalyptic and prophetic communities in the post-exilic period as they related to Judaism as a whole.[22] The developing dualism between this age and the new order to come, and references to inner-Jewish conflicts, suggested to Plöger and Hanson in particular that a fundamental split developed in the post-exilic period between prophetic-eschatological circles and those more oriented to a theocratic priestly administration. According to them, the more pragmatic priestly groups dealt with the pressure of minority status in the diaspora by emphasizing the temple cult and the torah regulations that helped maintain a separate Jewish identity (see pp. 102–10). These pragmatists periodically ostracized or oppressed the prophetic-eschatological circles, which accentuated the latter's otherworldly, countercultural orientation. And finally, the dispossessed prophetic circles were quite influential in the development from eschatologically oriented prophecy in the post-exilic period to the rise of the apocalypticism represented in the book of Daniel.

---

[21] See Hag 2:23; Zech 2:15; 3:10; 9:16; 12:3, 4, 6, 8, 9; 13:1–4; 14:1, 4, 6, 9, 13, 16, 20, 21; Isa 61:2; 62:11; 63:4; see also those things which are to come in 65:17–25; 24:21; 25:9; 26:1; 27:1, 12, 13; Joel 1:15; 2:1, 11, 31 (3:4H); 3:14 (4:14H); Obadiah 8, 15; Mal 3:2, 17; 4:1, 5 (Heb 3:19, 23).

[22] See the various reconstructions discussed by O. Plöger, *Theocracy and Eschatology* (Atlanta: John Knox, 1968); P. Hanson, *The Dawn of Apocalyptic*; M. E. Stone, *Scripture, Sects, Visions* (Philadelphia: Fortress Press, 1980); J. Blenkinsopp, "Interpretation and the Tendency to Sectarianism: An Aspect of Second Temple History," in Sanders, ed., *Jewish and Christian Self-Definition*, vol. 2, 1–26; and S. Talmon, "The Emergence of Jewish Sectarianism in the Early Second Temple Period," in Miller, et al., eds., *Ancient Israelite Religion*, 587–616.

Although the two scholars differ substantially on many details, their basic reconstruction of post-exilic "party conflict" has been influential in the investigation of apocalypticism.[23] Their proposals—that socially marginalized and oppressed communities gave rise to apocalypticism—do find some points of agreement in the general study of nineteenth- and twentieth-century millenarian and utopian communities.[24] And the link they propose between the apocalypticism of Daniel and post-exilic prophecy seems firm whatever additional factors require consideration. Nevertheless, considerable work remains to be done in investigating the social location of the particular communities responsible for post-exilic Jewish apocalypses.[25] It is unlikely, for example, that such clear-cut distinctions between prophetic and priestly groups in the post-exilic period can be made on the basis of the surviving literature; also there appears to be no simple connection between the prophetic-eschatological groups identified by Plöger and Hanson and the community responsible for the production of Daniel.[26]

The current scholarly trend, therefore, has moved away from an emphasis on apocalypticism as the eschatological child of prophecy to the consideration of other contributions to its emergence.[27] There are several reasons for this trend. First, there remains the difficulty in moving from relatively obscure prophetic oracles to the reconstruction of apocalyptically oriented communities; this becomes especially tenuous

---

[23] This is clear from the survey of research done by E. Nicholson, "Apocalyptic," *Tradition and Interpretation* (ed. G. W. Anderson; Oxford: Clarendon Press, 1979), 189–213. Hanson's own views have developed since the publication of *The Dawn of Apocalyptic*, as can be seen in two more recent articles, "Apocalyptic Literature," *The Hebrew Bible*, 465–488; and "Israelite Religion in the Early, Postexilic Period," in Miller, et al., eds., *Ancient Israelite Religion*, 485–508.

[24] For examples, see V. Lanternari, *The Religions of the Oppressed* (New York: New American Library, 1963); K. Burridge, *New Heaven, New Earth: A Study of Millenarian Activities* (Oxford: Blackwell, 1969); N. Cohn, *The Pursuit of the Millennium* (rev. ed.; New York: Oxford Press, 1970); W. La Barre, "Materials for a History of Studies of Crisis Cults: A Bibliographic Essay," *Current Anthropology* 12 (1971): 3–44; B. R. Wilson, *Magic and the Millennium. A Sociological Study of Religious Movements of Protest Among Tribal and Third-World Peoples*.

[25] For the period and setting in question, see also S. Isenberg, "Millenarianism in Greco-Roman Palestine," *Religion* 4 (1974): 26–46; G. Nicklesburg, "Social Aspects of Palestinian Jewish Apocalypticism," in Hellholm, ed., *Apocalypticism in the Mediterranean World and the Near East*, 641–54; S. B. Reid, *Enoch and Daniel. A Form Critical and Sociological Study of Historical Apocalypses* (BMS 2; Berkeley: BIBAL Press, 1989).

[26] In particular see the essay by Blenkinsopp, "Interpretation and the Tendency to Sectarianism" in Sanders, ed., *Self Definition*, and the two surveys by Collins and Davies referred to in the following note.

[27] This trend is clear from the surveys by Collins, "The Place of Apocalypticism" in Miller, et al., eds., *Ancient Israelite Religion*; and Davies, "The Social World," in Clements, ed., *The World of Ancient Israel*.

when the differences between texts and communities have been blurred
by designating both as (proto) apocalyptic. Even though apocalypticism
owes much to prophecy, there are significant differences in form and
content between a prophetic book such as Ezekiel or Haggai and a
pseudonymous, historical apocalypse like Daniel, not to mention the
communities which produced and preserved them. Second, there is a
distinct difficulty in defining the apocalypticism of Daniel by reference to
literary traditions and cultural movements that originate before the
advent of Hellenism. This is generally admitted by scholars who, nevertheless, have pushed the search for the origins of apocalypticism back
centuries from the advent of Hellenism in the ANE. Understanding the
impact of Hellenism upon Judaism is indispensable for interpreting the
book of Daniel in its cultural context. To take one example: Persian
dualistic philosophy may have influenced incipient Jewish apocalypticism, but the dualism represented in Daniel probably owes more to
Hellenistic influence on Jewish thinking. Finally, there are several contributions to apocalypticism (e.g., priestly/scribal divination; forms of
Hellenistic/Babylonian science; mantic wisdom) that are as crucial for its
understanding as that of prophetic eschatology.

The Contribution of Wisdom

G. von Rad proposed that the apocalyptic stress on the divine
determination of times was an out-growth of the wisdom movements in
the post-exilic period.[28] He suggested that both Ecclesiastes and the
Wisdom of Jesus son of Sirach contained assumptions about the determination of history that compared closely to the emphasis on divine
sovereignty in Daniel. He noted that in the pseudonymous book of
Ecclesiastes one finds the affirmation of "Solomon" that God has determined the times and seasons (Eccl 3:1–8), as well as a pessimism
concerning the human condition and the affairs of the current age (see
pp. 219–26). The book polemicizes against the view that human insight
has definitive access to divine mysteries (Eccl 6:10). The epilogue (12:14)
affirms that whatever is hidden God will eventually bring to light and
judge; it is a statement of faith that waits for the divine gift of insight to
interpret future, divine activity. Similarly, Ben Sira records that a wise
scribe must penetrate the secrets in prophecy and other literature (39:1–11)
because the creator has built a purpose into all things which cannot be
undone (42:15–25). The wise among the apocalyptic circles, then, offer
pseudonymously in the book of Daniel what "Solomon" himself lacked

---

[28] *Theologie des Alten Testaments* (vol. 2; 4th ed.; Munich: Chr. Kaiser, 1965),
316–38 [this section is expanded from the treatment given in the earlier edition
used for the English translation]; *Wisdom in Israel*, 263–83.

and what Ben Sira hinted at—a revelation informing them of God's timing and the advent of judgment/deliverance.

One can argue in response to von Rad that neither Ecclesiastes nor Sirach—perhaps the wisdom documents closest to Daniel in time of composition—possess the eschatological sense so pronounced in Daniel.[29] Also, the terminology for the sages in Daniel differs somewhat from that used in Proverbs or Ecclesiastes. Daniel and his friends are described as insightful (*maśkîlîm*),[30] but the sages of the gentile courts are described in different terminology (see discussion below). And finally, an apocalypse like Daniel is form-critically quite different from either Ecclesiastes or Ben Sira. It must be admitted, therefore, that von Rad's proposal for the origins of apocalypticism is not completely satisfactory. On the other hand, his essential point about the connection between wisdom and apocalypticism regarding the divine determination of the times is still valid and remains an indication of a common intellectual matrix for the two cultural movements.

Esoteric and Mantic Wisdom

With the discovery and analysis of fragments of the book of 1 Enoch from the Qumran documents, there emerged a new basis for the development of apocalypticism in the post-exilic period.[31] Enoch had long been acknowledged as an apocalyptic work, and Milik demonstrated that some of these Aramaic texts of 1 Enoch (4Q Enastr; 4QEn) are most plausibly dated to the end of the third century and the first half of the second centuries B.C.E. Thus portions of Enoch (The Watchers, chapters 1–36; The Astronomical Book, chapters 72–82) are likely older than the final form of the book of Daniel—at least according to the consensus of critical scholarship.[32] Apparently the figure of Enoch became prominent in Jewish circles interested in apocalyticism, particularly among those interested in eschatology, astronomical lore, and others forms of esoteric

---

[29] See the volume by von der Osten-Sacken, *Die Apokalyptik in ihrem Verhältnis zu Prophetie und Weisheit*. Other scholars such as Davies, "The Social World," in Clements, ed., *Ancient Israel*, 263–64; and J. D. Martin, "Ben Sira—A Child of His Time," in Martin and Davies, eds., *A Word in Season. Essays in Honour of William McKane*, 141–61, have proposed that Ben Sira does indeed have certain affinities with eschatological and scribal lore related to apocalypticism.

[30] Dan 1:4; cf. 11:33, 35; 12:3, 10. Proverbs does make several references to the wise or discerning one (*maśkîl*); cf. 10:5, 19; 14:35; 15:24; 16:20; 17:2; 21:12.

[31] J. T. Milik, *The Books of Enoch* (Oxford: Clarendon Press, 1976); and J. VanderKam, *Enoch and the Growth of an Apocalyptic Tradition* (CBQMS 16; Washington: Catholic Biblical Association, 1984).

[32] See also M. E. Stone, "The Book of Enoch and Judaism in the Third Century B.C.E.," *CBQ* 40 (1978): 479–92.

wisdom. A pseudonymous work attributed to him, therefore, began to take shape before the compiling of the book of Daniel.[33]

Other scholars proposed even before the publishing of the Enoch fragments that the kind of wisdom circles suggested by von Rad for the origins of apocalypticism did not represent the variety of wisdom movements in the Hellenistic period.[34] Müller linked apocalypticism with "mantic wisdom," a phrase which refers to those forms of divination (interpretation of entrails, omens, dreams, astronomy)[35] and priestly-scribal lore in the ANE. The figure of Joseph interpreting dreams in Egypt is one example of mantic wisdom, and the figure of Daniel is another. Müller noted that many biblical references to divination and mantic wisdom are set in foreign lands (e.g., Joseph, 2 Isaiah), and that Israelites had sustained contact with forms of mantic wisdom during the exilic and post-exilic periods. As a result of this contact, Jewish scribes and sages developed their own forms of manticism. Smith downplayed divination in his description of Babylonian scribal lore which is based in part on the writings of a scribal-priest of the Seleucid era named Berossus.[36] Smith's description of the Hellenistic-Babylonian scribal schools is quite revealing:[37]

> the major activities of a Babylonian intellectual were astronomy, astrology, mathmatics, historiography and the recovery of ancient lore . . . the scribes were an elite group of learned, literate men, an intellectual aristocracy which played an invaluable role in the administration of their people in both religious and political affairs . . . they projected their scribal activities on high, on a god who created by law according to a written plan, on a god who was a teacher in his heavenly court . . . they speculated about hidden, heavenly tablets, about creation by divine word, about the beginning and the end, and thereby claimed to possess the secrets of creation.

One cannot take over this statement about the Hellenistic-Babylonian scribes uncritically and apply all characteristics to Jewish scribes and

---

[33] J. Greenfield, M. E. Stone, "The Books of Enoch and the Traditions of Enoch," *Numen* 26 (1979): 89–103; VanderKam, *Enoch*.

[34] H. P. Müller, "Magisch-mantische Weisheit und die Gestalt Daniels," *UF* 1 (1969): 79–94; idem, "Mantische Weisheit und Apokalyptik," *VT Sup* 22 (1972): 268–93; J. Smith, "Wisdom and Apocalyptic," *Visionaries and Their Apocalypses* (IRT 2; ed. P. Hanson; Philadelphia: Fortress Press, 1983), 101–21 [first published in 1975]. Von Rad stated that the wisdom elements most crucial to apocalypticism were those concerned with the interpretation of dreams and the investigation of oracles and signs (*Theologie* [4th edition], vol. 2, p. 331), but he didn't make any sustained effort at locating these concerns among specific wisdom circles in Israel.

[35] On diviners and seers in the ANE see M. S. Moore, *The Balaam Traditions. Their Character and Development*, 20–65.

[36] S. Burstein, *The Babyloniaca of Berossus* (SANE 1/5; Malibu: Udena, 1978).

[37] Smith, "Wisdom and Apocalyptic," in Hanson, ed., *Visionaries and Their Apocalypses*, 103.

mantic sages in Babylon, Jerusalem, or Alexandria (Egypt), but the general tone is quite suggestive for the kinds of people who produced apocalypses like Enoch or Daniel. The intellectual concerns and professional duties for these people are somewhat different from the representatives of proverbial-court wisdom, even though both movements use sapiential terminology. There is some evidence, furthermore, to suggest that the Hellenistic-Jewish portraits of Enoch are intended as a polemical counterpart to the great Babylonian tradition of wise men and diviners from the past.[38] To a degree, the portrait of Daniel and his friends in Dan 1–6 has a similar and polemical function over against the wisdom represented in the Babylonian and Persian courts.[39] In the Wisdom of Ben Sira, which represents the learning and world view of one wise scribe in Jerusalem of the early second century B.C.E., are two references to Enoch in the famous list of praiseworthy men (Sir 44:16; 49:14).[40] The books attributed to Enoch and Daniel, then, probably reflect the standing of these figures in those sapiential-scribal circles influenced by manticism and eschatological speculation.[41]

Summary: The Roots of Apocalypticism

On the one hand, no one community or social movement produced the types of apocalyptic literature in Judaism of the pre-Christian era. There is simply too much variety among the texts to describe apocalypticism in any monolithic fashion. And one should treat cautiously any of the theories which identify apocalypticism with particular groups or institutions in the post-exilic period. On the other hand, it is likely that "prophecy" contributed an eschatological orientation and an emphasis on the interpretation of visions to the development of apocalypticism. "Wisdom" likely contributed an accent on the divine determination of times and seasons, an interest in astronomy and the cosmos, and the interpretive principles of mantic-scribal lore. But by the Hellenistic period, one should hesitate to draw firm distinctions between those circles interested in prophecy and those associated with sapiential-scribal concerns. Surely one scribal concern in the post-exilic period was the interpretation of prophecies from previous generations.

---

[38] See the thorough treatment in VanderKam, *Enoch.* It is possible that the priestly genealogy in Gen 5:21f. already portrays Enoch as the counterpart to Enmeduranki, the Akkadian founder of divination (*Enoch,* 23–51).

[39] On Daniel's "wisdom," see J. Collins, "The Sage in the Apocalyptic and Pseudepigraphic Literature," in Gammie and Perdue, eds., *The Sage in Israel,* 347–53.

[40] The two references occur at the beginning and end of the list of praiseworthy men. See also Wisd 4:10–15.

[41] For an edition of the Ethiopic book of Enoch, see M. Knibb, *The Ethiopic Book of Enoch: A New Edition in Light of the Aramaic Dead Sea Fragments* (2 vols; Oxford: Clarendon Press, 1978).

Apocalypticism, therefore, is more than the outgrowth of Israelite prophecy and wisdom movements. There are at least two additional factors that contribute to its development, factors that are particularly germane to an analysis of religion and culture. (1) Apocalypticism, generally speaking, is one response to the diaspora. It is the product of the exilic and post-exilic periods in which Israel found itself under the control of foreign empires. Already in the Babylonian exile, Jews had experienced life in which they were the cultural minority, and this experience would grow with the passing of the centuries and various foreign rulers. (2) Apocalypticism is decisively shaped by the Jewish encounter with Hellenism in which political control, speculation about the nature of the cosmos, and cultural hegemony were closely allied.[42] As is clear from the Jewish literature produced as a result, the encounter with Hellenism produced political and cultural rifts of crisis proportions among Jews—and apocalypticism was one response.

APOCALYPTICISM AND THE BOOK OF DANIEL

Several things can be said by way introduction to the book of Daniel and its approach to religion in a period of turmoil and oppression. First, the canonical form of the book (in the Hebrew Bible) does not cover all the written material about Daniel which is known from the Hellenistic period. It is more accurate to speak of Daniel cycles or Daniel books.[43] There are additions to the book in the LXX[44] and fragments of Daniel cycle(s) among the Qumran documents.[45] One can compare the Daniel cycle(s) to the growth of the Enoch traditions (as noted above)[46] and also those about Ezra.[47] In each case references in the OT to these persons become the basis for the growth of cycles in the later post-exilic period. A Daniel is mentioned in Ezekiel 14:14, 20; 28:3 as a righteous (ṣdq) and wise (ḥkm) man. The exilic figure appears in a list of heros in 1 Macc 2:60

---

[42] J. Collins, "Cosmos and Salvation: Jewish Wisdom and Apocalyptic in the Hellenistic Age," *HR* 17 (1977–78): 121–42.

[43] Josephus, *Ant.* 10.11, 7, speaks of books by Daniel. On the interpretation of Daniel in Josephus, see F. F. Bruce, "Josephus and the Book of Daniel," *ASTI* 6 (1965): 148–62.

[44] The Prayer of Azariah and the Song of the Three Young Men; Susanna; Bel and the Dragon.

[45] F. F. Bruce, "The Book of Daniel and the Qumran Community," *Neotestamentica et Semitica* (ed. E. Ellis, M. Wilcox; Edinburgh: T & T Clark, 1969), 221–35; A. Mertens, *Das Buch Daniel im Lichte der Texte vom Toten Meer* (SBM 12; Stuttgart: Echter Verlag, 1971); J. Trever, "The Book of Daniel and the Origin of the Qumran Community," *BA* 48 (1985): 89–102.

[46] See notes 31–33 above.

[47] E.g., the Ezra/Esdras traditions reflected in the Greek and Slavonic Bibles and the Latin Vulgate (1, 2 Esdras, 4 Ezra).

as one who was delivered from the lions' den. A Daniel of old is the father-in-law of Enoch in the intertestamental book of Jubilees (Jub 4:20). It seems impossible that these various references could be related to a single figure, but they point to the stature of a Daniel figure over a period of centuries,[48] and they suggest that the canonical book of Daniel is an abbreviation of a wider collection of stories.

Second, the book presents Daniel as someone with prophetic and sapiential characteristics. The book itself uses the wisdom vocabulary explicitly to describe him, but Matt 24:15, the Qumran community, and Josephus all consider Daniel to be a prophet.[49] As noted above, the vision reports in Daniel (as in apocalyptic literature as a whole) owe much to earlier vision reports in the prophets. Chapter 1 has Daniel living at the royal court in Babylon as a torah-observant exile from Jerusalem. It would be unwise to overemphasize a court or temple setting for the author(s) of Daniel, but his sapiential (and priestly-scribal?) activity probably is a clue to the author's social setting.

Third, the book may be divided into two parts on the basis of genre and language. Chapters 1–6 are narratives concerned with Daniel and his companions in the royal court. Chapters 7–12 are primarily vision reports of revelations given to Daniel. These elementary form-critical observations relate to a conclusion widely shared by investigators, namely, that the court narratives in chs. 1–6 are older than the vision reports in chs. 7–12.[50] This does not mean the book is an artificial unity; there are many points in which the court narratives are closely related by theme and vocabulary to the visions in 7–12. It does mean that not all of the description of Daniel and friends necessarily corresponds to those circles responsible for the book, since the author(s) possibly adapted some stories of known figures. The book has its own integrity, and it should go without saying that Daniel's author(s) clearly intended for the court narratives and vision reports to be read together.[51]

---

[48] See further, Müller, "Magisch-mantische Weisheit," 87–94; J. Day, "The Daniel of Ugarit and Ezekiel and the Hero of the Book of Daniel," *VT* 30 (1980): 174–84.

[49] See further, K. Koch, "Is Daniel Also Among the Prophets?" *Int* 39 (1985): 117–30. 4QFlor II, 3, makes reference to the book of Daniel the prophet.

[50] For the history of discussion see J. Collins, *The Apocalyptic Vision of the Book of Daniel* (HSM 16; Missoula: Scholars Press, 1977), 7–11, 27–65. See also A. R. Millard, "Daniel 1–6 and History," *EQ* 49 (1977): 67–73; J. Gammie, "On the Intention and Sources of Daniel i–vi," *VT* 31 (1981): 282–92; P. W. Coxon, "The 'List' Genre and Narrative Style in the Court Tales of Daniel," *JSOT* 35 (1986): 95–121. Two recent, literary studies of the court tales in Daniel are D. N. Fewell, *Circle of Sovereignty. A Story of Stories in Daniel 1–6* (BLS 20; Sheffield: Almond Press, 1988); L. Wills, *The Jew in the Court of the Foreign King* (HDR 26; Minneapolis: Fortress Press, 1990), 75–152.

[51] For a strong statement on the integrity of the book as a whole see P. R. Davies, "Eschatology in the Book of Daniel," *JSOT* 17 (1980): 33–53, esp. 33–34.

The book is also written in two different languages. Chapters 1:1–2:4a and 8:1–12:13 are in Hebrew, while the material between is written in Aramaic. No completely satisfactory explanation exists for this bilingual form. It obviously does not follow the form-critical division between narratives and vision reports. Apparently the author was bilingual, but the reasons for writing in this fashion remain mysterious.[52]

Fourth, the canonical book of Daniel was produced during the period of the Maccabean revolt (ca. 165 B.C.E.).[53] This has long been recognized in general terms by interpreters. The book is opposition literature that arose in a period of turmoil and oppression. The impact of the diaspora and of Hellenism took the form of a political and cultural crisis during the rule of Antiochus IV Epiphanes, and the book of Daniel is one Jewish response (see pp. 116–21). But why the pseudonymity and the depiction of court life in Babylon? Pseudonymity was a characteristic of apocalyptic literature, since attribution to a famous figure in the past granted the authors a certain authority. And such past attribution also played well with the theme that God had determined epochs from the beginning of creation and had revealed such information in advance. But why the Babylonian exile in particular? The suggestion proposed by Müller is perhaps the most satisfactory: the Babylonian exile was the "beginning period" (*Urzeit*) of the diaspora,[54] the beginning of a time of cultural imperialism imposed on Israel which reached its acute form in the circumstances of the Maccabean revolt. Daniel is the figure who lives at the beginning of this period and the wise seer to whom God reveals the historical events which will follow. Daniel's four-world empire scheme in chs. 2 and 7 fits this proposal, since the first of the four kingdoms represents the power of Babylon. Chapter 9 also fits a scheme whereby the effects of exile work themselves out over a period of years. At the same time, Daniel and his friends represent the struggles Israel would face in the diaspora and in Hellenistic Palestine. Earlier forms of the court narratives likely preserved stories of how faithful Jews could survive at a gentile court. As a result of the crisis under Antiochus IV they become examples of survival and courage in the face of oppression. The visions preserve the conviction that God had given evil only a limited reign on earth and had revealed this merciful decision in advance to the wise.

---

[52] For suggestions and bibliography on reasons for the bilingualism of Daniel, see Collins, *Apocalyptic Vision*, 15–19; and LaCocque, *Daniel in His Time*, 8–12.

[53] J. C. H. Lebram, "Konig Antiochus im Buch Daniel," VT 25 (1975): 737–72; H. Gese, "Die Bedeutung der Krise unter Antiochus IV. Epiphanes für die Apokalyptik des Danielbuches," ZTK 80 (1983): 373–88.

[54] Müller, "Mantische Weisheit und Apokalyptik," 289. See also his discussion in "Märchen, Legende und Enderwartung: Zum Verständnis des Buches Daniel" VT 26 (1976): 338–50.

THE COURT NARRATIVES IN THE BOOK OF DANIEL

Chapter One

According to the first chapter, Daniel and his three friends are selected from among the exiled Judeans to receive training in the royal court of Babylon. There is no hint that the young men volunteered; they are taken by a Babylonian official and are duly enrolled in the training resources of the royal court. It is an obvious example of cultural imperialism where (human) resources are taken from a subject people and trained for use in the imperial court. A second example of dominance comes with the giving of Babylonian names to each Jew. Daniel, Hananiah, Mishael, and Azariah become respectively Belteshazzar, Shadrach, Meshach, and Abednego. Although renaming was not uncommon in a court setting, the renaming of Daniel and his friends symbolizes their involuntary incorporation into an alien culture.

The young men are required to have certain characteristics (1:3–4): they should be Israelites from the royal or noble families, with no defects, good of appearance, learned in wisdom (*maśkîlîm bəkol ḥokmāh*), having knowledge (*yōdə'ê da'at*) and insight (*məbînê maddā'*). These last named characteristics mark out the young men as sages at the court, since they are described in typical sapiential terms. They are also required to learn the Babylonian tongue which suggests some typically scribal duties, i.e., they must read, write, and interpret for the work of the court.

The use of the term *maśkîlîm* (hiphil participle from *śkl*) is a significant clue not only for the identification of the young men but probably for the writer(s) of the book as well. At a minimum, these characteristics represent the ideals of the author(s). In 1:4 *maśkîlîm* is not a title but a description of the young men that takes an object.[55] Elsewhere in Daniel, *maśkîlîm* is used as a title or description of a group (11:33, 35; 12:3, 10). In 11:33f. those who are learned or discerning among the people (*maśkîlîm 'am*) will cause many to have insight, though some of these *maśkîlîm* will face persecution, and will stumble and fall. In 12:3, the *maśkîlîm* will shine like the firmament as a result of the resurrection from the dead. And in a period of persecution and crisis, these *maśkîlîm* had the discernment to know that God had decreed an end to wickedness (12:10).

The problem of the royal diet is another illustration from the first chapter (1:8–16) that has cultural conflict as its basis. Daniel and his friends do not want the defilement that will come as the result of their

---

[55] On the term, see H. Kosmala, "Maśkil," *JANESCU* 5 (1973): 235–41; C. Newsom, "The Sage in the Literature of Qumran: The Functions of the *maśkil*," in Gammie and Perdue, eds., *The Sage in Israel*, 373–82. See also the comments below on Daniel 11–12.

eating the food provided at the royal court. The account contrasts the power of the practices of a religious minority with the assumed superiority of the dominant culture. According to the account, God worked through a court steward who acquiesed to Daniel's request to have his own appearance measured against that of the other courtiers who ate of the king's meat and drank his wine. Moreover, at the end of a ten-day trial period, the appearance of Daniel and his friends is better than that of their peers.

Such an account fits not only the crisis period under Antiochus IV Epiphanes, where Jewish kosher laws were an issue (1 Macc 1:62–64); it is also a more general example of a court narrative which instructed Jews on the importance of maintaining their identity in the diaspora,[56] and one which instructed them that God's sovereignty could be seen even in a gentile court.[57] The account is quite revealing for what it implies about Jewish identity. To be a Jew in an imperialistic culture requires commitment to a distinctive lifestyle in spite of the pressures to conform. There is no question as to which culture and political system is dominant or, in the mind of the author(s), no question as to which lifestyle is better. The God of heaven watches over those who maintain their identity in a gentile court, and he sees to it that they succeed. The account presupposes the confession that, in spite of its minority status, Jewish identity is superior to that of the dominant culture because it reflects the wisdom of the God of heaven.

Daniel 1:17–20 describes the scribal wisdom of the Babylonian court as a way of introducing the wisdom of Daniel and its superiority to that possessed by other members of the court. In 1:17 the emphasis falls on two points; the first is that the young men have a wisdom that God has given them, and the second is that their wisdom is used in interpreting other forms of divine revelation. God gave them knowledge, "the means to make wise through documents" (haśkēl bəkol sēper),[58] and wisdom. Daniel is also given the ability to provide understanding for every kind of vision (bəkol ḥazôn) and dreams (ḥalōmôt). There are two kinds of interpretation noted, that of documents or books and that of dreams and visions. The former is classical scribal activity and the latter is that of mantic wisdom, though perhaps the latter was also considered scribal

---

[56] The issue of a proper diet for Jews is widely noted in later, post-exilic literature. Cf. Tob 1:10–12; Add Esth 14:17; Jdt 11:12–13; 12:1–4; 2 Macc 5:27; Jub 22:16.

[57] Several scholars have proposed that Daniel 1 is written after the narratives in 2–6 as an introduction to the stories. See, for example, the comments in Wills, *The Jew in the Court of the Foreign King*, 79–81.

[58] The phrase is difficult to translate literally into English. The phrase, and particularly the verb *haśkēl* (hiphil inf. abs. of śkl) reminds the reader of the *maśkîlîm bəkol ḥokmāh* in 1:4.

activity. The Babylonian interpreters are described as diviners,[59] i.e., practitioners of mantic wisdom, whose knowledge is considerably less effective than that of the four young men. This account is also essential for the interpretive position Daniel assumes in the book as a whole because it defines his role as a mantic sage and seer.

Chapter Two

Chapter 2 is vital for both the court narratives and the vision reports which follow. New vocabulary is introduced which underscores the role of mantic interpretation and the superiority of Daniel's wisdom to that of the Babylonian diviners. Nebuchadnezzar has a dream and requires an interpretation of it from his diviners. It is a task that none of them can fulfill. The dream and its interpetation is a "mystery" (*rāz*), a term used several times in the chapter.[60] According to 2:19 the mystery of the dream's contents and its interpretation are revealed (*glh*) to Daniel in a vision (*hzw*). The Aramaic term used for "interpretation" in chapter two is *pəšar*. It is a cognate of a term *pešer* used in post-exilic Hebrew and popularly employed in the Qumran documents.[61] The comment at the end of chapter 1—that the wisdom of Daniel and his friends was ten times superior to that of the Babylonian diviners—finds a noteworthy example in the ability of Daniel to interpret the king's dream.

Nebuchadnezzar's dream concerns a statue made of composite materials that is struck by a rock and destroyed (2:31–45). Daniel's interpretation (*pəšar*) of the dream finds that the statue is a symbol of world empires. In this interpretation, Daniel follows a widely recognized form of depicting world history.[62] The large statue in the dream had a head of gold, its torso and arms were made of silver and bronze, its legs of iron, and its feet of iron and clay. Although there is some variance of opinion, most likely the composite statue represents Babylon, Media, Persia, and Greece, and the periods of their rule.[63] Babylon is specifically

---

[59] *harṭummîn* and *'ašəpîn*. The former term is probably Egyptian in origin (cf. Gen 41:8) and the latter is Akkadian and used in Babylonian texts for the interpreter of dreams. Additional terms are used in 2:2, 27; 4:7 (4H). On the mantic terminology in the OT and particularly Daniel, see Müller, "Magisch-mantische Weisheit und die Gestalt Daniels," 79–85; "Mantische Weisheit," 271–72, 275–80.

[60] 2:18, 19, 27, 30, 47 (plural). The other occurence of the Aramaic term in Daniel is in 4:6.

[61] 2:4–6, 9, 16, 24–26, 30, 36, 45. G. J. Brooke, "Qumran Pesher," *RevQ* 10 (1981): 483–503.

[62] J. W. Swain, "The Theory of the Four Monarchies: Opposition History Under the Roman Empire," *Classical Philology* 35 (1940): 1–21; D. Flusser, "The four empires in the Fourth Sibyl and in the Book of Daniel," *IOS* 2 (1972): 148–75; G. Hasel, "The Four World Empires of Daniel 2 against Its Near Eastern Environment," *JSOT* 12 (1979): 17–30.

[63] In addition to the bibliography and discussion in the studies noted above,

described as the head of gold and thus the first kingdom in the series (2:37–40). The rock that topples the statue is "not handled" yet it grows to fill the earth. It represents the everlasting kingdom of the God of heaven (2:44).

According to the account, Nebuchadnezzar reacts to Daniel's interpretation with praise and an acknowledgment that Daniel's deity is God of gods and Lord of lords, the one who reveals mysteries (2:47). The account is another claim for the sovereignty of the God of heaven (=Yahweh the God of Israel for the readers) who grants wisdom to the elect in a gentile court. Nebuchadnezzar may praise the high god of heaven, but the readers of Daniel know that this is none other than Yahweh whose secret rule will be made manifest in the coming kingdom not made with [human] hands.

The perception of world rule in the interpretation of the dream is much discussed among scholars. One should begin with the observation of Swain that such a scheme for representing the course of history is a type of opposition literature in the ancient world that stood against the dominant political order. The literary portrait of Daniel and his friends represents the view that the current world order is only a prelude to the in-breaking of the kingdom of the Most High. One can also read the interpretation of the dream provided to Nebuchadnezzar in comical terms: the king praises Daniel and the God of heaven even though Jewish readers understand the scheme to represent gentile rulers (such as Nebuchadnezzar) whose reign is limited and will be overthrown! The account is not, however, hostile to Nebuchadnezzar. Jeremiah had called Nebuchadnezzar Yahweh's servant (e.g., Jer 25:9), and within those bounds decreed by God for the historical process, the court narratives recommend an acceptance of a minority status.

It is unlikely that the symbolism of the individual kingdoms is as important as what the four kingdoms stand for as a whole. In 2:44 the rock appears in the days of the rulers—as if the rock's destructive power hits all the kingdoms at once. Most likely this means each kingdom not only represents a distinct epoch in world history but stands as an example of a pretentious human kingdom that must give way to the rule of the God of heaven. Such an interpretation fits with the sequence of four beasts in chapter 7 who also represent the succession of world empires. Even though the fourth beast is singled out for its destructiveness, all of the creatures are mentioned together at the end of the description of their respective roles (7:12).

Von Rad, in particular, has proposed that this scheme of world empires in Daniel is quite different from the salvation-history scheme of

---

see the reconstruction offered by J. Walton, "The Four Kingdoms of Daniel," *JETS* 29 (1986): 25–36.

the classical prophets. The prophetic scheme presupposes the saving acts of God in history, but the apocalyptic scheme represented in Daniel depicts world history as a time of evil and gentile rule until the reign of God breaks in at the end.[64] Von Rad's contrast between prophecy and apocalypticism is too sharply drawn, although significant differences remain between the two schemes. Both understand that God is sovereign over the historical process and both share a conviction that God's decisive act still lies in the future. Daniel, however, has a more deterministic element to its understanding of historical periods, and it does not reflect the view that the "mighty acts" of Yahweh in the past (e.g., the exodus or the raising up of David) are about to be repeated in typological fashion in the future. More specifically, it is true that the world-empire scheme represents post-exilic history as a period of judgment (made clear by the confessional prayer in 9:4–19),[65] a time of gentile hegemony, and an opportunity for the purification of the wise. But it is also true that the authors of Daniel believe God had acted in the historical process and continued to do so in the period of evil by vindicating Daniel and his friends at the gentile court. It is as if there are two kingdoms to acknowledge, one ruled by the gentiles and one ruled by the Most High who has granted gentile hegemony a period of time in which to exercise sovereignty.[66] Israel was and remained God's elect ("your people," 9:16, 19; cf. 7:27). God had delivered them from the power of Egypt and given them instruction through Moses (9:4–19). The kosher laws alluded to in 1:8–16 presuppose such divine instruction was valid for life in the diaspora. Daniel faced Jerusalem when he prayed (Dan 6:11; v. 10A). This presupposes the importance of God's choice of Jerusalem and that the temple service there represents all Jews (cf. 9:16–17, 20). The piety of Daniel and his friends reflects the conviction that Jews might serve in a gentile kingdom while acknowledging the sovereignty of the Most High over all.

---

[64] A similar, one-sided emphasis is expressed by J. Lebram, "The Piety of the Jewish Apocalypticists," in *Apocalypticism in the Mediterranean World and the Near East* (Uppsala: International Colloquium on Apocalypticism, 1979), 176: "The world has now become a place of all-pervading profanity from which there is no escape. In this last period of universal history holiness is basically impossible, and evil, wickedness, will inevitably triumph." His comments on the purification and spiritual discipline in Daniel as responses to evil are quite insightful (pp. 178–87).

[65] Some scholars propose that the confessional prayer in 9:4f. is a redactional element and does not reflect the viewpoint of the primary author(s) of Daniel, but the evidence for this is not decisive. See the comments of J. Collins, *Daniel, With an Introduction to Apocalyptic Literature*, 90–96. In an earlier study, *The Apocalyptic Vision of Daniel*, 185–87, Collins proposed that the confessional prayer could not have been composed by those responsible for the visions in 7–12, but he reconsiders the matter in his later work. See also G. H. Wilson, "The Prayer of Daniel 9: Reflection on Jeremiah 29," *JSOT* 48 (1990): 91–99.

[66] P. R. Davies, "Eschatology in the Book of Daniel," 40–41.

The historical scheme of Daniel suggests a three-part arrangement: the period of Israel's formation, the period of domination where Israel is under the control of gentile empires, and an eternal period of the kingdom of God.[67] In the second period, the emphasis switches from God's acts in the formation of Israel to the stage of world history where the remnants of Israel exist in the diaspora. Although it is a period of judgment, it is also a period of preparation for the culmination of world history when the eschaton breaks in. The in-breaking of the kingdom of God is also the culmination of world history; it introduces a time when the salvation history of Israel, which seemed at an end during the period of gentile hegemony, is transformed along with the rest of world history. Chapter 7 makes explicit what is only hinted at in chapter 2—the eschatological kingdom includes people from every nation and tongue (7:14). The inclusive nature of the eschatological kingdom suggests the threefold historical scheme has been influenced by the mythic symbolism of correspondence between Urzeit and Endzeit.[68]

Chapter Three

The account of persecution in 3:1–30 is another example of a court narrative that may have antecedents in the diaspora but takes on new significance in the persecutions by Antiochus IV.[69] Nebuchadnezzar constructs a statue of gold and requires veneration of it among his subjects. In the previous chapter his kingdom is represented by a head of gold on a statue comprised of different materials; this image is comprised entirely of gold and is likely a boastful symbol of his reign.[70] Daniel's three friends will not commit apostasy and are punished by being cast into a fiery furnace. As in the previous accounts, God vindicates them; on this occasion God sends an angel[71] to protect them from the fire.

The conversation between the three young men and Nebuchadnezzar confirms that the conflict is based on a different understanding of how to serve God. Nebuchadnezzar questions whether there is an intention on the part of the young men to worship the statue he has erected, and then asks if they are prepared at that point to do so in his presence

---

[67] See further the comments in K. Koch, "Spätisraelitisches Geschichtsdenken am Beispiel des Buches Daniel," in K. Koch, ed., Apokalyptik, 276–310, who proposes a similar threefold scheme.

[68] This point is discussed further in the analysis of Daniel 7.

[69] See E. Haag, "Die drei Manner im Feuer nach Dan 3, 1–30," TTZ 96 (1987): 21–50.

[70] This symbolic interpretation comes from the lack of specificity in the text concerning the statue's role. The statue does not represent a specific deity for the Israelite reader so much as it represents the idolatrous pretension of the gentile empire.

[71] The Aramaic phrase is bar 'elāhîn; literally "a son of God(s)."

(3:14–15).[72] Verse 3:17 contains the reply of the three young men which begins: "If our God whom we worship exists, he can deliver us. . . ."[73] The difficult reply is less the questioning of whether their deity exists— since that has been established in the previous chapter with Nebuchanezzar's affirmation of Daniel's God—and more a reflection of the way Nebuchadnezzar questioned them. Their answer literally takes words from the king's mouth. However, the question still remained whether or not God would deliver the young men from the fiery furnace. Perhaps the highest affirmation comes in the following verse (3:18), when the young men confess that evn if God does not deliver them, they will not worship Nebuchadnezzar's statue.

Daniel 3:18 gives the response of the author(s) to the cultic enforcements of Antiochus IV. It is not so different from the accounts of the martyrs in 2 Macc 7. Regardless of the outcome, there must be no compromise with idolatry. The religion and culture offered to Jews by Antiochus and his supporters were incompatible with the convictions of Daniel's author(s). This account in 3:1–30 is somewhat different from that of the previous stories in that the young men needed more than kosher food or mantic skills in the interpretation of dreams to prosper at the royal court. They needed all the courage they could muster to keep themselves from idolatry and to prepare themselves to die as a result of their convictions. The end result, however, is similar to that of 2:46–49. When the young men are delivered from the fiery furnace, Nebuchadnezzar praises the God who delivered them and gives them places of influence in the royal administration.

Chapters Four–Six

The various accounts in chs. 4–6 seem to have a complex pre-history, though they are linked together in their canonical form by common vocabulary and theme.[74] For example, the account of Nebuchadnezzar's illness in chapter 4 has a parallel in a fragmentary text from Qumran (4QPrNab), where it is Nabonidus, the last king of Babylon, who is cured by a Jewish sage or seer (gzr).[75] The relationship between this text and

---

72 The Aramaic text of 3:14–15 twice uses the particle 'îtay, which means "there is" or "there exists" in the questions of 3:14–15. The initial clause of v. 15 literally asks "if there is to you preparation?" (hn 'ytykwn 'tydyn).

73 Verse 17 employs the same particle îtay used in 3:14–15 and picks up the "if" (hēn) from 3:15. See the careful study by P. Coxon, "Daniel iii 17: A Linguistic and Theological Problem," VT 26 (1976): 400–409.

74 E. Haag, "Der Traum des Nebukadnezzar in Dan 4," TTZ 88 (1979): 194–220; idem, Die Errettung Daniels aus dem Löwengrabe (SBS 110; Stuttgart: Katholisches Bibelwerk, 1983); Wills, The Jew in the Court of the Foreign King, 87–152.

75 J. T. Milik, "Prière de Nabonide et autres écrits d'un cycle de Daniel," RB 63 (1956): 407–15.

the canonical account is unclear. Also, the various Greek versions may reflect dependence on one or more Aramaic texts that differ from the present MT. Whatever the literary pre-history of these chapters, in their current form they continue the themes of the idolatrous nature of the Babylonian and Persian courts and the miraculous means used by the God of heaven to sustain the faithful Jewish courtiers.

Chapter Four. In chapter 4 Daniel interprets a dream for Nebuchadnezzar sent by God Most High (*'elāhā' 'illā'â*). Daniel is even described as the chief of the king's diviners (*rab ḥarṭummîn*). His interpretation can be summarized as follows: because the king has failed to acknowledge the sovereignty of the God Most High—who rules over human kingdoms and can grant authority to anyone (4:27, 32; 22, 29a)—the king will become like an animal. When the period decreed by the Most High is complete, Nebuchadnezzar will be restored.

Nebuchadnezzar is led by these events to acknowledge the sovereignty of the Most High who rules forever (4:34–35; 31–32a). He praises the King of Heaven (*melek šamayyā'*) and confesses that the ways of the Most High are just. At one level of reading the account is simply another echo of the theme of divine sovereignty. But the point is made quite artfully for the Jewish audience. Nebuchadnezzar's sojourn among the animals, for example, may be a play on the announcement of Jeremiah that God had granted sovereignty to the Babylonian king, and that even the animals in the land would serve him (Jer 27:6). The reversal of roles is comical. Now the pretentious king eats straw like an animal. The language for deity is also subtle. Appellatives such as Most High and King of Heaven could be used in the post-exilic period in either polytheistic or monotheistic circles; but for Jewish readers, the Most High who revealed secrets to Daniel is Yahweh the God of Israel (see pp. 111–14).

Chapter Five. Chapter 5 continues the theme of divine sovereignty and revealed wisdom with the account of the fall of Babylon. The mysterious handwriting on the wall, which signals the demise of Belshazzar's kingdom, remains a storyteller's delight. Daniel's interpretation plays explicitly on the hubris of Nebuchadnezzar described in the previous chapter, and the fact that Belshazzar has not understood the rule of the Most High. Belshazzar's own idolatrous pride emerges in his use of the Jerusalem temple vessels when drinking wine (5:2). As a result the kingdom is given over to the Medes. One should note the similarity between the interpretive wisdom needed to comprehend the mysterious handwriting and that needed to interpret the significance of Jeremiah's prophecy in Daniel 9. Neither text is comprehensible apart from the wisdom given to Daniel by God or an angelic mediator. Perhaps this similarity is the most vivid illustration of the mantic-scribal lore of interpretation in the late post-exilic period. It assumes that God communicates knowledge of the future through present signs (dreams, strange writings) and the words of the past.

Chapter Six. Chapter 6 has Daniel under threat of death in the new Persian court. Darius, the first ruler in the realm, places Daniel in a high administrative post, a position which makes other officials jealous. They conclude that they will be unable to find corruption in Daniel unless it concerns the practice of his religion (6:5; 6a). Their opportunity comes as a result of Daniel's ritual of prayer, which is in violation of a new edict forbidding the invoking of any deity or individual except the king for thirty days. Daniel habitually faces Jerusalem when he prays to "his God" (6:10–11; 11–12a). One should not overlook the link in this account with the reference to the temple vessels from Jerusalem in the previous chapter. As the site of the temple and the dwelling place of Yahweh, "his God," Jerusalem is the symbol of the unity and the uniqueness of Judaism over against gentile religions. And Daniel, whatever his position in the Persian court, is a faithful Jew who acknowledges the significance of Jerusalem. The description of Daniel's crime is another case showing the conflict between the minority religion of Judaism and the dominant religion of a gentile empire in the diaspora. For the writer(s) there can be no compromise between the exercise of piety and the position of honor at the gentile court held by Daniel. If the Most High grants wisdom and success to Daniel, then so be it, but wisdom and success would not come at the cost of Daniel's fidelity to Judaism.

The conclusion to the court narratives comes in the rescue of Daniel from the lion's den and the praise of Daniel's God by Darius. The king is the third gentile ruler discussed, and like his two predecessors in the story line, he too acknowledges the sovereignty of God. Darius confesses that the God of Daniel is the living God, one who will exist forever and whose kingdom will not be destroyed. This confession is much like the affirmation of God's kingdom in 2:44 and 7:14. The verb translated as "destroyed" (*ḥbl*) in 2:44, 6:26 (27a), and 7:14 is used also by Daniel in his claim that the lions have not destroyed him because God had protected him 6:22 (23a). The word play joins together the person of Daniel and the manifestation of God's rule. Daniel represents the rule of the Most High by his faithfulness at the Persian court.

THE COURT NARRATIVES IN DANIEL AS A "DIASPORA THEOLOGY OF TWO KINGDOMS"

P. R. Davies proposes the phrase "two kingdoms" in his description of the world view represented by the court narratives in Dan 1–6.[76] It is a helpful description of the faith and world view represented in these

---

[76] P. R. Davies, "Eschatology in the Book of Daniel," 40–41. The court narratives are examples of "the theology of the two kingdoms as a creed of Diaspora Judaism." See also the comments above in the analysis of Dan 2.

accounts. Judaism had come to grips theologically with the diaspora and the extended periods of gentile rule by positing a two-kingdom theology, that of human rule with its succession of provisional empires and that of God which would come in fullness when the gentile kingdoms had run their course. In good times there could be harmony between the two kingdoms; the wisdom of God communicated to the elect would enable them to cope if not to prosper since they understood that even the gentile kingdoms ruled as a result of God's permissive will. During Israel's periods of persecution or oppression the narratives express the conviction that God's sovereignty would vindicate the righteous.

The concept of the "two kingdoms" can be used profitably to underscore the relationship between religion and culture represented in the court narratives. Daniel and his friends represent a different religion and culture than the gentile empires because they worship a different God. Throughout the narratives there is a tension between the religion of the exiles and that of the gentile court. The tension is always there, whether it is a private matter of refusing to eat the food of the royal court, whether one speaks of the reign of the Most High rather than that of Yahweh, the God of Israel, or whether one is under threat of execution by the empire because of cultic practices.[77]

One might say that the religion practiced by Daniel and his friends could coexist with the religious and cultural imperialism represented at the gentile courts, but their religious practices called into question the legitimacy of the dominant culture. Coexistence between the two is not necessarily impossible, but the inherent hubris and idolatry represented in the ruling kingdoms make the practice of Judaism difficult, and at times impossible, without conflict. The religious practices of Judaism are ultimately superior to those of the gentile court, but there is no evidence that the wisdom of the ruling court will respond adequately to this fact.

In summary, the court narratives in Daniel 1–6 have some common features in their description of human kingdoms which illustrate the reasons for ongoing tension in matters of religion and culture.

(1) The rule of gentile kingdoms is a derivative one; Babylon or Persia rules by the permissive will of the Most High, and the period for their rule is determined by God.

(2) They are not themselves examples of the kingdom of God except that they rule by divine permission. Through them or among them, God manifests his power and wisdom.

---

[77] Davies' statement—that "the normal state of affairs is one of harmony and not tension; the acts of persecution against Daniel and his friends are isolated incidents in an otherwise harmonious coexistence" (p. 40)—undervalues the tensions and acts of persecution in the canonical stories as we now have them. Harmonious coexistence does not describe the court narratives when read in light of the vision reports which follow.

(3) Although the God of Israel may be acknowledged in the gentile praise of the Most High or of the King of Heaven, the hubris and idolatry of the gentle kingdoms render them unfit as places where Judaism can flourish unhindered.

(4) The kingdom of the Most High will come when the gentile empires have run their course.

(5) The truth of God Most High is made manifest in the gentile courts by the religious practices of Daniel and his friends, and by their vindication in matters of wisdom and accuracy in interpreting dreams.

THE APOCALYPTIC VISIONS IN DANIEL 7–12

The vision reports in Dan 7–12 depend on the portraits of Daniel the mantic seer in the court narratives for their correct interpretation. Vision reports and court narratives share the theme of a two-kingdom theology, though the visionary accounts are more explicit about the threat to Judaism than the narratives.

Chapter Seven

Chapter 7 begins with the description of a dream with visions granted to Daniel. The account has two parts; the first contains the description of the vision (7:1–14)[78] and the second its interpretation (7:15–27). Both the two-part nature of the account and its contents are similar to the description of Nebuchadnezzar's dream and its interpretation in chapter 2.[79] Daniel sees four beasts emerge from the sea. In order they are: a winged lion, a bear, a four-headed leopard with four wings, and a ferocious beast with iron teeth and ten horns. Each beast stands for a gentile empire (7:17) just as the various parts of the statue in chapter 2. The fourth beast—represented by one horn in particular—oppresses the saints (qaddîšîn="holy ones")[80] of the Most High and seeks to change the religion (dāt) mandated by him (7:25).[81] The horn is described as a fourth king who subdues three previous rulers, a description that identifies the king as Antiochus IV. Instead of a stone not-made-by-hands, which represented the eternal kingdom of God in chapter 2, there is a vision of a regal figure described as the Ancient of Days, who is enthroned and surrounded by myiads of beings (7:9–10, 13). The Ancient

---

[78] 7:2 uses the singular form "vision" (ḥzw) for the dream. Visions are mentioned in 7:1.

[79] Both chapters are also written in Aramaic. For an extended comparison of themes from chapter seven with chapters two–six, see A. Lenglet, "La structure littéraire de Daniel 2–7," *Bib* 53 (1972): 169–90.

[80] 7:18, 21, 22, 25, 27, 28.

[81] The word dāt can be translated law or custom, but it apparently serves as a synonym for religion in 7:25 and in 6:5 (6A).

of Days is approached by one "like a son of man" (*kəbar 'enāš*) who draws near to him (7:13). This Ancient of Days is the Most High whose dominion overcomes that of the fourth beast and lasts forever (7:25, 27).

Chapter 7 is a central chapter for an overall interpretation of the book of Daniel. It catches many themes from the court narratives, especially the theme of world empires in chapter 2, and it sets a pattern for the visionary material which follows. It also refers to two terms, the "saints (holy ones) of the Most High"[82] and the one "like a son of man,"[83] which are central to the interpretation of the chapter but which remain enigmatic nevertheless. The terms have rich tradition histories in the ancient world; it is their connection with one another in chapter 7, however, that is of most interest in this investigation.

Saints and One like a Son of Man

Both the saints and the son of man are symbols which stand in distinction to the animals in the vision. Since the animals are symbols of the ruling gentile kingdoms, the saints and one *like* a son of man represent the kingdom of the Most High. The animals are described as *like* a lion, in the likeness (*dāməyāh*) of a bear, and *like* a panther (7:4–6). They come from the sea, the one *like* a son of man comes with the clouds from the opposite direction. Both the saints and the one like a son of man will share in the eternal rule of the Ancient of Days (=the Most High), but they are not alone. This kingdom also includes people from every nation and tongue (7:14).[84] Thus chapter 7 (and chapter 2) implies that the kingdom of God will be established on earth, a transcendent and eternal rule, the antithesis of the gentile empires.[85] These are the most critical elements in identifying the saints and the one like a son of man—they have a representative, symbolic character in opposition to the beasts who represent a succession of world empires.

---

[82] For bibliography and discussion, see L. Dequeker, "The 'Saints of the Most High' in Qumran and Daniel," *OTS* 18 (1973): 108–87; V. Poythress, "The Holy Ones of the Most High in Daniel vii," *VT* 26 (1976): 208–13; J. Collins, *Apocalyptic Vision*, 123–52; J. Goldingay, " 'Holy Ones on High' in Dan 7:18," *JBL* 107 (1988): 495–97.

[83] The bibliography on this topic is enormous. The following books give a good discussion of the issues and contain additional bibliography. See J. Coppens, *Le Fils d'homme vétéro-et intertestamentaire* (BETL 61; Leuven: University Press, 1983); A. J. Ferch, *The Son of Man in Daniel 7* (Berrien Springs: Andrews University Press, 1983); H. Kvanvig, *Roots of Apocalyptic: The Mesopotamian Background of the Enoch Figure and of the Son of Man* (WMANT 61; Neukirchen-Vluyn: Neukirchener Verlag, 1988).

[84] And perhaps also "the 'people' (*'am*) of the saints on high" (7:27) are considered a separate component of the kingdom, but it is not clear whether the phrase "people of the saints on high" should be differentiated from the "saints on high" already mentioned in 7:18, 22, 25.

[85] The eschatological nature of the kingdom is illustrated by the prediction of resurrection from the dead in chapter 12.

Can one be more specific about their respective identities in Daniel 7? The description of holy (qdš) in the OT can be applied to objects animate and inanimate, but the plural noun "holy ones" (qədōšîm) typically describes angelic beings.[86] In Jewish literature of the intertestamental period, the Hebrew or Aramaic term denotes both angelic and human beings.[87] The use of the relevant terms elsewhere in Daniel would suggest angelic figures for the saints in chapter 7;[88] however, the evidence remains suggestive and not conclusive. "Saints" could be a reference to righteous Jews, especially if the term "people" ('am) in the phrase "people of the saints on high" ('am qaddîšê 'elyônîn) in 7:27 defines the saints as human.[89] The visible rule of God is predicted as the eternal successor to the rule of gentile empires—and one naturally expects human participation in the kingdom of God (cf. 7:14). Angels are unmistakably referred to in 7:10 with its reference to the myriads in the presence of the Ancient of Days. Furthermore, the beast makes war on the saints, a remark which suggests the saints are righteous Jews oppressed because of their faith. One doubts that the gentile kingdoms themselves could oppress the angelic host. In short, the evidence is inconclusive, and the only reason a compromise solution (saints in chapter 7 refers to both humans and angels) is not supported by more interpreters is the lack of parallels in second temple literature where saints includes both angelic and human beings.[90] On balance, the saints of chapter 7 likely represent faithful Israelites defined by their eschatological identity—they are "holy ones" and inhabitants of the kingdom of the Most High, and thus similar to the angelic hosts.

The figure of the one like a son of man is even more complicated than the identity of the saints on high. In the OT the phrase "son of man" means "mortal one." Ezekiel, for example, is addressed repeatedly as "son of man"[91] to distinguish him from the appearance of God, angels, and strange beasts who were a part of his visionary experiences (cf. Ezek 1:2f.). Daniel too is addressed as a son of man to distinguish him from an

---

[86] E.g., Job 5:1; Psa 89:5, 7 (6, 8 MT). For additional references and discussion, see note 82 above.

[87] Angels in Sir 42:17; Jub 17:11. Humans in Tob 12:15; 1 Macc 1:46. Both in 1QM 12:8–9?

[88] 4:10=Aramaic, masc. sing. (13E); 4:13=Aramaic, masc. pl. (17E); 8:13=Hebrew, masc. sing; 8:24= Hebrew, masc. pl. There are, however, textual problems with the last reference, and it is not clear whether the "people of the saints" ('am qədōšîm) refers to angelic beings or humans. Cf. BHS and commentators.

[89] Cf. the "holy people" in 12:7.

[90] Davies, "Eschatology in the Book of Daniel," 43, suggests that the saints in chapter 7 may refer to both humans and angels. See also Collins, Apocalyptic Vision, 142–44.

[91] Koch, Das Buch Daniel, 217, defines ben 'ādām as "an individual representative of the human species" (die Gattung Menschheit). See Ezek 2:1, 3, 6, 8; 3:1, 3, 4, 10, 17, 25.

angelic companion.[92] Anthropomorphic references for God are particularly circumscribed in Ezek 1:26; God is described as "upon the likeness (dəmût) of the throne, a representation like the appearance of a man" (dəmût kəmar'ēh 'ādām). This throne scene can be compared to the brief and circumscribed description of the appearance of the Ancient of Days in Dan 7:9–10 who takes his seat on one of several thrones. The appearance of the one like a son of man, then, takes place in a visionary "throne scene";[93] the figure comes with the clouds of heaven, is presented to the Ancient of Days, and is accorded authority to rule in the eternal kingdom (7:13–14).

The brief reference to this one like (kə) a son of man suggests two things about his identity. First, the term son of man is not a title as it developed in intertestamental Judaism (1 Enoch 37–71, 2 Esdras 13–14) and early Christianity. He is referred to as like a son of man, not as the son of man; there seems to be no assumption of a title in the phrase. Second, the comparison is to the human species, not to the animals who symbolize gentile kings or empires. This suggests the one like a son of man is a symbol of those who will comprise the eternal kingdom of the Most High or, if the figure is not a corporate symbol (like the "saints"), he represents the people as their head.[94]

There are, of course, other possibilities for the identity of the one like a son of man; the brief reference to him is remarkably allusive.[95] For example, the function of the figure would remain essentially the same if he is identified as an angel who represents the coming eternal kingdom of the Most High, since the kingdom extends to the human and angelic spheres.[96] What should be stressed is the representative, symbolic nature of the figure. To use the language of the two kingdoms, the one like a

---

[92] Dan 8:15–17. The angel Gabriel is described as "manlike" (kəmar'ēh gāber) while Daniel is addressed as a "son of man" (ben 'ādām). The angel in 10:16–18 is described as one of "human likeness" (kidmût bənē 'ādām, kəmar'ēh 'ādām), though at first sight he is described as a man ('îš) in 10:5. In 3:25 the fourth, non-human figure in the fire is described as "seemingly divine" (ləbar 'elāhîn) to distinguish him from the three young men.

[93] M. Black, "The Throne-Theophany Prophetic Commission and the 'Son of Man': A Study in Tradition-History," Jews, Greeks and Christians: Religious Cultures in Late Antiquity. Essays in Honor of William David Davies (SJLA 21; ed. R. Hamerton-Kelly; R. Scroggs; Leiden: E. J. Brill, 1976), 57–73.

[94] Black, "The Throne-Theophany Prophetic Commission," in Hamerton-Kelly and Scroggs, eds., Jews, Greeks and Christians, 61, writes somewhat overconfidently: "there is no doubt that Daniel intended his Son of Man to symbolise the Saints of the Most High, i.e., the purified and redeemed Israel."

[95] See the list of proposed identifications provided by Koch, Das Buch Daniel, 216–34.

[96] The identifications of the holy ones as angels and the one like a Son of man as an angel (probably Michael) are discussed at length by Collins, Apocalyptic Vision, 123–52.

son of man embodies the kingdom of the Most High as surely as the beasts and horns embody the gentile kingdoms. The world empires are inhumanly arrogant, while the kingdom of God is represented by the symbolic figure of restored humanity.[97] The figure is *like* a human being, because he represents the *eschaton* which has not yet arrived. He is a symbol of that which is to come. Seen from the perspective of the eternal kingdom, the rule of the gentile kingdoms is incompatible with that proposed for restored humanity.

The one like a son of man, however, embodies more than just humanity restored from the domination of arrogant empires. His description has royal overtones from the OT combined with the mythic theme of the correspondence between primal humanity (*Urzeit*) and eschatological humanity (*Endzeit*). The implication of the account is that the one like a son of man is enthroned beside the Ancient of Days (7:9–10, 13–14). The enthronement scene reminds one of the earlier traditions of Davidic rule from Zion and the predicted incorporation of other peoples in a new world order,[98] although any specifically Davidic characteristics for the figure are missing. And just as the first Adam had an exalted place in creation (Sir 49:16; Wisd of Sol 2:23), so too has the eschatological man in the new age.[99] In the context of these royal and mythic themes, the "son of man" represents the "true Israel . . . in whom Israel [i.e. the people of God] attains an inner identity with its messianic representative."[100] In turn, the true Israel as a corporate entity looked forward to a place of honor in the new age of the kingdom which included redeemed people from every nation and tongue.

In conclusion, chapter 7 is "the hinge of the book of Daniel as a whole."[101] It depends on the description of the seer Daniel given in the court narratives, and the vision it describes picks up the theme of world empires also taken from the earlier chapters. The themes of oppression, the suffering of the saints, and the triumph of God's rule can be found in these earlier chapters, but chapter 7 elaborates best on these themes and sets a tone for the visions which follow.

Chapter Eight

Chapter 8 elaborates on the theme of the animal empires, providing more specifics to the description of the Greek empire and the oppression

---

[97] It is important to note the connection between the approach of the one like a Son of man and the reference to the people from every nation and tongue (=restored humanity) in 7:13–14.

[98] Pss 2, 72, 110; Isa 2:1–4, 9:5–6.

[99] A. LaCocque, *Daniel in His Time*, 94–95.

[100] So H. Gese, "Die Bedeutung der Krise unter Antiochus IV. Epiphanes für die Apokalyptik des Danielbuches," 381. See his treatment of chapter 7, 377–86.

[101] J. Goldingay, *Daniel* (WBC 30; Waco: Word Publishing Co., 1989), 159.

of Israel under Antiochus IV. The visionary account concerns two animals, a ram with two horns, and a goat, and it is interpreted by an angel who names the ram as the symbol of Media and Persia and the goat as the kingdom of Greece. The goat has one large horn which, when broken off, is replaced by four more. One of the four horns persecutes the heavenly host (ṣəbā' haššāmayim) and brings to an end the daily offering (tāmîd) in the temple.[102] Truth will be thrown to the ground (8:10–12; cf. 8:23–24). These oppressive acts describe the work of Antiochus IV, while the emphasis on the temple underscores its significance to the author(s) of Daniel.

Chapters Ten–Eleven

Chapters 10–11 heighten both the sense of persecution by Antiochus and the expectation of the end when God will thwart the Greek king's oppression. According to Dan 10:1f., Daniel has a vision that contains reference to a great struggle (ṣābā' gādôl). Daniel mourns for three weeks before he meets an angel who supplies him with additional details of struggle yet to come. It is a clue to the cosmic nature of the struggle between God and the forces of evil; the oppression of Daniel and his friends is but one aspect of widespread rebellion against the will of the Most High. The best indication of the cosmic nature of the struggle against the Most High is the report that the angel who came to Daniel was delayed three weeks in coming because of opposition from another angel described as the "prince of Persia" (10:12–14). The angel reports that the events to come are already written in a book, a statement that is supposed to comfort Daniel in a time when the outlook seems hopeless (10:19–21).

Chapter 11 provides the most detailed account in the book concerning the rule of Alexander the Great's successors and the persecution of the Jews by Antiochus Epiphanes (the "northern king" of 11:21f.). Although Antiochus is arrogant, idolatrous, and strong, he will come to an end with no one to help him (11:45; cf. 8:24b). It is a succinct statement, but one consistent with the deterministic features of the book as a whole. God has decreed a time for the exercise of gentile dominion, even the time of persecution by Antiochus, but the oppression and evil at work in the world order will come to an end at the appointed time (8:14; 9:24–27; 12:11–12). Antiochus represents in extreme form what the Babylonian and Medio-Persian rulers represent in the court narratives, a hubris that leads such rulers to exalt themselves and their kingdoms above the rule of the Most High, who is the true sovereign over human destiny.

---

[102] The combining of these two acts—struggle with the heavenly hosts and profaning the temple—suggests that the heavenly host includes humans. Perhaps the heavenly hosts is another reference to the saints mentioned in chapter 7.

The acts of Antiochus IV and various responses to them are recorded in the historical commentary of 11:21–45 (see pp. 116–21). The king acts against the "holy covenant" (bərît qōdeš), likely a reference to the faithful among the Jewish community who opposed his activities, though he is attentive to those among the community who had forsaken ('zb) this covenant (11:28–30).[103] When he intervenes in the affairs of the temple, he brings to an end the daily sacrifice and sets up an "abomination of desolation" (šiqqûṣ məšōmēm).[104] There are cryptic references to his deceiving those who have abandoned the covenant, while those who know "their God"[105] remain strong against these acts (11:31–32). Apparently the reference is to the hubris of Antiochus, who also promotes a form of the ruler cult for himself at the Jerusalem temple (11:36–37).[106] Among those who resist are the discerning ones among the people (maśkîlîm) who instruct the many (rabbîm). Their opposition is not described as a military resistance, but it is a costly resistance nevertheless, and some of the maśkîlîm suffer defeat and failure. In their resistance they receive only a "little help,"[107] but they persevere because the appointed end of the wickedness will come (11:33–35).

The references to the maśkîlîm in 11:33–35 are clear reminders of the discernment of Daniel and his friends in the court narratives; they too are maśkîlîm and models of piety and insight (1:4). In the face of a seemingly overwhelming force, the wise know that the kingdom of the Most High will ultimately prevail. This is the wisdom communicated in the visions and represented in the righteous sages of the court narratives. The term maśkîlîm probably does not refer to a separate party, nor is it quite a title, though it is used elsewhere as a description of certain

---

[103] See the references to the violation of the "holy covenant" in 1 Macc 1:11–15 and 1QM 1:2.

[104] The phrase is likely a pun on the name Ba'al Shamem, the Lord of Heaven, who would be known in Hellenistic circles as Zeus Olympus (2 Macc 6:2). Cf. Dan 8:13 (happeša' šōmēm); 9:25–27 (šiqqûṣîm məšōmēm); 12:11 (šiqqûṣ šōmēm). Probably the reference in 11:39 to a "foreign deity" ('elōah nēkār) is also to Zeus Olympus/Ba'al Shamem, but the identification is complicated by the cryptic reference to the "god of fortresses" ('elōah mā'uzzîm) in 11:38. The latter reference is possibly to the fortified citadel in Jerusalem used by people loyal to Antiochus. Cf. 1 Macc 1:33–40 which connects the citadel with lawless men and the defilement of the temple.

[105] Although the book understands Yahweh to be the God Most High, the identification of Yahweh with Ba'al Shamem/Zeus Olympus (the "abomination of desolation") is rejected as unacceptably syncretistic.

[106] "He shall do as he pleases, raising himself (yitrōmēm) and exalting (yitgaddēl) himself against every deity" (11:36a). See also the conclusion to 11:37. Antiochus had his full title printed on many coins in his realm. The title included a reference to himself as "the manifestation of God" (ΘΕΟΥ ΕΠΙΦΑΝΟΥΣ). See the references and discussion in Hengel, Judaism and Hellenism, 285–86.

[107] Perhaps this is a reference to the military activities of the Maccabees.

levitical teachers (2 Chron 30:22), of cult officials in particular psalm headings,[108] and in the community rule of the sectarian inhabitants of Qumran as a reference to teachers/leaders.[109] It is a description used by the author(s) of Daniel to identify faithful Jews in the period of the crisis. It is also likely a term the authors would use to describe themselves.

There are at least four groups identified in the symbolic description of 11:21f. (1) There are the maśkîlîm who resist and instruct others. They represent the community of the holy covenant profaned by the policies of Antiochus IV. (2) Those instructed are the "many" (rabbîm), probably a term to describe the Jewish community as a whole,[110] a number of whom are confused and uncertain about the meaning of events. (3) The third group (or assorted movements) is mentioned in the oblique reference to the "little help" in 11:34. Apparently these are Jews who opposed the policies of Antiochus IV, but whose opposition took a different form than that of the maśkîlîm. They too may be part of the "many." Both the second and the third groups would represent membership in the "holy covenant" in spite of their differing reactions to the Seleucid policies. (4) Finally, there are the apostates, those who cooperated with or even assisted Antiochus.

Chapter Twelve

It is plain from the references to suffering and failure that the resistance to Antiochus cost dearly. This background of suffering and political oppression forms the context in which the future resurrection from the dead is announced (12:1–3). Those who died maintaining their faithfulness will rise to everlasting life; those who were wicked will rise to live in shameful disgrace. Whatever the author(s) of Daniel think about an eschatological doctrine of the resurrection, the specific comments in 12:2f. are influenced by two factors: the suffering of the righteous and the unrequited nature of the wicked, and more explicitly, the fate of the righteous who died in the struggle to maintain their faith. Also the future resurrection is part of the two-kingdom theology of the book. The kingdom of God is transcendent and eternal, two characteristics which differ from the great gentile powers and two characteristics which furnish a proper setting for the eschatological vindication

---

[108] Pss 32, 42, 44, 45, 52–55, 74, 78, 88–89, 142.

[109] 1QS 3:13; 9:12, 21; 1QSb 1:1; 5:20. See the conclusion of C. Newsom, "The Sage in the Literature of Qumran: The Functions of the maśkîl," in Perdue, *The Sage in Israel*, 382: "The superior gift of knowledge that God had given to the maśkîl made him also the one who could guide the members of the community into the experience of the wonders of the heavenly realm and even show them how such knowledge might be used to protect themselves against the powers of evil until the time when God would put a final end to its dominion."

[110] In the community rule at Qumran, the assembly of the inhabitants is known as the many (rabbîm); see 1QS 6:20–23.

of the saints through resurrection. The *maśkîlîm*, therefore, will shine like the firmament, suggesting that a process of transformation is expected in the age of resurrection.[111]

Daniel concludes with the statement that the things to come are sure, and all written in a book. It is a conclusion fully consistent with the scribal-mantic background proposed for the author(s). It is also a confessional statement on the part of the author(s). The visions of the book are written in the conviction that they communicate the future God has decreed will come. The heavenly book contains this information, and it is the privilege of "Daniel" to communicate this wisdom to the faithful.

DANIEL AS OPPOSITION LITERATURE

The book of Daniel represents opposition to the world order of its day, an order that was either indifferent or hostile to the faith of the apocalypticists. The opposition is not necessarily derived from the op-pressed, lower classes who have given up hope for the betterment of their circumstances and who look to a new age for their salvation, although such a socio-cultural context is frequently claimed for apocalypticism. Daniel does project salvation to come with the kingdom of the Most High, but the best indication for the socio-cultural setting of the author(s) comes in the portrait of the sages at the gentile courts (Dan 1–6) and from learned, scribal circles responsible for the compilation and interpre-tation of the vision reports (Dan 7–12). Of course, the book of Daniel intended to instruct more than the learned classes; it is intended for the "many" (*rabbîm*), Jews who need guidance in a time of oppression. Collins's description of the vision reports fits the outlook of the book as a whole:

> They are a "political manifesto, produced by one section of the intelligen-tsia but designed to affect the populace. Daniel was not addressed to only one social class. . . . The manifesto which we find in Daniel is one of resistance. . . . However, the resistance evoked is not military action, but the non-violent assertion of their [the readers'] religious loyalty and submission to martyrdom if necessary. . . . The visions of Daniel are designed to promote this response to the political situation. They constitute a political manifesto because they demand a specific reaction to the existing political state. However, they differ sharply from other contemporary political oracles insofar as their alternative to the current kingdom is not a restored national kingship, even an idealized one depicted in religious terms. Rather it is a transcendent kingdom where the *maśkîlîm* share the eternal angelic life."[112]

---

[111] Perhaps this transformation is to a form of existence like that of the angels; see Collins, *Apocalyptic Vision*, 142–44.

[112] Collins, *Apocalyptic Vision*, 213–14.

We might expand on these conclusions by recourse to the study of sectarian movements whose very existence often represents a form of protest or resistance against the dominant order of their society. B. Wilson offers a widely used typology of sects defined by their respective "responses to the world" and their "search for salvation."[113] His definition of a sect is perhaps too broad—it is "a self-distinguishing protest movement"—but his typology is a heuristic device that allows one a better grasp of religious movements in their cultural setting.[114] He proposes a sketch of seven ideal sects.

(1) Conversionist. This model concentrates on the conversion or change of heart required for an individual to oppose evil and find salvation.

(2) Revolutionist. This model stresses the supernatural change of the world order, the coming of a new, eschatological age. The revolution is brought about by divine forces, not human activity.

(3) Introversionist. This approach uses a withdrawal from the evil nature of the world.

(4) Manipulationist. This approach relies on the transmission of new or secret knowledge. The recipient is then able to deal more effectively with life's problems.

(5) Thaumaturgical. These communities use miracles and magic as a means to cope with evil.

(6) Reformists. This model proposes changes in social structure and human activity as an aid to progress and the overcoming of evil.

(7) Utopian. These movements claim the key to salvation is no less than the complete remaking of the social order along ideal lines.

Of his seven ideal types, the conversionist, the revolutionist, and the thaumaturgical place greater emphasis on direct, divine activity. None of them, however, advocates a completely passive ethic. The other four place more emphasis on the human contribution, though none of them lacks a role for divine activity.

In his sociological analysis of the vision reports in Dan 7–12, S. B. Reid proposes the community of the author(s) of Daniel fits most closely in the revolutionist model of Wilson.[115] His analysis is plausible if not convincing. One might say that the sages, the intelligentsia responsible for the book, opposed cultural oppression by insisting that the eschaton was God's responsibility but fidelity to the ancestral traditions was their responsibility. They point to an eschaton only God can create and sustain,

---

[113] See his *Religious Sects: A Sociology Study* (London: Weidenfeld and Nicholson, 1970); and *Magic and the Millennium.* His typology is not limited to Christian sectarian movements, and he seeks to avoid the bias inherent in the distinction between church and sect.

[114] See the helpful introduction to Wilson's thought in D. E. Miller, "Sectarianism and Secularization: The Work of Bryan Wilson," *RSR* 5 (1979): 161–74.

[115] Reid, *Enoch and Daniel,* 77–136.

while their resistance to the political and cultural imperialism of Antiochus takes seriously the possibility of martyrdom before the eschaton finally comes. Reid also notes the importance Wilson attaches to sectarian reactions to social and cultural change, and he suggests that the community behind Daniel was a declining elite, sages and scribes who lost status and possessions in the reforms of Antiochus IV. In this view Reid sharpens the conclusions of others that the apocalypticism of Daniel originated among oppressed classes, but more specifically among educated and formerly well-to-do classes, and not the poor and uneducated elements of society. His suggestion may provide insight into the comment that some of *maśkîlîm* would stumble and fail (11:32–35), and it helps account for the elements of asceticism in the book (1:8–16; 9:3; 10:2–3). The sage can use ascetic practices as a means of cultural protest over the loss of possessions and as a means of spiritual discipline.

Daniel, therefore, is sectarian literature according to Wilson's definition, representing essentially a revolutionist's protest against the oppressive imperialism of Antiochus IV. One hesitates, however, to describe Daniel as a sectarian work without further qualification. If by sectarian one means a viewpoint that defines the true Israel by excluding the religion of most Jews in the diaspora and that of all gentiles without further qualification, then Daniel is not sectarian. The book of Daniel is more concerned to define the separateness and the distinctiveness of Judaism over against the dominant (and often oppressive) gentile empires and to instill hope for the end to suffering in a time of crisis. This is a major element of the book's approach to the relationship between religion and culture, and it is different from a blanket exclusion of other Jews who differ, or of gentiles. True, what the God of heaven requires sets the Jew apart from the non-Jew, even if the Jew serves in a gentile court. But that is not all. In its emphasis on the sovereignty of God Most High among the gentiles, the book of Daniel sets the stage for the revelation that the eternal kingdom of God transcends any human effort at social order or political rule. This is a second element to its approach regarding religion and culture. The Jew must live faithfully in response to what God has revealed, regardless of circumstances, yet with the anticipation of the kingdom to come as a divine gift. And far from excluding Jews or gentiles, the book represents the possibility of gentiles acknowledging the rule of the Most High, even as it depicts the symbolic unveiling of the kingdom as inclusive of saints and peoples from every nation and tongue.

In the book of Daniel, the *maśkîlîm* labor on behalf of the many, to instruct them (11:33) and to set them right (12:3). They do so in anticipation of the time when they will shine like the firmament, when the days appointed for travail and purification have come to pass, and when the Ancient of Days has taken his seat among a holy people (7:9–10, 14, 27; 12:7) to rule in the eternal kingdom. In light of that eschaton, religion in any culture is at best a penultimate expression of service to the Most High.

SELECT BIBLIOGRAPHY

ISRAELITE RELIGION

Ackroyd, P. R. *Studies in the Religious Tradition of the Old Testament.* London: SCM Press, 1987.

Ahlström, G. "An Archaeological Picture of Iron Age Religions in Ancient Palestine." *Studia Orientalia* 55/3 (1984): 3–31.

_____. *Aspects of Syncretism in Israelite Religion.* Horae Soederblomianae 5. Lund: Gleerup, 1963.

Ancient Israelite Religion. Essays in Honor of Frank Moore Cross. Edited by P. D. Miller, Jr., P. D. Hanson, S. D. McBride. Philadelphia: Fortress, 1987.

Bickerman, E. *The Jews in the Greek Age.* Cambridge: Harvard University Press, 1988.

Collins, J. "The Place of Apocalypticism in the Religion of Israel." In *Ancient Israelite Religion. Essays in Honor of Frank Moore Cross.* Edited by P. D. Miller, Jr., P. D. Hanson, S. D. McBride. Philadelphia: Fortress, 1987. Pages 539–58.

Cross, F. M. *Canaanite Myth and Hebrew Epic.* Cambridge: Harvard University Press, 1973.

De Moor, J. C. *The Rise of Yahwism. The Roots of Israelite Monotheism.* BETL 91. Leuven: University Press, 1990.

de Vaux, R. *Ancient Israel.* 2 vols. New York: McGraw Hill, 1965.

Eissfeldt, O. "Baʿalšamēm und Jahwe." *Kleine Schriften.* Volume 2. Pages 171–98. Tübingen: Mohr, 1963.

Fohrer, G. *A History of Israelite Religion.* Nashville: Abingdon, 1972.

Gammie, J., and L. Perdue. *The Sage in Israel and the Ancient Near East.* Winona Lake: Eisenbrauns, 1990.

Haran, M. *Temples and Temple Service in Ancient Israel.* Oxford: Clarendon, 1978.

Hengel, M. *Judaism and Hellenism: Studies in Their Encounter in Palestine during the Early Hellenistic Period.* 2 vols. Philadelphia: Fortress Press, 1974.

Herrmann, S. "Die konstruktive Restauration. Das Deuteronomium als Mitte biblischer Theologie." In *Probleme Biblischer Theologie. Gerhard von Rad zum 70. Geburtstag.* Edited by H. W. Wolff. Pages 155–71. Munich: Kaiser, 1971.

Lang, B. *Monotheism and the Prophetic Minority.* SWBAS 1. Sheffield: Almond Press, 1983.

The Listening Heart. Essays in Wisdom and the Psalms in honor of Roland E. Murphy, O. Carm. Edited by K. Hoglund et al. JSOTSS 58. Sheffield, JSOT Press, 1987.

Maag, V. *Kultur, Kulturkontakt und Religion.* Göttingen: Vandenhoeck & Ruprecht, 1980.

Mettinger, T. N. D. "The Elusive Essence. YHWH, El and Baal and the Distinctiveness of Israelite Religion." In *Die Hebräische Bibel und ihre zweifach Nachgeschichte. Festschrift für Rolf Rendtorff.* Edited by E. Blum, C. Macholz, E. Stegemann. Pages 393–417. Neukirchen-Vluyn: Neukirchener Verlag, 1990.

Miller, P. D., Jr. "Israelite Religion." In *The Hebrew Bible and its Modern Interpreters.* Edited by D. Knight, G. Tucker. Pages 218–32. Chico: Scholars Press, 1985.

Müller, H. P. "Mantische Weisheit und Apokalyptik." *VTSup* 22 (1972): 268–93.

Murphy, R. *The Tree of Life. Exploration of Biblical Wisdom.* New York: Doubleday, 1990.

Nicholson, E. *God and His People. Covenant and Theology in the Old Testament.* Oxford: Clarendon Press, 1986.

_____. "Israelite Religion in the Pre-exilic Period. In A Debate Renewed." In *A Word in Season. Essays in Honour of William McKane.* Edited by J. D. Martin, P. R. Davies. Pages 3–34. JSOTSS 42. Sheffield: JSOT Press, 1986.

Ringgren, H. *Israelite Religion.* Philadelphia: Fortress Press, 1966.

Schmid, H. H. *Altorientalische Welt in der alttestamentlichen Theologie.* Zurich: Theologischer Verlag, 1974.

_____. *Wesen und Geschichte der Weisheit. Eine Untersuchung zur altorientalischen und israelitischen Weisheitsliteratur.* BZAW 101. Berlin: A. Töpelmann, 1966.

Schroer, S. *In Israel gab es Bilder.* OBO 74. Göttingen: Vandenhoeck & Ruprecht, 1987.

Sievers, J. *The Hasmoneans and Their Supporters. From Mattathias to the Death of John Hyrcanus I.* SFSHJ 6. Atlanta: Scholars Press, 1990.

Smith, M. S. *The Early History of God.* San Francisco: Harper and Row, 1989.

Tigay, J. *You Shall Have No Other Gods: Israelite Religion in Light of Hebrew Inscriptions.* HSS 31. Atlanta: Scholars Press, 1986.

Vincent, A. *La religion des judéo-araméenes d'Eléphantine.* Paris: Geuthner, 1937.

Weinfeld, M. *Deuteronomy and the Deuteronomic School.* Oxford: Clarendon Press, 1972.

Wilson, R. R. *Prophecy and Society in Ancient Israel.* Philadelphia: Fortress, 1980.

Zimmerli, W. "The History of Israelite Religion." In *Tradition and Interpretation.* Edited by G. W. Anderson. Pages 351–84. Oxford: Clarendon Press, 1979.

THE MATERIAL CULTURE AND HISTORY OF ANCIENT ISRAEL

Ahlström, G. "An Archaeological Picture of Iron Age Religions in Ancient Palestine." *Studia Orientalia* 55/3 (1984): 3–31.

Coogan, M. "Of Cults and Cultures: Reflections on the Interpretation of Archaeological Evidence." *PEQ* 119 (1987): 1–8.

de Geus, C. H. J. "Die Gesellschaftskritik der Propheten und die Archäologie." *ZDPV* 98 (1982): 50–57.

Delcor, M. "Les cultes étrangers en Israel au moment de la réforme de Josias d' après 2 R 23: Etude de religions sémitiques comparées." *Mélanges bibliques et orientaux en l'honneur de M. Henri Cazelles.* Edited by A. Caquot, M. Delcor. Pages 91–123. AOAT 212. Neukirchen-Vluyn: Kevelaer, 1981.

Dever W. G. "The Contribution of Archaeology to the Study of Canaanite and Early Israelite Religion." In *Ancient Israelite Religion. Essays in Honor of Frank Moore Cross.* Edited by P. D. Miller, Jr., P. Hanson, D. McBride. Pages 209–47. Philadelphia: Fortress, 1987.

_____. "Material Remains and the Cult in Ancient Israel: An Essay in Archaeological Systematics." In *The Word of the Lord Shall Go Forth. Essays in Honor of David Noel Freedman in Celebration of His Sixtieth Birthday.* Edited by C. Meyers, M. O'Connor. Pages 571–87. Philadelphia: ASOR, 1983.

_____. *Recent Archaeological Discoveries and Biblical Research.* Seattle: University of Washington Press, 1990.

Finkelstein, I. *The Archaeology of the Israelite Settlement.* Jerusalem: IEJ, 1988.

Gottwald, N. *The Tribes of Yahweh. A Sociology of Religion of Liberated Israel (1250–1050 B.C.).* Maryknoll: Orbis, 1979.

Herzog, Z. et al. "The Israelite Fortress of Arad." *BASOR* 254 (1984): 1–34.

Holladay, J. S. "Religion in Israel and Judah Under the Monarchy: An Explicitly Archaeological Approach." *Ancient Israelite Religion. Essays in Honor of Frank Moore Cross.* Edited by P. D. Miller, Jr., P. D. Hanson, S. D. McBride. Philadelphia: Fortress, 1987. Pages 249–99.

Kenyon, K. *Royal Cities of the Old Testament.* London: Barrie and Jenkins, 1971.

Lemche, N. P. *Ancient Israel. A New History of Israelite Society.* Sheffield: JSOT, 1988.

Mazar, A. *Archaeology of the Land of the Bible.* New York: Doubleday, 1990.

Negbi, O. *Canaanite Gods in Metal. An Archaeological Study of Ancient Syro-Palestinian Figurines.* Tel Aviv: Institute of Archaeology, 1976.

Porten, B. *Archives from Elephantine. The Life of an Ancient Jewish Military Colony.* Berkeley: University of California Press, 1968.

Shiloh, Y. "Judah and Jerusalem in the Eighth-Sixth Centuries B.C.E." *Recent Excavations in Israel: Studies in Iron Age Archaeology.* Edited by S. Gitin, W. Dever. Pages 71–96. AASOR 49. Winona Lake: Eisenbrauns, 1989.

_____. "The Material Culture of Judah and Jerusalem in Iron II: Origins and Influences." In *The Land of Israel: Crossroads of Civilization.* Edited by E. Lipinski. Pages 113–46. OLA 19. Leuven: Uitgeverij Peeters, 1985.

Stern, E. *Material Culture of the Land of the Bible in the Persian Period 538–332 B.C.* Jerusalem: IEJ, 1982.

Tcherikover, V. *Hellenistic Civilization and the Jews.* Philadelphia: Jewish Publication Society, 1959.

RELIGION IN THE ANCIENT NEAR EAST

Albertz, R. *Persönliche Frömmigkeit und offizielle Religion. Religionsinterner Pluralismus in Israel und Babylon.* CTM 9. Stuttgart: Calwer Verlag, 1978.

Apocalypticism in the Mediterranean World and the Near East. Edited by D. Hellholm. Tübingen: J. C. B. Mohr, 1983.

Caquot, A., and M. Sznyer. *Ugaritic Religion.* Iconography of Religions 15. Leiden: Brill, 1980.

Clifford, R. J. *The Cosmic Mountain in Canaan and in the Old Testament.* HSM 4. Cambridge: Harvard, 1971.

Culican, W. "The Iconography of Some Phoenician Seals and Seal Impressions," *AJBA* 1 (1968): 50–103.

De Moor, J. C. "The Semitic Pantheon of Ugarit." *UF* 2 (1970): 187–228.

Eddy, S. K. *The King is Dead. Studies in the Near Eastern Resistance to Hellenism 334–31 B.C.* Lincoln: University of Nebraska Press, 1961.

Gese, H., M. Höfner, and K. Rudolph. *Die Religionen Altsyriens, Altarabiens und der Mandäer.* Die Religionen der Menschheit 10/2. Stuttgart: Kohlhammer, 1970.

Huldberg-Hanson, F. O. *La Deesse TNT. Une étude sur la religion canaanéo-punique.* 2 vols. Copenhagen: Gad's Forlag, 1979.

Metzger, M. "Gottheit, Berg und Vegetation in vorderorientalischen Bildtradition." *ZDPV* 99 (1983): 54–94.

Miller, P. D., Jr. "El, the Creator of Earth." *BASOR* 239 (1980): 43–46.

Moscati, S., ed. *The Phoenicians.* New York: Abbeville Press, 1988.

Müller, H. P. "Religionsgeschichtliche Beobachtungen zu den Texten von Ebla." *ZDPV* 96 (1980): 1–19.

Stadelmann, R. *Syrisch-palästinensische Gottheiten in Ägypten.* Leiden: Brill, 1967.

Tarragon, J. M. *Le culte a Ugarit. D'après les textes de la pratique en cunéiformes alphabetiques.* Cahiers de la Revue Biblique 19. Paris: Gabalda, 1980.

Xella, P. "Le polytheisme phenicien." In *Religio Phoenicia.* Edited by C. Bonnet et al. Pages 29–39. Studia Phoenicia 4. Namur: Societé des études classiques, 1986.

Zijl, P. J. van. *Baal. A Study of Texts in connexion with Baal in the Ugaritic Epics.* AOAT 10. Neukirchen-Vluyn: Kevelaer, 1972.

INDEX OF MODERN AUTHORS

Select Index of Ancient Texts